ZAGATSURVEY®

2005/06

PARIS
RESTAURANTS

**Local Editors: Alexander Lobrano,
Mary Deschamps**

Local Coordinator: Claire Fitzpatrick

Editor: Troy Segal

Published and distributed by
ZAGAT SURVEY, LLC
4 Columbus Circle
New York, New York 10019
Tel: 212 977 6000
E-mail: paris@zagat.com
Web site: www.zagat.com

Acknowledgments

We thank Erica Curtis, Amy Jeryl, Bruno Midavaine, Bibi Scuba, Steven Shukow and the Skoi family. We also thank our associate editor, Anne Cole, and our editorial assistant, Melissa Brewster, as well as the following members of our staff: Reni Chin, Schuyler Frazier, Jeff Freier, Shelley Gallagher, Natalie Lebert, Mike Liao, Dave Makulec, Emily Parsons, Robert Poole, Robert Seixas, Thomas Sheehan, Joshua Siegel and Sharon Yates.

Contents

About This Survey

Over the past 26 years, Zagat Survey has reported on the shared experiences of diners like you. This *2005/06 Paris Restaurant Survey* is an update reflecting significant developments as reported by our editors since our last *Survey* was published. For example, we have added important new restaurants, and indicated new addresses, chef changes and other major developments. All told, this guide now covers 993 restaurants on the scene or, in this case, on the Seine. It is worth noting that our own experience living in Paris, from 1968 through 1970, inspired all our surveys.

What started in 1979 as a hobby involving 200 friends rating local restaurants has come a long way. Today we have over 250,000 surveyors and now cover entertaining, golf, hotels, resorts, spas, movies, music, nightlife, shopping, sites and attractions as well as theater. All of these guides are based on consumer surveys. Our *Surveys* are also available on PDAs, cell phones and, by subscription, at zagat.com, where you can vote and shop as well.

By regularly surveying large numbers of avid customers, we hope to have achieved a uniquely current and reliable guide. A quarter-century of experience has validated this. For this book, over 4,300 restaurant-goers participated. Our editors have synopsized our surveyors' opinions, with their comments shown in quotation marks. We sincerely thank each of these surveyors; this book is really "theirs."

Of course, we are especially grateful to our editors, Alexander Lobrano, European correspondent for *Gourmet* and a food and travel writer based in Paris, and Mary Deschamps, a freelance writer in Paris. Our thanks also go to our coordinator, Claire Fitzpatrick, and to *Le Figaro*'s François Simon for his help and advice along the way.

To help guide our readers to Paris' best meals and best buys, we have prepared a number of lists. See Most Popular (page 9), Top Ratings (pages 10–15) and Best Buys (page 16). In addition, we have provided 44 handy indexes and have tried to be concise.

To vote in any of our upcoming *Surveys*, just register at zagat.com. Each participant will receive a free copy of the resulting guide when published. Your comments and even criticisms of this guide are also solicited. There is always room for improvement with your help. Just contact us at paris@zagat.com.

New York, NY
April 18, 2005

Nina and Tim Zagat

What's New

Dining in Paris may be a nonpareil experience, but for Americans it can also seem a pricey one: at 50.65€, the average cost of a meal equals $67.92. But take heart: the city's ever-changing culinary scene means that less costly alternatives always abound. In fact, out of the 76 restaurants added to this edition, 55 offer moderately priced menus (26€ to 45€), and 13 are downright inexpensive (25€ or less) – thanks to a crop of chefs with a common commitment to eating at reasonable prices.

Bistro Boom: One result of their efforts is that the neighborhood bistro, which once seemed to be in terminal decline, is back in all its chalkboard-menu glory. Ground zero for the renaissance lies in the 11th, home to such ambitious arrivals as Le Marsangy, Le Sot l'y Laisse and Le Temps au Temps. Two other novices do bistro with a Basque-Southwestern flair: L'Ourcine in the 13th and Les Papilles in the 5th.

For Adults Only: After progressively thinning out for a decade, serious French establishments – whether Classic, Contemporary or Haute Cuisine – are also making a comeback, albeit with a fresher, less fusty look. Such rejuvenated veterans include Jean-Pierre Vigato's Apicius, with a stylishly understated setting and revamped menu; Chiberta, relaunched by Guy Savoy; and Gérard Faucher's Faucher, renamed 123 (after its street address, another trend du jour). Yohann Marraccini, chef-owner of the hit De Lagarde, is reviving Beauvilliers, the mythic Montmartre table that shuttered last year. There are also newcomers in the old style, both from chefs with a hotel background: Auguste, operated by Gaël Orieux, ex-second at the Meurice, and Dominique Bouchet, the Crillon's former top toque. Leisurely and elegant, all are aimed at adults who are definitely not going to a disco after dinner.

Party Time: Not that the hot scenes show any signs of cooling off. The hippest new spot in town is probably Le Murano, where diners enjoying the New French cuisine are inevitably wearing sunglasses, day and night – perhaps as protection from the dazzling white decor. Even among Paris party animals, however, good food is in fashion. Among the more interesting culinary contenders is Musichall, with a spectacular computer-generated light system, grand piano and an appealing mix of Asian and New French fare.

A Votre Santé: Though notorious for their devotion to smoking and fat-rich foods, Parisians are getting almost as health-obsessed as New Yorkers. Menus all around town now offer more steamed dishes, more low-cal options and an explosion of organic produce – even at new quick-eat places like BIOArt in the 13th and Scoop in the 1st.

Paris   Alexander Lobrano
April 18, 2005

Ratings & Symbols

Name, Address, Métro Stop, Phone* & Fax Numbers, & Web Site

Zagat Ratings

Hours & Credit Cards

	F	D	S	€C
Tim & Nina's ◗🖾⊄	▽ 23	9	13	15

604, rue de Buci, 6ᵉ (Odéon), 01 23 45 54 32; fax 23 44 55 66; www.zagat.com

🖾 *Jamais fermé*, this "crowded" 6th arrondissement cafe started the "Swedish-French craze" (e.g. herring and foie gras on tiny toasts with a choice of sauces); though it looks like a "garage" and T & N "never heard of credit cards or reservations" – yours in particular – the *très* "*merveilleuse* Stockholm-Lyonnaise cuisine" draws demented "debit-account" diners to this "deep dive."

Review, with surveyors' comments in quotes

Restaurants with the highest overall ratings and greatest popularity and importance are printed in CAPITAL LETTERS.

Before reviews a symbol indicates whether responses were uniform ■ or mixed 🖾.

Hours: ◗ serves after 11 PM
🖾 closed on Sunday

Credit Cards: ⊄ no credit cards accepted

Ratings are on a scale of **0** to **30. Cost (€C)** reflects our surveyors' estimate of the price of dinner with one drink and tip, in euros.

F	Food	D	Decor	S	Service	€C	Cost
23		9		13		€15	

0–9 poor to fair	**20–25** very good to excellent	
10–15 fair to good	**26–30** extraordinary to perfection	
16–19 good to very good	▽ low response/less reliable	

For places listed without ratings, such as a newcomer or survey write-in, the price range is indicated as follows:

I	25€ and below	**E**	46€ to 75€
M	26€ to 45€	**VE**	76€ or more

---

* When calling from outside France, dial code +33, then omit the first zero of the number. The fax number appears as if dialed from Paris, minus the 01.

Most Popular

Paris

- Chez L'Ami Louis
- Ambroisie
- Bofinger
- Opéra de Paris Bastille
- Benoit
- Café Marly
- Hippopotamus*
- Tour d'Argent
- Notre Dame
- Detail at left
- Coupole
- Régalade
- N. 12
- Michel Rostang
- Av des Champs-Elysees
- Hiramatsu
- Astrance
- Bois de Boulogne
- Av de Villiers
- La Seine
- Rue de Convention
- Av Jean Moulin
- Rue de Vaugirard
- * Check for other locations

Paris

- Chez Georges
- Grand Véfour
- Musée du Louvre
- Bouquinistes
- Rôtisserie d'en Face
- Allard
- Café Les Deux Magots
- Brasserie Lipp
- Hélène Darroze
- Angelina
- Atelier de Joël Robuchon
- Epi Dupin
- Ladurée*
- Maxim's
- Lucas Carton
- Buddha Bar
- Ambassadeurs
- Arpège
- Bristol
- Market
- Laurent
- Lasserre
- Esplanade des Invalides
- Taillevent
- Pierre Gagnaire
- Cinq
- Plaza-Athénée
- Violon d'Ingres
- Guy Savoy
- Arc de Triomphe
- Tour Eiffel
- Jules Verne
- Palais de Chaillot
- Champ de Mars
- Boundary of arrondissement
- Bd Malesherbes
- Bd Haussmann
- Rue du Faubourg St. Honoré
- Av des Champs-Elysees
- Av Kléber
- Av de Wagram
- La Seine
- quai Voltaire
- Bd St. Germain
- Bd Raspail
- Rue de Varenne
- Rue de Sèvres
- Bd des Invalides
- Av Duquesne
- Av Rapp
- Rue des Petits Champs
- Km 1/2

Most Popular

1. Taillevent
2. Tour d'Argent
3. Guy Savoy
4. Lucas Carton
5. Grand Véfour
6. Jules Verne
7. Bouquinistes
8. Cinq
9. Pierre Gagnaire
10. Arpège
11. Epi Dupin
12. Buddha Bar
13. Bofinger
14. Ladurée
15. Rest. Alain Ducasse
16. Lasserre
17. Atelier Joël Robuchon
18. Benoît
19. Ambassadeurs
20. Ambroisie
21. Hélène Darroze
22. Bristol
23. Chez L'Ami Louis
24. Brass. Lipp
25. Violon d'Ingres
26. Astrance
27. Michel Rostang
28. Chez Georges
29. Laurent
30. Market
31. Régalade
32. Rôtiss. d'en Face
33. Coupole
34. Hippopotamus
35. Hiramatsu
36. Café Les Deux Magots
37. Angelina
38. Café Marly
39. Allard
40. Maxim's*
41. Costes
42. Georges*
43. Ze Kitchen Galerie
44. Relais/l'Entrecôte
45. Carré des Feuillants
46. Brass. Balzar
47. Bastide Odéon
48. Angle du Faubourg
49. Pied de Cochon*
50. Procope

It's obvious that many of the restaurants on the above list are among Paris' most expensive, but if popularity were calibrated to price, we suspect that a number of other restaurants would join the above ranks. Given the fact that both our surveyors and readers love to discover dining bargains, we have added a list of 80 Best Buys on page 16. These are restaurants that give extraordinary quality at extremely modest prices.

---

* Indicates a tie with restaurant above

Top Ratings

Excludes places with low voting, except where indicated by a ∇.

Top 50 Food

28 Taillevent
   Guy Savoy
   Cinq
   Pierre Gagnaire*
   Grand Véfour
   Hiramatsu
27 Michel Rostang
   Bristol
   Rest. Alain Ducasse
   Lucas Carton
   Apicius
   Gérard Besson
26 Ambroisie
   Ambassadeurs
   Chez L'Ami Louis
   Astrance
   Arpège
   Lasserre
   Relais Louis XIII
   Elysées
   Magnolias
   Pré Catelan
   Atelier Joël Robuchon
   Relais d'Auteuil/Pignol
25 Ledoyen

   Sormani
   Carré des Feuillants
   Espadon
   Tour d'Argent
   Régalade
   Jamin
   Trois Marches
   Jacques Cagna
   Troquet*
   Truffière*
   Meurice
   Duc
   Grande Cascade
   Moulin à Vent
24 Angle du Faubourg
   Violon d'Ingres
   Réminet
   Passíflore
   Amphyclès
   Goumard*
   Trou Gascon
   Laurent
   Jules Verne
   Epi Dupin
   Marée

By Cuisine (French)

Bistros (Contemporary)
26 Astrance
25 Troquet
24 Epi Dupin
23 Beurre Noisette
22 Ardoise

Bistros (Traditional)
26 Chez L'Ami Louis
25 Régalade
   Moulin à Vent
23 Christine
   Petit Marguery

Brasseries
21 Relais Plaza
20 Brass. du Louvre
19 Brass./l'Ile St. Louis
18 Costes
   Chien qui Fume

Classic
27 Villaret
   Gérard Besson
26 Relais Louis XIII
25 Paul Chêne
   Espadon

Contemporary
28 Hiramatsu
27 Michel Rostang
   Bristol
   Rest. Alain Ducasse
   Lucas Carton

Haute Cuisine
28 Taillevent
   Guy Savoy
   Cinq
   Pierre Gagnaire*
   Grand Véfour

Top Food

Lyon
23 Benoît
22 Lyonnais
21 Moissonnier
20 Vieux Bistro
   Aub. Pyrénées Cévennes

Other Regions
27 Bath's/*Auvergne*
21 Comte de Gascogne/*Gascony*
   Pamphlet/*Basque*
20 Ambassade d'Auv./*Auvergne*
   Bascou/*Basque*
   Bistro d'Hubert*/*Basque*

Provence
22 Sept Quinze
21 Bastide Odéon
   Fish La Boissonerie
   Jardin
   Olivades

Seafood
25 Duc
24 Goumard
   Marée
   Cagouille
   Luna

Shellfish
22 Dôme
   Dessirier
   Marius*
   Maison Prunier
21 Marée de Versailles

Southwest
24 Trou Gascon
   Hélène Darroze
22 Maison Courtine*
   Bistrot Baracane
21 Oulette

Steakhouses
23 Relais/l'Entrecôte
   Boeuf Couronné
21 Gavroche
   Gourmets des Ternes
20 Relais de Venise

Wine Bars/Bistros
21 Bourguignon du Marais
   Vin sur Vin
19 Willi's Wine Bar
18 Cave de l'Os à Moëlle
   Caves Pétrissans*

By Cuisine (Other)

Chinese
22 Passy Mandarin
21 Chez Vong
   Tang
   Tong Yen*
20 Mirama

Eclectic
23 Ze Kitchen Galerie
22 Spoon, Food/Wine
   Market
21 Chamarré
   Relais Plaza

Greek/Mediterranean
20 Il Baccello
   Délices d'Aphrodite
19 Mavrommatis
16 7ème Sud
15 16 Haussmann

Italian
25 Sormani
23 Ostéria
   Il Cortile
22 Chez Vincent
21 Romantica

Japanese
24 Isami
23 Benkay
22 Kinugawa
20 Yen
19 Orient-Extrême

Lebanese
21 B-Café
20 Al Dar
   Al Diwan
19 Noura
16 Fakhr el Dine

Moroccan
23 Timgad
22 Mansouria
21 Atlas
   404
   El Mansour

Thai
22 Thiou
21 Erawan
20 Blue Elephant
   Baan-Boran
19 Sawadee

Top Food

Vietnamese
24 Coin des Gourmets▽
23 Kim Anh▽
22 Tan Dinh
21 Lac-Hong
20 Kambodgia▽

Wild Cards
24 Anahuacalli/*Mexican*
22 Caviar Kaspia/*Russian*
21 Copenhague/*Danish*
19 Anahï/*South American*
18 Flora Danica/*Danish*

By Special Feature

Breakfast
22 Dôme
   Dalloyau
21 Ladurée
   Gavroche
   Hédiard

Newcomers/Unrated
   Auguste
   Dominique Bouchet
   Ourcine
   Table du Lancaster
   Table/Joël Robuchon

Hotel Dining
28 Cinq
   Four Seasons George V
   Pierre Gagnaire*
   Hôtel Balzac
27 Bristol
   Hôtel Bristol
   Rest. Alain Ducasse
   Hôtel Plaza-Athénée
26 Ambassadeurs
   Hôtel de Crillon

Sunday Dining
28 Cinq
   Pierre Gagnaire*
27 Bristol
26 Ambassadeurs
   Chez L'Ami Louis

Tea & Desserts
22 Dalloyau
21 Ladurée
19 Mariage Frères
18 Angelina
17 A Priori Thé

"In" Places
28 Guy Savoy
26 Astrance
   Atelier Joël Robuchon
25 Régalade
23 Ze Kitchen Galerie

Teen Appeal
24 Isami
   Anahuacalli
23 Ostéria
22 Spoon, Food/Wine
   Sept Quinze

Late Dining
22 Caviar Kaspia
21 Gavroche
   Coupe-Chou
20 Al Diwan
19 Gamin de Paris

Wine Lists
28 Taillevent
   Guy Savoy
   Cinq
   Pierre Gagnaire*
   Grand Véfour

By Arrondissement

1st
28 Grand Véfour
27 Gérard Besson
25 Carré des Feuillants
   Espadon
   Meurice

3rd
26 Chez L'Ami Louis
21 Pamphlet
   404
20 Chez Janou
   Ambassade d'Auv.

2nd
23 Chez Georges
22 Lyonnais
   Céladon
21 Gavroche
   Drouant

4th
26 Ambroisie
24 Isami
23 Ostéria
   Benoît
22 Orangerie

5th

- **25** Tour d'Argent
  Truffière
  Moulin à Vent
- **24** Réminet
  Anahuacalli

6th

- **26** Relais Louis XIII
- **25** Jacques Cagna
- **24** Epi Dupin
  Hélène Darroze
- **23** Christine

7th

- **26** Arpège
  Atelier Joël Robuchon
- **24** Violon d'Ingres
  Jules Verne
  Petrossian

8th

- **28** Taillevent
  Cinq
  Pierre Gagnaire*
- **27** Bath's
  Bristol

9th

- **27** Muses
- **23** Chez Jean
  Table d'Anvers
- **21** Ladurée
- **20** Bistrot Papillon

10th

- **21** Chez Michel
  Deux Canards
- **18** Brass. Julien
- **17** Brass. Flo
  Terminus Nord

11th

- **27** Villaret
- **22** Mansouria
- **21** C'Amelot
  Astier
- **20** Blue Elephant

12th

- **24** Trou Gascon
- **21** Oulette
  Biche au Bois
- **17** Square Trousseau
  Train Bleu

13th

- **23** Petit Marguery
- **22** Avant Goût
- **21** Chez Paul
- **18** Terroir
  Nouveau Village Tao▽

14th

- **25** Régalade
  Duc
- **24** Cagouille
- **22** Dôme
  Maison Courtine

15th

- **25** Troquet
- **23** Os à Moëlle
  Beurre Noisette
  Benkay
- **22** Tire-Bouchon

16th

- **28** Hiramatsu
- **26** Astrance
  Pré Catelan
  Relais d'Auteuil/Pignol
- **25** Paul Chêne

17th

- **28** Guy Savoy
- **27** Michel Rostang
- **25** Sormani
- **24** Amphyclès
- **23** Timgad

18th, 19th & 20th

- **23** Boeuf Couronné
- **22** Chez Vincent
- **19** Zéphyr
- **16** Wepler
- **15** Rughetta

Outside Paris

- **26** Magnolias
- **25** Trois Marches
  Tastevin
- **22** Dalloyau
- **21** Comte de Gascogne

Top 50 Decor

28 Cinq
  Ambassadeurs
  Grand Véfour*
  Meurice
  Train Bleu
  Grande Cascade
  Tour d'Argent
27 Taillevent
  Espadon
  Pré Catelan
  Jules Verne
  Bristol
  Lasserre
  Ledoyen
26 Lucas Carton
  Lapérouse
  Georges
  Rest. Alain Ducasse
  Ambroisie
  Blue Elephant
  Laurent
25 China Club
  Bar Vendôme
  Costes
  Chalet des Iles

  Coupe-Chou*
  404
  Buddha Bar
  Guy Savoy
  Bon
  Pierre Gagnaire
  Fermette Marbeuf 1900
24 Trois Marches
  Jacques Cagna
  Pershing
  Elysées
  Brass. Julien
  Jardin des Cygnes
  Maison Blanche*
  Toupary
  Relais Louis XIII
  Pavillon Montsouris
23 Bofinger
  Atelier Joël Robuchon
  Café Marly
  Orangerie
  Christine
  Michel Rostang
  Brass. Mollard
  Coupole

Outdoors

Bristol
Café Lenôtre
Café Marly
Copenhague
Délices de Szechuen
Espadon
Georges

Jardins de Bagatelle
Laurent
Maison de l'Amér. Lat.
Pavillon Montsouris
Pré Catelan
Rest./Palais Royal
Tastevin

Romance

Allard
Ambassadeurs
Caviar Kaspia
Copenhague
Costes
Dôme
Espadon
Flora Danica
Grande Cascade

Grand Véfour
Jardins de Bagatelle
Jules Verne
Lapérouse
Lasserre
Ledoyen
Orangerie
Pré Catelan
Tour d'Argent

Rooms

Alcazar
Bon 2
Cristal Room
Gare

Kong
Ladurée (8ᵉ)
Maison Blanche
Train Bleu

Views

Altitude 95
Copenhague
Georges
Jules Verne
Kong

Maison Blanche
R.
Rest./Musée d'Orsay
Terrasse
Toupary

Top 50 Service

28 Taillevent
   Cinq
   Guy Savoy
27 Lasserre
   Hiramatsu
   Grand Véfour
   Bristol
   Espadon
   Ambassadeurs
   Pierre Gagnaire
26 Michel Rostang
   Tour d'Argent
   Rest. Alain Ducasse
   Meurice
   Ambroisie
25 Lucas Carton
   Grande Cascade
   Relais d'Auteuil/Pignol
   Apicius
   Arpège
   Bar Vendôme
   Ledoyen*
   Carré des Feuillants
24 Florimond
   Elysées

   Obélisque*
   Pré Catelan
   Truffière
   Laurent
   Astrance
   Gérard Besson
   Jamin
   Jacques Cagna
   Relais Louis XIII
   Ferme St-Simon
   Jules Verne
23 Angle du Faubourg
   Marée
   Jardin des Cygnes
   Relais Plaza
   P'tit Troquet
   Magnolias
   Trois Marches
   Christine*
22 Chez Georges
   Violon d'Ingres
   Sormani
   Lapérouse
   Caviar Kaspia
   Trou Gascon

Best Buys

1. Cosi
2. Crêperie de Josselin
3. Chartier
4. Lina's
5. BE Boulangépicier
6. Higuma
7. Angelina
8. A Priori Thé
9. Mariage Frères
10. B-Café
11. Zéphyr
12. P'tit Troquet
13. Ladurée
14. Café Charbon
15. Anahuacalli
16. Domaine de Lintillac
17. Polidor
18. Aub. du Champ de Mars
19. Dalloyau
20. Brass./l'Ile St. Louis
21. Bistrot du Peintre
22. Water Bar Colette
23. Petit Rétro
24. Chez Paul (13e)
25. Florimond
26. Loir dans la Théière
27. Camille
28. Cave de l'Os à Moëlle
29. Beurre Noisette
30. Troquet
31. Chez Janou
32. Petit Prince de Paris
33. Brass. du Louvre
34. Sept Quinze
35. Languedoc
36. Mirama
37. Tire-Bouchon
38. Bistrot d'Henri
39. Atlas
40. Aub. Pyrénées Cévennes

Other Good Values

Alivi
Astier
Avant Goût
Baan-Boran
Bistrot Baracane
Biche au Bois
Café de Flore
Café de la Musique
Café du Commerce
Cafetière
Café Very/Dame Tart.
C'Amelot
Chez Marianne
Chez Omar
Chez Paul (11e)
Chicago Pizza
China Club
Christine
Coffee Parisien
Délices d'Aphrodite
Deux Canards
Editeurs
Fish La Boissonnerie
Flore en l'Ile
Fumoir
Gamin de Paris
Grand Louvre
Juvéniles
Matsuri
Monsieur Lapin
Nemrod
Pamphlet
Passy Mandarin
Petit Bofinger
404
Relais/l'Entrecôte
Rest./Musée d'Orsay
Scheffer
Villaret
Wadja

Restaurant Directory

Absinthe (L') ☒   19 | 16 | 15 | 43

24, pl du Marché St-Honoré, 1er (Pyramides), 01 49 26 90 04; fax 49 26 08 64; www.michelrostang.com
☑ "On Paris' seemingly only traffic-free square" (the Place du Marché-Saint Honoré), this "pleasantly situated bistro" offers "open-air delight" in summer and year-round "authentic" atmosphere, all agree; however, while devotees declare it "delivers" with often "innovative", "consistent Classic French food" at "quite reasonable" prices, doubters demur, saying "it's hard to believe it's owned by Michel Rostang"; "if only they could serve the real absinthe", maybe the disagreements would be dispelled.

A et M Le Bistrot ☒   15 | 14 | 15 | 39

136, bd Murat, 16e (Porte de St-Cloud), 01 45 27 39 60; fax 45 27 69 71
■ "No miracles, but no disappointments" sums up this contemporary bistro, "an honest table with attentive service and justifiable prices" in the 16th arrondissement; though "inventive", the fish-heavy menu can be "a little boring", but "you can't do better in the Porte de Saint-Cloud area", especially when "lunching with executives of the TF1" TV station nearby.

Affiche (A l') ☒   – | – | – | M

48, rue de Moscou, 8e (Rome), 01 45 22 02 20
In the up-and-coming Europe district, this storefront bistro with a Contemporary French chalkboard menu is "a nice addition to a neighborhood that badly needed a decent, reasonably priced" place, even if a few find that the namesake old "movie poster–themed" decor is "an unnecessary gimmick."

Affriolé (L') ☒   21 | 13 | 18 | 41

17, rue Malar, 7e (La Tour-Maubourg/Invalides), 01 44 18 31 33; fax 44 18 91 12
☑ Chef Thierry Verola's table in a quiet corner of the 7th may be "noisy", but who cares when his "small but varied menu" of "inventive" contemporary Bistro cooking is so "sublime" – an "exceptional value for the money"; and if many judge the "decor drab", the "charming service" helps "warm up" the room.

Aiguière (L') ☒   – | – | – | E

37 bis, rue de Montreuil, 11e (Faidherbe-Chaligny), 01 43 72 42 32; fax 43 72 96 36; www.l-aiguiere.com
Maybe because it's tucked away in the 11th, not many know this "lovely, romantic" auberge with a "cozy atmosphere" created by exposed beams and a cheerful blue-and-yellow color scheme; "served with savoir faire" (the plates come covered with a dome), the "excellent" "albeit a bit pricey" Traditional French food is backed up with a 400-label wine list.

Ailleurs ●🗷
11 | 13 | 13 | 38

26, rue Jean Mermoz, 8ᵉ (Franklin D. Roosevelt), 01 53 53 98 00; fax 53 53 98 01; www.ailleurs-fr.com

🗷 "You're not really someplace else [*ailleurs*], you're in the heart of the Champs-Elysées" smirk smarties about this Eclectic, a "fashion restaurant" that they claim is "fading away", its in-crowd clientele "like a flock of birds who've migrated to other places", due to the "uneven cuisine"; still, fans of this fusion fiesta find the "menu exotic" and the "staff nice", and the noise makes it "a good place to go when you really don't want to talk."

Aimant du Sud (L') ●🗷
– | – | – | M

40, bd Arago, 13ᵉ (Les Gobelins), 01 47 07 33 57

"A very-good, well-priced local" bistro is the sunny summary of this modest place in the 13th, whose Med menu features standards (as its name hints) for lovers of the south of France, plus a "nice Southwestern wine list"; in summer, "reservations are indispensable" if guests want to Basque on the "lovely terrace."

Al Caratello
– | – | – | M

5, rue Audran, 18ᵉ (Abbesses/Pigalle), 01 42 62 24 23

Though some might find this shop-front dining room off the rue Lepic over-lit and plain, the generously served Italian cooking has made the place a hit with trendy theater, TV and film-industry locals; friendly service and reasonably priced wines from The Boot add to the appeal, so be sure to reserve.

Alcazar ●
16 | 21 | 16 | 48

62, rue Mazarine, 6ᵉ (Odéon), 01 53 10 19 99; fax 53 10 23 23; www.alcazar.fr

🗷 Most admire the "soaring ceilings, ultramodern decor" and "exceptional open kitchen" that characterize Sir Terence Conran's "big" bi-level brasserie for the beautiful people, despite its un-Gallic air – kind of "like Santa Monica in the 6th arrondissement"; though it's "more a scene than a meal", the New French eats are, "if not inspired, consistent" (do try the "signature shellfish sampler"), and the hip types are "fun to watch", if hard to talk to (it's "a little noisy, even for a noisy place").

Al Dar ●
20 | 10 | 16 | 37

8, rue Frédéric Sauton, 5ᵉ (Maubert-Mutualité), 01 43 25 17 15
93, av Raymond Poincaré, 16ᵉ (Victor Hugo), 01 45 00 96 64; fax 45 01 61 67

🗷 Falafel fans and meze mavens acclaim the "always-fresh", "super-good" food at these Lebanese tables in the 5th and the 16th – so it's a pita that the dining-room decor (think pastels and mirrors) is "a bit depressing" and the service slightly "stuffy"; of course one can always take advantage of the "absolutely amazing take-out section."

Al Diwan ◐   20 | 14 | 16 | 42

*30, av George V, 8ᵉ (Alma-Marceau/George V), 01 47 23 45 45;
fax 47 23 60 98*

■ For a "little Beirut in Paris", fans flock to this "dining
room with a modern Middle Eastern–style decor", which
provides "possibly the most tasty Lebanese food in town"
("I even ate a goat's testicle, and it was delicious"); some
feel the fare "in no way compensates" for the prices
("justified only by" the swanky Avenue George V address)
or the "slow staff" – though it helps if you "wear black
leather to fit in with the local" Arabic crowd.

Alivi (L') ◐   19 | 16 | 19 | 36

*27, rue du Roi de Sicile, 4ᵉ (Hôtel-de-Ville/St-Paul), 01 48 87 90 20;
fax 48 87 20 60; www.restaurant-alivi.com*

■ Perfect "for discovering Corsican cooking" ("don't miss
the fish soup or the charcuterie plate") carol converts
about this "intimate" island in the Marais; equally "fine" is
the "friendly welcome" and "sweet service", all at tabs
that are as easy to swallow as the native wines.

ALLARD ◐ 🗷   22 | 17 | 19 | 52

*41, rue St-André-des-Arts, 6ᵉ (Odéon), 01 43 26 48 23;
fax 46 33 04 02*

■ Despite a few "too many Americans", this Saint-Germain
stalwart "exudes" "a consummate old-time bistro" vibe,
starting with its "delicious, hearty" Classic French food,
especially "the best duck with olives (who knew you could
eat that many at once?)" and "superb wine list"; adding to
the "authentic" ambiance are the "jam-packed tables" and
"servers who can be crusty – but in a friendly way"; "it's
thanks to places like this that Paris will always be Paris."

Allobroges (Les) 🗷   – | – | – | M

*71, rue des Grands Champs, 20ᵉ (Maraîchers/Nation),
01 43 73 40 00; fax 40 09 23 22*

It's "in the boondocks, but that keeps prices relatively low for
a genteel ambiance and well-prepared nouvelle-ish food"
insist the intrepid who've journeyed to this "little jewel
in the 20th"; the "welcome is warm" as you enter the wall-
papered dining room to savor the contemporary Bistro
delights, preferably on one of the prix fixes ("a real deal").

Al Mounia   19 | 22 | 19 | 44

*16, rue de Magdebourg, 16ᵉ (Trocadéro), 01 47 27 57 28;
fax 41 44 73 63; www.al-mounia.com*

■ A meal at this Moroccan near the Trocadéro is "almost
as good as going to Marrakesh" since stylistically the
"exotic" "decor is pure riad" (a North African villa); equally
"respectful of tradition" is the "earnest food" and "caring
service"; visual verisimilitude notwithstanding, however,
some say that "the hammered brass tables are not the
most comfortable to eat at" when seated on leather poufs.

Alsace (L') ⊘   16 | 15 | 14 | 44
39, av des Champs-Elysées, 8ᵉ (Franklin D. Roosevelt),
01 53 93 97 00; fax 53 93 97 09; www.restaurantalsace.com
◪ "It's brassy, noisy and filled with tourists", but "at 3 AM
in the 8th", you're "always glad this place is around" note
night-owls of this 24/7 "nonstop brasserie" that's generally
"good" "for an Alsatian fix" of "delicious choucroute" or a
"raw seafood platter on ice"; on the down side, often "the
waiters act like you're invisible" and several say it strikes
them as "pricey, due to its location" – an admittedly "grand"
one "on the Champs-Elysées."

Alsaco (L') ⊠   18 | 10 | 17 | 38
10, rue Condorcet, 9ᵉ (Gare du Nord/Poissonnière),
01 45 26 44 31; www.alsacoparis.com
■ "Excellent Alsatian cooking and a remarkable collection
of eaux-de-vies" attract hearty eaters to this "out-of-the-
way" corner of the 9th (leaving no doubt this is a "bona
fide *winstub*"); it's "ideal on a winter night", when you can
expect "personal service from the chef" and get cozy over
"wonderful choucroute" without spending a fortune.

Altitude 95   15 | 23 | 18 | 45
Tour Eiffel, Champ-de-Mars, 1st level, 7ᵉ (Bir-Hakeim/
Champ-de-Mars), 01 45 55 20 04; fax 47 05 94 40
◪ The "fabulous" panorama of Paris is the chief lure of
this Eiffel Tower eatery; but many "pleasantly surprised"
surveyors say the place "has changed": if it once seemed
"Paris' highest tourist trap", it now offers "decent" Classic
French eats and, as a score rise attests, the service has
gained altitude too; and if it still seems "overpriced" to
several, remember you get "the best view in town at a
fraction of the cost of the Jules Verne" (its sibling one
flight up); P.S. "call 15 days in advance" for a window table.

Ambassade d'Auvergne   20 | 16 | 20 | 46
22, rue du Grenier St-Lazare, 3ᵉ (Rambuteau), 01 42 72 31 22;
fax 42 78 85 47; www.ambassade-auvergne.com
■ If some "don't think of the Auvergne beyond Michelin
tires and volcanoes", the "consistently excellent food" at
"one of the best regional restaurants" in Paris will certainly
put that province on the map; the "cordial welcome" and
"attentive service" are almost as appetizing as the "hearty"
fare that includes the must-have "aligot, that elastic mashed
potato/cheese/garlic compound", and "chocolate mousse
to die for"; it also offers "great value" in a "country-style"
setting paradoxically "close to the Pompidou."

AMBASSADEURS (LES)   26 | 28 | 27 | VE
Hôtel de Crillon, 10, pl de la Concorde, 8ᵉ (Concorde),
01 44 71 16 16; fax 44 71 15 02; www.crillon.com
■ The Food score may not reflect the post-*Survey* arrival of
chef Jean-François Piège to this "marbled", "magnificent"

dining room with a "million-dollar view of the Place de la Concorde", but given his Plaza-Athénée pedigree, it's probably safe to say its renown for New French "delicious entrees and whimsical desserts" will continue – as perhaps will the "fawning" service ("never have there been so many to serve so few"); just "hold on to your wallet" because this "extraordinarily elegant" experience is also "evisceratingly expensive."

AMBROISIE (L') ☒   26 | 26 | 26 | VE

9, pl des Vosges, 4ᵉ (Bastille/St-Paul), 01 42 78 51 45
■ Chef-owner Bernard Pacaud's "jewel box" of Haute Cuisine in the tony Place des Vosges is not only "one of the most beautiful in Paris", with a "spectacular" "Petit Versailles"–style decor, but the cooking, a "creative" riff on classic dishes, is "ambrosial" – "truly the food of the gods" "served by people determined to please you"; "little extras help lessen the blow of the bill", but "if you can get in", go no matter what the state of your savings ("what would your children learn in college anyway?").

Amici Miei ☒≠   – | – | – | M

53, bd Beaumarchais, 3ᵉ (Chemin Vert), 01 42 71 82 62
Parisian pie-heads say yes, it *is* worth "waiting in the street" until a table opens up ("they don't take reservations") at this hole-in-the-wall Marais Italian; "the pizza's excellent", so don't be put off by the "tiny", bright Formica-finished dining room and somewhat "lamentable" service.

Ami Marcel (L') ☒   – | – | – | M

33, rue Georges-Pitard, 15ᵉ (Plaisance/Convention),
01 48 56 62 06; fax 48 56 62 06
The chef at this contemporary bistro on a quiet corner of the 15th formerly cooked at L'Espadon in the Ritz, and the precision and elegance of that kitchen show up in dishes like Salers steak with hand-cut fries; the simple, *crème*-colored dining room is staffed by a group who also worked at a variety of famous high-altitude tables before becoming part of this ambitious, but still earthbound, team.

Ami Pierre (A l') ◕☒   – | – | – | M

5, rue de la Main d'Or, 11ᵉ (Ledru-Rollin), 01 47 00 17 35
This "atmospheric" *bistrot à vins* near the Bastille is like being "propelled into France during the 1950s" with all the fixings: "friendly" atmosphere, "elbow-to-elbow" seating and "generous portions" of Southwestern–classic Bistro "eats that are very Gallic" ("divine cheese plate"); don't forget to start out or "finish up at the zinc-clad bar."

Amognes (Les) ☒   19 | 10 | 15 | 44

243, rue du Faubourg St-Antoine, 11ᵉ (Faidherbe-Chaligny),
01 43 72 73 05
☑ For anyone who likes "wonderfully inventive" Bistro cooking and "a really good buy", to boot, this "amazingly

creative little home near the Bastille is still waiting to be discovered"; a few doubters demur, citing a "lack of consistency", but most appreciate the "discreet service" that makes it "a good place for a tranquil discussion."

Ampère (L') 🖾   – | – | – | M
1, rue Ampère, 17ᵉ (Wagram), 01 47 63 72 05; fax 47 63 37 33
🔲 Chef Philippe Detourbe, a gastronomic star of the late '80s and early '90s (his numerous tables included an eponymous establishment in the 15th), has taken over this long-running, "popular" neighborhood spot near the Place Péreire; his new menu mixes Eclectic dishes such as shrimp tempura and wild mushroom risotto with Bistro classics such as pan-roasted duck breast or steak with morels.

Amphyclès 🖾   24 | 17 | 22 | VE
78, av des Ternes, 17ᵉ (Porte Maillot), 01 40 68 01 01; fax 40 68 91 88
■ With "cooking that's just as inventive as ever" ("don't miss the sea crab specialty") at this New French in the 17th, you can expect a "delicious" meal in the company of a "chic crowd" in a pleasant, pale-hued dining room; N.B. at press time, it had closed temporarily for renovation.

Amuse Bouche (L') 🖾   ▽ 17 | 16 | 18 | 43
186, rue du Château, 14ᵉ (Gaîté/Mouton-Duvernet), 01 43 35 31 61; fax 45 38 96 60
🔲 In a quiet part of the 14th, this "amusing little" place "just buzzes, especially after 10 PM"; but while lovebirds chirp it's "ideal for a romantic night out", given the "good New French cuisine" and "charming staff", sourpusses pout it's gotten "overpriced" for the quality on hand.

Anacréon 🖾   ▽ 17 | 12 | 16 | 38
53, bd St-Marcel, 13ᵉ (Les Gobelins), 01 43 31 71 18; fax 43 31 94 94
🔲 This "good neighborhood" establishment near the Place d'Italie is run by chef André Le Letty, ex Tour d'Argent, which explains why the Traditional French cooking is "intelligent, unusual" and "definitely not the kind of food you do at home"; the nonexistent decor gets nonexistent comments, but the fare is "served nicely" and the prices are especially gentle.

Anahï ●   19 | 14 | 17 | 48
49, rue Volta, 3ᵉ (Arts et Métiers/Temple), 01 48 87 88 24; fax 48 87 93 04
🔲 Ever since they took over an old-fashioned butcher's shop in the 3rd, sisters Carmen and Pilar (the chef) have been the "welcoming team" at this South American specializing in "succulent" Argentinean beef; however, whether they chose to pampa you or not seems to depend on your "beautiful-person" quotient, causing some to carp "your choice is simple: be a fashion victim or a victim of the manager"; many also moan that "the value-for-money ratio doesn't work here."

Anahuacalli
24 | 15 | 21 | 35

30, rue des Bernardins, 5ᵉ (Maubert-Mutualité), 01 43 26 10 20; fax 42 53 06 82

■ "It's not easy to find good Mexican food in Paris", which is why the hordes are so high on this 5th arrondissement "charmer", hailing its "original" "real cuisine" as a welcome antidote to "Tex-Mex rip-offs"; "killer margaritas" and "warm service" from the "adorable lady owners" add to the "convivial" ambiance of the yellow-painted dining room, and prices are pretty easy to swallow, too.

Andy Whaloo ●🗵
- | - | - | I

69, rue des Gravilliers, 3ᵉ (Arts et Métiers), 01 42 71 20 38; fax 42 74 03 41

Not many surveyors have noted this North African nibbles-and-drinks annex of the popular 404 in the 3rd; those who have hail the "super atmosphere" achieved by a '70s-funky, pop-Moroccan decor (stools made from old paint-drums, lots of bright colors) and "really nice service", even if the food's "a bit weak."

ANGELINA
18 | 20 | 14 | 25

226, rue de Rivoli, 1ᵉʳ (Concorde/Tuileries), 01 42 60 82 00; fax 42 86 98 97

🖾 Since 1903, this "old-world tea salon" across from the Tuileries has attracted sweet-toothed tourists for its "frighteningly decadent" hot chocolate, "so thick you almost have to scoop it", and "delectable" desserts; those au courant cavil the rest of the menu – salads, sandwiches, etc. – is "nothing special" and the "perennially stressed" staff seems often "on autopilot"; but if this "grande dame" is "past her prime" (and charging primo prices for pastries), she's still "a wonderful Parisian experience."

Angle du Faubourg (L') 🗵
24 | 19 | 23 | E

195, rue du Faubourg St-Honoré, 8ᵉ (Charles de Gaulle-Etoile/ Ternes), 01 40 74 20 20; fax 40 74 20 21; www.cavestaillevent.com

■ "Fabulously" "fresh, inventive" New French cooking and an "excellent selection of lesser-known wines" have made this "classy" "young sister to the big champ" Taillevent in the 8th "another success for M. Vrinat" (the owner); the terra cotta–colored "modern, sleek" decor strikes some as "sterile" – "I thought I was in a department store" – but the service, including the "delightful female sommelier", is generally "gracious"; it's "perfect for a business lunch", thanks to "a wonder" of a prix fixe menu.

Angl'Opera
- | - | - | M

Hotel Edouard VII, 39, av de l'Opéra, 2ᵉ (Opéra/Pyramides/ Quatre Septembre), 01 42 61 86 25; fax 42 61 47 73; www.anglopera.com

Gilles Choukroun, who built a reputation for audacious spices and textures at Café des Délices, has opened a second outlet for his edgy Contemporary French cooking in the 2nd; friendly waitresses animate the large, sleekly decorated dining room and patiently explain the novel menu, which needs explaining because it reads like Surrealist poetry, incorporating ingredients that range from foie gras to supermarket brands.

Annapurna ●◖🖾
18 | 16 | 18 | 48

32, rue de Berri, 8ᵉ (George V/St-Philippe-du-Roule), 01 45 63 91 62
◪ "Good Indian cooking", "attentive service" and a "kitschy" decor "complete with a bearded sitar player" and "low tables" curry favor with fans of this 8th arrondissement Brahmin; but antagonists argue "for the price", everything "could be better", particularly the "portions (a bit small)."

AOC (L') 🖾
– | – | – | M

14, rue des Fossés St-Bernard, 5ᵉ (Cardinal Lemoine/Jussieu), 01 43 54 22 52; fax 43 25 80 16; www.restoaoc.com
Specializing in pedigreed produce "as the name implies" (the prestigious AOC label denotes a "distinctive" food that meets strict government standards), this Latin Quarter bistro lives up to its name with "memorable" classic dishes, "graciously" and "generously served" (specifically recommended: "the rotisseried suckling pig, tender and crispy at the same time"); "prices are fair for such quality."

APICIUS 🖾
27 | – | 25 | VE

20, rue d'Artois, 8ᵉ (Franklin D. Roosevelt/St-Philippe-du-Roule), 01 43 80 19 66; fax 44 40 09 57; www.relaischateaux.com
■ In partnership with filmmaker Luc Besson, chef Jean-Pierre Vigato has moved his 20-year old Haute Cuisine haven to an elegant new townhouse on a quiet street in the 8th; well-spaced tables and calm, masculine colors set the scene for his "exquisite updated classics" that are "worth every euro"; complementing the "grand finesse" in the kitchen is the "professional", "no-attitude" service out front; small surprise that some say this "original has evolved into a classic."

Apollo
∇ 10 | 20 | 8 | 34

3, pl Denfert Rochereau, 14ᵉ (Denfert-Rochereau), 01 45 38 76 77; fax 43 22 02 15
■ Located in the street-level concourse of a métro station in the 14th, this "trendy" site with groovy '70s retro decor wins kudos for its "superb terrace, in the middle of Paris but sheltered from traffic"; antagonists think it should apollo-gize for the "uninteresting" New French fare that seems "a little expensive" given its "disappointing" nature.

Appart' (L') ●
14 | 18 | 14 | 46

9, rue du Colisée, 8ᵉ (Franklin D. Roosevelt), 01 53 75 42 00; fax 53 75 42 09; www.lappart.com
◪ Just off the Champs, this "fashionable" Classic French is "decorated to resemble a real Parisian apartment", hence

the name; if most like the "warm" look and "amusing" concept, many add that's the "only memorable thing" about this place, since the food is "decent" but "nothing to write home about" and the service from an all-female staff seems "very slow."

Appennino (L') ⬨ — | — | — | M

61, rue de l'Amiral Mouchez, 13ᵉ (Cité Universitaire), 01 45 89 08 15

Maybe because it's hidden away in the 13th, few know this Northern Italian with a "modest setting", but those who do praise the "quality cooking" and "excellent wines at what may be the best prices to be found anywhere in Paris"; even if "the welcome's a little chilly", the "service is professional."

A Priori Thé ⬨ 17 | 18 | 15 | 25

35, Galerie Vivienne, 2ᵉ (Bourse/Palais Royal-Musée du Louvre), 01 42 97 48 75

■ With a "great location" in the "beautiful Galerie Vivienne", this "cozy" tearoom is nearly everyone's cuppa with crumble, "scones and pastries to die for", one of the "best cheesecakes in Paris" and "inventive homemade" "light meals"; the waiters are "sometimes overwhelmed" during the "abundant brunch" on weekends, "but the charm" of the place takes priority over any glitches.

Arbuci (L') ◐ 13 | 14 | 13 | 40

25, rue de Buci, 6ᵉ (Mabillon), 01 44 32 16 00; fax 44 32 16 09; www.arbuci.com

◪ They may serve "delicious" "all-you-can-eat oysters" at this Saint-Germain "bustling" brasserie that got a "*très* chic" but "too modern" makeover awhile back, but many mutter the rest of the "traditonal menu" seems "mediocre" and "disorganized service" doesn't help; still, they offer dancing to DJ-spun and live tunes toward the end of the week, leaving some to ponder "maybe the jazz is a better value than the food."

Ardoise (L') 22 | 12 | 17 | 38

28, rue du Mont Thabor, 1ᵉʳ (Concorde/Tuileries), 01 42 96 28 18

■ When you're "taking a break from the Louvre" nearby, this "tiny place with huge flavors" offers a weekly changing "appetizing chalkboard menu" of "hearty" innovative Bistro fare that has the crowds crowing over chef-owner Pierre Jay; despite its "being flooded with tourists", the "service is lightning fast"; and "at such affordable prices" (especially for the "overpriced 1st"), "it's easy to overlook" the near-"nonexistent" decor and "elbow-bumping" seating.

Argenteuil (L') 23 | 18 | 21 | 47

9, rue d'Argenteuil, 1ᵉʳ (Palais Royal-Musée du Louvre/ Pyramides), 01 42 60 56 22

■ "In a sort of lost corner of the 1st", this "intimate" New French delights devotees with "delicious" food, service that's "courteous without any irritating chumminess" and a

"trim but handsome decor"; its "subtly exciting" charms are
lost on some, but most find it "perfect if you're Louvre-d out."

Aristide ☒ — | — | — | M |
121, rue de Rome, 17ᵉ (Rome), 01 47 63 17 83; fax 47 54 97 55
With a gorgeous interior dating to 1893, this "good",
moderately priced place in the 17th is "packed at noon"
with a business crowd, but quiet in the evening – which
makes it a fine "rendezvous for an intimate dinner" of
"solid Classic" French dishes made with first-rate foodstuffs.

Armand au Palais Royal ☒ 21 | 21 | 23 | 48 |
*4-6, rue du Beaujolais, 1ᵉʳ (Bourse/Palais Royal-
Musée du Louvre), 01 42 60 05 11; fax 42 96 16 24*
■ "Housed in the 17th century stables of the Palais Royal",
this "agreeable" Traditional French filly has a loyal
following of local and foreign fans who "recommend"
the "intimate ambiance" created by its "pretty" vaulted
ceilings, "attentive and genuinely friendly service" and
"marvelous" food (including a signature crêpe that contains
"some of the best foie gras in Paris").

ARPÈGE (L') ☒ 26 | 23 | 25 | VE |
*84, rue de Varenne, 7ᵉ (Varenne), 01 45 51 47 33; fax 44 18 98 39;
www.alain-passard.com*
☑ His cooking tastes "the way God intended it to" acclaim
acolytes of chef-owner Alain Passard, whose "exceptional",
if "esoteric", vegetable-oriented Haute Cuisine is "styled like
a haute couture designer's"; the decor at this "sophisticate"
in the 7th is "sparse, but impressive", and the "staff is
superb"; admittedly, the whole experience can be an
"intellectual challenge", and "prices have soared out of
control" – maybe that's why some would "be willing to work
as a waiter to get the food free."

Asian 14 | 21 | 13 | 45 |
*30, av George V, 8ᵉ (Alma-Marceau/George V), 01 56 89 11 00;
fax 56 89 11 01; www.asian.fr*
☑ A "professional clientele" finds the glamorama decor –
a sort of Disneyesque take on diverse decorative idioms of
the Far East – "wonderful" at this "chic", "cavernous" Pan-
Asian place off the Champs-Elysées; in fact, "you come here
more for the pretty setting than the mediocre", "pricey"
"theme cuisine" (though some "original" offerings have their
advocates); all agree, however, that the staff "seems as if
it's merely part of the decoration" – "beautiful" but "slow."

Assiette (L') ∇ 26 | 16 | 16 | 74 |
*181, rue du Château, 14ᵉ (Gaîté/Mouton-Duvernet),
01 43 22 64 86; fax 45 20 54 66*
■ "Off the beaten path" in Montparnasse, this traditional
bistro is sort of like "a private club with loyal, very-flush
clients" (including the late President François Mitterrand)
who love the "really good Southwestern cooking" of "Lulu

Rousseau, the cigar-smoking chef"; "you get food from her heart and the pick of her region" in a simple dining room with tile floors, but an "astronomical price tag" as the price of admission.

Assiette Lyonnaise ● 16 | 11 | 14 | 31
21, rue Marbeuf, 8ᵉ (Franklin D. Roosevelt), 01 47 20 94 80; fax 47 23 53 94
■ A roaring rise in the Food score makes this "charmer" of a regional bistro the Lyon king of Paris, given its "delicious", "honest" and "filling" fare that's "solid value for the money" and "for the area" (the 8th, where eating cheap isn't always easy); though the decor remains "unassuming", the atmosphere's "warm", thanks to "increased friendliness" on the staff's part.

Astier ☒ 21 | 12 | 17 | 35
44, rue J.P. Timbaud, 11ᵉ (Oberkampf/Parmentier), 01 43 57 16 35
■ It gets a little "hot, temperaturewise" and "it's not the place for quiet conversation", but this site "off the beaten (tourist) path" in the 11th packs 'em in with its "pleasing" classic Bistro food "for a modest price", especially on the "extensive prix fixe" whose "mind-blowing cheese tray" is "nearly the same size as the table"; though "precise", the servers speak "minimal English", but one's "friendly fellow customers are only too happy to guide the uninitiated."

Astor (L') 22 | 21 | 21 | 90
Hôtel Astor, 11, rue d'Astorg, 8ᵉ (St-Augustin), 01 53 05 05 20; fax 53 05 05 30; www.hotel-astor.net
☑ This Haute Cuisine hotel dining room in the 8th is favored by a business clientele for its "ambitious, delicious" New French cuisine, a "lunch menu that's a good buy" and the "elegant, art deco–style decor"; however, several say the "quality has become uneven" since a "chef change", and the service, while "artful", bears "a touch of the scornful."

ASTRANCE ☒ 26 | 21 | 24 | VE
4, rue Beethoven, 16ᵉ (Passy), 01 40 50 84 40
■ Provided you "book months ahead of time", "an exquisite experience" awaits at chef/co-owner Pascal Barbot's New French table "with a luminous gray decor" in a quiet street near the Trocadéro; his "food from out of a fantasy" has many "gasping in awe", with due appreciation for the "wonderful, accommodating staff" too; some suggest success has made it "self-important" (expecting their money "would buy me more fun than this"), but most say it's "still an extraordinary bargain for this level of cooking."

Astrée (L') ☒ – | – | – | E
3, rue du Général Lanzerac, 17ᵉ (Charles de Gaulle-Etoile), 01 45 72 27 00; fax 45 72 03 21
Located not far from L'Etoile, this dressy little dining room with steel-gray painted walls brightened by modern floral

arrangements has quickly gained a following for its original New French dishes (e.g. mackerel marinated in a finely spiced marinade); a business crowd at noon gives way to a stylish flock of gourmets in the evening, who don't find the pricey tab off-putting considering the intricate preparations.

Astuce (L') ☒   – | – | – | M

138, rue de Vaugirard, 15ᵉ (Duroc/Falguière), 01 47 83 29 52; fax 08 25 17 08 25; www.lastuce.fr

A large mirror dominates this snug Left Bank dining room where the creative Bistro fare is starting to draw a stylish, young crowd as word gets around the *quartier*; friendly service and a warm atmosphere make it easy to linger on the banquettes here.

Atelier Berger (L') ◐☒   21 | 17 | 17 | 50

49, rue Berger, 1ᵉʳ (Louvre-Rivoli), 01 40 28 00 00; fax 40 28 10 65

▨ Dueling opinions duke it out about this "quiet" duplex dining room with "modern decor"; devotees declare Norwegian chef-owner Jean Christiansen's New French cuisine, a "carefully crafted" "combination of the inspired and the traditional", makes this "modern" place "among the best addresses in Les Halles"; but the "disappointed" deplore the "indifferent service" "and zero scene."

ATELIER DE JOËL   26 | 23 | 21 | E
ROBUCHON (L') ◐

5, rue de Montalembert, 7ᵉ (Rue du Bac), 01 42 22 56 56; fax 42 22 97 91

▨ From the day it opened in the 7th, chef Joël Robuchon's comeback has been a "real culinary hot spot"; within a "sleek", black setting, diners "sit around a counter" "overlooking the kitchen" (think "glorified diner") to sample "tapaslike", "tasty morsels" ("plus some mains") of his "tongue-popping" Haute Cuisine; fans find it "fabulous", with the only "flat note" being that the limited-reservations policy often causes a "long wait at the door" (which "doesn't open from the outside"); best advice: "eat early."

Atelier Gourmand ☒   – | – | – | M

20, rue de Tocqueville, 17ᵉ (Villiers), 01 42 27 03 71; fax 42 27 03 71

Though it's not very well known, this "fairly priced" New French in the 17th is "a neighborhood jewel" that's "always worthy of your confidence", even if its menu changes often; the owners, a "husband-wife team, provide good service", though the setting, decorated in a hybrid of Second Empire and artist's atelier styles, is "not *très* fun."

Atelier Maître Albert (L') ◐   – | – | – | M

1, rue Maître Albert, 5ᵉ (Maubert-Mutalité), 01 56 81 30 01; fax 53 10 83 23

Now under the command of chef Guy Savoy, this "warm" and "very Latin Quarter" (read: noisy) bistro has gotten a

F | D | S | €C

dramatic revamp by his preferred decorator Jean-Michel Wilmotte since the last *Survey*; the new look is all exposed stone walls and cobalt-blue beams overhead, but the Maître's old pupils will be glad to hear that the large Renaissance fireplace and rotisserie have not been touched – in fact, the short menu stars roasted-on-a-spit fowl, fish and meats, served by a young staff.

Atlas (L') 21 | 16 | 18 | 36
12, bd St-Germain, 5ᵉ (Maubert-Mutualité), 01 46 33 86 98; fax 40 46 06 56

■ "Generous" helpings of "savory tagines" and other "classics", served by a "most welcoming and eager staff", keep the crowd coming to this long-running couscous casbah in the Latin Quarter; sure, it's "more expensive than the clip joints off the Boulevard Saint-Michel", but that's because you're paying for "atmospheric decor", "like something from an early *James Bond* film shot in Morocco."

Auberge Aveyronnaise ● – | – | – | M
40, rue Gabriel Lamé, 12ᵉ (Cour St-Emilion), 01 43 40 12 24; fax 43 40 12 15

"Good regional dishes" from the Aveyron district of the Auvergne acquire admirers to this "sweet bistro" in the 12th not far from Bercy; if the bill-of-fare runs to sturdy dishes like aligot (potatoes whipped with cheese curds), prices are light as a feather, making it a good choice for groups; all can enjoy the "jovial service."

Auberge Bressane (L') 21 | 16 | 19 | 43
16, av de La Motte-Picquet, 7ᵉ (Ecole Militaire/ La Tour-Maubourg), 01 47 05 98 37; fax 47 05 92 21

■ "A great place to beat the Sunday-night blues" ("go in hungry, and come out ready to face the work week") attest those "addicted" to this "excellent auberge" in the 7th, which serves "hearty", "rustic" Classic French "quality cuisine" from Lyon and Burgundy; "almost-familial" service further "warms the heart and soul" of the well-heeled clientele here, which even smiles on the "outdated but charming" digs "decorated with heraldic emblems", wood paneling and wrought-iron light fixtures.

Auberge Dab (L') ● 16 | 14 | 16 | 52
161, av de Malakoff, 16ᵉ (Porte Maillot), 01 45 00 32 22; fax 45 00 58 50

◪ "The aroma of shellfish is heady" at this huge haven near the Porte Maillot, which offers a "classic brasserie experience" in that it's "always reliable for a seafood platter" and "people-watching by the window" in a "decor from a Jean Gabin film" of the '50s; but faultfinders feel it's a "factory"-like experience – from the food to the "pleasant, but often distracted" service – and a "relatively expensive" one to boot.

30 **subscribe to zagat.com**

Auberge du Champ de Mars ☒   19 | 17 | 18 | 32
18, rue de l'Exposition, 7ᵉ (Ecole Militaire), 01 45 51 78 08
■ Converts champion this "small, family-run" place, with a "romantic", "dark and mysterious setting", and a husband-wife team – "he's the chef, she's the hostess" – "who make you feel like guests in their home"; it's "great value for the money" in an expensive part of the 7th, especially given such "good" Classic French cooking ("loved the duck").

Auberge du Clou (L') ●⇗   – | – | – | M
30, av Trudaine, 9ᵉ (Anvers/Pigalle), 01 48 78 22 48; fax 08 70 24 22 48
At this fashionable table in the up-and-coming 9th, the "second floor with the fireplace is charming in winter" and the Eclectic–New French cooking is "interesting" and "original" year-round (though it's "too bad the menu doesn't change more" often, some sigh); "service is amiable", if "a little stuffy."

Auberge Etchégorry ☒   – | – | – | E
41, rue Croulebarbe, 13ᵉ (Corvisart/Les Gobelins), 01 44 08 83 51; fax 44 08 83 69
Tucked away in the 13th, this vintage Basque isn't exactly basking in the attention of surveyors; but those who know insist it's "super" "for Southwestern cooking in Paris", even for "a spontaneous meal"; however, the folkloric, whitewashed decor strikes a "sort of miserable" note for several, especially given the expensive tabs.

Auberge et Cie ☒   – | – | – | M
23, rue Clauzel, 9ᵉ (St-Georges), 01 48 78 74 40; fax 48 78 20 96; www.aubergecompagnie.com
While its exposed stone walls, wood beams and candlelit tables evoke a cozy, rustic auberge, this newcomer is actually located in the stylish, arty Saint-Georges area; run by three friends, none of whom are professionally trained chefs, it puts Southwestern dishes at center stage, supported by seafood and other lighter possibilities.

Auberge Nicolas Flamel ☒   ▽ 16 | 16 | 14 | 44
51, rue de Montmorency, 3ᵉ (Etienne Marcel/Rambuteau), 01 42 71 77 78; fax 48 04 58 36
◪ "The decor alone is worth coming for" at this Marais mansion, purported to be "the oldest house in Paris", which offers a "warm welcome" to visitors; while folks feel cooler about the "so-so" classic Bistro kitchen, they praise the "not-to-be-missed lamb that's slow-roasted for seven hours" and "a wonderful bargain-filled wine list."

Auberge Pyrénées Cévennes (L') ☒   20 | 16 | 18 | 35
106, rue de la Folie-Méricourt, 11ᵉ (République), 01 43 57 33 78
■ "On a small street near the Place de la République" lies this "very-good country restaurant" serving "big portions"

of "hearty", "old-fashioned" Southwestern dishes like "thick foie gras" and possibly "the best cassoulet ever"; a "happy staff" makes for "soigné service", and best of all, it offers "an enjoyable experience without having to take a second mortgage on the house."

Auguste 🖾
- | - | - | E

54, rue de Bourgogne, 7e (Varenne), 01 45 51 61 69
Fine linens, a vivid color scheme and well-spaced tables lend this Classic French – just steps from the Assemblée Nationale – an aura of understated contemporary chic that draws government types, Condé Nast editors and the local discreet bourgeoisie; at the stove, chef Gaël Orieux (ex Le Meurice) conjures up a short market-driven menu that changes seasonally.

Authenti© 🖾
- | - | - | M

81, av du Segur, 15e (Cambronne/Ségur), 01 43 06 20 20
Banquettes, vaguely retro decor and moderately priced Bistro cooking (try the côtes de boeuf with béarnaise) have helped this newcomer across the street from the headquarters of UNESCO in the 15th quickly become a hit; it fills up fast with a cosmopolitan crowd of functionaries at noon, replaced by well-heeled local couples in the evening.

Auvergne Gourmande (L') ⊄
- | - | - | M

127, rue St-Dominique, 7e (Ecole Militaire), 01 47 05 60 79; fax 47 05 11 13
This vest-pocket–size annex of the popular Fontaine du Mars a few doors down in the 7th is a "fun place", a *table d'hôte* usually populated with "friendly table partners" who can make for "a delightful evening"; everyone sits together on "high stools", dining on "delicious" Auvergnat edibles; it's "excellent value for the money", too.

Avant Goût (L') 🖾
22 | 14 | 18 | 36

26, rue Bobillot, 13e (Place d'Italie), 01 53 80 24 00; fax 53 80 00 77
🗷 It's "quite a schlep" to the Butte-aux-Cailles quarter of "the far-flung 13th", but the crowds still come to this "deservedly popular" New French "neo-bistro" where chef-owner Christophe Beaufront, "a Guy Savoy protégé, offers excellent, creative cooking" for near-"bargain" prices (especially on the "frequently changing set menus"); since it's "hard to do better for the money" and the "welcome is warm", it's easy to overlook the "close tables"; just "book ahead" since it's "always full"; N.B. the Decor score may not reflect a post-*Survey* modernization.

Avenue (L') ◖
16 | 18 | 13 | 56

41, av Montaigne, 8e (Franklin D. Roosevelt), 01 40 70 14 91; fax 40 70 91 97
🗷 Kind of a "Paris version of a *Sex and the City* place", this "trendy" "hangout" on the Avenue Montaigne comes "courtesy of the Costes brothers" and bears all their

"typical" features, from a "hip" decor by Jacques Garcia to "stylish" "servers who have a lot of room for improvement"; the "light" New French fare is "expensive for what you get", especially given the "tiny portions" geared for "young women to stay thin and still eat"; but "food is not the point here", and many find it all "fun" and "sexy . . . until you're put in a corner for not being sexy enough."

Azabu ⁻ | ⁻ | ⁻ | M |
3, rue André Mazet, 6ᵉ (Odéon), 46 33 72 05; fax 44 07 38 32
Near the Odéon, this "excellent teppanyaki restaurant where the chef cooks your food in front of you" is such a reasonably priced crowd-pleaser that it's worth visitors "giving up a French meal for"; with specialties such as "okonomiyaki (fish and vegetable pancake) that's heaven", this may be "the best non-sushi Japanese in town"; be forewarned that service can be "slow", especially on weekends, but you can kill time by checking out the "must-see Zen-style bathrooms."

B*fly ● 13 | 18 | 11 | 48 |
49-51, av George V, 8ᵉ (George V), 01 53 67 84 60; fax 53 67 84 67
☑ Populated by an "affluent" "twenty-to-fiftysomething" singles crowd, plus "wanna-be models" waiting for "pomaded Euros to buy them" "expensive" drinks, this restaurant-bar on the swank Avenue George V defines the label "has-been"; but it's admittedly more about the "great bartending" and people-watching than the Eclectic cuisine, and the service is about as helpful as a fly on the wall.

Baan-Boran ●⊠ 20 | 14 | 19 | 35 |
43, rue de Montpensier, 1ᵉʳ (Palais Royal-Musée du Louvre), 01 40 15 90 45; fax 40 15 90 45
■ Across the street from the Palais Royal, this "intimate", "good-quality" Siamese is "one of the only restaurants in Paris that cooks to real Thai tastes, rather than toning it down for French palates" (though it's still "not spicy enough" for some); all agree "the presentation and service are colorful", though, and prices are tasty, too.

Babylone (Au) ⊠⇗ ⁻ | ⁻ | ⁻ | M |
13, rue de Babylone, 7ᵉ (Sèvres-Babylone), 01 45 48 72 13
Only open during the day, this "wonderful" classic bistro near Sèvres-Babylone has the "atmosphere of a real old-fashioned hole-in-the-wall, plus succulent home cooking"; it's "good for a quick lunch after shopping at the Bon Marché" store, but come early because "just 40 minutes after opening, most of the *plats du jour* run out."

Bacchantes (Les) ●⊠ ⁻ | ⁻ | ⁻ | M |
21, rue de Caumartin, 9ᵉ (Havre-Caumartin/Opéra), 01 42 65 25 35; fax 47 42 65 87
Near the Opéra Garnier and the big department stores, this "convivial", "debonair *bistrot à vins*" is "a good address

for those who like Traditional French cooking at affordable prices" – not to mention a "menu that changes daily"; "be sure to book or come early, since it fills up quickly at noon."

Baie d'Ha Long (La) 🗷   – | – | – | E
164, av de Versailles, 16ᵉ (Porte de St-Cloud), 01 45 24 60 62; fax 42 30 58 98
Maybe it's because this "cozy, little" Southeast Asian is on the outer edges of the16th that so few know it; those who travel the long way praise the "high quality", if slightly "high-priced", "original specialties" (tip: "choose a dish that originates in the aquarium"), "efficiently" served by the *maîtresse de maison,* a veritable Vietnamese "princess."

Bains (Les) ◑   9 | 13 | 9 | 53
7, rue du Bourg l'Abbé, 3ᵉ (Etienne Marcel/Réaumur Sébastopol), 01 48 87 01 80; fax 48 87 13 70; www.lesbainsparis.com
◤ "If you eat here, you get into the disco without braving the door policy" – the main reason citizens "suffer the club food" on a New French–Thai menu and the "pretentious personnel" at this venerable but still viable nightspot in the 3rd; otherwise, just "go for the bar" and the "jam-packed dance floor" with its "definite see-and-be-seen" scene; naturally, it's "overpriced, but by how much depends upon what wine one orders."

Ballon des Ternes (Le) ◑   15 | 15 | 15 | 43
103, av des Ternes, 17ᵉ (Porte Maillot), 01 45 74 17 98; fax 45 72 18 84
■ "Well situated" near the Porte Maillot, this "find" of a "neighborhood brasserie" offers "especially good shellfish and fish", along with other traditional dishes like veal kidneys; its attractive ambiance stems equally from the "knowledgeable", "English-speaking", "unpretentious" waiters and the "beautiful" belle-epoque decor, complete with "a nice terrace" for the summer; it's "good value for the money", too.

Ballon et Coquillages   – | – | – | M
71, bd Gouvion St-Cyr, 17ᵉ (Porte Maillot), 01 45 74 17 98; fax 45 72 18 84
Eight different varieties of bivalves star at this shellfish-only annex of the nearby Ballon des Ternes, where customers sit at a stylish round bar (there are no tables, this is a real oyster bar) that promotes a certain degree of conviviality; with obliging service and an appealing decor enlivened by red stools, this Porte Maillot place is perfect to bear in mind for a quick, casual meal.

Banyan ◑🗷   – | – | – | M
24, pl Etienne Pernet, 15ᵉ (Félix Faure), 01 40 60 09 31; fax 40 60 09 20
A former chef at the Blue Elephant and Asian goes out on his own with this pleasant little Thai in a quiet corner of the

15th; beautiful flower arrangements and soft lighting transform the storefront space into an appealing dining room that's instantly drawn locals for the quality of the authentic cooking and friendly service.

Baptiste 🗷 — | — | — | M
51, rue Jouffroy d'Abbans, 17ᵉ (Malesherbes/Wagram), 01 42 27 20 18; fax 43 80 68 09
"All-around excellent" is the word from the few who know this Contemporary French near the Place Wagram; "clever" cooking from "a team that obviously cares about what it's doing", "cozy" vintage 1930s decor and prices that are moderate for this part of town make it ideal for "business or pleasure."

Bar à Huîtres (Le) 🌑 17 | 15 | 15 | 42
33, bd Beaumarchais, 3ᵉ (Bastille), 01 48 87 98 92; fax 48 87 04 42
33, rue St-Jacques, 5ᵉ (Maubert-Mutualité), 01 44 07 27 37; fax 43 26 71 62
112, bd du Montparnasse, 14ᵉ (Raspail/Vavin), 01 43 20 71 01; fax 43 20 52 04
www.lebarahuitres.com
◪ "It's all about the oysters" at this trio of strategically located seafooders with shell-themed interiors by decorator Jacques Garcia; while they are undeniable "tourist" havens, most praise the "remarkably fresh" shellfish and "reasonable prices", but "ignore the cooked offerings", which are "nothing special", and snarl about "rushed" service that can "take the pleasure out of a meal."

Bar des Théâtres 🌑 14 | 10 | 14 | 39
6, av Montaigne, 8ᵉ (Alma-Marceau), 01 47 23 34 63; fax 45 62 04 93
◪ For more than 50 years, Théâtre des Champs-Elysées patrons have found this "classic" on the Avenue Montaigne handy for "relaxing with friends" "after a show" (or before, given the "remarkably efficient service"); alas, "it's not what it used to be", now that the "entertainment and model crowd" is diluted by lesser-known faces, a remodeling has "diminished the atmosphere" and aside from one of "the best steak tartares" around, the Traditional French food's "without interest."

Baron Bouge (Le) ∇ 13 | 19 | 15 | 25
(fka Le Baron Rouge)
1, rue Théophile Roussel, 12ᵉ (Ledru-Rollin), 01 43 43 14 32
■ For a sip of "Old Paris", try this "superb *bar à vins* near one of the prettiest markets in the city" – the Marché d'Aligre in the 12th; join "regulars" gathered around "wine casks" or at the bar to "chat" and nibble "salty" charcuterie (and fresh oysters on Sunday mornings) and tipple "high quality" varietals that can be purchased to take home; a "warm welcome" and easy prices make it an ongoing hit.

Barramundi ◐ ⊠
— | — | — | E

3, rue Taitbout, 9ᵉ (Richelieu-Drouot), 01 47 70 21 21; fax 47 70 21 20

"You come for the decor", which features elements from all over the world, including African masks, but "the loud music" can "make it hard to talk" at this "trendy" restaurant/club in the 9th; it's "fun for a night out with friends" of a wild stripe – assuming no one's really hungry, since the "expensive" Eclectic menu incites minimal enthusiasm.

Barrio Latino ◐
8 | 22 | 9 | 37

46-48, rue du Faubourg St-Antoine, 12ᵉ (Bastille), 01 55 78 84 75; fax 55 78 85 30

☑ "Sexy" Latin atmosphere, "excellent music" and zingy mojitos rev up the "young" dance-ready crowd at this multilevel club/eatery near the Bastille; as for dining, most advise bypassing "the banal food", since even "supermarket guacamole is better" than its ilk here; a "rude door policy" doesn't whet appetites either.

Barroco ◐
— | — | — | M

23, rue Mazarine, 6ᵉ (Odéon/St-Germain-des-Prés), 01 43 26 40 24; fax 55 04 86 19; www.restaurant-latino.com

Not far from the Odéon, this Nuevo Latino taverna pulls in a stylish international crowd to sip good cocktails and Chilean wines and to sample a diverse menu that takes inspiration from Spain, Portugal and Latin America; "the pretty decor" reminiscent of a refined Brazilian home pleases, but service tends to be more "sexy than classy."

Bar Rouge ⊠
— | — | — | M

Galeries Lafayette Gourmet, 97, rue de Provence, 9ᵉ (Havre-Caumartin/Opéra), 01 40 23 52 59; fax 40 23 52 60

Tucked in the Galeries Lafayette in the 9th, this wine bar pairs the potables with first-rate tapas and other Spanish nibbles in a contemporary setting; open only during store hours, it's very busy at lunchtime, sating local business types and "the shopping-weary" with a quick bite or a "coupe de champagne."

Bartolo ◐⊅
17 | 9 | 11 | 39

7, rue des Canettes, 6ᵉ (St-Germain-des-Prés), 01 43 26 27 08

☑ The word on this long-running Italian in Saint-Germain is decidedly mixed: most laud the "delicious pastas" and wood-oven fired pizzas but the "noisy", unremarkable room and the sullen service get the boot; P.S. "come with cash because they don't take credit cards."

Bar Vendôme ◐
20 | 25 | 25 | 59

Hôtel Ritz, 15, pl Vendôme, 1ᵉʳ (Concorde/Opéra), 01 43 16 33 63; fax 43 16 33 75; www.ritzparis.com

■ "Feel like a character in an old Elizabeth Taylor movie" while taking tea or relishing apéritifs and "the best club sandwiches in Paris" at this "grand" bar in the Hôtel Ritz; expect "class, class, class" and "gracious" service; despite some comparatively ritzy prices, if you're looking to "indulge your desire for luxury while maintaining your budget" with a light meal, this is an "exquisite" option; P.S. enjoy the "enchanting terrace" in fair weather.

Bascou (Au) 🏛   20 | 14 | 16 | 42
38, rue Réaumur, 3ᵉ (Arts et Métiers), 01 42 72 69 25; fax 42 72 69 25

■ "A warm welcome and savory cooking" greet diners at this "exceptional" "Basque bistro" near the Place de la République; "interesting wines" are paired with the "rich", "distinctive" cuisine of the Southwest; add in a room that's "humanly scaled" and "sensible prices" and you get satisfied surveyors musing "what else can you ask for?"

Basilic (Le)   13 | 15 | 12 | 43
2, rue Casimir Périer, 7ᵉ (Invalides/Solférino), 01 44 18 94 64; fax 44 18 33 97

☒ Like the "imposing Sainte-Clothilde church" nearby in the 7th, this Classic French upholds the bourgeois status quo with "simple" offerings, of which "the house special roast lamb" is the star; other than that, "the cooking's not terribly interesting", and "the service on par with that at a bar-tabac", but the "quiet terrace" always assuages.

Bastide Odéon (La) 🏛   21 | 18 | 19 | 45
7, rue Corneille, 6ᵉ (Odéon), 01 43 26 03 65; fax 44 07 28 93; www.bastide-odeon.com

☒ "Like a trip to Provence without the train ride" say contented armchair travelers of this "modern" bistro near the Luxembourg Gardens that turns out "original" but "not intimidating" southern-minded dishes in a "cheerful" yellow-and-red-accented bi-level space; a few suggest that it's "over-hyped" and "touristy" and have mixed feelings about the service, but all "appreciate the air-conditioning" and the relatively "reasonable" prices.

Bath's 🏛   27 | 21 | 24 | 90
9, rue de La Trémoille, 8ᵉ (Alma-Marceau), 01 40 70 01 09; fax 40 70 01 22; www.baths.fr

■ For such a *petit* "father-son operation", this contemporary bistro in the swank 8th is a startlingly "major address", "working wonders" with "excellent" Auvergnat cuisine that can be enjoyed à la carte or on a "remarkable" tasting menu; owner Jean-Yves Bath "greets all guests warmly", the room is "cozy with well-spaced tables" and service is "stellar", all of which makes the "steep" prices easier to swallow.

Bauta (La) 🏛   – | – | – | E
129, bd du Montparnasse, 6ᵉ (Vavin), 01 43 22 52 35; fax 43 22 10 99

"The cooking's very good" at this classic Venetian in Montparnasse, so "it's a shame that this place lacks a certain charm" in its decor and service that would make a meal here more of an occasion; it's also unlikely to be a frequent pleasure, since it's "expensive" – although the two-course prix fixe isn't a bad deal.

B-Café (Le)   21 | 17 | 20 | 31

(fka Byblos Café)

6, rue Guichard, 16ᵉ (La Muette), 01 42 30 99 99; fax 42 30 54 54

■ "Polite", "charming people" serving "delicious Middle Eastern specialties" "make this upscale Lebanese a must for aficionados"; the "modern decor" and "sure values" mean it's a "bustling lunch spot", though others appreciate that, compared to many establishments in the 16th, "they're open late, too."

Béatilles (Les) ⌧   – | – | – | E

11 bis, rue Villebois-Mareuil, 17ᵉ (Charles de Gaulle-Etoile/ Ternes), 01 45 74 43 80; fax 45 74 43 81

It's worth sleuthing out this "lost corner" in the 17th, since chef Christian Bochaton's New French cooking is "a sure bet" and "notable for its clean, well-defined" flavors; his wife Catherine oversees the "attentive" staff in a modern dining room that unfortunately "lacks the zip" that's found on your plate.

Beato ⌧   ▽ 15 | 15 | 18 | 52

8, rue Malar, 7ᵉ (Invalides), 01 47 05 94 27; fax 45 55 64 41

◪ This well-heeled Italian in the 7th serves "very good" food ("taste the squid's ink pasta with langoustines") and is "popular with politicians at lunchtime" who rightly recognize that "the business prix fixe is a great deal" but are too busy to notice that "the decor could use an update"; P.S. "it's much more expensive in the evening."

Beaujolais d'Auteuil (Le)   17 | 11 | 13 | 39

99, bd de Montmorency, 16ᵉ (Porte d'Auteuil), 01 47 43 03 56; fax 46 51 27 81

■ You may be packed "tight like sardines" at this "red-check-tableclothed" spot on the edge of the 16th, "but you always return for the good times" and "solid" "Classic" French dishes like "eggs poached in red wine and calf's liver", not to mention the "pretty terrace" in summer.

BE Boulangépicier ⌧   19 | 14 | 14 | 22

73, bd de Courcelles, 17ᵉ (Courcelles/Ternes), 01 46 22 20 20; fax 46 22 20 21

■ "Alain Ducasse strikes again", in cahoots with master baker Eric Kayser, with this luxury bread and gourmet-food shop in the 17th; "it's chic and expensive but so good that you want to buy everything"; and while "it's not easy to have a meal on the spot" due to scant seating, you can pack the "creative" sandwiches for a "snob"-style picnic at nearby Parc Monceau.

Bel Canto
14 | 17 | 20 | 50

*72, quai de l'Hôtel de Ville, 4ᵉ (Hôtel-de-Ville/Pont-Marie),
01 42 78 30 18; fax 42 78 30 28*
*88, rue de la Tombe-Issoire, 14ᵉ (Alésia), 01 43 22 96 15;
fax 43 27 09 88* ⌧
*6, rue du Commandant Pilot, Neuilly (Les Sablons), 01 47 47 19 94;
fax 47 38 60 49* ⌧
www.lebelcanto.com
☑ "Combine a show with dinner" – but not in the usual
sense – at these Italians, where "young, energetic" students
from the Opéra de Paris Conservatory "perform between
taking orders"; while the kitchen gets no encores and not all
servers can multitask so ably, "it's worth coming back" for
the "jolly" ambiance and "charming" "musical program."

Bélier (Le) ⌧
– | – | – | M

*L'Hôtel, 13, rue des Beaux-Arts, 6ᵉ (St-Germain-des-Prés),
01 44 41 99 01; fax 43 25 64 81; www.l-hotel.com*
Situated in the Saint-Germain hotel where Oscar Wilde
passed away and chanteuse Mistinguett rested up, this
"intimate" spot allows jet-setters to refuel on "well-
presented", though slightly "pretentious", Classic French
fare against a "*très chic*" and pleasurably louche backdrop
designed by decorator Jacques Garcia; "accommodating"
service rounds out the generally positive experience.

Bellini ⌧
19 | 14 | 18 | 49

*28, rue Lesueur, 16ᵉ (Argentine), 01 45 00 54 20;
fax 45 00 11 74*
■ "No pretense, just really nice food" say *amici* of this
"neighborhoody" little Italian in the 16th that serves up
"savory" "classic" dishes including "tagliatelle flambéed
in a Parmesan wheel that's not to be missed"; all also
appreciate the "attentive" reception and "good wine list";
N.B. a recent revamp may outdate the Decor score.

Bellotta-Bellotta ⌧
– | – | – | M

*18, rue Jean-Nicot, 7ᵉ (La Tour-Maubourg), 01 53 59 96 96;
fax 53 59 70 44*
"Authentic tapas" and "incredible" Iberian ham are the
draws at this "cute, little" Spaniard in the heart of the 7th;
but while moderately priced, several rounds of those tiny
plates can end up being "pricey", so most use it as a place
to "meet friends" for snacks over a glass of wine or sherry.

Benkay
23 | 17 | 21 | 79

*Hôtel Novotel Tour Eiffel, 61, quai de Grenelle, 15ᵉ (Bir-Hakeim/
Charles Michels), 01 40 58 21 26; fax 40 58 21 30;
www.novotel.com*
☑ "Miracles on your plate and a fabulous view of the Seine"
summarizes the scene at this Japanese in the 15th; "having
a semi-private chef prepare [sushi and teppanyaki] in front
of you is a dream", and polished service helps offset the

"chilly decor"; "if you're looking for an inexpensive" meal, however, you won't find it here.

BENOÎT
23 | 20 | 22 | 72

20, rue St-Martin, 4ᵉ (Châtelet-Les Halles), 01 42 72 25 76; fax 42 72 45 68

⬛ One of the town's most popular and "just what a bistro should be" say cassoulet-cravers about this family-run homage to Lyon in the 4th that smacks of "Paris from the bygone days"; though seating may be "segregated" for natives "and foreigners" and the service, while filled "with gusto", can be "chilly", few quibble about the "fancy prices", deeming it all "worth it, in an old-time luxury way"; N.B. at press time, Alain Ducasse was in talks to acquire the place.

Berkeley (Le) ◑
10 | 15 | 10 | 42

7, av Matignon, 8ᵉ (Franklin D. Roosevelt/Miromesnil), 01 42 25 72 25; fax 45 63 30 06; www.leberkeley.com

⬛ With its stripe-tent ceiling and slightly over-the-top decor, this "extremely chic" Costes brothers Classic French–Eclectic hangout is a colorful locale for "drinks and dessert" or Sunday brunch on the "pretty terrace" after a stroll on the nearby Champs-Elysées; too bad service is more "snooty" "than the food quality merits" ("they treat us like tourists, even though we're not").

Beudant (Le) Ⓢ
– | – | – | M

97, rue des Dames, 17ᵉ (Rome/Villiers), 01 43 87 11 20; fax 43 87 27 35

The "owners really know what they're doing", so "follow their advice and you'll be happy" tip informants on this little-known Classic French near Villiers whose kitchen has a particular talent with fish; the lunch prix fixe is a particularly good value, and if the salmon-colored dining room's "a bit sad", this doesn't deter the local patrons.

Beurre Noisette (Le) Ⓢ
23 | 15 | 19 | 35

68, rue Vasco de Gama, 15ᵉ (Lourmel/Porte de Versailles), 01 48 56 82 49; fax 48 56 82 49

⬛ This "excellent little" bistro "tries hard to make dining a pleasure", which explains why its reputation is growing despite a location "deep in the 15th"; the "chef is a true chef – no fooling around"; service is "personal" and "it's a great buy for the money" too.

Biche au Bois (A la) Ⓢ
21 | 10 | 20 | 36

45, av Ledru-Rollin, 12ᵉ (Gare de Lyon), 01 43 43 34 38

⬛ Since 1925, this "clubby" corner near the Gare de Lyon has fed generations of "regulars" "generous" portions of the "real thing": Classic French cooking highlighted by "seasonal game"; while no one swoons over the decor, everyone "loves the buzz" and "the jovial waiters", making it "always crowded" and reservations essential.

BIOArt ● ◑ ☒
— | — | — | M

3, quai François Mauriac, 13ᵉ (Bibliothèque François Mitterrand),
01 45 85 66 88; fax 45 85 04 24; www.bioart.fr
This vast dining room in the emerging neighborhood
surrounding the dramatic Bibliothèque Nationale claims
to be the city's largest organic food restaurant; and with
Parisians becoming more health conscious, it's no surprise
that it's popular with a fashionable young crowd which
appreciates the menu's avoidance of stereotypical sprouts
in favor of such Contemporary French concoctions as
fricassee of chicken in coconut milk.

Bistro 121 ●
— | — | — | M

121, rue de la Convention, 15ᵉ (Boucicaut/Convention),
01 45 57 52 90; fax 45 57 14 69; www.bistro121.com
A coterie of loyal "locals" appreciates the "simple" but
"satisfying" "traditional" Bistro cooking, "nice choice of
wines" and "amiable" service at this 15th arrondissement
stalwart; "the lights are bright for late-night dining" and the
decor could use some sprucing up, but a "warm welcome"
and fair prices compensate.

Bistro de Breteuil (Le)
14 | 15 | 14 | 38

3, pl de Breteuil, 7ᵉ (Duroc), 01 45 67 07 27; fax 42 73 11 08;
www.bistro-et-cie.fr
☑ "The lovely terrace" and "all-inclusive" formula by
bargain-master Willy Dorr keep this epitomic "idea of a
typical bistro" in the chic 7th arrondissement "jam-packed";
not everyone is spellbound, citing "ordinary" Classic
French food, a "limited wine selection" and brusque
service, but they're overwhelmed by those who claim it a
"stuff-your-face steal."

Bistro de Gala ☒
∇ 18 | 15 | 17 | 42

45, rue du Faubourg Montmartre, 9ᵉ (Grands Boulevards/
Le Peletier), 01 40 22 90 50; fax 40 22 98 30
■ It "may not be one of the big guns yet, but it's not far off"
say savvy scouts of this contemporary bistro in the slightly
scruffy Faubourg Montmartre; as proof, they point to
its "market-based" cooking, "appealing wine list" and
"professional" service, all of which equals "excellent
value for the money."

Bistro de l'Olivier (Le)
20 | 15 | 19 | 46

13, rue Quentin Bauchart, 8ᵉ (George V), 01 47 20 78 63;
fax 47 20 74 58
■ For a "mini-vacation in the center of Paris", let this
"cozy" Provençal-Mediterranean bistro transport you to
the land of "lavender and thyme" via its fish-centric menu
and "sunny" atmosphere; "the new management has done
wonders", which explains why the crowd also chirps
about "good cheer" from the staff and "bargain" bills for
the pricey 8th.

Bistro des Deux Théâtres (Le) ●   16 | 13 | 16 | 35
18, rue Blanche, 9ᵉ (Trinité), 01 45 26 41 43; fax 48 74 08 92;
www.bistro-et-cie.fr
☑ Popular with a business crowd at lunch, this purely prix
fixe Classic French in the theater district in the 9th is "a
handy place to dine after a show"; critics pan the food as
"pedestrian" and the decor as even more so; but no one
complains about getting "value for their euro", which is
why it regularly plays to a full house.

Bistro d'Hubert (Le) ⌀   20 | 17 | 18 | 45
41, bd Pasteur, 15ᵉ (Pasteur), 01 47 34 15 50; fax 45 67 03 09;
www.bistrodhubert.com
■ "Bridging the gap between Bistro fare and inventive
cooking" this "casual" address in the 15th specializes in
"savory" Southwestern-inflected New French cuisine;
diners can view the "open kitchen from most tables" or the
bar in the "charming" blue-and-yellow room, making things
"a little noisy" but nonetheless "fun."

Bistro du 17ème (Le)   16 | 15 | 15 | 34
108, av de Villiers, 17ᵉ (Péreire), 01 47 63 32 77; fax 42 27 67 66;
www.bistro-et-cie.fr
■ "Bargain" hunters "line up" to "eat a lot for a little"
at this Willy Dorr–owned traditional bistro that offers
the "best prix fixe (including bottle of wine)" in the 17th
arrondissement"; such a winning formula also means that
the room can be "hectic" and not a suitable place for
"a quiet dinner."

Bistro Melrose ●   – | – | – | M
5, pl Clichy, 17ᵉ (Place de Clichy), 01 42 93 61 34; fax 42 93 76 45;
www.bistro-et-cie.fr
It may be "touristy" given its location on the edge of
Montmartre overlooking the Place Clichy, but this traditional
bistro belonging to Willy Dorr's prix fixe empire is both
"lively" and a "good value", turning out serviceable food
at a fast, efficient clip.

Bistro St. Ferdinand ●   ▽ 15 | 15 | 16 | 33
275, bd Péreire, 17ᵉ (Porte Maillot), 01 45 74 33 32;
fax 45 74 33 12; www.bistro-et-cie.fr
■ Sure it's a bit of a "food factory", but this bistro that's
"practical" for Palais des Congrès events is a "success"
thanks to prix fixe pasha Willy Dorr's "well-priced" start-
to-finish formula of a "consistent" Classic French meal
that "includes wine."

Bistrot à Vins Mélac ⌀   16 | 15 | 14 | 39
42, rue Léon Frot, 11ᵉ (Charonne), 01 43 70 59 27; fax 43 70 73 10;
www.melac.fr
■ Seated at "big wooden tables", groups of friends and a
cast of "neighborhood characters" merrily sip wine "by

the bottle or the glass" and partake of "simple" Aveyronnais eats at Jacques Mélac's "boisterous" *bistrot à vins* in the 11th; N.B. abstainers stay home, since (so a posted sign claims) the water is strictly reserved for cooking.

Bistrot Baracane ●🅾️   22 | 13 | 21 | 36
38, rue des Tournelles, 4ᵉ (Chemin Vert), 01 42 71 43 33;
fax 40 02 04 77; www.L-oulette.com
■ Lucky are those who "fall into" this "cheerful", little sibling of L'Oulette near the Place des Vosges, specializing in "lick-your-plate" traditional Southwestern dishes like "cassoulet" and "awesome house wine" at "terrific value"; given that there's "little room to exhale" in the tight but "homey" space, reservations are "highly recommended."

Bistrot Bigorneau (Le)   − | − | − | E
71, av Paul Doumer, 16ᵉ (La Muette), 01 45 04 12 81;
fax 45 04 00 50
Showcasing an upmarket sea-shack look that one might find featured in the French decorating magazine *Maisons Côté Ouest* – "so *comme-il-faut* for the 16th" – this fashionable seafooder "from the owner of Marius et Jeanette" is winning over well-heeled locals with its high-quality "catch-of-the-day" menu, served by swift staffers.

Bistrot d'à Côté   21 | 16 | 20 | 47
16, av de Villiers, 17ᵉ (Villiers), 01 47 63 25 61; fax 48 88 92 42 🅾️
10, rue Gustave Flaubert, 17ᵉ (Péreire/Ternes), 01 42 67 05 81;
fax 47 63 82 75
4, rue Boutard, Neuilly (Pont-de-Neuilly), 01 47 45 34 55;
fax 47 45 15 08 🅾️
www.michelrostang.com
■ Chef Michel Rostang's "mini-chain" purveys "hearty" Bistro "classics" for those who "don't want to re-mortgage the house"; if they've become "too popular" for an "informal" meal, the "welcome" remains "warm" for all.

Bistrot d'Alex 🅾️   14 | 12 | 13 | 42
2, rue Clément, 6ᵉ (Mabillon/Odéon), 01 43 54 09 53;
fax 43 25 77 66
🔳 An "excellent location" across from the Marché Saint-Germain and its "quintessential bustling bistro" profile keep the "tourists" coming to this 31-year-old spot, despite what dissidents deem "dull" dishes, aging digs, "surly service" and "excessive" prices for the quality of the Classic French–Med meals and Provençal wines.

Bistrot d'André (Le) 🅾️   ∇ 15 | 16 | 12 | 38
232, rue St-Charles, 15ᵉ (Balard), 01 45 57 89 14; fax 45 57 97 15
■ Inhabiting the former workers' canteen of the long-defunct Citroën plant in the 15th, this "typical" bistro is of "a type we'd like to find many more of in Paris": "good-value" Traditional French cooking and a backdrop that makes it "great for people-watching and a romantic drink."

Bistrot de l'Etoile Lauriston ●🅵   20 | 14 | 18 | 53
*19, rue Lauriston, 16ᵉ (Charles de Gaulle-Etoile/Kléber),
01 40 67 11 16; fax 45 00 99 87*
🅵 This "lively, attractive" spot near the Etoile in the 16th is a perpetual winner with both tourists and a "regular" crowd thanks to "no-nonsense" but "elegant" Contemporary French food, "efficient" service and prix fixe formulas for lunch and on select nights; the only quibble here is that "you're squeezed in" at "tightly spaced tables."

Bistrot de l'Etoile Niel ●🅵   21 | 15 | 17 | 49
75, av Niel, 17ᵉ (Péreire), 01 42 27 88 44; fax 42 27 32 12
🅵 "A comfortable place to eat and linger", this bistro near the Etoile in the 17th chalks up its continued success to "very good products" and a "relaxed" vibe; some lament the "tightly spaced tables" and find it on the "expensive" side but concede that the contemporary cooking is consistently "tasty."

Bistrot de l'Université 🅵   – | – | – | M
*40, rue de l'Université, 7ᵉ (Rue du Bac), 01 42 61 26 64;
fax 42 61 26 64*
Though it's decked with pretty stucco moldings and offers gentle prices, this "pleasant, neighborhood" classic bistro with a practical 7th arrondissement location remains little known; maybe it's "nothing special", but you can count on the "simple, old-fashioned dishes."

Bistrot de Marius (Le)   17 | 12 | 15 | 46
6, av George V, 8ᵉ (Alma-Marceau), 01 40 70 11 76; fax 40 70 17 08
🅵 Given its situation in the "golden triangle" of the 8th, this "casual" but "animated" offshoot of Marius et Janette next door is judged a good catch for "high-quality" seafood at "a fraction of the cost" of the *maison mère*; if a few find it too "noisy", "cramped" and "touristy", more say it's "perfect for lunch" or "after a concert."

Bistrot de Paris (Le) ●🅵   17 | 15 | 16 | 43
*33, rue de Lille, 7ᵉ (Rue du Bac/St-Germain-des-Prés),
01 42 61 16 83; fax 49 27 06 09*
🅵 Located near the Musée d'Orsay, this place embodies the "definition of a friendly, noisy" classic bistro; although it's "nothing spectacular", neighborhood types find it "reliable" "for hosting a spontaneous" dinner at fair prices.

Bistrot des Capucins 🅵   – | – | – | M
*27, av Gambetta, 20ᵉ (Père Lachaise), 01 46 36 74 75;
fax 46 36 74 89; www.le-bistrot-des-capucins.com*
"Filled with personality and cheer", chef-owner Gérard Fouché's (ex Grand Véfour) Southwestern bistro is deemed "delightful" by denizens of the 20th; while the decor may "need some work", the "efficient" service and moderate prices are fine as they are.

Bistrot des Dames (Le) ◑
– | – | – | I

*Hôtel El Dorado, 18, rue des Dames, 17ᵉ (Place de Clichy),
01 45 22 13 42; fax 43 87 25 97*

The "laid-back" ambiance and "great caipirinhas" get
Batignolles "locals" "talking to the people at the next table"
at this "neighborhood haunt" of a classic bistro; although
it's not a gastronomic destination, service is "friendly",
prices are low and there's a "private" little garden patio.

Bistrot des Vignes (Le)
▽ 17 | 18 | 20 | 43

*1, rue Jean-de-Boulogne, 16ᵉ (La Muette/Passy), 01 45 27 76 64;
fax 45 27 76 64*

■ "This is the kind of little restaurant that we like" –
"unpretentious" atmosphere, "solid" classic Bistro dishes
(think blanquette de veau), "fast" service and an "excellent
value for the money" proclaim patrons of this "lighthearted"
locale in tranquil Passy.

Bistrot d'Henri (Le) ◑
20 | 14 | 17 | 33

*16, rue Princesse, 6ᵉ (Mabillon/St-Germain-des-Prés),
01 46 33 51 12*

■ For "old-fashioned comfort food" like that served for
"Sunday lunch in the country" (ah, the "mouthwatering"
roasted-for-seven-hours lamb), you can hardly best this
"tiny" classic bistro; it's "terribly popular", so prepare to
be "short on elbow room" in exchange for "one of the best
buys" in "jumping" Saint-Germain.

Bistrot du Cap (Le)
– | – | – | M

*30, rue Peclet, 15ᵉ (Convention/Vaugirard), 01 40 43 02 18;
fax 40 43 02 18*

"Bravo!" say the few who know this modestly priced
contemporary bistro on a quiet pedestrian street in the
15th; the "great terrace" helps make it a "favorite casual
spot" for summer fare of Provençal inspiration, such as
"great fish soup" or "memorable tuna with tapenade."

Bistrot du Dôme (Le)
19 | 15 | 17 | 44

1, rue Delambre, 14ᵉ (Vavin), 01 43 35 32 00

Dôme Bastille (Le)

2, rue de la Bastille, 4ᵉ (Bastille), 01 48 04 88 44; fax 48 04 00 59

▨ Spawned by Le Dôme, this seafood duo in Montparnasse
and Bastille and features an "impressive" roster of "fab"
"no-frills" gills at "unbeatable prices"; "prompt" service
and a "value-laden wine list" are additional baits, but if
some regret the "tight tables" and decor ready for an
"upgrade", the fact that "they're jammed" says it all.

Bistrot du Peintre (Le) ◑
15 | 20 | 14 | 29

*116, av Ledru-Rollin, 11ᵉ (Bastille/Ledru-Rollin), 01 47 00 34 39;
fax 46 36 13 09*

■ The "old-fashioned" beauty of the art nouveau interior
overshadows the kitchen's "solid" efforts at this "really

cool" classic bistro near the Bastille; since the "setting is so romantic" and "it's a good value", most "would go back."

Bistrot du Sommelier ⊠   19   14   20   62
97, bd Haussmann, 8ᵉ (St-Augustin), 01 42 65 24 85;
fax 53 75 23 23; www.bistrodusommelier.com
☑ Amateur sommeliers "have fun" letting the staff "match the wines to each course and then trying to guess" their provenance at "foremost expert" Philippe Faure-Brac's classic bistro in the 8th; a few sour grapes squirt that it's "expensive" and "pretentious", but they're outvoted by oenophiles thrilled to sample a range that includes some "little-known" vintages.

Bistrot La Catalogne ⊠   ∇ 13   10   17   26
Maison de la Catalogne, 4-6-8, Cour-du-Commerce-St-André, 6ᵉ
(Odéon), 01 55 42 16 19; fax 52 42 16 19
☑ Since it's run by the Catalan tourist office as a cultural and culinary showcase, perhaps reviewers expect more of this brightly lit Spaniard in a cobbled passageway just off the Odéon; if you're "in a hurry", they do "decent" if "not exceptional" tapas accompanied by "some very nice wines"; it's rather inexpensive for the neighborhood, but some still say "a bit overpriced for what one gets."

Bistrot Papillon (Le) ⊠   20   15   18   41
6, rue Papillon, 9ᵉ (Cadet/Poissonnière), 01 47 70 90 03;
fax 48 24 05 59
☑ Bargain hunters flutter to this traditional bistro in a "hard-to-find" corner of the 9th that's named for the slightly "freaky butterfly collection on the wall"; for some, it's a "wonderful discovery", but others shrug it's "nothing special" and fly from the often "indifferent" service and "sad" decor.

Bistrot Paul Bert (Le) ⊠   ∇ 19   16   17   56
18, rue Paul Bert, 11ᵉ (Faidherbe-Chaligny), 01 43 72 24 01;
fax 43 72 24 66
■ "Be sure to have a meal" at this "unfussy" classic bistro in the 11th arrondissement, as the portions are "generous", the wine list over 300-labels strong and the owners "good folks"; the patina-ed decor might be "a bit shabby but what's on the plate more than makes up for it"; just please remember to "reserve."

Bistrot Vivienne ⊠   17   16   12   43
4, rue des Petits Champs, 1ᵉʳ (Bourse/Palais Royal-
Musée du Louvre), 01 49 27 00 50; fax 49 27 00 40
☑ This classic bistro entices those "shopping in the Galerie Vivienne" who love "the feeling of being outdoors without the car exhaust"; maybe management "should make more of an effort", because the "cooking's neither here nor there" and service can be "indifferent" – but a "good spirit" survives, nonetheless.

Blue Elephant ◐
20 | 26 | 18 | 53

*43-45, rue de la Roquette, 11ᵉ (Bastille/Voltaire), 01 47 00 42 00;
fax 47 00 45 44; www.blueelephant.com*

■ Take a "fantasy trip" to the jungles of Thailand via this "superb" link in a global chain near the Bastille whose "over-the-top" interior is "lush" with "plants and exotic trappings"; "refined" dishes "adapted to a Western palate", plus "graceful" service, offer a welcome "break from French" cooking, but prices much higher than "in a Thai village" help re-orient you.

Bocconi (Trattoria) ☒
– | – | – | M

*10 bis, rue d'Artois, 8ᵉ (St-Philippe-du-Roule), 01 53 76 44 44;
fax 45 61 10 08*

Elegant decor and generous portions of fresh, housemade pastas contribute to the appeal of this trattoria that's popular with financial executives at lunchtime; in the evening it pulls in a stylish, young clientele that includes many Italian expats.

Boeuf Couronné (Au) ◐
23 | 20 | 21 | 58

*188, av Jean Jaurès, 19ᵉ (Porte de Pantin), 01 42 39 44 44;
fax 42 39 17 30*

■ This king of beef "merits its crown (*couronne*)" and is "worth the trip" to the remote 19th for a knee-weakening côte de boeuf and other Classic French cuts; some come for the historic ties, as it "preserves" the "mythic aura of the slaughterhouses" (located here until 1974) and because it "bucks the tides of fashion and restaurant standardization."

Boeuf sur le Toit (Le) ◐
17 | 19 | 15 | 48

*34, rue du Colisée, 8ᵉ (Franklin D. Roosevelt/
St-Philippe-du-Roule), 01 53 93 65 55; fax 53 96 02 32;
www.boeufsurletoit.com*

◪ This Flo Group-owned brasserie off the Champs-Elysées is "always enjoyable" thanks to its "consistent" classic menu and shellfish bar, "noisy", "theatrical" vibe and "historic clout" (it dates to 1870); if some snip it should be called "Le Touriste sur le Toit" and warn that the "corporate ownership is wearing thin", others detect "improvement over the past few years."

BOFINGER ◐
18 | 23 | 18 | 50

*5, rue de la Bastille, 4ᵉ (Bastille), 01 42 72 87 82; fax 42 72 97 68;
www.bofingerparis.com*

◪ Near the Bastille, this "old friend" is as "picturesque" and "Parisian" as brasseries come, with its "beautiful belle-epoque space" that's capped by a "spectacular" cupola ("don't forget to look up!"); the eye-popping "three-tiered shellfish platters" and "terrific choucroute" dazzle tourists and natives alike, and if sauer-pusses hiss its "setting surpasses the food and service", it remains a "classic experience."

Bon ●🗹   – | 25 | 16 | M

25, rue de la Pompe, 16ᵉ (La Muette), 01 40 72 70 00;
fax 40 72 68 30; www.bon.fr

🗹 Some changes have occurred at this "hipster" spot: while decorator and former owner Philippe Starck's "radically" baroque decor ("you're not sure if you're in a restaurant or on a stage") remains, the team behind Copenhague has taken over, instituting an exotic, New French menu (e.g. hibiscus-infused bass) at more moderate prices.

Bon Accueil (Au) 🗹   23 | 19 | 20 | 51

14, rue de Monttessuy, 7ᵉ (Alma-Marceau/Ecole Militaire),
01 47 05 46 11

■ Practically "in the shadow of the Eiffel Tower", this Classic French "lives up to its name" (which means 'warm welcome') thanks to the "hospitable" host and "helpful" if sometimes "overburdened" service that ministers to folks "jammed" into the "smallish" space and spilling out to sidewalk tables; the "fresh ingredients and imagination" go a long way here, as do your euros at bill time.

Bon 2 ●   14 | 19 | 12 | 49

2, rue du Quatre Septembre, 2ᵉ (Bourse), 01 44 55 51 55;
fax 44 55 00 77; www.bon.fr

🗹 Co-owner and designer Philippe Starck's address near the Bourse may be "visually stunning" with "private booths, chandeliers and contrasting colors", but the Contemporary French–Med "food does not live up" to the surrounds; at least "you can be served coming out of a show after 11 PM."

Bon Saint Pourçain (Le) ≠   19 | 12 | 20 | 37

10 bis, rue Servandoni, 6ᵉ (Odéon/St-Sulpice), 01 43 54 93 63

■ Imagine you're "dining with a French family, except you get to choose what you eat" at this "little wonder" of a Classic French "tucked" "behind Saint-Sulpice"; the "sign outside advertises bourgeois cuisine, and that's what we get in the best sense" say patrons who also laud the "good-natured" staff and "reasonable" cash-only tabs.

Bons Crus (Aux) 🗹   – | – | – | M

7, rue des Petits-Champs, 1ᵉʳ (Bourse/Palais-Royal-
Musée du Louvre), 01 42 60 06 45

The "atmosphere and satisfying" Lyonnais eats make this 1905 hole-in-the-wall wine bar a hit with the fashion and business people who traffic the Place des Victoires; "unpretentiously Parisian" and "a great lunch spot", it's also "a bargain" in a pricey part of town.

Bouche à Oreille (De) 🗹   – | – | – | M

34, rue Gassendi, 14ᵉ (Denfert-Rochereau/Mouton-Duvernet),
01 43 27 73 14

The name means 'word of mouth', and that's exactly what's starting to build about this spot set in a simple Montparnasse dining room; its talented young chef turns out inventive Bistro dishes on a menu that follows the market.

Bouchons de François Clerc (Les) ⌂   17 | 15 | 16 | 45

12, rue de l'Hôtel Colbert, 5ᵉ (Maubert-Mutualité), 01 43 54 15 34; fax 46 34 68 07
6, rue Arsène Houssaye, 8ᵉ (Charles de Gaulle-Etoile), 01 42 89 15 51; fax 42 89 28 67
7, rue du Boccador, 8ᵉ (Alma-Marceau), 01 47 23 57 80; fax 47 23 74 54
22, rue de la Terrasse, 17ᵉ (Villiers), 01 42 27 31 51; fax 42 27 45 76
www.lesbouchonsdefrancoisclerc.com
☑ "The best wine value going" is the draw at this chain that provides varietals "at store prices"; foes fume "the remarkable list" "doesn't save the insipid dishes", which seem "expensive" for the quality; but friends, who find the New French fare "respectably creative", think of it as "paying for the wine, then the food is free"; "all the locations are different in decor", but the Latin Quarter branch located in a medieval "stone vaulted cellar" is "a favorite."

Bouillon Racine   13 | 22 | 13 | 35

3, rue Racine, 6ᵉ (Cluny-La-Sorbonne/Odéon), 01 44 32 15 60; fax 44 32 15 61; www.bouillonracine.com
☑ "If only the food and service could live up to the decor" bemoan boosters of this Belgian "buried in the backstreets of the 6th"; its setting, "as if you're on a glittering art nouveau stage", remains "absolutely charming" and the beer selection "far out"; but it's a "better bet for a drink than a meal", as the cuisine, which has forsaken its Flemish roots in favor of Classic French fare, is "disappointing."

Boulangerie (La) ⌂   ▽ 15 | 19 | 18 | 25

15, rue des Panoyaux, 20ᵉ (Ménilmontant), 01 43 58 45 45; fax 43 58 45 46; www.restaulaboulangerie.com
■ It's "way off the beaten track in the 20th" and, aside from some nice mosaics by local artists, "the setting is simple"; but those who know this classic bistro praise its "homestyle cooking" at "a fraction of the cost" of the guidebook stars – a combination that makes it popular with trendy, arty, young Menilmontant types (think *La Bohème*) who create a "relaxed atmosphere."

Boulangerie-Restaurant-EK-Odéon ⌂   – | – | – | M

10, rue de l'Ancienne Comédie, 6ᵉ (Odéon), 01 43 25 71 60
Ambitious baker Eric Kayser answers the honest need for good (and good-value) eats in Saint-Germain with this three-meal-a-day venue emphasizing salads, sandwiches and New French *plats du jour*; the interior has the '60s retro look one associates with this master baker's other

outlets, but the overall feel is Left Bank hip, with white porcelain, low lighting and attention-grabbing lollipop-red and tangerine tables; it also offers take-out meals.

BOUQUINISTES (LES) 🖾   22 | 19 | 19 | 54
53, quai des Grands-Augustins, 6ᵉ (St-Michel), 01 43 25 45 94; fax 43 25 23 07; www.guysavoy.com
▪ "Delicious" market-fresh fare prepared under the auspices of owner Guy Savoy, plus "a fun modern decor" (think "New York in Paris"), attract a "good mix of Parisians and tourists" to this New French with a "pretty view of the Seine" in Saint-Germain; some scold the service as "spotty", and penny-pinchers pout "you pay for [Savoy's] name rather than what's on your plate"; but most feel they're getting a good buy, given the "inventive" cooking.

Bourguignon du Marais (Au) 🖾   21 | 17 | 19 | 42
52, rue François Miron, 4ᵉ (Pont-Marie/St-Paul), 01 48 87 15 40; fax 48 87 17 49
▪ Maybe he's *un peu* "pushy", but "the owner really knows his Burgundies and is willing to share his knowledge with you" at this *bistrot à vins* that tops off a "small but excellent wine list" with "truly rustic", "great classic Bistro food" in the Marais; the "modern decor is nice for a change", too.

B4 ◐   – | – | – | E
6-8, sq Ste-Croix de la Bretonnerie, 1ᵉʳ (Hôtel-de-Ville/ Rambuteau), 01 42 72 16 19; fax 42 72 16 19
As its punning name implies, this "animated", "upscale" Marais Mediterranean-Provençal is a pre-clubbing table par excellence; with "good foreign wines" and "pleasant fusion cooking", it pulls a young, "discreetly gay" crowd, though its "trendy but friendly" atmosphere welcomes all; b-ware – it can get "expensive, but then that's the price you pay for seeing and being seen."

Braisière (La) 🖾   – | – | – | E
54, rue Cardinet, 17ᵉ (Malesherbes), 01 47 63 40 37; fax 47 63 04 76
This "charming family-run" spot serves New French cooking with Gascon overtones, a "combination that's out-of-the-ordinary but not bizarre"; "a popular lunch place for people who work in the area" near the Parc Monceau, it's also "agreeable for a dinner with friends", since service is attentive and fresh flowers bedeck the recently renovated, homey dining room.

Brasserie Balzar ◐   18 | 19 | 18 | 40
49, rue des Ecoles, 5ᵉ (Cluny-La Sorbonne/St-Michel), 01 43 54 13 67; fax 44 07 14 91; www.brasseriebalzar.com
▪ "The Parisian brasserie par excellence", this "classy classic" across the street from the Sorbonne is popular with writers, university professors and "people who might be somebody"; most like the "old-fashioned decor", while

the "professionalism" of the "seasoned, insouciant" servers is much appreciated ("our waiter didn't even flinch when my husband accidentally shot a snail across the dining room"); if some say "it's not as good as it always was, it's pretty close", and most would "go back in a heartbeat."

Brasserie de la Poste ☒   14 | 14 | 15 | 40
54, rue de Longchamp, 16ᵉ (Trocadéro), 01 47 55 01 31; fax 47 55 01 31
◪A "great hangout" near the Trocadéro, this "true neighborhood brasserie" boasts "cordial service" and "straightforward, standard fare"; malcontents mutter a "change in ownership [a while back] has ruined the atmosphere", but for this expensive neighborhood, it's certainly a "sure value."

Brasserie de l'Ile St. Louis ◐   19 | 18 | 18 | 33
55, quai de Bourbon, 4ᵉ (Cité/Pont-Marie), 01 43 54 02 59; fax 46 33 18 47
■ "Not one of the chains", this "bustling", "authentic old brasserie" on the Ile Saint Louis "in the shadow of Notre Dame" not only has a "wonderful setting", but also Alsatian-oriented cooking that's "surprisingly good for such a touristy place" – and "at reasonable prices" as well; the "waiters are fun", too, and the wood-paneled decor "quaint."

Brasserie du Louvre ◐   20 | 21 | 20 | 39
Hôtel du Louvre, pl André Malraux, 1ᵉʳ (Palais Royal-Musée du Louvre), 01 42 96 27 98; fax 44 58 38 00; www.hoteldulouvre.com
■ The "great location" of this brasserie across the street from the Louvre makes it ideal "*après musée*" or "if you're pressed for time", since the service is "courteous, friendly and prompt"; the "lovely atmosphere", augmented by the "good traditional food", adds up to a fine "break from fancy places."

Brasserie Flo ◐   17 | 21 | 16 | 45
7, cour des Petites-Ecuries, 10ᵉ (Château d'Eau), 01 47 70 13 59; fax 42 47 00 80; www.flobrasseries.com
◪ "Buried in an alley in the 10th", this "lively" brasserie with an Au Printemps branch is "touristy" but tempting with an art nouveau "decor worth a detour" and "harried but professional waiters flying by with massive trays" of "fabulous shellfish"; some shrug "a chain is a chain is a chain"; but even if "the reputation is better than the food", it's still "more fun than just about any place else in Paris."

Brasserie Julien ◐   18 | 24 | 17 | 50
16, rue du Faubourg St-Denis, 10ᵉ (Strasbourg-St-Denis), 01 47 70 12 06; fax 42 47 00 65; www.flobrasseries.com
■ "Get out your monocle, wax your moustache and pretend you're living in the Third Republic" when you visit this "art-nouveau gem" of a brasserie with "exceptional decor"

"among the shish-kebab stands around the Porte Saint-Martin"; "a bit noisy", it's "still pleasant" "for a quick lunch", "romantic dinner" or a "late supper"; while the food plays second fiddle, it's on a "decent level", particularly the profiteroles in "creamy hot-chocolate sauce."

Brasserie La Lorraine ◐   — | — | — | E
2, pl des Ternes, 8ᵉ (Ternes), 01 56 21 22 00; fax 56 21 22 09;
www.brasserielalorraine.com
This Frères Blanc–owned "classical brasserie" in the 8th has recently received a renovation, updating the authentic '20s "charm" with a grand Hollywood-does-art-deco interior, formal service (the staff used to be, "shall we say, leisurely") and some fusion fare to augment the "traditional dishes" (shellfish platters, choucroute garni); it's "terrific on Sundays, for business lunches" or for dinner before or after a concert", especially on the "fun terrace from which to watch the world go by."

BRASSERIE LIPP ◐   17 | 20 | 15 | 46
151, bd St-Germain, 6ᵉ (St-Germain-des-Prés), 01 45 48 53 91;
fax 45 44 33 20; www.brasserie-lipp.fr
☑ "If you don't get sent to second-floor Siberia", but sit in the "art nouveau main dining room", this Saint-Germain brasserie can be "fun", with "waiters straight out of central casting" – e.g. "long aprons and big moustaches" – who manage to be "rude yet polite"; though "the food doesn't live up to the setting", it's still "solid" ("onion soup's so good you'd swim in it if it weren't so hot"); sure, it's "overpriced and touristy", but for "a thoroughly Parisian experience" à la Hemingway, you gotta "love the Lipp."

Brasserie Lutétia   15 | 16 | 17 | 49
Hôtel Lutétia, 23, rue de Sèvres, 6ᵉ (Sèvres-Babylone),
01 49 54 46 76; fax 49 54 46 00; www.lutetia-Paris.com
■ "Good and reliable" is how most brasserie buffs would sum up this "pleasant if not brilliant" example of the species with a "great location" just steps from the Bon Marché department store; the seafood platters "in particular are well done" and "breakfast is good", too, in this dining room designed by Sonia Rykiel in "chic" art deco style.

Brasserie Mollard ◐   18 | 23 | 14 | 52
115, rue St-Lazare, 8ᵉ (Auber/St-Lazare), 01 43 87 50 22;
fax 43 87 84 17; www.mollard.fr
☑ It's the "beautifully preserved" "Ecole de Nancy mosaics" and other 1900 art nouveau decorations that make "this brasserie in front of the Gare Saint-Lazare a real institution"; though "a little expensive", the "humongous seafood platters" are "good" enough (in particular, the "lobster prix fixe is worth it") to "outweigh any shortcomings of the staff"; theatergoers also appreciate that "it's one of the [few] in the area open late."

Breakfast in America
– | – | – | I

17, rue des Ecoles, 5ᵉ (Cardinal Lemoine/Jussieu), 01 43 54 50 28;
www.breakfast-in-america.com
With a baseball-cap-wearing owner from Connecticut, red
vinyl banquettes and "a true diner feel", this Latin Quarter
site with is "the only place in town to find a real American
breakfast, with all the coffee you can drink"; but while the
bottomless cup and the "friendly service" "transport the
homesick back to the States", dissenters dis it as strictly
a drive-by.

BRISTOL (LE)
27 | 27 | 27 | VE

Hôtel Le Bristol, 112, rue du Faubourg St-Honoré, 8ᵉ (Miromesnil),
01 53 43 43 40; fax 53 43 43 01; www.hotel-bristol.com
■ "A wonderful restaurant in a wonderful hotel" sums up
this Haute Cuisine establishment in the Bristol that hits
"irreproachable" "heights of luxe"; served by a "cosseting
staff", chef Eric Fréchon's New French cooking is "superb,
refined, even artistic"; "the garden dining room is splendid"
during the summer, while "the marvelous oval room" with
oak paneling is one of the most "elegant" spaces in Paris;
it all "makes for a delightful evening" or lunch – expensive,
oui, but "worth every penny."

BUDDHA BAR ●
16 | 25 | 14 | 58

8, rue Boissy-d'Anglas, 8ᵉ (Concorde), 01 53 05 90 00;
fax 53 05 90 09; www.buddha-bar.com
◩ "Amazing atmosphere" and "spectacular decor" that
includes a "magnificent" gold-painted Buddha are the lures
at this "trendy" Asian in the 8th; but even if it's "more scene
than cuisine", "the food's actually pretty good", especially
if you groove on the DJ's "awesome sounds" and overlook
the often-"absent" service; some sniff that it's "not as 'in'
as it once was" (witness the "tour operators and business
groups"), but for most it's "a sexy, hip place for a romantic
meal"; be a little Zen when the check comes, though.

Buffalo Grill
7 | 8 | 10 | 24

15, pl de la République, 3ᵉ (République), 01 40 29 94 98
1, bd St-Germain, 5ᵉ (Jussieu), 01 56 24 34 49
3, pl Blanche, 9ᵉ (Blanche), 01 40 16 42 51
36, bd des Italiens, 9ᵉ (Opéra), 01 47 70 90 45
9, bd Denain, 10ᵉ (Gare du Nord), 01 40 16 47 81
2, rue Raymond Aron, 13ᵉ (Quai de la Gare), 01 45 86 76 71
117, av du Général-Leclerc, 14ᵉ (Porte d'Orléans), 01 45 40 09 72
154, rue St-Charles, 15ᵉ (Javel), 01 40 60 97 48; fax 40 60 17 48
6, pl du Maréchal-Juin, 17ᵉ (Péreire), 01 40 54 73 75
29, av Corentin-Cariou, 19ᵉ (Porte de la Villette), 01 40 36 21 41;
fax 53 26 88 17
www.buffalo-grill.fr
◩ Specializing in a "fast-food version of steak", these
"cheap" "cafeterias for cowboys" are "ok for the kids" or
when you "have to have some American food"; the "decor's

very basic" and the service, though "fast", is somewhat
lacking (they "couldn't keep beer cold during a heat wave"),
but the health-conscious "appreciate seeing the chart,
updated daily, that specifies the provenance of the meat."

Buisson Ardent (Le) ⊠ —| —| —| M |
25, rue Jussieu, 5ᵉ (Jussieu), 01 43 54 93 02;
fax 46 33 34 77
It may not be very widely known, but this contemporary
bistro in the 5th "near Jussieu" – "an area that doesn't
have a lot of good eating" – gets raves from those who've
found it; fans order "don't change a thing", since the food
is "hearty and inventive", the "service nice" and the setting
a pretty 1920s-style dining room that's "traditional and
welcoming"; "it's a pleasure to sit down at the table here",
especially since it's capped off by an easily digested check.

Butte Chaillot (La) 20| 18| 17| 50 |
110 bis, av Kléber, 16ᵉ (Trocadéro), 01 47 27 88 88;
fax 47 27 41 46; www.guysavoy.com
■ "Convenient to the Trocadéro", this "Guy Savoy–owned
bistro" boasts "sleek decor" and "a lively scene"; if "not
grand gourmet", the menu offers a "good mix" of classics
like the "incredible roast chicken and mashed potatoes"
along with "more adventurous" New French dishes, served
by a "friendly young staff"; and while this "neighborhoody,
casual spot" is perhaps a bit "expensive for what it is", it
remains "reliable", and a "safe bet for business luncheons."

Ca d'Oro ⊠ ▽ 16| 11| 15| 33 |
54, rue de l'Arbre-Sec, 1ᵉʳ (Louvre-Rivoli), 01 40 20 97 79
■ "Very good and very authentic", this "neighborhood
Italian" near the Louvre serves "fine Venetian cooking";
though the "setting is simple", the "welcome is warm",
and it's pretty "good value for the money."

Café Beaubourg ● 14| 19| 12| 35 |
100, rue St-Martin, 4ᵉ (Châtelet-Les Halles/Rambuteau),
01 48 87 63 96; fax 48 87 81 25
◪ "Wonderful people-watching" and a "great terrace"
make this cafe with a "fun setting" in front of the Centre
Pompidou a "pleasant stop" and "a perfect place to meet
people since everyone knows where it is"; however, the
"fashionable arty crowd" advises "stick to drinks" since,
aside from "very good brunches", the Classic and New
French "food is like what they serve" on airlines and the
staff "slow and unfriendly."

Café Burq ●⊠ —| —| —| M |
6, rue Burq, 18ᵉ (Abbesses), 01 42 52 81 27
Tucked away in a steep Montmartre street, this *bistrot à
vins* is a "totally unpretentious place – but it works", thanks
to "very good" contemporary Bistro fare and "some great
quaffs", along with "wonderful atmosphere and music";

there's also a "bar scene with a hip, young, slightly grungy crowd" of "locals avoiding the tourist" scene.

Café Charbon ◑
14 | 24 | 14 | 30

109, rue Oberkampf, 11ᵉ (Parmentier/Rue St-Maur), 01 43 57 55 13; fax 43 57 57 41

☑ "You go to see and be seen" at this "cafe with a limited menu" in the 11th, whose "magnificent decor" and "cool crowd" make it an ideal "spot for afternoon lounging"; but those expecting more may be "disappointed", since the traditional Bistro fare, many maintain, is merely "mediocre" and lacking the "spice of good service."

Café Constant ⊠
– | – | – | l

139, rue St-Dominique, 7ᵉ (Ecole Militaire), 01 47 53 73 34

Low-budget eating doesn't have to be a letdown, as proven by this friendly corner cafe that's come to the cheerful precincts of the rue Saint Dominique; a hit for its daily changing menu of inexpensive but high-quality traditional Bistro cooking, including a variety of comforting treats *à la grandmère*, it's owned by chef Christian Constant, whose more expensive Le Violon d'Ingres is just down the block.

Café d'Angel (Le) ⊠
▽ 18 | 11 | 15 | 40

16, rue Brey, 17ᵉ (Charles de Gaulle-Etoile/Ternes), 01 47 54 03 33; fax 47 54 03 33

■ Citing the "creative" Bistro cuisine, converts carol this cozy, homey place with "a charming lady owner" deserves its halo; granted, the "tables are a little tight", but it's a pretty "great buy", so "bring your friends from out-of-town" to this "trendy" corner near the Etoile.

Café de Flore ◑
14 | 19 | 14 | 33

172, bd St-Germain, 6ᵉ (St-Germain-des-Prés), 01 45 48 55 26; fax 45 44 33 39; www.cafe-de-flore.com

☑ Even though "the only thing left of the Existentialists is their mention in the menu, it's still amusing to watch the crowd" (often "loaded with tourists") at this "Paris landmark cafe" with "a great location in the heart of Saint-Germain"; though "breakfast is good" and it's "a must for a drink", "no one really comes here for the Brasserie food", which is "way overpriced" for what you get, fume foes who also find the waiters "tedious"; but despite all, this "mythic" place "still retains" "that je ne sais quoi."

Café de la Musique ◑
14 | 17 | 12 | 29

213, av Jean Jaurès, 19ᵉ (Porte de Pantin), 01 48 03 15 91; fax 48 03 15 18

☑ The "stylish crowd", trendy soundtrack and "big terrace" strike a chord at this Villette-area cafe; a harsher note is sounded when it comes to the Brasserie cuisine, which seems "rather pricey" given its "ordinary" nature; still, most find it pleasant, especially "before a concert, or to people-watch on the weekend."

Café de la Paix ⬤

17 | 22 | 17 | 52

Grand Hôtel Inter-Continental, 12, bd des Capucines, 9ᵉ (Auber/Opéra), 01 40 07 30 20; fax 40 07 35 29; www.paris.intercontinental.com

☑ At this reopened, perpetually "busy" address, "they've made some real efforts, especially in refurbishing the sublime 1882 decor" – and a Food score climb confirms they've "equally improved" the Classic French cuisine, to the extent that some quip "go for the people-watching, stay for the fare"; opponents opine it's "overpriced" and "living on its memories", but they're outvoted by those who say "it remains essential Paris", and "the perfect place for champagne after the Opéra" Garnier, across the street.

Café de la Poste ⬤ 🖾

– | – | – | I

13, rue Castex, 4ᵉ (Bastille), 01 42 72 95 35

As restaurants in the Marais become ever more concept-driven, it's reassuring to find a good ol', good-value Classic French, whose menu runs to a solid roster of favorites (from confit de canard to chocolate mousse), served in an old-time atmosphere of mirrored walls and cracked tile floors; taking its name from the art moderne post office (one of Paris' grandest) nearby, it serves a mixed crowd of well-behaved postal workers, arty types and vintage intellectuals.

Café de l'Esplanade (Le) ⬤

14 | 19 | 9 | 47

52, rue Fabert, 7ᵉ (Invalides/La Tour-Maubourg), 01 47 05 38 80; fax 47 05 23 75

☑ "The Costes brothers strike again with another of their triumphs of haute attitude over dining" is the general take on this table with an "elegant crowd, good-looking staff", "sophisticated" Jacques Garcia–designed decor and "great location across from Les Invalides"; it's the boys' "same old, same old menu" (a combo of Classic and Contemporary French cuisine), however, and "you need to be a movie star" or "to wear black" "to get any attention" from those comely servers; still, it's "not bad for a trendy."

Café de l'Industrie ⬤

▽ 11 | 17 | 11 | 23

16-17, rue St-Sabin, 11ᵉ (Bastille/Bréguet-Sabin), 01 47 00 13 53; fax 47 00 92 33

☑ Near the Bastille (and hence very busy), this bar/eatery has "rather nice decor" and a "convivial", "authentic intellectual-cultural atmosphere" "reminiscent of post-war cafes"; most find the traditional Bistro bites a bit "banal", but "on the other hand, the bill is light" on the wallet.

Café de Mars ⬤

▽ 17 | 12 | 15 | 29

11, rue Augereau, 7ᵉ (Ecole Militaire), 01 47 05 05 91; fax 45 55 76 99; www.cafe-de-mars.com

■ "Great for a quick bite", this "always-smoky and crowded" cafe offers "eating in the rue Cler area at its best"; the Bistro menu, augmented with some Eclectic innovations (from cheeseburgers to a brunchtime Caesar salad), offers "good food for the price", especially on the evening prix fixe.

✗ Café des Délices (Le) ◑⊠   21 | 14 | 17 | 43
87, rue d'Assas, 6ᵉ (Port-Royal/Vavin), 01 43 54 70 00; fax 43 26 42 05; cafedesdelices.lesrestos.com
■ Chef-owner Gilles Choukroun is a "rising star" with his increasingly popular address near the Luxembourg Gardens that serves a "short but delicious menu" of innovative "Bistro food with Middle Eastern" and other "influences from all over the world" (among the typical offerings, locals "love the langoustines with finely chopped pistachio nuts" and "the fantastic 'tomato in all its forms' appetizer"); a "warm welcome" and a "colorful setting" have *amis* advising "don't miss this gem."

Café des Lettres   – | – | – | M
53, rue de Verneuil, 7ᵉ (Rue du Bac/Solférino), 01 42 22 52 17; fax 45 44 70 02; www.cafedeslettres.com
"Located in a paved interior courtyard, a nice and quiet terrace" makes this "cozy" Scandinavian in the 7th "perfect for a summer meal with friends" before or after a visit to the Musée d'Orsay nearby; "discreet, efficient service" handles a clientele that's "very French with lots of locals" feasting on the "simple but good" cuisine.

Café du Commerce (Le) ◑   10 | 18 | 11 | 28
51, rue du Commerce, 15ᵉ (Emile Zola), 01 45 75 03 27; fax 45 75 27 40; www.lecafeducommerce.com
☑ "Edible, easy, unmemorable" summarizes the "standard Bistro food" at this "huge" 1920s brasserie in the 15th with "nice decor" ("especially during the summer when they open the roof") and "picture-perfect waiters" who can be "grumpy" but are "so Parisian"; true, it gets "noisy and overcrowded", but most find it "for all the hustle and bustle, fun" and "the prices right", making it ideal for "simple dinners with large groups of friends"; N.B. the scores may not fully reflect a recent change of ownership.

Café du Passage (Le) ◑   – | – | – | I
12, rue de Charonne, 11ᵉ (Bastille/Ledru-Rollin), 01 49 29 97 64; fax 49 29 97 64
Not far from the Bastille, this *bistrot à vins* is "a hole-in-the-wall well worth finding" for its "excellent wine list" (380 different labels) and "very welcoming host"; the "ancient, cozy space", a former workshop in a mews, is animated with taped jazz and regulars devouring the *andouillette* (tripe sausage), along with other light fare for affordable prices.

Café Etienne Marcel ◑   ▽ 17 | 17 | 15 | 45
34, rue Etienne Marcel, 2ᵉ (Etienne Marcel), 01 45 08 01 03; fax 42 36 03 44
☑ Surveyors' views diverge on just about every facet of this establishment on the edge of Les Halles, from the retro

'60s a-go-go decor ("nice" vs. "outdated after the first week") to the Eclectic cuisine ("quality" vs. "leaves a lot to be desired") to the prices ("affordable" vs. "excessively expensive"); suffice to say that, while the scene has its merits, it's "certainly not the best of the Costes brothers'" addresses; even "the staff seems less beautiful than those in their other restaurants."

Café Faubourg
18 20 20 47

Sofitel Le Faubourg, 11 bis, rue Boissy-d'Anglas, 8ᵉ (Concorde/Madeleine), 01 44 94 14 24; fax 44 94 14 28; www.sofitel.com

■ Located in the Sofitel Le Faubourg, just off the Place de la Concorde, this Classic French serves "nice food" with a Southwestern accent in an "elegant", "airy" atrium dining room popular with a business crowd at noon and fashion execs at dinner; many appreciate the "refined", "serene atmosphere" created by the friendly, professional service and a pianist at night.

Café Flo ⊠
14 19 12 37

Au Printemps, 64, bd Haussmann, 9ᵉ (Auber/ Havre-Caumartin), 01 42 82 58 84; fax 45 26 31 24; www.flobrasseries.com

■ "Strictly a shoppers' lunch spot" (though they do dinner on Thursday), this Flo Group–run restaurant on the top floor of the Au Printemps department store serves up a "good enough" Traditional French menu amid a "beautiful space" with "great views of Paris"; no surprise, "there are long waits during the height of the lunch hour", but it's fun to "go for a sundae just to see" the "exquisite glass ceiling."

Café Fusion ◑⊠
– – – M

12, rue de la Butte aux Cailles, 13ᵉ (Place d'Italie), 01 45 80 12 02; fax 47 00 53 53

With a striking fluorescent-orange decor, aluminum-topped tables and tubular lighting fixtures, this fusion food fixture in a trendy corner of the 13th has a decidedly '70s-retro look; the mixed, lively crowd loves the terrace out front for dining in good weather, as well as the moderately priced menu that skates all over the world with a variety of wok-cooked Eurasian dishes.

Café Guitry
– – – M

Théâtre Edouard VII, 10, pl Edouard VII, 9ᵉ (Auber/Opéra), 01 40 07 00 77; fax 47 42 77 68

Located in one of the most famous playhouses in Paris, this 9th-arrondissement eatery is filled with framed theater posters, wooden tables and wicker chairs; the sepia-toned atmosphere is amplified by Traditional French favorites such as rabbit terrine, steak tartare and fruit tart, all being consumed by theatergoers pre-curtain and bankers and brokers post-workday.

Café la Jatte   15 | 19 | 14 | 43
60, bd Vital Bouhot, Neuilly (Pont-de-Levallois), 01 47 45 04 20;
fax 47 45 19 32; www.cafelajatte.com

◪ You can enjoy what's probably the "best view in Neuilly"
at this contemporary bistro with a "fabulous setting
complete with dinosaur skeleton" on the Ile de la Jatte;
the "scene is beautiful", especially from "the tables
overlooking the river", the "food decent" and the "service
fast"; so even if the bill gets "a little expensive for what
you find on your plate", it's no surprise that the "vibrant
atmosphere" pulls in a "business crowd at noon and fashion
folks at night."

Café Lenôtre (Le)   19 | 19 | 16 | 43
Pavillon Elysée, 10, av des Champs-Elysées, 8ᵉ
(Champs-Elysées-Clémenceau), 01 42 65 85 10;
fax 42 6576 23; www.lenotre.fr

◼ Located in the Pavilion Elysée, a pretty wedding-cake of
a building in the gardens of the Champs-Elysées, this "very
trendy place" by the Lenôtre group has "a great terrace" for
summer dining, but is also "fun indoors on a rainy autumn
day"; the New French menu is "decent", but those in the
know "go just for the divine desserts" brought by "charming
servers"; P.S. there's also an "original" cookware boutique
and cooking school offering daily lessons in French and
English on the premises.

CAFÉ LES DEUX MAGOTS ◑   14 | 19 | 14 | 33
6, pl St-Germain-des-Prés, 6ᵉ (St-Germain-des-Prés),
01 45 48 55 25; fax 45 49 31 29; www.lesdeuxmagots.fr

◪ "About as Left Bank as it gets", this Saint-Germain literary
"landmark" remains the "quintessential cafe experience"
and a "touristy must" – if only "to add 'been there' to your
résumé", since the Classic French "food's not that great"
("breakfast is best"), the waiters are "typically rude" and
for the quality, "prices are high"; still, even if "you pay to
sit" and sip "something sinfully rich" on that "wonderful
glassed-in terrace", "it's worth every penny", since it's "the
perfect spot to contemplate the start of a new day in Paris."

Café M   19 | 18 | 17 | 52
Hôtel Hyatt, 24, bd Malesherbes, 8ᵉ (Madeleine/
St-Augustin), 01 55 27 12 34; fax 55 27 12 35;
www.paris.madeleine.hyatt.com

◼ Being located in the Hyatt near the Madeleine causes
a "lack of Paris feeling" perhaps, but otherwise life is
"surprisingly good" at this "simple, sleek" hotel dining
room; the "fresh", fusion-y New French food is "even a
little imaginative", and the effort of the staffers, who are
often "interns, is sometimes tentative but always gracious";
the business-oriented believe it works well "for a low-key
lunch with a client", especially if you snag a table in front
of the fireplace.

CAFÉ MARLY ❶
15 | 23 | 14 | 43

93, rue de Rivoli, 1ᵉʳ (Palais Royal-Musée du Louvre),
01 49 26 06 60; fax 49 26 07 06

◪ "If it didn't have the best location and view in Paris, I'd give this place up" sigh surveyors about this "fashionable" Costes brothers' cafe overlooking the I.M. Pei pyramid entrance to the Louvre – and indeed, a "staff that's more stylish than helpful" and "mediocre" meals mar the experience for many; still, a gallery-full of fans finds the Classic and New French fare "nice" enough, advising "the best thing is breakfast – you'll never taste a better omelette than the you-have-to-ask-for-it herb one they do here."

Café Max ⊠
– | – | – | M

7, av de La Motte-Picquet, 7ᵉ (Ecole Militaire/La Tour-Maubourg),
01 47 05 57 66

Only a happy few know this traditional bistro with an endearing flea-market decor in the 7th, but they're not shy about vaunting its charms – it's not only "great fun" but "an honor to be invited to this convivial atmosphere"; namesake chef-owner Max Gerchambeau has left, but the menu still offers many "decadent, hearty" Southwestern specialties.

Café Moderne ⊠
– | – | – | M

40, rue Notre-Dame-des-Victoires, 2ᵉ (Bourse), 01 53 40 84 10;
fax 53 40 84 11

Just across the street from the old Bourse (Paris stock market), this slick address with a long, narrow dining room overlooking an interior courtyard has a pleasant atmosphere that's at once hip and cozy; parquet floors, butter-colored walls and jewel-tone velvet upholstery create a modern urban backdrop for a stylish, young crowd to enjoy a Classic French-Med menu, recently re-done by a new young chef.

Café Ruc ❶
13 | 16 | 12 | 42

159, rue St-Honoré, 1ᵉʳ (Palais Royal-Musée du Louvre),
01 42 60 97 54; fax 42 60 94 81

◪ "Want to see a model? come here to look at the staff" advise the amorous about this "self-consciously trendy" "Costes brothers outpost" "in the center of everything" (well, "near the Louvre" and the Comédie Française, at least); skeptics sneer it's all "sizzle but no steak", citing "indifferent service and food" of the contemporary and classic Bistro variety, and all agree it's "too expensive", but at least there's "good people-watching", "sitting on the terrace."

Café Terminus
∇ 19 | 13 | 17 | 39

Hôtel Concorde St-Lazare, 108, rue St-Lazare, 8ᵉ (St-Lazare),
01 40 08 43 30; fax 40 08 43 65; www.concordestlazare-paris.com

◪ This "surprising establishment in a location [Saint-Lazare] not known for cuisine" is "a solid hotel restaurant" that's a "nice little place to dine" on Brasserie cooking; the "dull transient atmosphere is as depressing as the food is good", but it's convenient before catching a train.

Cafetière Corse (La) ●☒   19 | 18 | 19 | 38
(fka La Cafetière)
21, rue Mazarine, 6ᵉ (Odéon), 01 46 33 76 90; fax 43 25 76 90
■ "Intimate and old-world", this "very cozy" Corsican, "nicely decorated" with a signature collection of antique, enameled coffeepots, serves up "excellent food and desserts" "with a touch of creativity"; its service is "delightful" and "efficient", prices are easy for Saint-Germain, and most judge it to be "worth every revisit."

Café Very   11 | 11 | 9 | 22
Jardin des Tuileries, 1ᵉʳ (Concorde/Tuileries), 01 47 03 94 84; fax 47 03 94 84

Dame Tartine
2, rue Brisemiche, 4ᵉ (Hôtel-de-Ville), 01 42 77 32 22; fax 42 77 32 22
■ Open-faced "sandwiches of every sort" star at these "simple" spots amid the Tuileries and "in the shadow of the Beaubourg"; "fast service" makes them popular with a "young, lively, noisy crowd"; and if some liken the experience to "eating in a cafeteria", it can be "fun" for a "light", "quick feed."

Caffe del Gattopardo   – | – | – | M
102, rue Lepic, 18ᵉ (Abbesses), 01 42 58 06 22; fax 42 58 08 24; www.lagorgone.com
Octopus carpaccio typifies the Sicilian-focused cooking at this tiny dining room, located on one of the trendiest streets in Montmartre and frequented by resident TV and show-biz types; adding to its almost-in-Palermo atmosphere are a high noise level, speedy waiters and brighter lighting than is usually found in Parisian dining spots; N.B. Italian groceries and cookbooks are sold at the front of the space.

Caffé Toscano   – | – | – | M
34, rue des Saints-Pères, 7ᵉ (St-Germain-des-Prés), 01 42 84 28 95; fax 42 84 26 36
Despite the fact that it's strategically located just off the Boulevard Saint-Germain, few seem to have found this "little piece of Italy in Paris"; but those who have say it's "a place we'd like to share", since "the owners receive you with real warmth" before you sit down to "simple and good", "authentic" eats with a Tuscan accent, "quickly served."

Cagouille (La)   24 | 14 | 18 | 49
10, pl Constantin Brancusi, 14ᵉ (Gaîté/Montparnasse-Bienvenüe), 01 43 22 09 01; fax 45 38 57 29; www.la-cagouille.fr
■ "Fish heaven" profess fans of this Montparnasse mainstay that specializes in "simply" and "honestly prepared" seafood that's as "fresh as the ocean's" latest catch; the modern black-slate-and-wood decor may be

just "average", but no one minds since a "warm", "casual atmosphere" pervades the room in winter, and there's "an agreeably tranquil terrace in the summer"; "service varies according to the team on duty", but most find it generally "pleasant and efficient."

Cailloux (Les) 🗷   – | – | – | I

58, rue des Cinq Diamants, 13ᵉ (Corvisart/Place d'Italie), 01 45 80 15 08; fax 45 65 67 09

Tucked away in the "charming and increasingly hip Butte-aux-Cailles neighborhood" of the 13th, this popular bit of The Boot with a "simple decor" sends out "generous plates" of pasta for low prices; a "sweet" "all-Italian staff and a relaxed atmosphere make it a local favorite."

Caïus 🗷   – | – | – | M

6, rue d'Armaillé, 17ᵉ (Charles de Gaulle-Etoile), 01 42 27 19 20; fax 40 55 00 93

Imaginative New French cooking has made this wood-paneled dining room in the 17th a huge hit; chef Jean-Marc Notelet loves to surprise with an inventive but judicious use of ingredients, especially peppers of different provenances; if his talent and modest prices attract businesspeople at noon, at night the crowd shifts to serious eaters from all over town in search of a good buy.

Caméléon (Le) 🗷   17 | 13 | 18 | 42

6, rue de Chevreuse, 6ᵉ (Vavin), 01 43 20 63 43; fax 43 27 97 91

■ Name aside, this "homey" spot is no chameleon, but rather "the real thing: a Parisian bistro" – one that after over 30 years on a "nice cozy" Montparnasse street remains "as good as ever", serving "solid, unpretentious Classic French food" that's "excellent for the price"; it's still "a sexy little nook", too, with an old-fashioned cracked-tile floor and offbeat floral wallpaper.

Camélia (Le) 🗷   ▽ 23 | 19 | 23 | 53

7, quai Georges Clémenceau, Bougival (RER La Défense), 01 39 18 36 06; fax 39 18 00 25; www.lecamelia.com

■ "Fantastic food" that's "very inventive for the price" make many "wanting to go as often as possible" to this "peaceful bourgeois house on the banks of the Seine" in suburban Bougival; an "incomparable welcome", plus "just the right touch of New French cooking in the classic dishes" bring surveyors to full bloom, well watered by "a wine list the length of a bible."

C'Amelot (Le) 🗷   21 | 11 | 18 | 35

50, rue Amelot, 11ᵉ (Chemin Vert), 01 43 55 54 04; fax 43 14 77 05

◪ For those seeking the best in "budget-priced gastronomy", the quest ends at this "quaint place" in the 11th, where "simple but sophisticated" Bistro fare is served on a "designated menu of the day" ("you only choose dessert"); most have "no problem" with the "no-choice" *carte,* since it is "incredibly priced", and the "warm atmosphere" created by the "cheerful husband (chef) and wife (hostess)" overcomes the drawback of the "small, cramped space."

Camille ◑   19 | 18 | 21 | 36
24, rue des Francs-Bourgeois, 3ᵉ (St-Paul), 01 42 72 20 50; fax 40 27 07 99
■ "All the Bistro standards are well executed" at this "quaint" lace-curtain corner in the Marais, which may be "small and crowded" but is "worth a visit" for fans of "homestyle food at reasonable prices", served by "funny, endearing" staffers; but book ahead, since its "popularity with the locals" can make "weekends impossible if you don't have a reservation."

Cantinella ⌧   – | – | – | I
30, rue du Faubourg St-Jacques, 14ᵉ (St-Jacques/Port Royal), 01 46 33 24 20
Generous portions of reasonable traditional Italian dishes are drawing Left Bank office workers to this new site for lunch (evening brings a more diverse 14th-arrondissement crowd); its lively atmosphere and hurried but good natured service make it reminiscent of popular urban trattorias throughout The Boot.

Can Tin'h ⌧   – | – | – | I
5, rue de Vanves, Boulogne (Porte de St-Cloud/Marcel Sembat), 01 46 08 14 12
In the quiet suburb of Boulogne, this new hole-in-the-wall (maximum capacity: 40) offers upscale Vietnamese fare at rock bottom prices; the bright decor, augmented with colorful Formica tables, a bar with changing lights, a sparkling concrete floor and lamps made of bowls sets the scene for such specialties as *bo bun,* soothing soups and a yogurt-based dessert, all served with a smile under the eyes of owners Irène Tran and Valérie Auczié.

Cap Seguin (Le) ⌧   ▽ 16 | 18 | 11 | 39
face au 27, quai le Gallo, Boulogne (Pont-de-Sèvres), 01 46 05 06 07; fax 46 05 06 88; www.lecapseguin.com
◪ With a breezy Seine-side location in Boulogne, this wood-paneled barge is the place to come for "proof that the long business lunch still exists – a tradition that the escargotlike service does nothing to challenge"; it's "a pleasant place", though, with a nice "nautical atmosphere" and decor, and the Traditional French cooking seems to please the "chic" crowd, so rather than let the slow-paced meal get you down, "count to 10 and enjoy the view."

Cap Vernet (Le) ⌧   16 | 13 | 14 | 52
82, av Marceau, 8ᵉ (Charles de Gaulle-Etoile), 01 47 20 20 40; fax 47 20 95 36
◪ Overlooking the Arc de Triomphe, this split-level, seafood "updated brasserie" is an "efficient" place for a business

meal, which makes it "very lively at lunch time"; but if the bait here is "good fish", there's some major crabbing about the New French menu, which seems "so-so" given the "high prices"; however, "disappointed" designers who believe the "boating decor could be renewed" will find it has indeed been changed, outdating the Decor score.

Carpe Diem ⊠   – | – | – | E

10, rue de l'Eglise, Neuilly (Pont-de-Neuilly), 01 46 24 95 01; fax 46 40 15 61

What a difference a day makes if you have a meal at this "small", homey suburbanite in Neuilly; "memories of great magret de canard" and other solid, carefully prepared classic Bistro dishes "always bring back" the customers, despite somewhat high prices.

CARRÉ DES FEUILLANTS ⊠   25 | 22 | 25 | VE

14, rue de Castiglione, 1er (Concorde/Tuileries), 01 42 86 82 82; fax 42 86 07 71; www.relaischateaux.com

☑ "Fantastic food and immaculate service – well-mannered and effortless" – mean a most "*magnifique*" meal at chef-owner Alain Dutournier's "superb Haute Cuisine" hangout in the 1st; the recently renovated sleek steel-gray setting is "a success" say most; of course, the usual minority of malcontents mutters about an "overrated reputation", but most happily hum along to this "song for the palate", "a place to visit often", provided you can swing a "splurge."

Carr's   – | – | – | M

1, rue du Mont Thabor, 1er (Tuileries), 01 42 60 60 26; fax 42 60 33 32

Those seeking "a sweet little corner of Ireland" can find it two steps from the Tuileries gardens, where lots of gab and Guinness make this Dublin denizen a friendly hangout; and even Gallic grumblers who grouse that Gaelic gastronomy "is not renowned" admit the grub's generally "very tasty", especially the "brunch on Sundays."

Cartes Postales (Les) ⊠   ∇ 20 | 12 | 15 | 54

7, rue Gomboust, 1er (Opéra/Pyramides), 01 42 61 02 93; fax 42 61 02 93

☑ Don't be misled "by the menu translated into Japanese and the numerous Nipponese tourists" – this sushi-sized spot in the 1st serves "excellent New French cuisine", albeit an Asian-fused version, since the chef-owner trained with Alain Dutournier after leaving his native Japan; regulars "really enjoy" "the chance to order half-size portions to sample a variety"; however, some stylists suggest "a little candlelight and flowers would improve the sterile decor."

Casa Alcalde   ∇ 16 | 14 | 13 | 39

117, bd de Grenelle, 15e (La Motte-Picquet-Grenelle), 01 47 83 39 71; fax 45 66 49 01

■ "Reservations are a must" if you want a table at this "always-full", "reliable address for paella" and other

Spanish specialties; the Iberian eats and wines, served in an "intimate" innlike setting, create a "vacation atmosphere" in the midst of the 15th.

Casa Bini

| 20 | 12 | 17 | 41 |

36, rue Grégoire de Tours, 6ᵉ (Odéon), 01 46 34 05 60; fax 40 46 09 71

☑ "Superb Tuscan cooking" and a "magnificent Italian wine list" pulls a chic crowd of Saint-Germain "habitués" to this popular place; admittedly, the simple decor "could use some updating", so regulars recommend reserving a table in the upstairs dining room, which is "nicer" and less filled with "heavy smoke."

Casa Hidalgo ◑

| – | – | – | I |

17, rue de la Forge Royale, 11ᵉ (Faidherbe-Chaligny/Ledru-Rollin), 01 40 24 10 54

With its yellow-painted walls and tile floor, this Spanish table brings a bit of southern sun to a neighborhood not far from the Bastille; owned by a friendly expat from Andalucia, the kitchen specializes in hot and cold tapas, paella and grills, and is attracting an enthusiastic neighborhood crowd with its cheerful decor and low prices.

Casa Olympe (La) ☒

| 19 | 12 | 16 | 50 |

48, rue St-Georges, 9ᵉ (St-Georges), 01 42 85 26 01; fax 45 26 49 33

☑ "Hidden" in the 9th near Saint-Georges, this "intimate" Med-Provençal bistro still wins medals from many for its "fresh", "inventive" cuisine that makes "reservations imperative"; however, some sterner judges have found the fare "disappointing lately", and even admirers critique the casa for its "too tightly spaced tables."

Casa Tina ◑

| ∇ 12 | 16 | 13 | 34 |

18, rue Lauriston, 16ᵉ (Charles de Gaulle-Etoile/Kléber), 01 40 67 19 24; fax 41 44 73 63; www.casa-tina.net

■ "Authentic atmosphere is guaranteed by Spanish-speaking waiters" at this "snug and noisy" outpost of Iberia in the 16th that's also "like Madrid" in its "copious tapas menu" (which some say are "better to order" than the mains), served late; though more inclined to Chanel than castanets, a young crowd finds it "great to go with a group to chat, drink and eat"; N.B. they recently opened Casa Paco, a similar sibling, in the 16th.

Casa Vigata

| – | – | – | M |

44, rue Léon Frot, 11ᵉ (Charonne), 01 43 56 38 66

"Pasta with all kinds of sauces and divine stuffed sardines" are among the homestyle Sicilian dishes that chef-owner Roberta Tringale ("she's charming and has real character") turns out at this little-known vest-pocket of a place in the 11th arrondissement; the "colored faience" creates some warm Mediterranean atmosphere in the small space.

Caveau du Palais (Le)
∇ 21 | 15 | 18 | 41

17-19, pl Dauphine, 1ᵉʳ (Cité/Pont-Neuf), 01 43 26 04 28; fax 43 26 81 84

■ Anyone hoping to "hang out with a legal crowd" will testify to this Classic French near the Palais du Justice (hence the name) in "one of the prettiest squares in Paris"; but even if you care more about tarts than torts, it's still an "appealing" destination for a "lovely meal" that'll let you "travel back in time" until the bill comes; N.B.closed on Sundays October–April.

Cave de l'Os à Moëlle
18 | 15 | 16 | 30

181, rue de Lourmel, 15ᵉ (Lourmel), 01 45 57 28 28; fax 45 57 28 00

■ "If you don't mind communal seating" and "helping yourself" from the dishes on tables and a stove, you'll probably love the "conviviality" of this wine-oriented bistro in the 15th; it "helps to speak *français*", since the stone-walled setting is packed with locals, but everyone enjoys the "high-quality" "Classic French food", including "succulent" all-you-can-eat terrines cooked at parent L'Os à Moëlle across the street, and "good selection of wines."

Cave Gourmande (La) - le Restaurant de Mark Singer ⊠
∇ 25 | 14 | 23 | 34

10, rue du Général Brunet, 19ᵉ (Botzaris), 01 40 40 03 30; fax 40 40 03 30

■ Though this "corner of the 19th isn't given to gastronomic highs", the bistro of Mark Singer, "an American who moved to Paris from Philadelphia at age seven and became an incredible chef", is "truly worth the métro ride"; as in any "inventive" kitchen, some ambitious dishes "can be confused", but overall the "attention given to detail" is "incredible"; Singer's French wife oversees the "welcoming staff", resulting in a "wonderful dining experience" that "offers spectacular value for the money."

Caves Miard (Les) ⊠
– | – | – | I

(aka La Crémerie)

9, rue des Quatre-Vents, 6ᵉ (Odéon), 01 43 54 99 30; fax 43 54 99 30

Customers were shocked when, after 40 years, the Miard family sold its wine bar on a pleasant corner of Saint-Germain; but the new owner has made an immediate impression, offering warm hospitality, a mostly French wine list and an Italian menu of light bites, plus a daily hot dish or two; the crowd runs from antique dealers and book editors to politicians – the Sénat is steps away – and the occasional movie star.

Caves Pétrissans ⊠
18 | 17 | 18 | 48

30 bis, av Niel, 17ᵉ (Péreire/Ternes), 01 42 27 52 03; fax 40 54 87 56

■ "Crusty and dusty", this "old-style *bistrot/bar à vins*" in the 17th is a "tourist-free" "Parisian gem" "just the way we like 'em"; with the advice of "the owners who are more than willing to share a couple of glasses discussing wine and food", "the formula is that you buy a bottle from the [adjacent] shop and just pay a corkage fee" to accompany the "fine Traditional French cuisine" ("ah, the tête de veau").

Caviar Kaspia ●🌑   22 | 17 | 22 | 98

17, pl de la Madeleine, 8ᵉ (Madeleine), 01 42 65 33 32; fax 42 65 09 55; www.kaspia.fr

■ "A luxurious trip to Russia" awaits when you "climb the stairs to caviar heaven" at this "elegant, expensive, decadent" dining room for a meal of "worldly treasures" and "a gorgeous view of the Madeleine across the street"; particularly perfect post-shopping or -theater, or just for a "special treat" of "a carafe of icy vodka, several hundred grams of sevruga, butter-splashed blini, smoked salmon and finally a tiny dish of wild strawberries"; it's "expensive", of course, but "what could be better?"

Cazaudehore La Forestière   18 | 21 | 18 | 54

1, av Kennedy, St-Germain-en-Laye (RER St-Germain-en-Laye), 01 30 61 64 64; fax 39 73 73 88; www.cazaudehore.fr

■ "Marvelous for an outdoor dinner during the summer" or "a romantic lunch", this "exclusive place in the middle of the Saint-Germain-en-Laye forest" "where Louis XIV used to hunt" serves up "very good" Contemporary and Classic French meals in a "cheerful and bright glass-paneled dining room"; a few find it "expensive relative to what you get", but to most, it's great for "a gallant moment in the greenery."

Céladon (Le)   22 | 22 | 21 | 81

Hôtel Westminster, 15, rue Daunou, 2ᵉ (Opéra), 01 47 03 40 42; fax 42 60 30 66; www.leceladon.com

■ A "sophisticated and gracious" experience awaits at this Classic French near the Place Vendôme; settled in a dining room with a slightly "crusty" restrained-pastel decor, the exigent extol not only the quality of the cooking ("the lobster special gave me a whole new appreciation of that marvelous food") but the "remarkable" value of the prix fixe menus; "a perfect spot for business lunches", it's also a charmer for "a special occasion or a special person."

182 Rive Droite 🌑   – | – | – | M

182, quai Louis-Bleriot, 16ᵉ (Porte de St-Cloud/Exelmans), 01 42 88 44 63; fax 42 88 79 17

The spacious, loftlike setting and "good, if not great" Mediterranean–New French cooking of this stylish site more than compensates for its location "in the middle of nowhere" in the 16th; for the few who have found it, "it's a nice surprise" with "friendly service", relaxed atmosphere and easygoing prices.

123 ⌧
– – – E

(fka Faucher)

*123, av de Wagram, 17ᵉ (Ternes/Wagram), 01 42 27 61 50;
fax 46 22 25 72*

Chef-owner Gérard Faucher has reinvented his long-running restaurant in the 17th, transforming it from a polite sort of place with bourgeois cooking to an aspiringly trendy, expense-account sort of place (though the overhauled New French menu is actually less pricey now); a sultry new decor of crystal chandeliers, parquet floors, striped walls and a back-lit red-laminate bar communicates the groovy mood to a fresh clientele of advertising and media types.

Chai 33
13 | 17 | 15 | 40

*33, cour St-Emilion, 12ᵉ (Cour St-Emilion), 01 53 44 01 01;
fax 53 44 01 02; www.chai33.com*

☑ Fans love "the incredible mix of old and new" – a historic stone-and-brick wine warehouse with an "original", "New Age-y" interior – that characterizes this sprawling wine bar/eatery in the popular Bercy district; oenophiles also "adore" "going down to the superb cave to choose their wine"; fewer corks pop over the "flavorless" Classic French fare, but smiling sippers outweigh sour grapers, even if you're paying "more for the place than for what's on your plate."

Chalet de Neuilly (Le)
– – – M

*14, rue du Cdt Pilot, Neuilly (Les Sablons/Porte Maillot),
01 46 24 03 11; fax 46 37 18 80*

No need to go to Courchevel or Val d'Isère when hearty mountain specialties (cheese fondue, raclette) are served in Neuilly's cozy, family-run enclave that evokes – as the name suggests – a chalet, with a stone-and-wood interior decorated with ski accessories and posters; Classic French meat dishes augment the affordable alpine offerings.

Chalet des Iles (Le)
13 | 25 | 13 | 52

*Lac Inférieur du Bois de Boulogne, 16ᵉ (Av Henri Martin/
Rue de la Pompe), 01 42 88 04 69; fax 42 88 84 09;
www.chaletdesiles.net*

☑ Maybe the Classic French "food's nothing special", but everyone loves escaping via a "brief but charming boat ride" to this "magical spot on an island in the Bois de Boulogne"; sure, the service can be "nonexistent" ("we had to call the main number by cell phone to ask them to take our order"), but "it's one of the most enchanting places around when the good weather comes"; make sure to get a terrace table, though, since if you sit "inside, the charm vanishes."

Chamarré (Le) ⌧
21 | 16 | 19 | 71

*13, bd de la Tour-Maubourg, 7ᵉ (Invalides/La Tour-Maubourg),
01 47 05 50 18; fax 47 05 91 21*

☑ Arpège-trained Jérôme Bodereau collaborates with co-chef/co-owner Antoine Heerah of Mauritius to produce this "truly original" storefront in the 7th; supporters say "while not cheap", it's "Paris' best exotic" eatery, whose "harmony of Franco-Mauritian flavors" "absolutely must be tasted"; but to critics, a "cold" tropical-wood decor and somewhat "snooty staff" mean a meal here "isn't *très* fun."

Chantairelle 🗷 — | — | — | E

17, rue Laplace, 5ᵉ (Maubert-Mutualité), 01 46 33 18 59; www.chantairelle.com
Hearty and "interesting food from an area not usually seen by tourists" – the rugged central Auvergne – pulls patrons to this "good-quality" table in the 5th; it cooks fresh, authentic dishes like *pounti* (pork, prunes and Swiss chard) without an overdose of kitschy decor – though the setting sweetly evokes this rural province with a well and a tape of birdsong; N.B. they also sell a nice selection of foodstuffs.

Chardenoux ▽ 16 | 22 | 20 | 44

1, rue Jules Vallès, 11ᵉ (Charonne/Faidherbe-Chaligny), 01 43 71 49 52
☑ The location in the 11th may be "obscure", but most surveyors find it "a pleasure" to "travel in time to the [early] 1900s", when this bistro with a charming decor of etched glass and swirling stucco moldings opened; the kitchen surfs between Traditional and New French cooking that's "fresh and tasty" if "not inspired", but the "service more than makes up for this", so it's "well worth the trip"; N.B. a post-*Survey* chef change may outdate the Food score.

Charlot - Roi des Coquillages ◑ 16 | 14 | 16 | 53

12, pl Clichy, 9ᵉ (Place de Clichy), 01 53 20 48 00; fax 53 20 48 09; www.charlot-paris.com
☑ Overlooking the Place Clichy, this brasserie is known for its "fresh and filling fruits-de-mer" plates, "even in summer"; some snap there's "not much else" on the Classic French menu, and "you need an archaeologist's eye to appreciate the kitschy '70s decor", but when it comes to "excellent seafood", the *roi* reigns on.

Charpentiers (Aux) ◑ 16 | 16 | 19 | 38

10, rue Mabillon, 6ᵉ (Mabillon/St-Germain-des-Prés), 01 43 26 30 05; fax 46 33 07 98
■ Established in 1856 in the "old Carpenter's Guild hall" – hence the "charming architectural models" on display – this "classic" in Saint-Germain offers "traditional Bistro fare", "prepared with nothing nouvelle in sight"; it's "down-home cooking", so there's little that's "spectacular", but the staff appropriately acts "like you're one of the family."

Chartier 12 | 22 | 15 | 20

7, rue Faubourg-Montmartre, 9ᵉ (Cadet/Grands Boulevards), 01 47 70 86 29; fax 48 24 14 68; www.bouillon-chartier.com
☑ This "huge barn" of a Classic French "hasn't changed in 100 years", which explains the "unbeatable atmosphere"

that has long made it "another check-the-box Paris
experience"; ok, maybe "the food could be better", but it's
very "cheap" and is served "fast" by "hurried" "waiters who
scribble your order on the corner of the paper tablecloth",
so "go for the history", if nothing else.

Chateaubriand (Le) ⌧   – | – | – | M
*129, av Parmentier, 11ᵉ (Concourt/Parmentier), 01 43 57 45 95;
fax 43 57 45 95*
With globe lamps, wooden tables, mosaic floors and a poster
that recalls its former life as a neighborhood *épicerie*
(grocery store), this bistro is as well-liked by a young
dressed-all-in-black set from the 11th for its atmosphere
as it is for its food; the blackboard menu, which changes
regularly, runs to a mix of classic Gallic dishes and modern
Mediterranean ones, all served by laid-back staffers.

Chen Soleil d'Est ⌧   20 | 11 | 16 | 86
*15, rue du Théâtre, 15ᵉ (Charles Michels), 01 45 79 34 34;
fax 45 79 07 53*
☒ Despite the demise of its namesake chef, friends find
this 15th-arrondissement Asian "the best Chinese in Paris",
praising its "refined", "sometimes startling" but "always
delicious" dishes that contain pedigreed French produce;
"the superiority of the cuisine more than makes up for the
pushy service" and somewhat "soulless" setting in a Seine-
side modern complex.

Cherche Midi (Le) ◑   18 | 14 | 16 | 41
*22, rue du Cherche-Midi, 6ᵉ (Sèvres-Babylone/St-Sulpice),
01 45 48 27 44*
☒ "Superb pastas" and a "nice-guy owner" have won
"loyal clients" to this "local hangout for famous actors and
politicians" in Saint-Germain that "hits the spot when you're
looking for an easy Italian meal"; a niche of noodle naysayers
note the "variable service" (perhaps "the regulars get
more attention") and "squishy" seating, but most have fun,
especially if they "get a table on the terrace."

Chez Albert ⌧   – | – | – | M
43, rue Mazarine, 6ᵉ (Odéon), 01 46 33 22 57
"Probably the best Portuguese in Paris", this long-running
Lusitanian near the Odéon offers "a warm welcome and
warming cooking", including myriad delicious takes on
cod; an off-white decor is the backdrop for decorative bits
of copper cookware, and the popularity of the place among
Left Bank yuppies means it's often very "noisy"; be warned:
"they put tourists in an upstairs Siberia."

Chez André ◑   18 | 13 | 17 | 46
*12, rue Marbeuf, 8ᵉ (Franklin D. Roosevelt), 01 47 20 59 57;
fax 47 20 18 82*
☒ The fact that it's one of those "increasingly rare" sites
for traditional Bistro cooking ("as good a *gigot* as you can

get anywhere") sells this stylishly "smoky", "humming" haven off the Champs; malcontents mutter the "menu is much more mundane" nowadays, and "you never know if the service will be great or terrible", but most are prepared to put up with ample "noise" and to "love thy neighbor" at thine elbow for a bona fide bistrot experience.

Chez Arthur ●☒   − | − | − | M

25, rue du Faubourg St-Martin, 10ᵉ (Strasbourg-St-Denis), 01 42 08 34 33; fax 42 08 34 33

In the same family for three generations, this venerable bistro exudes a solid 19th-century charm with immaculate starched white tablecloths, wood-paneled walls and courtly, avuncular waiters to serve the lively clientele, many of whom work in the theaters of the 10th; the menu is a veritable textbook of the classics, all generously served.

Chez Catherine ☒   21 | 18 | 22 | 67

3, rue Berryer, 8ᵉ (George V/St-Philippe du Roule), 01 40 76 01 40; fax 40 76 03 96

☑ Surveyors are split on chef/co-owner Catherine Guerraz's relocation to a swank spot in the 8th, with some lamenting the "lost charm" of the old digs, and the "higher prices" that have come with "catering to an expense-account crowd"; but most maintain "the move is a major improvement", with a New French menu that "mixes well-prepared bistro classics with modern inspirations" (plus "wonderful wines"), "high-quality service" and elegant, dove-gray decor accented with orchids and antique silver.

Chez Clément ●   13 | 15 | 13 | 32

17, bd des Capucines, 2ᵉ (Opéra), 01 53 43 52 00; fax 53 43 82 09
21, bd Beaumarchais, 4ᵉ (Bastille/Chemin Vert), 01 40 29 17 00; fax 40 29 17 09
9, pl St-André-des-Arts, 6ᵉ (St-Michel), 01 56 81 32 00; fax 56 81 32 09
123, av des Champs Elysées, 8ᵉ (Charles de Gaulle-Etoile), 01 40 73 87 00; fax 40 73 87 09
19, rue Marbeuf, 8ᵉ (Franklin D. Roosevelt/George V), 01 53 23 90 00; fax 53 23 90 09
106, bd du Montparnasse, 14ᵉ (Vavin), 01 44 10 54 00; fax 44 10 54 09
407, rue de Vaugirard, 15ᵉ (Porte de Versailles), 01 53 68 94 00; fax 53 68 94 09
47, av de Wagram, 17ᵉ (Charles de Gaulle-Etoile/Ternes), 01 53 81 97 00; fax 53 81 97 09
99, bd Gouvion-St-Cyr, 17ᵉ (Porte Maillot), 01 45 72 93 00; fax 45 72 93 09
98, av Edouard Vaillant, Boulogne (Marcel Sembat), 01 41 22 90 00; fax 41 22 90 09
www.chezclement.com

☑ "Locals love to trash this chain", but since it pops up in "convenient locations", each invoking a "quaint" rusticity with copper pans, "silverware sculpture" and wood paneling, it's often "filled with budget-conscious eaters"; aside from the assorted "rotisseried meats", the "diverse", "no-frills" Classic French menu is "without culinary interest" and the "service seems tired" – but it's "consistent" ("ah, reliability") and "hey, for the price what do you expect?"

Chez Denise - La Tour de Montlhéry ❶🖾

22 | 17 | 19 | 45

5, rue des Prouvaires, 1er (Châtelet-Les Halles), 01 42 36 21 82; fax 45 08 81 99

■ "Raffish, friendly" and "fun", this all-night classic bistro on the edge of Les Halles serves up "great traditional dishes that seem to fall off chicer menus: pot-au-feu, tripe stew", along with "the best frites on the planet"; "the waiters make a big difference with their sense of humor"; P.S. it's "the best of the real after-dark Paris", so book ahead.

Chez Diane 🖾

19 | 15 | 21 | 43

25, rue Servandoni, 6e (St-Sulpice), 01 46 33 12 06

◪ Before or "after a walk in the Luxembourg Gardens", many wander into this "wonderful, warm, welcoming place" in a pretty cobbled lane nearby; while some shrug over the "so-so" eats, the classic Bistro cooking served by candlelight wins more friends than foes for its "delicious" flavors.

Chez Francis ❶

15 | 17 | 15 | 52

7, pl de l'Alma, 8e (Alma-Marceau), 01 47 20 86 83; fax 47 20 43 26

◪ With a "beautiful location" at the Place de l'Alma providing a "fabulous view" of the Eiffel Tower, this "bright and flashy" brasserie offers a "romantic setting" in which to sample seafood and other "reliable" "comfort food" ("the oysters outclass the rest"); too bad that "rude service has apparently become a trademark here."

Chez Françoise ❶

15 | 15 | 18 | 43

Aérogare des Invalides, 7e (Invalides), 01 47 05 49 03; fax 45 51 96 20; www.chezfrancoise.com

■ "Beyond the tides of fashion", this Classic French located in the *aérogare* of Les Invalides is the haunt of politicians from the nearby ministries, who endorse the "surprise-free, for-your-mother-in-law" cuisine and "attentive service"; all of it, including the decor, is somewhat "solemn", but then, "that's probably the image of the clientele too."

Chez Fred 🖾

▽ 18 | 10 | 15 | 43

190 bis, bd Péreire, 17e (Péreire/Porte Maillot), 01 45 74 20 48

■ "A bouchon [bistro] like you find in Lyon" exclaim enthusiasts of the "good terrines and charcuterie" and "wonderful steak" served at this traditional table ("not a hint of nouvelle cuisine") near the Porte Maillot; "the granite-topped tables and floors make for cold decor" but "nice service" warms things up a bit.

Chez Gégène
▽ 15 | 24 | 19 | 48

162 bis, quai de Polangis, Joinville (RER Joinville-le-Pont),
01 48 83 29 43; fax 48 83 72 62; www.chez-gegene.fr

■ In suburban Joinville, this barn on the Marne is "one of
the rare surviving *guinguettes*" (restaurant/dance halls)
that thrived in Paris circa 1900; "it's all about atmosphere"
here, so come on weekends to dance and "dream", but
"forget about" the Classic French food, which runs to
mussels and fries served with cheap house wine.

CHEZ GEORGES ⌧
23 | 19 | 22 | 54

1, rue du Mail, 2ᵉ (Bourse), 01 42 60 07 11

■ "Such fun", this "venerable" "bistro par excellence" just
off the Place des Victoires, with its "charming" waitresses
serving a stylish crowd ("we saw Anna Wintour") that
comes for "*oh-mon-Dieu*, what delicious" Classic French
fare, from that "big ol' boat of béarnaise with the steak frites"
to the "baba-au-rhum swimming in alcohol"; sure, the long,
narrow dining room gets "a little crowded and noisy, but
it's all part of the experience" where "authenticity reigns."

Chez Georges-Porte Maillot ◖
18 | 13 | 15 | 49

273, bd Péreire, 17ᵉ (Porte Maillot), 01 45 74 31 00;
fax 45 74 02 56; www.chez-georges.com

◪ It's "hard to be disappointed" by "old-fashioned" classics
like "good roast lamb" and tête de veau, which is why this
"traditional brasserie" ("any more so, and you'd die") near
the Porte Maillot has become "an institution"; "the friendly
service compensates for the rather lugubrious decor", if
not completely for the "not-cheap" tabs.

Chez Gérard ⌧
▽ 18 | 18 | 16 | 44

10, rue Montrosier, Neuilly (Porte Maillot), 01 46 24 86 37;
fax 46 37 21 72

■ "Very fresh" fare that includes "many selections from
the Auvergne" makes this "warm" classic bistro "a real
find in Neuilly"; it's "lively at any time of day, with the most
convivial waiters" and walls lined with "circus posters
and framed cartoons."

Chez Gildo ⌧
▽ 18 | 14 | 22 | 50

153, rue de Grenelle, 7ᵉ (La Tour-Maubourg), 01 45 51 54 12;
fax 45 51 54 12

◪ Long "one of the best Italians in Paris", this "fashionable"
place in the 7th offers *la dolce vita* on the Left Bank for the
fans who say "from the pasta to the zabaglione, everything
is good"; the outvoted parsimonious posit that perhaps "the
portions could be more generous, in view of the prices."

Chez Janou ◖
20 | 19 | 17 | 35

2, rue Roger Verlomme, 3ᵉ (Bastille/Chemin Vert), 01 42 72 28 41

◪ "Just a stone's throw from the Place des Vosges", this
Provençal bistro with a "decor of old movie posters" and

"a young, hip, but not pretentious crowd" brings the taste of the Med to the Marais with "a stunning list of anise-flavored drinks"; "one of the loveliest terraces" in Paris makes this an ideal summer address – "if you can get a place"; but year-round it's easy on the wallet with "excellent prices for the prix fixes and great carafe wines."

Chez Jean 🏿   23 | 17 | 21 | 47
8, rue St-Lazare, 9ᵉ (Notre-Dame-de-Lorette), 01 48 78 62 73; fax 48 78 66 04

■ "Under the management of Jean-Frédéric Guidoni, formerly maître d'hotel at Taillevent", "and his lovely wife, Delphine", this New French in the 9th has "lots of natural style"; the "creative", "limited menu is all about fresh and seasonal, and the chef, also a Taillevent alum, knows exactly what to do with it"; "the service is perfectly professional" and regulars say this young address "is continuously improving" – although it's already "really a bargain for what you get."

Chez Jenny ◑   18 | 19 | 18 | 40
39, bd du Temple, 3ᵉ (République), 01 44 54 39 00; fax 44 54 39 09; www.chez-jenny.com

■ Since the Alsacian decor has been updated, the "very good choucroute" is no longer the only reason to make tracks for this sprawling "sturdy standby" of a brasserie just off the Place de la République; the spiffing-up didn't ruffle the "wonderful fish selections", "well chosen wines" from the region or the "welcoming" service, either.

Chez L'Ami Jean ◑🏿   16 | 9 | 14 | 38
27, rue Malar, 7ᵉ (Invalides/La Tour-Maubourg), 01 47 05 86 89

◪ Following the "much-publicized" arrival of "a new chef-owner" a while back, the food is still Southwestern, but now it's "much more sophisticated" at this snug, rustic dining room with "tightly spaced tables" in the 7th; and if a few complain that "the atmosphere has evaporated due to the changes", the majority come to Basque in pleasure; P.S. "it's always packed", "so make sure to have a reservation."

CHEZ L'AMI LOUIS ◑   26 | 14 | 21 | VE
32, rue du Vertbois, 3ᵉ (Arts et Métiers), 01 48 87 77 48

■ "The best roast chicken, the best foie gras", "the best bistro in the world" are just some of the superlatives this "classic" in the 3rd garners; geared for "trenchermen on high doses of cholesterol-lowering drugs", the "portions are immense", so do share (which, given the "outrageous prices", "allows you to become a regular without being a Rockefeller"); "service is gruff but effective" and while it "looks like the decor hasn't changed since they opened 80 years ago", this is "a place to return to again and again."

Bastide Odeon (*)
Belier
* Bistrot d Henri
* Bon Saint Pourcain
(€) Cafe des Delices >
* Cafetiere Corse
* Camoleon ⊖
Chez Viane
* Chez Maitre Paul *
* Christine —
* Maison du Jardin ✗
Marlotte   27 Rue de
                Vaugirard

π̄

Friday - Cafe des Delices

Saturdy Chez Maitre Paul
01-43-54-7459 au gourmand
         that icon
Sunday Raaminet
         (quai)

Chez la Vieille ☒
— — — M

1, rue Bailleul, 1er (Louvre-Rivoli), 01 42 60 15 78; fax 42 33 85 71
"Great homestyle food", occasionally with a Corsican accent, is the lure at this "little classic bistro" near Les Halles that's "saved its old-fashioned charm" but left its decor basically untouched since World War II; it's "no longer as fashionable as it was 10 years ago, but so much the better, since now it's easier to get a table" at this lunch locale that only serves dinner on Thursdays.

Chez Léon ☒
— — — M

32, rue Legendre, 17e (Villiers), 01 42 27 06 82; fax 46 22 63 67
While it may be "hard to find", this classic bistro in the 17th arrondissement "near the Rue de Levis street market" is worth seeking out for the "reliably delicious regional cooking" at "reasonable prices"; some still miss the old owners, but most find the cozy room with a honeycomb-tile floor "professionally run."

Chez Livio
12 11 13 34

6, rue de Longchamp, Neuilly (Pont de Neuilly), 01 46 24 81 32; fax 47 38 20 72
✔ "A warm welcome from Alfio and Vittorio Innocenti" keeps 'em coming back to this "noisy" Italian reputed for its pizzas and "reasonable prices"; for most of the regulars, however, the "convivial atmosphere" counts for as much as the "ordinary" kitchen – as well as the fact it's "one of the rare places open on Sunday in Neuilly."

Chez Maître Paul
21 16 19 44

12, rue Monsieur-le-Prince, 6e (Odéon), 01 43 54 74 59; fax 43 54 43 74
■ "A don't-miss" near the Odéon for its "delicious, fragrant cooking from the Jura" region (i.e. "wonderful chicken in a *vin jaune* sauce"), fawn fans of this "quintessential neighborhood" bistro; it's still "cozy", "precious" and "not-so-touristy" (though visitors should "avoid the upstairs", also known as "the American ghetto").

Chez Marcel ☒
— — — M

7, rue Stanislas, 6e (Notre-Dame-des-Champs), 01 45 48 29 94
"The owner's personality is everywhere" at this "somewhat undiscovered" classic bistro in Montparnasse, and that's good, since "he cares a great deal about his customers' experience"; "traditional-at-its-best" Lyonnais eats are dished up by "friendly service" amid "just a handful of tables, so you feel like you're eating in someone's home."

Chez Marianne
15 10 12 25

2, rue des Hospitalières St-Germais, 4e (St-Paul), 01 42 72 18 86; fax 42 78 75 26
✔ "The decor is nothing to write home about" and "service is a little gruff", but that's "part of the charm" of the "old-

fashioned, bare-bones" personality of this "cramped,"
"little slice of the Middle East in the middle of the Marais";
pedestrians find it "perfect after touring the area for a
light meal", since "you can graze on the Jewish equivalent
of tapas", i.e. pastrami, a variety of different salads
and falafel sandwiches.

Chez Michel ●⊠   21 | 13 | 18 | 45

*10, rue de Belzunce, 10ᵉ (Gare du Nord/Poissonnière),
01 44 53 06 20; fax 44 53 61 31*

◪ It may be "out of the way" "near the Gare du Nord", but
this doesn't deter "a clientele that's more concerned with
food than frills" from trying chef Thierry Breton's "delicious"
"reinventions of the dishes of his native Brittany", along
with New French favorites; the digs are a little "cramped"
and "cold, but the service isn't"; N.B. Chez Casimir, a more
casual cousin, has opened just down the street.

Chez Nénesse ⊠   – | – | – | M

*17, rue de Saintonge, 3ᵉ (Filles-du-Calvaire/République),
01 42 78 46 49; fax 42 78 45 51*

"Don't let the plastic-coated menus frighten you" – "this is
the real thing" if you're looking for "a calm neighborhood"
classic bistro in the Marais; few may have found it, but
enthusiastic regulars "love this inimitable corner of old
Paris" whose welcoming personnel "take you in."

Chez Ngo ●   ∇ 19 | 17 | 13 | 42

*70, rue de Longchamp, 16ᵉ (Trocadéro), 01 47 04 53 20;
fax 47 27 81 06*

■ It's "difficult to be disappointed" by this "authentic"
Asian in the 16th, whose "refined Chinese cooking", along
with some Thai delicacies, makes it more than a won-ton
success; "come as a couple" for "the best Peking duck in
Paris" while you relax in a cosseted, almost stereotypical
decor of wood panels and calligraphic wall hangings.

Chez Omar ●⊟   20 | 12 | 14 | 31

47, rue de Bretagne, 3ᵉ (République/Temple), 01 42 72 36 26

■ Anyone who wonders why this North African near
République is "always packed" with "trendy" types hasn't
sampled the "best couscous in Paris", which come in
several different varieties, "even a vegetarian one"; "they
don't take reservations", so prepare to stand at the bar for
a while unless you "come before 8 PM or after 10 PM."

Chez Papa ●   12 | 7 | 9 | 21

*29, rue de l'Arcade, 8ᵉ (Madeleine/St-Lazare), 01 42 65 43 68
206, rue La Fayette, 10ᵉ (Louis Blanc), 01 42 09 53 87
6, rue Gassendi, 14ᵉ (Denfert-Rochereau/Raspail), 01 43 22 41 19
101, rue de la Croix Nivert, 15ᵉ (Commerce/Félix Faure),
01 48 28 31 88*

◪ "Cheap, copious" dishes from the Southwest make
bargain hunters with big appetites happy at this "noisy",

"smoky" chain perpetually packed with "a lot of students, who are part of the decor"; foes warn "fragile stomachs, abstain" (the fare "is all heavy, even the [giant] salads"), and dis the "deplorable service", but at least "you'll be stuffed for a small amount of euros."

Chez Paul ◑   20 | 17 | 18 | 36
13, rue de Charonne, 11ᵉ (Bastille/Ledru-Rollin), 01 47 00 34 57; fax 48 07 02 00

■ "A pretty postcard of why Paris will always be Paris", this "hip, lively" traditional bistro near the Bastille is "authentic right down to the swirling [cigarette] smoke and the two cognacs after lunch", with "a very impressive kitchen" and prices that "don't make you feel ripped off"; its tendency to be "always packed" may be alleviated by a recent expansion, but you should still "call ahead" and prepare to stand your ground against service that can be "a little too speedy (to free up the table)."

Chez Paul ◑   21 | 17 | 21 | 37
22, rue de la Butte-aux-Cailles, 13ᵉ (Corvisart/Place d'Italie), 01 45 89 22 11; fax 45 80 26 53

■ "This is what Paris is all about" proclaim patrons who find this classic bistro in the "charming Butte-aux-Cailles neighborhood" "worth the detour from Downtown", given its "very good regional cooking" and "high-quality service"; it's "ideal", whether you're a "middle-aged lady dining alone" or taking part in "a binge among buddies."

Chez Pauline ⊠   18 | 17 | 19 | 59
5, rue Villedo, 1ᵉʳ (Pyramides/Palais Royal), 01 42 96 20 70; fax 49 27 99 89; www.chezpauline.com

☑ From the Classic cuisine to the "pleasant" red banquettes, "everything screams authentic French" at this "favorite" "on a quiet side street" near the Palais Royal; sure, it's "old-fashioned" and "overpriced for what you get", foes fume; but fans find it a "wonderful place to cocoon while dining on retro food" and enjoying service "that confounds stereotypes of unfriendly" staffers; P.S. make sure you "stay at ground level" to avoid sitting in the bland upstairs.

Chez Prune ◑   14 | 16 | 11 | 31
36, rue Beaurepaire, 10ᵉ (Jacques Bonsergent/République), 01 42 41 30 47; fax 42 00 32 28

☑ "It's pleasant to have a drink on the terrace overlooking the Canal Saint-Martin" at this "unpretentious" place in the 10th, "a part of town not known for great restaurants"; the scene "seems more about being trendy than about really good food" – e.g. the "weird sauces and mixes of sweet and sour" on the Eclectic menu – and "the service could be better", but none of these shortcomings dismay the "noisy twenty- and thirtysomething crowd" that is revivifying this *quartier.*

Chez Ramulaud ◗
▽ 18 | 13 | 16 | 33

*269, rue Faubourg-St-Antoine, 11ᵉ (Faidherbe-Chaligny/
Nation), 01 43 72 23 29*

■ "Stylish, noisy and animated", this bistro is the kind of
place where you might see agricultural activist "José
Bové meeting with top Chirac advisors", a pretty strong
recommendation for the "inventive", often organic food; the
"knowledgeable staff" compounds the "guaranteed fun",
even if some beef "there are so many supplements on the
prix fixe that it doesn't make sense to have a prix fixe."

Chez René ⊠
20 | 15 | 20 | 45

*14, bd St-Germain, 5ᵉ (Maubert-Mutualité), 01 43 54 30 23;
fax 43 26 43 92*

■ This Saint-Germain "jewel" is "a step back in time" with
"doting waiters", a "homey", lace-curtained atmosphere
and "marvelous", "hearty Lyonnaise cooking" ("don't come
if you're on a diet"), especially "the best boeuf bourguignon
that tastes like they boiled a whole ox to make" "rich, thick
dark syrup" of a sauce; with decor and "waiters that
seemingly have been here since the Korean War", "it never
changes" – "and that's a compliment."

Chez Savy ⊠
– | – | – | M

*23, rue Bayard, 8ᵉ (Franklin D. Roosevelt), 01 47 23 46 98;
fax 47 23 46 98*

"Hiding in plain sight" for anyone who wants "great
traditional cuisine and good-value wines" in the 8th, this
"nice, quiet, little bistro" "specializes in super-fresh meat
delivered directly from the Auvergne"; small wonder its 1923
interior often seems "reserved for the devoted regulars."

Chez Vincent ⊠
22 | 9 | 18 | 36

*5, rue du Tunnel, 19ᵉ (Botzaris/Buttes-Chaumont), 01 42 02 22 45;
fax 40 18 95 83*

■ "When you really want to eat Italian you absolutely must
come here" to this "super-convivial" corner in the 19th,
where chef-owner Vincent Cozzoli, alias "the Picasso of
antipasti", whips up an artful menu of "abundant and tasty
food" and "occasionally breaks into an aria", to boot;
though it seems to be "frequented only by regulars", "don't
be afraid to step inside" the unpretentious digs.

Chez Vong ◗⊠
21 | 20 | 19 | 64

*10, rue de la Grande Truanderie, 1ᵉʳ (Etienne Marcel),
01 40 26 09 36; fax 42 33 38 15; www.chez-vong.com*

◤ "Perhaps the most beautiful Chinese extant" – full of
foliage, Buddhas, lacquered screens and low lights that
create a "very different ambiance than the usual Paris
restaurant" – this upmarket table in Les Halles promises
"a delicious, exotic trip that doesn't disappoint" supporters
say; however, doubters declare it goes vong when it comes
to the cuisine ("routine and merely acceptable").

Chiberta 🗷
| – | – | – | E |

3, rue Arsène Houssaye, 8ᵉ (Charles de Gaulle-Etoile/George V), 01 53 53 42 00; fax 45 62 85 08; www.lechiberta.com

Legendary chef-owner Guy Savoy is now running this popular 8th arrondissement spot, revamping it with a low-fat, high-flavor menu of New French cuisine, from inventive starters like crabmeat with celery and beet chips to a more mainstream veal shank slow-cooked with peaches; businesspeople traveling solo will appreciate full service at the slate-faced bar, while Jean-Michel Wilmotte's high-powered, black-and-leather redo reels in showbiz folks and captains of industry alike.

Chicago Pizza Pie Factory ◑
| 9 | 12 | 11 | 22 |

5, rue de Berri, 8ᵉ (George V), 01 45 62 50 23; fax 45 63 87 56

☑ Just off the Champs, this "enjoyable" but "noisy" "American-style pizzeria" "decorated with Chicago street signs" is the "place to go if you need a deep-dish fix in Paris"; antagonists argue "you've got to be mighty desperate or homesick to pick this poor imitation of the vaunted" Chi pie, but "it's fun every once in a while" if you don't "expect a setting or service" (though the "dancing" "staff "will be happy to sing you a birthday song").

Chieng Mai ◑
| 18 | 8 | 13 | 31 |

12, rue Frédéric Sauton, 5ᵉ (Maubert-Mutualité), 01 43 25 45 45

☑ "Authentic and spicy Thai" eats make this "nice local" Latin Quarter table "near Notre Dame" "a sure bet" for "good food at a good price" profess fans; but pessimists point to "small portions", "anonymous" "decor that's a bore" and service that's "pretty dire" (unless you're "regular customers") as reasons to "go somewhere else."

Chien qui Fume (Au) ◑
| 18 | 19 | 16 | 43 |

33, rue du Pont-Neuf, 1ᵉʳ (Châtelet-Les Halles), 01 42 36 07 42; fax 42 36 36 85; www.au-chien-qui-fume.com

■ "Sit outside and watch the world of Les Halles unfold around you" or take a table in the dining room with a decorative motif of "dogs dressed as people" at this "good example of a brasserie"; "service can suffer from the crowds", but most are mollified by such "well-executed French classics" as a "delicious braised rabbit presented in a copper pot" or "outstanding onion soup."

China Club ◑
| 17 | 25 | 17 | 41 |

50, rue de Charenton, 12ᵉ (Bastille/Ledru-Rollin), 01 43 43 82 02; fax 43 43 79 85

☑ While it's "a little out of the way" in a quiet street near the Bastille, the "marvelous decor" reminiscent of "an old opium den" or "a brothel" and "a happening scene" make this Asian well worth seeking out; some clubbers cavil "it's best just for a drink in the cozy bar on the first floor", styled like an old-fashioned *fumoir*, or one of the weekend "jazz concerts in the basement" because the Chinese "cooking, although good, is not really interesting."

China Town Olympiades ◗   − | − | − | I |

44, av d'Ivry, 13ᵉ (Porte d'Ivry), 01 45 84 72 21; fax 45 84 74 52; www.chinatownolympiades.com

"The famous Peking duck carved before your eyes and the lazy Susans on the tables create some atmosphere" at this 300-seater, maybe "the best-known Chinese in the 13th"; but this Olympian's opponents opine it's become "a factory", with "mediocre food" and "slow service"; and while it's cheap, its "run-down" decor really needs some work.

Christine (Le) ◗ ⍉   23 | 23 | 23 | 47 |

1, rue Christine, 6ᵉ (Odéon/St-Michel), 01 40 51 71 64; fax 42 18 04 39

■ "They do quaint just right" at this "charming" Classic French with a "lovely" courtyard-garden view; recently redone, with an open kitchen, "the elegant decor matches the cuisine" ("simple", but "exquisitely prepared"), "the prix fixes are good value" and the young staff, often "art-history students who speak English", is "friendly"; though usually it's "only found by those in-the-know", it's worth beating a path to this "wonderful place" in Saint-Germain.

Ch'Ti Catalan ⍉   − | − | − | M |

4, rue de Navarin, 9ᵉ (Pigalle/St-Georges), 01 44 63 04 33

The name of this flame-colored dining room in the 9th refers to its owners' origins: one hails from French Catalonia, and the other is a Ch'Ti (the slang term for someone from the north of France); their roots are also reflected in a menu which ranges from Northern French staples like steak in a Maroilles cheese sauce to Catalonian grilled fishes.

CINQ (LE)   28 | 28 | 28 | VE |

Four Seasons George V, 31, av George V, 8ᵉ (Alma-Marceau/ George V), 01 49 52 71 54; fax 49 52 71 81; www.fourseasons.com/paris

■ "Exceptional from every point of view" aver acolytes of the George V's Haute Cuisine haven; start with "original, fresh", "exquisite food" from Philippe Legendre (ex Taillevent) and a "splendid" wine list, add a "majestic" setting "blooming with beautiful flowers", finish with "impeccable" "yet not haughty service" and the total comes to a "very special experience"; true, it "gives expensive a whole new meaning", but what wouldn't you pay for a place of utmost "class without pretension"?

59 Poincaré ⍉   21 | 22 | 21 | 81 |

Hôtel Le Parc, 59, av Raymond Poincaré, 16ᵉ (Victor Hugo/ Trocadéro), 01 47 27 59 59; fax 47 27 59 00; www.alain-ducasse.com

☑ "Steps from the Place Victor Hugo", this "stylish" duplex – the original location of Alain Ducasse, who still acts as consultant – sets a Contemporary French table known for (but not limited to) "high-quality" beef and lobster; but while the cooking is "tasty", critics call the cost "crazy" "for what it is", and sticklers think the service could be "better drilled"; however, the "beautiful courtyard dining" in summer mollifies many.

Cloche des Halles (La) ⊠⊅   – | – | – | I
28, rue Coquillière, 1er (Les Halles/Louvre-Rivoli), 01 42 36 93 89
"There's no better Saturday lunch than sharing plates of charcuterie and cheese with a bottle of Chiroubles or Chénas" in this intimate, atmospheric wine bar, "one of the best in Paris"; named for the bell that used to ring the opening and closing hours of the old Les Halles market, it's a happy place and a "real bargain", to boot.

Clos des Gourmets (Le) ⊠   22 | 17 | 19 | 49
16, av Rapp, 7e (Alma-Marceau/Ecole Militaire), 01 45 51 75 61; fax 47 05 74 20
■ "One of the biggest little tables in Paris" rave reviewers of this New French run by a "charming husband-wife team"; though it's not bargain-priced, the "unbelievably creative" quality of the cuisine makes it "good value for this quarter" of the 7th, and despite "sardine-can seating", the room is "cozy and bright" and the "service warm" (though "one more *serveur* could increase efficiency").

Closerie des Lilas (La) ◐   17 | 22 | 17 | 58
171, bd du Montparnasse, 6e (Port Royal/Vavin), 01 40 51 34 50; fax 43 29 99 94
◪ This "mythic" Montparnasse table offers "two separate dining experiences: the brasserie for lunch and late-night and the restaurant for dinner"; while "both offer a chance to relive the Lost Generation life", it's the former, with its "famous steak tartare" and "piano-bar atmosphere", that fans favor, since otherwise the Classic French "food leaves a little to be desired"; but even if this "overpriced" place is "resting on its laurels", it remains "as romantic as all of Paris"; P.S. in summer, "the terrace is still the place to be."

Clos Morillons (Le) ⊠   ∇ 17 | 12 | 13 | 42
50, rue des Morillons, 15e (Porte de Vanves), 01 48 28 04 37; fax 48 28 70 77
■ With a renovated, sunny-yellow decor that's "simple, but bright and neat", this New French in the 15th now allows customers to concentrate on the "inventiveness" of such "succulent" dishes as kidneys in a juniper-berry *jus*; "moderate prices" are appreciated, too.

Clos Saint-Honoré (Le) ⊠   – | – | – | M
3, rue St-Hyacinthe, 1er (Tuileries), 01 40 15 09 36; fax 40 15 09 56
Despite a handy location near, or rather beneath, the Tuileries (the dining room is a 17th-century cellar that extends under the gardens), only a handful of surveyors

have dug into the delights of this "quiet, romantic place that's perfect for a non-bank-breaking but delicious meal" of Classic French dishes, prepared by a buried "treasure" of a chef; the "attentive" service and modest prices are worth joining the underground movement for, too.

Clovis (Le)   ∇ 26 | 25 | 24 | 81
Sofitel Arc de Triomphe, 14, rue Beaujon, 8ᵉ (Charles de Gaulle-Etoile), 01 53 89 50 53; fax 53 89 50 51; www.accorhotels.com
■ It speaks volumes that this New French in the Sofitel Arc de Triomphe "doesn't feel like it's in a hotel, with its subdued and tasteful decor, creative and well-presented dishes and helpful staff", especially the "great sommelier" – all of which "make this an awesome experience", one that more folks "should discover"; it's "expensive", but "excellent for business lunches and dinners" or just "a real nice meal."

Clown Bar ◑⚑   ∇ 17 | 23 | 16 | 28
114, rue Amelot, 11ᵉ (Filles-du-Calvaire), 01 43 55 87 35
☑ The "wonderful antique decor" of landmarked circus-themed art nouveau tiles is more memorable than the fare at this *bar à vins* next to the Cirque d'Hiver in the 11th; still, it's a "comfortable, homey" place that's "fun for a light meal and drink" of comfort food like grilled andouillette; the major drawback is a staff that won't stop clowning around, necessitating that you "wave briskly for service."

Cô Ba Saigon ☒   – | – | – | M
181, rue du Faubourg St-Honoré, 8ᵉ (Charles de Gaulle-Etoile/ George V), 01 45 63 70 37; fax 45 63 70 37; www.cobasaigon.com
Lacking the kitsch common to Asian restaurants in Paris, this black-decorated dining room in the 8th is popular with a well-traveled cosmopolitan clientele, which can attest to the authenticity of the regional specialties from Saigon and Hue (others just appreciate the light touch and fresh seafood); service and prices are equally gentle.

Coco de Mer ◑☒   – | – | – | M
34, bd St-Marcel, 5ᵉ (Les Gobelins/St-Marcel), 01 47 07 06 64; fax 47 07 41 88
☑ "You'd think you were in the Seychelles (which might explain the indolent service)" at this site featuring Indian Ocean islands' cuisine; there's definitely a "vacation vibe", what with the "cocktails, colorful dishes and [having] your feet in the sand" that's sprinkled across the enclosed patio; "the cooking lacks genius", but hey, a meal here will set you back a lot less than a plane ticket to Mahé.

Coconnas   17 | 18 | 19 | 50
2 bis, pl des Vosges, 4ᵉ (Bastille/St-Paul), 01 42 78 58 16; fax 42 78 16 28
☑ Despite the valiant efforts of proprietor Claude Terrail of La Tour d'Argent, opinions on this Classic French with "a

fabulous location in the Place des Vosges" cleave into two camps: converts crow "it's a real find" for "pleasant" standards, while critics carp "the cooking is, frankly, of no interest whatsoever"; all agree, however, that you should "go for the memories" of "eating outdoors" amid the arcades of "the most beautiful square in Paris."

Coffee Parisien ●
| 14 | 13 | 11 | 26 |

4, rue Princesse, 6ᵉ (Mabillon), 01 43 54 18 18; fax 43 54 94 96
7, rue Gustave-Courbet, 16ᵉ (Trocadéro/Victor Hugo), 01 45 53 17 17; fax 45 53 48 33
46, rue de Sablonville, Neuilly (Les Sablons), 01 46 37 13 13; fax 46 37 55 15

■ "You'd think you were in a little college town" in the U.S., but "it's actually the 16th", Saint-Germain or Neuilly, the locations of this trio of "noisy", "smoky" "coffee shops", "favorites of expats" and "a young crowd"; though lauded "for Sunday brunch, American-style", they frustrate foes who call the eats "just average" and slam the "slow", "irritating" service; still, they're "good if you're craving a burger, cheesecake" or other Yankee staples, though they're "not cheap considering the quality of the fare."

Coin des Gourmets (Au)
| ▽ 24 | 10 | 19 | 30 |

5, rue Dante, 5ᵉ (Cluny-La Sorbonne/Maubert-Mutualité), 01 43 26 12 92

■ This tiny Latin Quarter corner is "one you shouldn't miss", because it's just the sort of place "you'd love to have just outside your door", with its "tasty, varied" Vietnamese vittles and "absolutely terrific" "Cambodian specialties"; it also offers "friendly" service and "great value – both hard to find in Paris" at times; "reserving is a must", since "it's always packed."

Comédiens (Les) ●🈯
| – | – | – | M |

7, rue Blanche, 9ᵉ (Trinité), 01 40 82 95 95; fax 40 82 96 95
Just after the curtain calls, this cozy place fills up with show-goers "coming out of the theaters of the 9th" and occasionally the namesake actors, giving the place sort of a Gallic Joe Allen buzz (as does the exposed-brick, self-styled 'NYC-like' decor); the Bistro fare "is no better than good", "but the ambiance is lively and fun", "making you want to be one of the regulars who get kissed when they come in."

. . . Comme Cochon 🈯
| – | – | – | E |

135, rue de Charenton, 12ᵉ (Gare de Lyon/Reuilly-Diderot), 01 43 42 43 36
Devotees are "never disappointed by the ambiance or the cooking", "washed down" with a "smart selection of Languedoc wines" at this "appealing classic bistro" near the Viaduc des Arts in the 12th; with a simple decor of

framed photographs and paintings, an arty, young crowd makes it "a fun place" where you're "always welcome."

Comptoir du Saumon

− − − M

60, rue François Miron, 4ᵉ (St-Paul), 01 42 77 23 08;
fax 42 77 44 75
21, rue Clément, 6ᵉ (Mabillon), 01 43 29 02 33;
fax 43 29 02 33
116, rue de la Convention, 15ᵉ (Boucicaut), 01 45 54 31 16;
fax 45 54 49 68
3, av de Villiers, 17ᵉ (Villiers), 01 40 53 89 00;
fax 40 53 89 89

This quartet of eat-in/take-out boutiques serves up a variety of hot and cold seafood plates that span the globe, from "very good Danish herring" to Scottish salmon to Iranian caviar; ambiancewise, they're "neither cozy nor warm" (the name doesn't mean 'salmon counter' for nothing), "but the food is very fresh, and your taste buds can't demand more than that."

Comptoir Paris-Marrakech ●

∇ 15 21 12 37

37, rue Berger, 1ᵉʳ (Les Halles/Louvre-Rivoli), 01 40 26 26 66;
fax 42 21 44 24

☑ Maybe "the Marrakesh branch is better than this Paris one – but it's a lot farther away", so most are happy to head for this Moroccan in Les Halles, and an atmospheric decor of "copper trays and leather hassocks" on which "a hip, young crowd" reclines; among the munchies, supporters single out the "very good tagines" with "special mention for the fig, mint and ginger ice creams"; "too bad that prices have been creeping up lately", though.

Comte de Gascogne (Au) ▣

21 20 20 80

89, av Jean-Baptiste Clément, Boulogne (Pont-de-St-Cloud),
01 46 03 47 27; fax 46 04 55 70

■ You can indeed dine like a count of Gascony on the "perfect foie gras" and other regional specialties at this swank spot in suburban Boulogne; its "original" greenhouse setting, a "pretty" courtyard with palm trees and fountains, makes a meal here "sort of like eating fantastic food in the middle of a tropical rainforest"; bear in mind, though, that while "very good", it's also "very expensive."

Congrès Maillot (Le) ●

12 15 9 53

80, av de la Grande-Armée, 17ᵉ (Porte Maillot), 01 45 74 17 24;
fax 45 72 39 80

☑ "Fresh shellfish" is the main reason to frequent this brasserie at the Porte Maillot; while useful "on Sundays or for events at the Palais des Congrès" close by, overall the place is "a far cry from what it used to be" all those opposed opine, complaining that "quantity has replaced quality" and the "service leaves a lot to be desired"; however, a luxurious renovation post-*Survey* may outdate the Decor score.

F D S €C

Contre-Allée (La) ⌸ ▽ 18 18 20 48
83, av Denfert-Rochereau, 14ᵉ (Denfert-Rochereau), 01 43 54 99 86; fax 43 25 05 28; www.contre-allee.com
■ Located in a quieter part of the 14th, this "tranquil" table is popular for its "excellent" Bistro fare that's "neither too Classic, nor too world-food" trendy; the inside is "a nice environment", but the smart money "snags an outside table" when the weather permits.

Cook Book ⌸ – – – M
9, rue Surcouf, 7ᵉ (Invalides), 01 45 51 92 82
This relaxed newcomer in the 7th illustrates how globe-trotting menus are seducing trendy, well-heeled young Parisians; specializing in choices for carnivores, its Eclectic array features steak from Argentina, kangaroo from Australia, lamb from Normandy and ham from Spain, complemented by a wine list that touches down on most major regions; the restrained interior of bare wood floors and red chairs is highlighted by open-shelf cabinets that display the vins available.

Copenhague ⌸ 21 18 19 60
142, av des Champs-Elysées, 8ᵉ (Charles de Gaulle-Etoile/ George V), 01 44 13 86 26; fax 44 13 89 44; www.restaurantfloradanica.com
■ "It's really worth a detour" to discover this delightful Dane, especially since "it's amusing to watch people" through the picture windows of the "quiet" dining room with red-leather chairs and a large oil of the Queen of Denmark "just a few steps from the bustle of the Champs"; it's "expensive", but the "sublime" food ("best salmon and herring in France"), "a great selection of aquavit" and "pleasant service" "conquer" the crowd, especially during the summer when they serve on a greenery-filled terrace.

Cordonnerie (La) ⌸ – – – M
20, rue St-Roch, 1ᵉʳ (Pyramides/Tuileries), 01 42 60 17 42; fax 40 15 97 21
Just behind the posh Place Vendôme, this tiny family-run site has for over 40 years been feeding hungry Parisians real, homey Classic French fare that changes according to the market, cooked in an open kitchen; a decor of wooden beams, tile floors and a bevy of traditional farm objects creates a historic atmosphere – appropriate for a building that dates from 1640.

Cosi ◗ 20 10 13 14
54, rue de Seine, 6ᵉ (Mabillon/Odéon), 01 46 33 35 36
■ "As sandwiches go, they don't get much better than this" say supporters of this sandwicherie/wine bar, a "fantastic stop while shopping the 6th" that offers "wonderful ingredients stuffed into tasty focaccia" "to the sound of opera" "music playing in the background"; furthermore,

all's quickly served up "at a price that makes you wish for a Cosi on every corner" – and ranks as the *Survey*'s No. 1 Best Buy among Paris restaurants.

Cosi (Le) 🗷   _|_|_| M

9, rue Cujas, 5ᵉ (Cluny-La Sorbonne/Luxembourg), 01 43 29 20 20; fax 43 29 26 40

Not to be confused with the popular sandwich shop, this "very pleasant" place near the Panthéon offers a wonderful little "taste of Corsica in Paris" (think braised kid, sheep-cheese–filled ravioli and a variety of island wines), served in a relaxed high-ceilinged setting.

Costes ◑   18 | 25 | 15 | 68

Hôtel Costes, 239, rue St-Honoré, 1ᵉʳ (Concorde/Tuileries), 01 42 44 50 25

✍ "It's rare for a fashionable spot to become an institution", but after nine years, this brasserie near the Place Vendôme is "still perceived as one of the 'in' places to be"; decorator Jacques Garcia's "sumptuous", "seductive" *fin-de-siècle* interior attracts more acclaim than the Eclectic eats, which, while "surprisingly good", remain just "a distraction" from "the fashionistas strutting by" – a group that includes the staff, "perfectionists in the art of treating you like dirt."

Côté Coulisses 🗷   _|_|_| M

1, rue Monsigny, 2ᵉ (Quatre Septembre), 01 42 96 16 61; fax 42 97 40 97; www.cote-coulisses.com

Red, velvet curtains and upholstery, plus a disco soundtrack, are providing a second act to this theater-district locale in the 2nd, whose name roughly translates as 'backstage'; despite the nightclub vibe and contemporary decoration, the French cooking is impeccably Traditional, with prompt, professional service and reasonable prices.

Cottage Marcadet (Le) 🗷   ∇ 24 | 19 | 25 | 46

151 bis, rue Marcadet, 18ᵉ (Lamarck-Caulaincourt), 01 42 57 71 22; fax 42 57 71 22

■ "A special dining experience" awaits those who make the effort of traveling to a remote, "charmless" corner of the 18th; "excellent value for the money" (especially on the 35-euro prix fixe, "which includes wine"), this "tiny" place "with a cozy atmosphere and very hospitable owner" wows and wins fans with New French "food to live for", such as red mullet in Balsamic vinegar in summer and raspberry *craquant* (a sugary 'sandwich' of the fruit and cookie discs).

Coude Fou (Le) ◑   16 | 12 | 16 | 36

12, rue du Bourg-Tibourg, 4ᵉ (Hôtel-de-Ville), 01 42 77 15 16; fax 48 04 08 98

■ Maybe depending on your neighbors, this Marais wine bar – reportedly the first one in Paris – is either cozy or "cramped", but most find the small room with stone walls a pleasant setting in which to enjoy "excellent" varietals and food that's "a cut above the usual" *bar à vins* including some "great duck dishes"; service is "friendly", prices are "middling" and "the crowd is mixed but respectable."

Couleurs de Vigne ⊠   – | – | – | I
2, rue Marmontel, 15ᵉ (Convention/Vaugirard), 01 45 33 32 96; fax 45 33 32 96
This charming, little wine bar with olive-green walls, cork-colored floors and shelves stocked with an impressive array of vinous treasures also offers reasonably priced plates of charcuterie and cheeses that are easily enough for two; patrons can also select one of the inexpensive regional labels to take home.

Coupe-Chou (Le) ●   21 | 25 | 21 | 49
9, rue de Lanneau, 5ᵉ (Maubert-Mutualité), 01 46 33 68 69; fax 43 25 94 15; www.lecoupechou.com
■ "A restaurant doesn't get any more romantic" than this Classic French situated "on one of the oldest streets" in the Latin Quarter; given the "marvelous decor" of candles, exposed stone walls, arched ceilings and a wood-burning fireplace, many "go more for the atmosphere than for the food", despite the many "mouthwatering" mains; still, its "charm" makes it a fine "place to begin a seduction" – unless, of course, "there's a tour bus out front."

Coupe Gorge (Le) ●   – | – | – | I
2, rue de la Coutellerie, 4ᵉ (Hôtel de Ville), 01 48 04 79 24; fax 42 46 11 72; www.coupegorge.com
Hidden away, this historic bistro (established 1905) charms with red velvet curtains, original fireplaces and a collection of framed paintings that rotates every two months; the simple fare has won a following among workers at the nearby Hôtel de Ville (City Hall), with the modest prices compensating for the sometimes rushed service.

COUPOLE (LA) ●   17 | 23 | 16 | 48
102, bd du Montparnasse, 14ᵉ (Vavin), 01 43 20 14 20; fax 43 35 46 14; www.flobrasseries.com
☑ "One of the eternal brasseries of Paris" resides in this "remarkable" Montparnasse "art deco beehive" that's "busy" until the wee hours with "efficient" if attitudinal "waiters traipsing through the huge", art-filled room, bearing platters of "superb" shellfish, steak frites and the like; admittedly, it's "noisy", something of "a tourist magnet" and many moan "the food is more fast than French"; but "it has tons of energy" and "a lot of history", and that "merits a visit" at least once.

Crêperie de Josselin (La) ●⋻   19 | 14 | 16 | 20
67, rue du Montparnasse, 14ᵉ (Edgar Quinet/ Montparnasse-Bienvenüe), 01 43 20 93 50
■ "Tasty crêpes" "so large they hang over the plate" have converts crowding into this bit of Brittany in Montparnasse;

given that "one of those puppies would feed three hungry people", it's an "incredible bargain", and a "more efficient staff won't be found anywhere else in the City of Light"; the "smoky" digs fall flat for a few, but that doesn't deter those who "go straight for" "one of the foremost crêperies in Paris" ("and don't forget the cider").

Cristal Room ⌧   — — — E

Baccarat, 11, pl des Etats-Unis, 16ᵉ (Boissière/Iéna), 01 40 22 11 10; fax 40 22 11 99; www.baccarat.fr

With chef Thierry Burlot running the kitchen, this intimate Philippe Starck–designed dining room in the Baccarat showroom in the 16th has become one of the harder-to-get-into addresses in Paris; amid decor that plays off the grandeur of the former mansion of eccentric aristocrat Marie-Laure de Noailles, with big, foppish plaster medallions and bare-brick walls in a sumptuous marble-accented salon, you can dine on New French dishes and drink from — what else? — Baccarat glasses.

Crus de Bourgogne (Aux) ⌧   — — — M

3, rue Bachaumont, 2ᵉ (Les Halles/Sentier), 01 42 33 48 24; fax 40 28 66 41

With red-checked tablecloths and red wine galore, this "old-style bistro" near Les Halles in the 2nd arrondissement is "a classic address"; some sigh the 73-year-old grandpa seems a tad "tired" — aside from a "spectacular lobster salad", the fare is rather "predictable" and the "service surly"; but if nostalgia is the best dish on the menu, at least it's moderately priced.

Cuisine (La)   — — — M

14, bd de La Tour-Maubourg, 7ᵉ (Invalides/La Tour-Maubourg), 01 44 18 36 32; fax 44 18 30 42

So discreet you could easily miss it, with low lighting, an Armaniesque decor and well-spaced tables, this solidly bourgeois table in the stolid 7th signals that it's for grown-ups — or at least people who can appreciate careful, impeccably executed New French cooking; artful service relaxes the dressy crowd.

Dagorno ●   — — — M

190, av Jean Jaurès, 19ᵉ (Porte de Pantin), 01 40 40 09 39; fax 48 03 17 23

The handful of folks willing to head up to this meat-oriented veteran in La Villette in the 19th arrondissement, once the location of Paris' slaughterhouses, think it's more than worth the trip, since this "beautiful establishment" (the decor dates from the turn of the century) offers heartily "excellent" Traditional French feed, complemented by a variety of vintage Armagnacs.

Dalloyau   22 16 16 32

5, bd Beaumarchais, 4ᵉ (Bastille), 01 48 87 89 88; fax 48 87 73 70

(continued)

Dalloyau

*2, pl Edmond Rostand, 6ᵉ (Cluny-La Sorbonne/Odéon),
01 43 29 31 10; fax 43 26 25 72
101, rue du Faubourg-St-Honoré, 8ᵉ (Miromesnil/
St-Philippe-du-Roule), 01 42 99 90 00; fax 45 63 82 92
69, rue de la Convention, 15ᵉ (Boucicaut), 01 45 77 84 27;
fax 45 75 27 99
65-67, av J.B. Clément, Boulogne (Boulogne-Jean Jaurès),
01 46 05 06 78; fax 46 03 90 30
www.dalloyau.fr*

☑ "Celebrate Aunt Marie's birthday" at one of these well-bred, old-fashioned tearooms famous for their "decadent desserts" – especially "the most amazing macaroons in the world" – plus a "cornucopia of wonderful small dishes", "excellent cocoa" and "a good selection of brews"; the service is sometimes "inclined to be icy", and you can end up "paying a lot", but a stop here is "for pastry lovers, like going to heaven"; P.S. there's a "magnificent view of the Luxembourg Gardens" in the 6th.

Da Mimmo ●🗷

▽ 19 9 12 35

*39, bd de Magenta, 10ᵉ (Gare de l'Est/Jacques Bonsergent),
01 42 06 44 47*

☑ Though it's located near the gritty Gare de l'Est, "a meal here is like going to Naples, with all that implies"; while advocates applaud the moderately priced "superb pizzas, the rest of the food is insolently expensive" – especially since the "often-absent servers" might fail to specify prices for "the daily specials" or mixed antipasti plates, "which can cause the bill to explode"; still, "if you're willing to spend" – as "a lot of people" are – "this is the place to go."

Dan Bau ●

‒ ‒ ‒ I

*18, rue des Trois-Frères, 18ᵉ (Anvers/Pigalle/Abbesses),
01 42 62 45 59*

It may be located in a touristy part of Montmartre, but this compact Vietnamese has become a hit with a motley crowd of locals for its easygoing prices, flavorful dishes and warm staff, including the friendly chef-owner who cooks out of a seriously tiny kitchen; tip: a visit works best for a quick, casual feed rather than a long tête-à-tête.

Daru (Le) 🗷

‒ ‒ ‒ E

*19, rue Daru, 8ᵉ (Courcelles/Ternes), 01 42 27 23 60;
fax 47 54 08 14; www.daru.fr*

Given that it's been around since the Russian Revolution, it's surprising how few surveyors have been to this venerable Slav, "a precious address to know about" in the 8th; those who have herald the cuisine – smoked salmon, blini and caviar (both fish and eggplant) – as "great", even if the candlelit decor, with lots of framed bits and pieces on the wood-paneled walls, seems "a bit stuffy", and the prices could deplete a czar's treasury.

Dauphin (Le)   19 | 16 | 19 | 40
167, rue St-Honoré, 1er (Palais Royal-Musée du Louvre), 01 42 60 40 11; fax 42 60 01 18
■ "Massive portions of fish", foie gras and other "simple" but "really solid" Southwestern eats "are served up in timely fashion" at this bistro from the team behind Biarritz's well-regarded Café de Paris; perhaps the vintage 1940 "interior is somewhat cold", but the "staff is friendly", and it offers "excellent value" "considering its location" "convenient to all the sights" in the 1st.

Davé   19 | 13 | 22 | 44
12, rue de Richelieu, 1er (Palais Royal-Musée du Louvre), 01 42 61 49 48; fax 42 61 49 48
◪ "If you want to meet real stars and top models in the flesh, then come here" to this Asian near the Palais Royal, where the "ever-present" owner Davé will "take the best care of you"; however, most visit more for the "beautiful-people" "atmosphere than the Chinese" and Vietnamese food – though "enjoyable", it's only "slightly better than the usual corner place" (and of course, "it costs more too").

D'Chez Eux ⌖   21 | 17 | 20 | 61
2, av Lowendal, 7^e (Ecole Militaire), 01 47 05 52 55; fax 45 55 60 74; www.chezeux.com
■ It's like being "in a time warp" to visit this "pleasant, casual neighborhood" place near Les Invalides, where "at tiny tables, enormous portions of Southwestern" and "classic Bistro food is delivered" "nonstop" by "waiters in blue smocks" who "treat everyone like a long-lost friend" – or perhaps a valued hand ("from the size of the servings, you'd think they were feeding you to do a full day's work in the fields"); it's all "great fun", and "even though it's expensive, it's good value" the satiated insist.

De Lagarde ⌖   – | – | – | M
83, av de Ségur, 15e (Ségur), 01 40 65 99 10; fax 40 65 99 10
Occupying a "quiet corner" of the 15th, this Classic French is "not to be missed", thanks to the "fantastic food" created by chef-owner Yohann Marraccini (ex Arpège), who just left to resurrect the late Beauvilliers; perhaps the "courteous staff" is "a little slow", but you should still "go quickly" to this little dining room decorated with coffeepots, because it already is "a grand restaurant, except it lacks an astronomical check."

Délices d'Aphrodite (Les) ●⌖   20 | 12 | 15 | 33
4, rue de Candolle, 5e (Censier-Daubenton), 01 43 31 40 39; fax 43 36 13 08; www.mavrommatis.fr
■ The "same as [sibling] Mavrommatis, but cheaper" agree acolytes of this "typically Greek" goddess, tucked away in

a quiet part of the Latin Quarter; it's become kind of "a Hellenic institution" for the "best moussaka in Paris" and other "inspired", "traditional" dishes, served in a somewhat "kitschy", "tightly spaced" taverna setting.

Délices de Szechuen — 18 | 12 | 17 | 38
40, av Duquesne, 7ᵉ (St-François-Xavier), 01 43 06 22 55
☑ Surveyors smile over the Szechuan servings, "freshly prepared with just the right [amount of] spice", at this Chinese "nestled in the heart of the 7th"; foes fret it's "kind of expensive" ("the fried dumplings should have been made of gold") compared to other Asians, and given the "gloomy" decor; however, a greenery-filled "good terrace in summer" compensates.

Dell 'Angelo ⊠ — – | – | – | M
6, av Rapp, 7ᵉ (Alma-Marceau), 01 44 18 90 12
Close to embassies and the Eiffel Tower in the 7th, this friendly trattoria caters to locals and tourists with Italian cooking, including a wide array of pizzas, served in a snug setting of wood paneling and freshly laundered tablecloths; the small but carefully selected wine list specializes in vino from The Boot.

Dell Orto ◑⊠ — – | – | – | E
45, rue St-Georges, 9ᵉ (St-Georges), 01 48 78 40 30
"Only open in the evenings, alas", this corner shop-front near the Place Saint-Georges has won a loyal following among a stylish, young crowd for its "exceptional", "original Italian cooking", served with a sense of "privilege" in a traditional Tuscan-style room; if the pasta is perfect, it's "too bad the prices have gone up since it became successful" – now, it's "expensive."

Dessirier — 22 | 17 | 21 | 69
9, pl du Maréchal Juin, 17ᵉ (Péreire), 01 42 27 82 14;
fax 47 66 82 07; www.michelrostang.com
■ "You pay dearly, but there are few better for fresh seafood" than this "refined", "old-fashioned" house near the Place Péreire (case in point: the signature "sea bass cooked in a crust of salt, which shows how a complex preparation can result in simple perfection" in a dish); "unpretentious", solicitous service nets accolades too, along with "much-appreciated valet parking."

Deux Abeilles (Les) ⊠ ▽ 14 | 12 | 15 | 26
189, rue de l'Université, 7ᵉ (Alma-Marceau), 01 45 55 64 04
☑ This well-mannered tearoom in the 7th is a place where "you run into attractive women who are watching their figures", as it's perfect for "a light lunch" of "specialty egg dishes" or an "original salad" – though then it tempts with "mouthwatering desserts"; the happy hum it's "worth a detour for the gracious service", even if the "unpretentious decor" "needs renovating."

Deux Canards (Aux) 🖉   21 | 20 | 23 | 41

8, rue du Faubourg-Poissonnière, 10ᵉ (Bonne Nouvelle),
01 47 70 03 23; fax 47 70 18 85; www.lesdeuxcanards.com
■ "Exceptional" "owner Gérard Faesch is cordial and
fun", "discoursing on his orange-based preparations" at
this Traditional French where the emphasis is on "regional
cooking made with fresh ingredients", which include the
namesake fowl; if most "love the menu", one or deux
critics quack over the costs ("it ain't a two-buck duck");
still, scores support those advocates who applaud this
friendly, moderate "favorite."

Devez (Le) 🌰   12 | 11 | 13 | 45

5, pl de l'Alma, 8ᵉ (Alma-Marceau), 01 53 67 97 53; fax 47 23 09 48
☑ "An original approach to meat" – specifically, the featured
Aubrac beef in the form of tapas, roasts or a 'MacD'Aubrac'
hamburger – plus a "rich wine cellar" pleases carnivores
at this "trendy steakhouse"; malcontents moo "you know
there are service problems when your vino arrives after
your dessert", but that doesn't "stop the 'in' crowd haunting
the outside tables", possibly because this is "one of the
few reasonably priced places" in the 8th.

Diamantaires (Les) 🌰   – | – | – | M

60, rue La Fayette, 9ᵉ (Cadet/Le Peletier), 01 47 70 78 14;
fax 44 83 02 73
Those who know this veteran in the 9th appreciate "the
complete repertory" of dishes from Armenia "and nearby
lands" on offer, including manti, "a seasoned ground lamb,
chopped onion and parsley-filled pastry boat served with
yogurt"; however, "you should avoid the nights they have
live music if you want a tranquil" evening, when the joint
jumps with members of Paris' large Armenian community.

Diep 🌰   18 | 11 | 13 | 55

55, rue Pierre Charron, 8ᵉ (Franklin D. Roosevelt), 01 45 63 52 76;
fax 42 56 46 56; www.diep.fr
☑ "One is never disappointed" is the Confucian judgment
on this "quite good" Chinese-Vietnamese in a "bustling"
"beautiful-people" corner of the 8th; however, you should
be someone who "wouldn't have trouble enjoying Peking
duck in a métro car at rush hour" as the place is "always
packed" and the "service is so quick it's stressful"; some say
wok on by, "there are better around for a lot less money",
but for most this "upscale" table "merits its prices."

Divellec (Le) 🖉   23 | 16 | 19 | 115

107, rue de l'Université, 7ᵉ (Invalides), 01 45 51 91 96;
fax 45 51 31 75
☑ "Superb seafood" – "the menu even states if it's wild or
farmed" – is the bait at this "old-fashioned" dining room
overlooking Les Invalides, favored by politicians, expense-
accounters and the occasional star "amenable to relaxed,

unhurried dining"; however, even advocates admit "the fish is definitely fresher than the decor" and that "year after year, prices become more prohibitive and the service increasingly stuffy"; still, it's "one of the best" poisson palaces in Paris, and rank has its privileges.

1728 ☒   18 26 17 56
8, rue d'Anjou, 8ᵉ (Concorde/Madeleine), 01 40 17 04 77; fax 42 65 53 87; www.restaurant-1728.com
☒ With a "surprising little jewel box" of a setting in an "exceptional 18th-century" townhouse in the 8th near Saint Augustin, this "beautifully decorated" place wins kudos from coo-ers for its Peking chef's "interesting cuisine", "a fusion of Japanese and New French trends"; "a must for romantic dinners", it's also "a pleasant place to meet for afternoon tea", though be forewarned that it's "expensive" – especially "for what it is" some naysayers note.

Dix Vins (Le) ☒⌿   ∇ 17 13 15 27
57, rue Falguière, 15ᵉ (Pasteur), 01 43 20 91 77; fax 43 20 91 77; www.les-dix-vins.com
■ The "prices are good and the food is decent" at this traditional bistro in the 15th; though it can get "crowded and loud" with all its habitués ("I've been here 20 times in the last two years"), the owners have made "marvelous use of the small space", with "flowers always on the tables"; throw in the "cheap" list of wines, and you have an "incredible value", making this ideal "for an inexpensive night out with friends."

Djakarta Bali   − − − M
9, rue Vauvilliers, 1ᵉʳ (Châtelet/Louvre-Rivoli), 01 45 08 83 11
Along with the "interesting" Indonesian cooking, acolytes admire the "absolutely adorable" service from the brother-and-sister team that runs this small place near Les Halles; it may be "a little hard to find", but it's worth it to sample the often "outstanding" eats served in a traditional native setting; P.S. "the Friday-night dancing is highly entertaining."

Djoon ☒   − − − M
22, bd Vincent Auriol, 13ᵉ (Quai de la Gare), 01 45 70 83 49; fax 45 70 83 57
The 13th has rarely seen anything quite as hip as this NYC loft-like restaurant-bar with polished cement floors, a faux Renaissance-style painted ceiling, lemon-yellow tub chairs and a large bay window; the Eclectic, wide-ranging menu covers Classic French dishes along with global-influenced renditions such as John Dory sautéed with Indian spices.

Domaine de Lintillac ☒   18 11 14 25
54, rue Blanche, 9ᵉ (Blanche/Trinité), 01 48 74 84 36; www.domainedelintillac-paris.com
■ "Simple but rich regional" "specialties from Southwestern France", including "everything from the duck", make even

the querulous quack with pleasure at this midsize table run by the Lintillac gourmet-food firm; not far from Pigalle, it's full of fun details like "a toaster on every table to ensure freshly crisped bread" and a reassuring "glow from the red lamp shades" to accompany the foie gras; virtually every visitor praises "the excellent value for the money" of the food and regional wine list.

Dôme (Le) ◗   22 | 21 | 20 | 67
108, bd du Montparnasse, 14ᵉ (Vavin), 01 43 35 25 81; fax 42 79 01 19

🔲 Suggestive of "something out of *A Moveable Feast*", this Montparnasse "grande dame" with "splendid decor" is "a pearl" serving up some of "the best oysters in the world", "other-worldly sole meunière" and other "fabulous seafood"; the crowd is a well-heeled mix of "regal, elegant, older" locals and tourists who appreciate that the "pro staffers" "don't rush you"; even admirers admit that it is "definitely too expensive", given the "careful rather than creative cuisine", but still, "it's a Paris institution."

Dôme du Marais (Le) 🖾   18 | 21 | 18 | 46
53 bis, rue des Francs-Bourgeois, 4ᵉ (Hôtel-de-Ville/ Rambuteau), 01 42 74 54 17; fax 42 77 78 17

🔲 Housed in a former church in the Marais, this "beautiful dining room with, of course, a dome above" "strikes an elegant balance, managing to be chic but not trendy", with a mix of "inventive" New and "Classic French food to match"; some find the scene a trifle "starchy", and snap the "personable service doesn't make up for the disappointing cuisine", but to most, it's ideal for "a romantic dinner" and offers one of the "rare good values in this quarter."

Dominique ◗🖾   – | – | – | E
19, rue Bréa, 6ᵉ (Vavin), 01 43 27 08 80
Once a fixture of the White Russian community in Paris, this long-running (est. 1928) Montparnasse citizen soldiers on, offering "various vodkas" – they have some 80 different varieties – to kick back with such Slav specialties as beef stroganoff and salmon koulibiaka in an intimate dining room that conjures up the old country.

Dominique Bouchet 🖾   – | – | – | E
11, rue Treilhard, 8ᵉ (Miromesnil), 01 45 61 09 46; www.dominique-bouchet.com
The former head chef at the Hôtel Crillon makes an impressive return with this eponymous 8th-arrondissement establishment where he offers his classic Haute Cuisine for merely high – as opposed to stratospheric – prices; the decor (exposed stone walls, black-stained wooden tables) is handsome, as are the well-trained young servers; oenophiles appreciate the policy of serving wines by the glass, carafe or bottle.

Doobie's
∇ 11 | 9 | 16 | 46

*2, rue Robert Estienne, 8ᵉ (Franklin D. Roosevelt),
01 53 76 10 76*

■ Just off the Champs, this site with a "trendy" New French–
Eclectic menu is *the* place to go for "the nicest brunch in
Paris", since it "achieves an unusual balance: fashionable
and kid friendly" at the same time; otherwise, the food's
"the least of your worries when you come here to show off
and be seen", and enjoy service that grooves to "lounge
music"; a few find the "velvet ropes up front" – designed to
imply exclusivity – a bit charm-killing.

Dos de la Baleine (Le) ⌧
14 | 10 | 15 | 38

*40, rue des Blancs-Manteaux, 4ᵉ (Hôtel-de-Ville/Rambuteau),
01 42 72 38 98; fax 43 45 43 34; www.ledosdelabaleine.com*

■ Reservations are recommended at this "noisy but nice"
Marais maven that has a sizable gay following, though
"heterosexuals are warmly welcomed, too"; maybe the
traditional Bistro "food is average", but given the cozy
ambiance and reasonable prices, it's a "good bargain."

Drouant ⌧
21 | 21 | 21 | 90

*18, rue Gaillon, 2ᵉ (Opéra/Quatre Septembre), 01 42 65 15 16;
fax 49 24 02 15*

■ As the venue of the prestigious Prix Goncourt (France's
highest annual prize for literature), this bastion of "refined
elegance" in "a historic structure" near the Opéra "doesn't
have to prove anything"; chef Louis Grondard's "fine"
Classic French cooking may not "merit the Goncourt of the
restaurant world" but it's "fashion-proof", particularly the
"fresh fish", and overall, this "mythic" table, for "what it
is", is "near perfect"; P.S. try eating in one of the "little
salons" "for a hint of literary holiness."

DUC (LE) ⌧
25 | 15 | 20 | VE

243, bd Raspail, 14ᵉ (Raspail), 01 43 20 96 30; fax 43 20 46 73

◪ It may be in Montparnasse, but a meal at this "delightful,
old standby" is "like a trip to Honfleur" because everything
is "sparkling fresh", as though it just landed on the docks
of that Norman port; "the best sole *meunière*", "sublime
oysters" and other "perfectly cooked (or uncooked) dishes"
send seafood fans sailing toward rapture; sure, the porthole
decor has "aged terribly", but the "genteel, accommodating
service" and the cuisine's "quality make you forget all,
even the exorbitant prices."

Duc de Richelieu (Le) ◕⌧
– | – | – | M

5, rue Parrot, 12ᵉ (Gare de Lyon), 01 43 43 05 64

The bistro boom in eastern Paris continues with this
newcomer from the former proprietor of Le Gavroche; just
down the street from the Gare de Lyon, it's convenient before
or after a train trip, but also worth seeking out for its cooking
alone, which features carefully prepared, traditional

Lyonnais dishes displayed on the equally traditional chalkboard menu; well-chosen wines and a spacious terrace for good-weather dining round out its appeal.

Durand Dupont ◑
9 | 15 | 11 | 46

14, pl du Marché, Neuilly (Les Sablons), 01 41 92 93 00; fax 46 37 56 79

☑ "Definitely still on the 'in' list", this "chic (and so much-too expensive)" Neuilly bistro has "a great terrace for self-display"; this "sunny" outdoor perch is in fact the reason "you really come here", since most say the "nothing-special" Eclectic eats are quite "variable", qualitywise, and the "pretty waitresses' efficiency leaves a lot to be desired."

Ebauchoir (L') ☒
– | – | – | M

43-45, rue de Citeaux, 12ᵉ (Faidherbe-Chaligny), 01 43 42 49 31

"Everyone is warmly welcomed at this bistro tucked away in the far reaches of the 12th", where the "delightfully unfussy" cuisine (Traditional French, with some "original" touches) and the company of an arty local crowd make "you jump back decades"; "the secret's out", however – "it's always packed" – so be sure to book.

Écaille de la Fontaine (L') ☒
– | – | – | E

15, rue Gaillon, 2ᵉ (Opéra), 01 47 42 02 99; fax 01 47 42 82 84

Not far from the Opéra Garnier, this dressy seafood specialist is the second establishment from thespians-turned-restaurateurs Gérard Depardieu and Carole Bouquet (La Fontaine Gaillon), and their menu strikes a balance between the current Parisian preference for minimalist preparations and the traditionally elaborate sauce-based stylings; the room's pale, soothing contemporary decor was designed by Bouquet as well.

Ecailler du Bistrot (L') ☒
– | – | – | M

20-22, rue Paul-Bert, 11ᵉ (Faidherbe-Chaligny), 01 43 72 76 77; fax 43 72 24 66

Not many have navigated their way to this seafooder in a quiet corner of the 11th, but those who have rave about "superb fish and shellfish", especially the "excellent oysters" from Brittany; an attractive tiled-and-painted-wood decor and "friendly service puts the client at ease", as do the reasonably priced tabs.

Ecluse (L') ◑
14 | 13 | 14 | 35

34, pl du Marché St-Honoré, 1ᵉʳ (Pyramides/Tuileries), 01 42 96 10 18; fax 42 96 10 17
15, quai des Grands-Augustins, 6ᵉ (St-Michel), 01 46 33 58 74; fax 44 07 18 76
15, pl de la Madeleine, 8ᵉ (Madeleine), 01 42 65 34 69; fax 44 71 01 26
64, rue François 1er, 8ᵉ (George V), 01 47 20 77 09; fax 40 70 03 33
13, rue de la Roquette, 11ᵉ (Bastille), 01 48 05 19 12; fax 48 05 04 88

(continued)
Ecluse (L')
1, rue d'Armaillé, 17ᵉ (Charles de Gaulle-Etoile), 01 47 63 88 29;
fax 44 40 41 91
www.leclusebaravin.com
☑ "Still the poster child for wine bars everywhere", this
mini-chain offers an "uneven" experience: there's a "vast
choice of *vins*", especially "Bordeaux by the glass", and the
"dark-wood, old-bar atmosphere" ("like a Gallic *Cheers*")
offers "a place to relax"; but "the good grape doesn't
excuse" a Classic French menu that's "serious but not really
appealing" and service that swings from "professional" to
"pretentious"; many say that valuewise, both the vino and
the vittles seem "pricey" too.

Editeurs (Les) ☽   13 | 22 | 16 | 34
4, carrefour de l'Odéon, 6ᵉ (Odéon), 01 43 26 67 76;
fax 46 34 58 30; www.lesediteurs.fr
☑ "It's charming to sit at a sidewalk table and watch the
passers-by" at this site with a prime setting overlooking
the Odéon – though the "comfortable", "library decor"
(full of "warm colors, filled bookshelves" and "comfy
nooks") is a best-seller too; alas, the "classic brasserie
cuisine" "is just decent", but a "hip, young crowd" finds it
"fine for a snack or drinks."

El Mansour ⌧   21 | 21 | 17 | 55
7, rue de La Trémoille, 8ᵉ (Alma-Marceau), 01 47 23 88 18;
fax 40 70 13 53
■ This "elegant" oasis off the Avenue George V serves
"refined Moroccan cooking" to a business crowd at noon
and Middle Eastern expats in the evening; a "traditional
setting" – North African art, "spacious tables" and oak
panels – contributes to the "quiet ambiance" of a room
peopled by "efficient, serious" servers; just expect to pay
princely prices for what's possibly Paris' "best tagine."

El Palenque ⌧⊘   ▽ 18 | 9 | 11 | 36
5, rue de la Mont. Ste-Geneviève, 5ᵉ (Maubert-Mutualité),
01 43 54 08 99
☑ "If you like meat", join the hungry gauchos who head for
"one of the best Argentineans in Paris" near the Panthéon;
but while all agree about the "impressively tender" beef
and prices, the rest "is a mixed bag": the "unpretentious"
decor offers rather "spartan comfort" and the "staff from
all over the continent" ranges from "friendly" to "rude."

ELYSÉES (LES) ⌧   26 | 24 | 24 | VE
Hôtel Vernet, 25, rue Vernet, 8ᵉ (Charles de Gaulle-Etoile/
George V), 01 44 31 98 98; fax 44 31 85 69;
www.hotelvernet.com
■ Chef Eric Briffard (ex Plaza-Athénée) has emerged as a
"winner" at this Haute Cuisine in the 8th; *amis* adore his

"delectable" earthy dishes ("if this is what heaven's like, I'll stop sinning now"), served by "staffers whose passion for food matches the chef's"; there's praise too for the dining room, recently redecorated but still dominated by a "gorgeous stained-glass ceiling" "by Gustave Eiffel (yes, he did the tower)"; it's "terribly expensive", but "there aren't enough superlatives to describe dining here."

Elysées Hong Kong   − | − | − | M
80, rue Michel-Ange, 16ᵉ (Exelmans), 01 46 51 60 99
An established staple for "regulars" from "the residences and the offices nearby", this award-winning Chinese is also starting to become "a destination beyond its quarters" of the well-upholstered 16th; "savory cooking and warm service" hold sway in a room decorated in antiqued 19th-century Asian style.

Emporio Armani Caffé ⊠   19 | 16 | 15 | 49
149, bd St-Germain, 6ᵉ (St-Germain-des-Prés), 01 45 48 62 15; fax 45 48 53 17
☑ "Nice pastas and light entrees", accessorized with a bit of "people-watching", make this "hip hangout" atop the Emporio Armani boutique an ideal "place to stop when you're out shopping" around Saint-Germain; except for "the stupid lamps hanging down over the tables", most find the "modern decor appealing"; granted, it is "expensive for basic Italian" – but then, so are Giorgio's clothes.

Enoteca (L') ◑   18 | 13 | 14 | 41
25, rue Charles V, 4ᵉ (St-Paul/Sully Morland), 01 42 78 91 44; fax 44 59 31 72
■ "Nestled in a quiet corner of the Marais", this wine bar of The Boot is "a polished comfort zone" with pretty "Murano lamps" under the massive beams of an ancient stone house; "as the name suggests, it's a place to drink rather than eat" – "all of the major vineyards are represented" – but the kitchen sends out "rustic", "reasonably good" pastas as well; toss in a "cozy atmosphere" and some "very Italian staffers" and most agree "we need more of these places."

Entoto ⊠   − | − | − | M
143-145, rue L.M. Nordmann, 13ᵉ (Glacière), 01 45 87 08 51
Tucked away in the 13th, this "nice, little exotic Ethiopian" lets you "go back to basics by eating with your bare hands", scooping up the vegetables and meats with pieces of flatbread just like they do in the old country; the owners are "sweet and generous", and the tabs modest, so "maybe we shouldn't make a lot of noise about it" whisper worshipers.

Entracte (L') (Chez Sonia et Carlos)   − | − | − | M
44, rue d'Orsel, 18ᵉ (Abbesses/Anvers), 01 46 06 93 41
At the foot of the funicular that ascends to Sacré-Coeur lies this "tiny and pleasant little bistro" where all the homestyle Traditional French dishes, from rack of lamb to

veal kidneys, are cooked to order in a broom closet of a kitchen by chef-owner Gilles Chiriaux; decorated with Montmartre artists' work, it's ideal "when you're going to the Théâtre de l'Atelier" nearby, but you better book to snag one of the 20-odd seats.

Entredgeu (L') ⊠   –| –| –| M|

83, rue Laugier, 17ᵉ (Porte de Champerret), 01 40 54 97 24; fax 40 54 96 62

Young chef-owner Philippe Tredgeu learned how to set a successful table by "working with the Chez Michel" team; now he and his wife have gone out on their own with this Classic French bistro in the 17th, and while their "little" home is not yet widely known, devotees deem it "a good find" with a "delicious", daily changing menu served by a "pleasant, energetic staff"; moderate prices make it a "definite come-back-to place."

En Vue (L') ◐⊠   –| –| –| M|

39, rue Boissy d'Anglas, 8ᵉ (Concorde/Madeleine), 01 42 65 10 49; fax 40 17 09 28

"Well-located in the rue Boissy d'Anglas", near Hermès, this posh spot boasts an "extremely original decor" of bird's-eye maple paneling, gray and rose hues, low lighting and "toilets worth a detour"; but despite "good cocktails", foes find the New French fare "frankly isn't very interesting", given the "desperately *petit* portions"; and while the service is "not unfriendly", overall the place is "trying to be too hip."

Epicure 108 ⊠   –| –| –| M|

108, rue Cardinet, 17ᵉ (Malesherbes), 01 47 63 50 91

"Interesting Asian-French fusion food" (think wasabi-flavored veal kidneys), from a Japanese chef-owner who trained in Alsace, makes for memorable meals at this little-known address near the Square des Batignolles; the site is small, but suits who flock here for lunch attest that the fare is "wonderful"; clean-air advocates should know, however, that "cigar-smoking guests" are encouraged to light up.

Epi d'Or (L') ⊠   ▽ 21| 18| 20| 47|

25, rue Jean-Jacques Rousseau, 1ᵉʳ (Louvre-Rivoli), 01 42 36 38 12; fax 42 36 46 25; www.epidor.fr

■ "Classy yet *sans* attitude", this old-fashioned bistro in a quiet street near the Palais Royal offers a "friendly family ambiance" and "good value" for Classic French food, like a "lovely beef salad"; it's also a plus – and "a pleasant surprise" – that "you're eating with Parisians, not tourists."

EPI DUPIN (L') ⊠   24| 15| 18| M|

11, rue Dupin, 6ᵉ (Sèvres-Babylone), 01 42 22 64 56; fax 42 22 30 42

☑ "It's tough to get reservations" at this 6th-arrondissement "madhouse with only 45 seats" offering "marvelously prepared, updated Bistro classics" at "bargain" rates; critics carp the "creative" chow "is overshadowed by the elbow-to-elbow" seating ("the closest tables in all Paris") and "friendly" but "frantic" service that "makes you feel rushed", but if "you can stand the hectic pace", you may well join the worshipers who warble it's "one of our favorites."

Erawan ⊠   21 | 11 | 14 | 36

76, rue de la Fédération, 15ᵉ (La Motte-Picquet-Grenelle), 01 47 83 55 67; fax 47 34 85 98

☑ "One of the best Thais in Paris" offers "prices that defy comparison" sing savants about this Siamese veteran where "beautiful silk dresses on the waitresses" enliven an otherwise "dated" decor of plants and posters; its location may be off the beaten path, but the "peaceful" 15th is closer to get to than Bangkok.

Escale du Liban (L') ◑   – | – | – | I

1, rue Ferdinand Duval, 4ᵉ (St-Paul), 01 42 74 55 70; fax 42 74 55 27

Occupying a bi-level space (downstairs is a take-out counter and tables, upstairs a dining room), this vest-pocket Lebanese has quickly become a popular spot in the Marais for a relaxed crowd of shopkeepers, city hall workers and arty types to partake in super-fresh shish kebab and meze.

Escargot Montorgueil (L') ⊠   ▽ 18 | 22 | 18 | 47

38, rue Montorgueil, 1ᵉʳ (Les Halles), 01 42 36 83 51; fax 42 36 35 05

■ In Les Halles, this classic bistro has always been "worth a detour for its decor", a "romantic", straight-out-of-a-Hollywood-set Second Empire scene; but after an ownership change, it's also on a roll for "creative dishes", including an "amazing escargot sampler" where the shelled slowpokes are cooked three different ways (the Roquefort version alone is "worth the flight across the pond"); it's a little "expensive" but worth it for the "lively location" and eats.

Espadon (L')   25 | 27 | 27 | VE

Hôtel Ritz, 15, pl Vendôme, 1ᵉʳ (Concorde/Opéra), 01 43 16 30 80; fax 43 16 33 75; www.ritz.com

■ Life "is ritzy" in all respects at the Hôtel Ritz's main restaurant where a mini-"orchestra plays quietly" and "waiters seem to float across" the "sumptuous" "circular room with mirrored walls" and "gorgeous garden" in summer – both of which offer "unparalleled people-watching of new money, old wealth", "beautiful women and handsome men"; if a bit "staid", chef Michel Roth's Classic French menu is "beautifully executed", so "if true love eludes you, come here for true romance at least."

Espadon Bleu (L') ⊠   21 | 19 | 17 | 44

25, rue des Grands-Augustins, 6ᵉ (Odéon/St-Michel), 01 46 33 00 85; fax 43 54 54 48; www.jacques-cagna.com

☑ "A good way of experiencing Jacques Cagna without paying Jacques Cagna prices" declare devotees of the celebrity chef-owner's Saint-Germain seafooder (facing his namesake establishment), which to them seems a "nice quiet place for a simple dinner" of "fresh, firm fish"; however, the less-happy harpoon "painfully slow" service and declare themselves "disappointed" in the fare.

Estaminet Gaya (L') 🗷 — | — | — | E
17, rue Duphot, 1er (Madeleine), 01 42 60 43 03; fax 42 60 69 35
"Hidden in a small street" near the Madeleine, this "simply excellent" seafooder reels 'em in with "really fresh fish" and "similarly scrumptious desserts"; the decor's "a bit like the métro stations, with nice mosaic tiles" and the service is "attentive"; it's "good for business lunches that don't have to be too fancy", and "although not horribly cheap" at night, it still qualifies as a "non-splurge dinner destination."

Etoile (L') ◑🗷 17 | 20 | 16 | 66
12, rue de Presbourg, 16e (Charles de Gaulle-Etoile), 01 45 00 78 70; fax 45 00 78 71
🗹 "A spectacular view of the Arc de Triomphe", aka the namesake Etoile, is the star attraction of this "exorbitant" fashion plate; but most find the Classic French cuisine surprisingly "nice" for "a nightclub restaurant (there's a real chef in the kitchen!)"; of course, the unconvinced still grumble its main merit comes after the meal, "when you go downstairs to dance"; perhaps they're put off by the "rich-kid crowd" with "an average age of 18."

Etoile Marocaine (L') ▽ 21 | 22 | 24 | 42
56, rue Galilée, 8e (George V), 01 47 20 44 43; fax 47 20 69 85
■ To be "treated like Moroccan royalty", head for this "small" place with a "really nice" North African–style decor off the Champs; the "authentic, interesting menu", which includes "excellent tagines and couscous", may be the "most succulent [of its kind] in Paris", and the "friendly staff" provides "efficient service"; all in all, a good deal for the dirham.

Excuse (L') 🗷 22 | 18 | 20 | 48
14, rue Charles V, 4e (St-Paul/Sully Morland), 01 42 77 98 97; fax 42 77 88 55
■ No excuses need be made by this "excellent find in the Marais" (and indeed, "it's worth going out of your way to find it"), since its "sophisticated and delicious" New French cooking is "presented with flair" by a staff that's "friendly to all" in "modern and romantic", albeit "snug", surroundings; "pricey but not outrageous", it has "an outstanding wine list", including some bottles from the "owner's Rhône Valley winery"; P.S. "the entire upstairs room is nonsmoking."

Fables de La Fontaine (Les) — | — | — | M
131, rue St-Dominique, 7e (Ecole Militaire), 01 44 18 37 55
On a busy shopping street in the 7th, this "really small" seafooder, now run by chef Christian Constant of Le Violon

d'Ingres, is "great for fresh shellfish", served amid a nautical blue-and-white-tiled decor; perhaps the *poisson*'s "a bit pricey" in some cases, but you can console yourself with the "good" signature dessert, a cream-filled pastry that commemorates a famed bike race between Paris and Brest.

Fakhr el Dine ●
16 | 13 | 16 | 48

3, rue Quentin Bauchart, 8e (George V), 01 47 23 44 42; fax 53 70 01 81
30, rue de Longchamp, 16e (Trocadéro), 01 47 27 90 00; fax 53 70 01 81
www.fakhreldine.com
■ Offering an "upscale Lebanese" experience, these two addresses in the 8th and the 16th are admittedly "expensive", but you'll enjoy "inspired" creations in a "friendly atmosphere" with "accommodating" service; they're also "great for takeout."

Famille (La) ⌧
– | – | – | M

41, rue des Trois-Frères, 18e (Abbesses/Anvers), 01 42 52 11 12
This funky site on a cobbled Montmartre street features the "astonishing" Eclectic cooking of young Basque chef Inaki Aizpitarte, whose "fresh, different" menus reflect both his experience in Latin America and his interest in North Africa; the simple loftlike space with a large table d'hôte and bar is already always packed with an internationally diverse, but uniformly cool, crowd.

Fauchon ⌧
– | – | – | M

26, pl de la Madeleine, 8e (Concorde/Madeleine), 01 70 39 38 78; fax 70 39 38 71; www.fauchon.com
It may not have the same wow-factor that it did a century ago, but this grande dame of a luxury grocer overlooking the Place de la Madeleine remains a "must-stop" for its striped-fabric tea salon, "an oasis of civility [before or] after a tough day of shopping"; in addition to the "fabulous" delicacies and brews, "the lobster salad is memorable", and though it can get a bit "pricey" for pastry, "the ladies who lunch" insist "it's worth every euro."

Fellini ⌧
21 | 14 | 20 | 43

47, rue de l'Arbre-Sec, 1er (Louvre-Rivoli), 01 42 60 90 66; fax 42 60 18 04
58, rue de la Croix Nivert, 15e (Commerce/Emile Zola), 01 45 77 40 77; fax 45 77 22 54
■ An "absolutely fantastic" cucina, including "excellent homemade pasta", has surveyors singing 'That's Amore' about this pair in the 1st and the 15th; "waiters who are always in a good mood (hard to find in Paris)" provide "a real Italian climate" along with "delightful, animated service"; this duo's usually "crowded with locals, so be sure to reserve."

Ferme (La)
— — — I

55-57, rue St-Roch, 1er (Opéra/Pyramides), 01 40 20 12 12; fax 40 20 06 06

It's "a bit of heaven" to bite into the "light preparations" at this "high-quality sandwich"-and-salad eatery located in an organic food shop in the 1st; all the dishes are made with "super-fresh produce", and the "charming" setting makes eating here both "a treat for the palate and the eye"; while "perfect for a quick stop", it's an equally good place "to go and relax with a great cup of coffee."

Ferme des Mathurins (La) ⊠
— — — M

17, rue Vignon, 8^e (Havre-Caumartin/Madeleine), 01 42 66 46 39; fax 42 66 00 27

You come to this "dark, rustic" 1945-vintage traditional bistro in the 8th – a favorite of the mystery writer Simenon – out of "nostalgia" for "an almost-forgotten style of cooking: the classics of the peasant kitchen"; "don't expect anything artistic" advise regulars, but rest assured that if you "order the special", it'll "taste wonderful."

Ferme St-Simon (La) ⊠
23   20   24   58

6, rue de St-Simon, 7e (Rue du Bac/Solférino), 01 45 48 35 74; fax 40 49 07 31; www.fermestsimon.com

■ "When you want a Traditional French experience", consider this "plushy establishment" in the 7th that feeds "government bigwigs" and "a professional clientele" by day and the local bourgeoisie in the evening; it's highly "reliable for well prepared" fare – in particular, the housemade "desserts are tops" – and the "elegant service" is always "welcoming" ("even if you aren't from one of the surrounding ministries"); "each of the three dining rooms has a different style", but all offer "enjoyable atmosphere."

Fermette Marbeuf 1900 (La) ●
17   25   18   56

5, rue Marbeuf, 8e (Alma-Marceau/Franklin D. Roosevelt), 01 53 23 08 00; fax 53 23 08 09; www.fermettemarbeuf.com

☑ Just off the Champs-Elysées, tourists find the "turn-of-the-century flamboyance" of this Frères Blanc–owned Classic French – "not a place the locals frequent" – to be the best part of a meal here, especially since a "badly needed refurbishment of the cutlery is now done"; while it's "too bad the food and service don't come close" to the "superb" "art nouveau setting", the former is "dependable" and the latter "surprisingly friendly."

Fernandises (Les) ⊠
— — — M

19, rue de la Fontaine-au-Roi, 11e (Goncourt/République), 01 48 06 16 96

"Simple and appealing", this established table in the 11th arrondissement serves up hearty, homemade dishes from Normandy, such as roast skate with Camembert sauce and Calvados-flambéed crêpes; although some deem the decor downright "distressing" – a huge mural depicting the Paris Commune dominates the brightly lit room – the food's of "reliably good quality."

Feuilles Libres ☒   <u>–</u> <u>–</u> <u>–</u> E
34, rue Perronet, Neuilly (Les Sablons), 01 46 24 41 41
Entrées Libres ◐☒
49, rue Madeleine Michelis, Neuilly (Les Sablons),
01 46 24 00 84; fax 46 40 77 61
www.feuilles-libres.com
Although few have found these New French enclaves helmed by a husband-and-wife team on a quiet Neuilly street, those who have know their "pleasant atmosphere" (especially on their linden-tree terraces in summer); the more "expensive" Feuilles restaurant where owner Emmanuel Laporte mans the stove is set up in a small house that sparkles with silver and colorful tablecloths; the brick bistro, run by Nathalie, serves up moderately priced seafood specialties in a more casual ambiance.

Filo Delle Stagioni (Au) ☒   <u>–</u> <u>–</u> <u>–</u> M
8, rue de Beauce, 3ᵉ (Temple/République), 01 48 04 52 24; fax 48 04 52 24
Situated in the ever-trendy northern Marais, this spare but intimate new Italian draws a creative crowd of journalists, fashion designers and musicians with an extensive menu of Sicilian-style pastas, risottos and pizzas – though it's the daily specials that best showcase the kitchen's ability, as attested to by the teasing waiters (many of whom are from The Boot themselves).

Findi ◐   17 15 14 48
24, av George V, 8ᵉ (Alma-Marceau/George V), 01 47 20 14 78; fax 47 20 10 08; www.findi.net
☑ With a "great location across the street from the Hôtel George V", this slightly pricey, "lively" Italian boasts "a modish setting", reminiscent of an updated Venetian palazzo; views vary about the food, ranging from "enjoyable" to "uninspired" and the same goes for the service; but that doesn't stop the place from being "packed with noisy thirtysomethings" and a few "famous faces and VIPs."

Fins Gourmets (Aux) ☒⇥   16 14 14 33
213, bd St-Germain, 7ᵉ (Rue du Bac), 01 42 22 06 57
☑ Second-generation spots pervaded by a "real" "old-fashioned bistro" atmosphere are becoming rare, and so in the 7th, this specialist in Southwestern cooking "should be preserved"; but even loyalists lament that, aside from an "unequalled pipérade" (a mélange of cooked onions, eggs, peppers, tomatoes and garlic), the kitchen "seems to be tired" of late and the waiters "are phoning it in"; even if it's "not great", though, this vet remains "cozy and reliable" for "regional", reasonable meals.

Finzi
16 | 10 | 12 | 41

182, bd Haussmann, 8ᵉ (St-Philippe-du-Roule), 01 45 62 88 68; fax 45 61 41 05

◪ Popular with bankers and brokers by day and the bourgeois locals by night, this "good Italian" in the 8th serves up pretty "authentic" pastas and a nice "selection of wines" to boot; but negatives note it's "not necessarily worth the trip if you're not in the neighborhood", especially since "the brash service" "leaves something to be desired."

Fish La Boissonnerie
21 | 16 | 20 | 37

69, rue de Seine, 6ᵉ (Odéon), 01 43 54 34 69; fax 43 54 33 47

■ "Co-owned by an American, this funky, fresh and flavorful fish stop" is fine when you'd adore an "accessible (emotionally and geographically)" spot in Saint-Germain for an "informal" meal of "Mediterranean food and wine"; its "friendly, English-speaking staff" makes it "a favorite of expat" Yanks, and the fact that it's "fantastic value for the money" doesn't hurt either.

Flandrin (Le) ◗
13 | 15 | 13 | 51

80, av Henri Martin, 16ᵉ (Rue de la Pompe), 01 45 04 34 69; fax 45 04 67 41

■ A terrace that's "*the* place to be seen – provided you arrive in a Porsche" – is the main interest of this "snobby" brasserie "in an old train station"; while it's "a must for certain well-off inhabitants" of the 16th and show-biz folks, the more culinary-minded moan the "food is not more than ok", and it comes with a helping of "haughtiness" from the staff; as for the prices, let's just say they're geared to the type of folks "that don't mind overpaying."

Flora ⊠
23 | 18 | 21 | 69

36, av George V, 8ᵉ (George V), 01 40 70 10 49; fax 47 20 52 87

■ "She is just so good" swoon supporters of chef-owner Flora Mikula, the namesake force behind this "small" but "sophisticated" address on the Avenue George V; her "imaginative", "internationally flavored New French menu" is "smartly presented" by "attentive servers" in a dining room that manages to be "elegant and informal at the same time"; here, for once, is a place that's "no flash, all substance", so "run", don't walk, to its "civilized" site.

Flora Danica
18 | 18 | 16 | 50

142, av des Champs-Elysées, 8ᵉ (Charles de Gaulle-Etoile/ George V), 01 44 13 86 26; fax 44 13 89 44; www.restaurantfloradanica.com

■ "An unexpected oasis in the wildness of the Champs-Elysées", this Classic French–Dane "keeps drawing you back for an unrivaled selection of salmon", "tasty herrings" and "aquavit, *vite!*"; more casual than cousin Copenhague upstairs, this Viking is vaunted also for a "Scandinavian decor that's clean-lined and tidy" (kind of "like a designer furniture store") and service that's friendly, if "a trifle slow"; P.S. bear in mind the backyard's "stunning terrace for hot summer days" and nights.

Flore en l'Ile (Le) ◑   17 | 20 | 17 | 36 |
42, quai d'Orléans, 4e (Hôtel-de-Ville/Pont-Marie), 01 43 29 88 27; fax 43 29 73 54
■ When you long for "that Ile Saint-Louis look", this "always crowded", "good neighborhood place" is "one of the most beautifully situated in Paris", with a spectacular "view of the back of Notre Dame"; it's "a favorite for a quintessential breakfast" *français* ("the flakiest croissants"), "afternoon tea", or "lovely" "late-night dessert"; less recommended are the Classic French dinners, but it's unbeatable for a "Berthillon ice cream with flying buttresses out the window."

Florimond (Le) ☒   22 | 16 | 24 | 39 |
19, av de La Motte-Picquet, 7e (Ecole Militaire), 01 45 55 40 38; fax 45 55 40 38
■ In the 7th, this "tiny" eatery is a "well-kept secret that deserves attention", thanks to a "courteous, kind chef/co-owner" and "service that goes the extra kilometer" with such Classic French comestibles as "delicious stuffed cabbage" and "ooh-la-la, puff-pastry dishes – Napoleons or langoustines"; "it's a funky setting, but most friendly."

Fogón Saint Julien ◑   ▽ 23 | 14 | 19 | 47 |
10, rue St-Julien-le-Pauvre, 5e (Maubert-Mutualité/St-Michel), 01 43 54 31 33; fax 43 54 07 00
■ "The best Spanish in Paris, no contest" contend converts who charge to this "quaint", "cozy place" in the 5th; the menu stars "wonderful paella", unsurpassed "not only in this country but in Europe", along with "amazing tapas" and "original wines"; prices may be a little "high", but this "is a must for Iberian cuisine lovers."

Fontaine de Mars (La)   19 | 18 | 20 | 44 |
129, rue St-Dominique, 7e (Ecole Militaire), 01 47 05 46 44; fax 47 05 11 13
■ In the "chic 7th", this "bustling little bistro" offers a "great experience" for fans of "consistently" "authentic", "hearty" Gascon-Southwestern cooking served in a dining room with "retro red-checked tablecloths" (though in good weather, "it's wonderful to sit outside next to the fountain"); creating an atmosphere that's "at once relaxed and sophisticated", "the service is so professional", especially "the warm welcome" from the proprietor; in short, it's "everything a meal in Paris should be."

Fontaine Gaillon (La) ◑☒   17 | 17 | 18 | 56 |
1, rue de la Michodière, 2e (Opéra/Quatre Septembre), 01 42 65 87 04; fax 47 42 82 84
■ The ratings may not reflect the regime of *propriétaires/* actors Gérard Depardieu and Carole Bouquet who have

lovingly rejuvenated this "old favorite" near the Opéra
Garnier; the chief coup was hiring chef Laurent Audiot
(ex Marius et Janette), whose knack for Classic French
cuisine is especially evident in seafood; "bursting with
atmosphere", it's a "great place to take visitors, as it looks
and tastes like their expectations" of a Gallic eatery.

Fontaines (Les) 🛐　　　20 | 9 | 16 | 35
*9, rue Soufflot, 5ᵉ (Cluny La Sorbonne/Luxembourg),
01 43 26 42 80; fax 44 07 03 49*
◪ "Copious – maybe too copious" quantities of "traditional
Bistro food" make this Latin Quarter table "an oasis in a
culinary desert"; certainly, the worn '70s "decor could be
nicer" and "the service can be a little slow", but that doesn't
daunt the "intellectual", "very French clientele that creates
a "bustling", "lively" scene.

Fontanarosa　　　▽ 21 | 13 | 18 | 41
*28, bd Garibaldi, 15ᵉ (Cambronne/Ségur), 01 45 66 97 84;
fax 47 83 96 30*
■ "Vive Sardinia!" shout supporters of this red-and-ochre-
colored Italian in the 15th, which re-creates the cucina of
the chef and owner's native land – much of it featured on
a "great serve-yourself antipasti table"; it's also renowned
for its "nice little terrace" "gorged with sunshine" and
potted olive trees that "keeps you returning with pleasure."

Foujita　　　16 | 6 | 11 | 39
*41, rue St-Roch, 1ᵉʳ (Pyramides), 01 42 61 42 93
7, rue 29 Juillet, 1ᵉʳ (Tuileries), 01 49 26 07 70; fax 49 26 07 60*
◪ When it comes to these veteran Japanese in the 1st,
sushi-lovers roll into two different camps; loyalists find the
fish "good" for a "quick", "exhausted-executive lunch";
but adversaries argue that "although the prices are still
reasonable, these places used to be so much better";
universally disliked, "depressing decor" doesn't help either.

Fouquet's (Le) ◗　　　16 | 19 | 15 | 62
*99, av des Champs-Elysées, 8ᵉ (George V), 01 47 23 50 00;
fax 47 23 60 02; www.lucienbarriere.com*
◪ Love it or hate it, this Classic French on the Champs is
"still going strong" after 105 years; foes fume "Fouquet about
it" – it's the "epitome of tourist joints", with "lackadaisical
service" and "ordinary" eats, while friends find the cuisine
"getting better" since a recent chef change and laud the
"classic" decor; all agree that "prices are scandalous", so
maybe it's best to "just come for a drink" and "nice people-
watching" along Paris' "main drag."

Fous d'en Face (Les) ◗🛐　　　▽ 12 | 13 | 12 | 32
*3, rue du Bourg Tibourg, 4ᵉ (Hôtel-de-Ville), 01 48 87 03 75;
fax 42 78 38 03*
■ With "a nice terrace and an appealing selection of
wines", this *bistrot à vins* "not far from the Hôtel de Ville"

(City Hall) in the 4th is a "good spot" for "simple" traditional Bistro "cooking using very fresh produce"; fans find it's fun "to discover a variety of [varietals] by the glass" amid a "pleasant atmosphere."

Frugier ⌧   – | – | – | M
137, av de Versailles, 16ᵉ (Mirabeau/Exelmans), 01 46 47 72 00; fax 46 47 72 00
Located near the Maison de Radio in the 16th, this new bistro is attracting media types and young folks with a daily changing chalkboard menu that mixes traditional grandmotherly dishes, such as rabbit in mustard sauce, with edgier, more modern ones like shrimp tartare; the white painted space has a simple charm, and service is brisk and friendly.

Fumoir (Le) ☽   15 | 20 | 15 | 35
6, rue de l'Amiral de Coligny, 1ᵉʳ (Louvre-Rivoli), 01 42 92 00 24; fax 42 92 05 05; www.lefumoir.com
☑ "Facing the Louvre (you can't get more central than that)", this Eclectic eatery attracts an "interesting crowd" of cognoscenti who "expressly ask to be seated in the calm, cozy library room" – with actual books! – in back; staffed by servers "who aren't great, but are at least alert", it's "famous mainly for" its "delightfully complete Sunday brunch" – at other meals, "drinks and starters are best"; just bear in mind that as it heats up, the scene gets "smoky (as its name implies)."

Gallopin ☽   15 | 20 | 16 | 46
40, rue Notre-Dame-des-Victoires, 2ᵉ (Bourse/ Grands Boulevards), 01 42 36 45 38; fax 42 36 10 32; www.brasseriegallopin.com
☑ "You feel as if you've stepped back in time" (1876 to be precise) at this antique "across the street from the old Bourse [stock market]" that boasts a "classic brasserie atmosphere with a large wooden bar and lots of mirrors"; like a blue-chip investment, the "traditional food is reliable rather than original", but at least it's a "constant" – unlike, alas, the "irregular service"; still, the "superb decor" remains a sure thing.

Gamin de Paris (Au) ☽   19 | 16 | 16 | 36
51, rue Vieille du Temple, 4ᵉ (Hôtel-de-Ville/St-Paul), 01 42 78 97 24
☑ "Always packed and noisy", this candlelit "bistro-type restaurant with a neighborhood feel" in the Marais is "an old-time favorite that never disappoints" for those who like its "funky and fun" atmosphere and typical but "tasty" Southwestern cuisine; some find the staff "competently rough" (or should we say 'roughly competent'?), and sometimes "you have to wait", but "the food delivers", and that "makes the queuing worthwhile."

Gare (La) ◐   13 | 19 | 12 | 41
19, chaussée de la Muette, 16ᵉ (La Muette), 01 42 15 15 31;
fax 42 15 15 23; www.restaurantlagare.com
▣ The "cool location of an old train station" and a "fantastic
terrace" are among the reasons that a "trendy, young
crowd" stops by this "large space" in the 16th; maybe "this
railroad won't bring you to gastronomic paradise", since the
classic French "food is just average", and the service is
"relatively inefficient"; but that doesn't derail its "popularity
with an interesting late-night crowd, for whom going home
with somebody else might be the dessert"; N.B. the Decor
score may not reflect a recent renovation.

Garnier ◐   18 | 15 | 15 | 67
111, rue St-Lazare, 8ᵉ (St-Lazare), 01 43 87 50 40; fax 40 08 06 93
■ Just across the street from the Gare Saint-Lazare, this
venerable brasserie is something of "a neighborhood
secret" for its "superb shellfish stand" of "fresh, fresh
fruits de mer"; blending Lalique lamps, '70s stylings and
modern furnishings, the "setting lacks real character"
some sigh; but the "service is courteous", and the overall
experience, while expensive, is "well worth every euro."

Gastroquet (Le) ◐   – | – | – | M
10, rue Desnouettes, 15ᵉ (Convention/Porte de Versailles),
01 48 28 60 91; fax 45 33 23 70
The "friendly chef-owner" "comes to the table and explains
the menu" at this "good example of a neighborhood
restaurant catering to locals" of the 15th; the Traditional
French cuisine is "solid, if not stellar" (though there are
some "fantastic desserts"), and that, combined with the
"pleasant" service, "provides a sense of well-being."

Gauloise (La)   17 | 17 | 19 | 38
59, av de La Motte-Picquet, 15ᵉ (La Motte-Picquet-Grenelle),
01 47 34 11 64; fax 40 61 09 70
■ For a "nice no-surprises meal" and a "typical" Second
Empire decor, disciples doff their berets to this traditional
bistro "near the Ecole Militaire and the Eiffel Tower"; amid
an atmosphere that's "as smoky as its name" suggests,
"you can meet members of Parliament" (the late President
Mitterrand was a regular); "friendly service" and "a pretty
little terrace" are additional pluses.

Gavroche (Le) ◐▨   21 | 17 | 17 | 43
19, rue St-Marc, 2ᵉ (Bourse/Richelieu-Drouot),
01 42 96 89 70
▣ "Calling all meat eaters" to this "vibrant" "institution" in
the 2nd, which carries "the charm of the classic bistros of
yesteryear"; there's a "good selection of Beaujolais" to
wash down that "good beef", and while it gets "a bit
crowded" with all the "close tables", it remains "perfect"
for those seeking that "Parisian atmosphere."

Gaya Rive Gauche ⌧   22 | 17 | 21 | 61
44, rue du Bac, 7ᵉ (Rue du Bac), 01 45 44 73 73; fax 45 44 73 73
■ In the rue du Bac, this "bastion for the chic and sleek" offers "absolutely superb seafood" in a blond-wood bi-level dining room (it's "Americans upstairs and French downstairs") with a "somber, elegant modern decor"; a "staff that knows when to arrive promptly and when to stay away" serves a clientele of "publishing people" and the occasional celebrity; not surprisingly, the "marvelously fresh fish" is "expensive", and you'll need to "book ahead."

Georges ◑   17 | 26 | 15 | 53
Centre Georges Pompidou, 19, rue Beaubourg, 4ᵉ (Hôtel-de-Ville/Rambuteau), 01 44 78 47 99; fax 44 78 48 93
◪ It's all about the "amazing" "360-degree" view atop the Pompidou Center ("dining on the Paris rooftops, wow") at this "wildly chic" creation, since the servers, seemingly "hired for their catwalk struts", "take haughty to new heights" and the "Eclectic food interpretations", while "good, are definitely second to the buzzing atmosphere generated by the 'in'-crowd" (and "overpriced" too); up to you to decide if the "high-tech" "panorama of the city makes up for an arrogant staff and [barely] above-par cuisine."

GÉRARD BESSON ⌧   27 | 22 | 24 | VE
5, rue Coq Héron, 1ᵉʳ (Louvre-Rivoli/Palais Royal-Musée du Louvre), 01 42 33 14 74; fax 42 33 85 71; www.gerardbesson.com
■ "Simply extraordinary but not overly precious" is how fans describe chef-owner Gérard Besson's "old-school Classic French with an updated twist" near Les Halles; "great detail in the preparation" of the "delicious fare", including "superb game dishes" and a "fabulous" truffle menu, make most happy in a dining room that's been renovated to "lovely" effect; despite "congenial service", however, a few find the prices "hard to swallow."

Gitane (La) ⌧   ▽ 18 | 13 | 18 | 35
53 bis, av de La Motte-Picquet, 15ᵉ (La Motte-Picquet-Grenelle), 01 47 34 62 92; fax 40 65 94 01
■ "Unpretentious" but "prime Southwestern"–Classic French fare, administered by "really nice service", ensures this bistro in the 15th is "always full" with a "mixed crowd of graying heads and hipsters"; "generous portions" for modest prices attract urban gypsies (*gitanes*) of all varieties.

Giulio Rebellato   20 | 14 | 20 | 53
136, rue de la Pompe, 16ᵉ (Victor Hugo), 01 47 27 50 26
■ "You'd think you were in Italy", except that the "properly spiced", "fresh dishes aren't as wonderful" there say fans of this "small" "well-kept secret" in the 16th; a "chic", "jet-setty" crowd and "good service" make "it always a treat to dine" here – and make "reservations necessary" too.

Gli Angeli ●
▽ 17 | 12 | 10 | 30

5, rue St-Gilles, 3ᵉ (Chemin Vert/St-Paul), 01 42 71 05 80
◪ Near the Place des Vosges, this "neighborhood Italian" gets mixed notices; certainly it's "always full" ("reservations are essential") with those who find the pasta and seafood "very nice"; but opponents argue "it's lost it", particularly when it comes to the "the nasty staffers – not a big draw."

Goumard
24 | 23 | 22 | VE

9, rue Duphot, 1ᵉʳ (Madeleine), 01 42 60 36 07; fax 42 60 04 54; www.goumard.fr
◪ Following a "change in owners" and chefs, this elegant, established seafooder in the 1st reels in a range of opinions; if scores side with fans fawning over the "fantasy fish" menu, "beautiful Lalique-insets room" and "choreographed" waiters, a sizable school is "disappointed" by "dishes that strive for more than they attain" and "pompous service"; perhaps the problem is that while everything is technically "excellent", "at these prices you want to be thrilled."

Gourmand (Au) ⊠
– | – | – | M

22, rue de Vaugirard, 6ᵉ (Odéon), 01 43 26 26 45; fax 43 26 26 45
Located in a simple yellow dining room just across the street from the Senat in Saint-Germain, this table features talented young chef Christophe Courgeau (ex Arpège and Les Ambassadeurs), who is pulling in a well-heeled crowd of politicians and publishing types enamored with his market-fresh Bistro cooking, offered on a brief, daily changing menu.

Gourmets des Ternes (Les) ⊠
21 | 12 | 12 | 43

87, bd de Courcelles, 8ᵉ (Ternes), 01 42 27 43 04
◼ In the 8th, "one of the last real bistros in Paris" is "the real McCoy" when it comes to some of "the best meat in town", followed by heavenly "homemade baba au rhum"; it's usually "crowded" with a bawdy bunch, kept in line by "surly servers", but most find it worth putting up with the macho atmosphere for "the intense pleasure of really good chow."

Graindorge ⊠
▽ 21 | 16 | 21 | 49

15, rue de l'Arc-de-Triomphe, 17ᵉ (Charles de Gaulle-Etoile), 01 47 54 00 28; fax 47 54 00 28; www.legraindorge.free.fr
◼ "Extraordinary" enthuse fans of this Northern French in a slightly "isolated" location in the 17th; the "tasty" Belgian "cooking is careful and refined", and "you have to try" their selection of Flemish beers and genièvre, a regional version of gin; if the "tables are a bit tightly spaced", it doesn't deter the "great service."

Grand Café (Le) ●
16 | 20 | 15 | 44

4, bd des Capucines, 9ᵉ (Opéra), 01 43 12 19 00; fax 43 12 19 09; www.lesfreresblanc.com
◪ Yet "another belle-epoque brasserie" owned by the Frères Blanc, this "grande dame" near the Opéra Garnier

boasts "beautiful" decor – now, "if only the food matched"
sigh stalwarts ("nothing wrong", but "nothing outstanding
either"); its sidewalk cafe offers "great people-watching",
though, and "you can have a hot meal any time of the day",
even if "uneven service" makes its delivery uncertain.

Grand Colbert (Le) ☻ 16 | 23 | 16 | 45
*2, rue Vivienne, 2ᵉ (Bourse/Palais Royal-Musée du Louvre),
01 42 86 87 88; fax 42 86 82 65*
▲ A bit "hard to find" in the Passage Vivienne arcade, this
"classic of the 2nd" "defines brasserie", with "superb"
"movie-set" decor of mosaic floors, "potted palms, lots of
mirrors, high ceilings, booths and waiters bustling about";
although the "traditional" food seems "standard" to savants,
this remains a "great place to take visitors" if you think
they'd like "to sample 'scary' French cuisine like escargots
and frogs' legs" amid an "appealing" ambiance.

Grande Armée (La) ☻ 12 | 15 | 13 | 47
*3, av de la Grande-Armée, 16ᵉ (Charles de Gaulle-Etoile),
01 45 00 24 77; fax 45 00 95 50*
▲ On "the wrong side of the Arc de Triomphe", this "little
foodie boudoir" (the Napoleon III decor is by ubiquitous
decorator Jacques Garcia) is an address where "young
Eurotrash and old aristocrats mingle" with "neighborhood
locals" of the 16th; "cuisinewise, it's the worst of the Costes
brothers'" establishments cavil critics "uninspired" by the
Classic French fare and the "pretentious service"; but
advocates "appreciate that they serve quite late", which
works well for an "informal", "naughty dinner for two."

GRANDE CASCADE (LA) 25 | 28 | 25 | VE
*Bois de Boulogne, allée de Longchamp, 16ᵉ (Porte Maillot),
01 45 27 33 51; fax 42 88 99 06; www.lagrandecascade.fr*
■ With a "spectacular setting" – "Napoleon III's former
hunting lodge in the Bois de Boulogne" – this Haute Cuisine
table is a "romantic dream", whether you dine "outdoors in
summer or in the round room in winter"; though "outshone"
by the locale, chef Richard Mebkhout's "original yet not
ostentatious" cooking is certainly "nothing to complain
about", and the same goes for the "stupendous wine list"
and "impeccable" staff; so when that "special occasion"
calls for "true luxury", this could be the one.

Grande Rue (La) ☒ – | – | – | M
*117, rue de Vaugirard, 15ᵉ (Falguière), 01 47 34 96 12;
fax 47 34 96 12*
In a vintage 1900 setting decorated with flea-market finds,
this tiny, off-the-beaten-track bistro is "a terrific discovery"
in the 15th; those who have tracked it down delight in the
contemporary twists that young chef-owner Emmanuel
Billaud, who worked with Alain Ducasse and Joël Robuchon,
gives to Classic French dishes (roast rabbit with green

anise, monkfish poached with coriander); "try the lemon tart" if it's available.

Grandes Marches (Les) ◐   17 | 17 | 14 | 51
6, pl de la Bastille, 12ᵉ (Bastille), 01 43 42 90 32; fax 43 44 80 02; www.flobrasseries.com
■ "Right next door to the Opéra Bastille", this "modern" brasserie equipped with "sleek decor" by architects Christian and Elizabeth de Portzamparc is "a good place to stop into" before or after a performance; otherwise, the "not-very-original" cooking and "maddeningly slow service" inhibit very many standing ovations from surveyors for this "expensive" locale.

Grand Louvre (Le)   16 | 18 | 17 | 36
Musée du Louvre, under the Pyramid, 1ᵉʳ (Palais Royal-Musée du Louvre), 01 40 20 53 41; fax 42 86 04 63
◪ For "a quiet respite from the museum crowds", culture vultures perch at this Classic French with "elegant decor" by Jean-Michel Wilmotte; but while admirers argue it'd be "a place to dine even if you weren't visiting the Louvre", the "not-so-impressed" paint a different picture, saying it's mainly "a time-out when you're tired of looking at art"; for most, though, this is "the only place to re-energize between Mona Lisa and Marie de Medici."

GRAND VÉFOUR (LE) ⌘   28 | 28 | 27 | VE
Palais Royal, 17, rue de Beaujolais, 1ᵉʳ (Palais Royal-Musée du Louvre), 01 42 96 56 27; fax 42 86 80 71; www.relaischateaux.com
■ At this "*sans pareil*" Haute Cuisine in the Palais Royal, the "divine" Directoire decor ("Napoleon and Josephine ate here") is "sublimely transforming", and as for chef Guy Martin's "mind-boggling" meals, "the gods don't eat any better"; many "expect to be intimidated by the staff, but they are kind and helpful"; in short, "everything is extraordinary, including the bill" ("to avoid a third mortgage, go for the prix fixe lunch").

Grand Venise (Le) ⌘   ▽ 24 | 17 | 24 | 72
171, rue de la Convention, 15ᵉ (Convention), 01 45 32 49 71; fax 45 32 07 49
■ "Don't eat for two days before going" to this Italian in the 15th, since the "gargantuan" portions are enough to fill a gondola – a plentitude that is reflected on the bill; still, it's "a truly wonderful experience", since "the family [of owners] makes you feel right at home" as does the "wonderful staff, including mama."

Grill (Le) ⌘   – | – | – | E
Hyatt Paris Vendôme, 5, rue de la Paix, 2ᵉ (Opéra), 01 58 71 12 34; fax 58 71 10 32; www.paris.vendome.hyatt.com
Dynamo decorator Ed Tuttle's modern, open-kitchen design – a refreshingly "unusual environment for a hotel

restaurant" – serves as a dramatic backdrop to chef Christophe David's Classic French grills menu; a "convivial staff" ensures a "pleasant and attentive meal", but beware of prices as stunning as the nearby Place Vendôme shops.

Grille (La) ☒ — │ — │ — │ M

80, rue du Faubourg-Poissonnière, 10ᵉ (Poissonnière), 01 47 70 89 73

Few know this "charming" bistro in the 10th, but those who do find it "just right for the price and a typical Paris experience"; expect a "tiny space" (30 seats) with friendly staffers, flea-market decor of antique lace, bric-a-brac and "very noisy" caged birds, along with an "admirable" Traditional French menu that never swerves from classics such as grilled turbot and profiteroles.

Grille St-Germain (La) ◕ 16 │ 15 │ 17 │ 36

14, rue Mabillon, 6ᵉ (Mabillon), 01 43 54 16 87; fax 43 54 52 88

◧ While this "comforting and conventional" corner in Saint-German has changed hands, all its aspects remain untouched, from the "interesting" decor of Studio Harcourt black-and-white photos and '30s "old movie posters" to the "old-fashioned" Bistro cuisine and "straightforward service"; a "low-key" party vibe prevails, reflecting its popularity with a Parisian nightcrawling crowd.

Guinguette de Neuilly (La) ▽ 12 │ 15 │ 14 │ 39

12, bd Georges Seurat, Neuilly (Pont de Levallois), 01 46 24 25 04; fax 47 38 20 49

◧ Foreigners find "this is what being French is all about" when it comes to the jolly sepia-tinted atmosphere of this 1920s veteran on the Ile de la Jatte; some scold the Classic French cooking as "bad, bad", but this remains an ideal place to "let yourself go on the edge of the Seine" like something straight out of Seurat (painterly homages to whom hang on the walls).

GUY SAVOY, RESTAURANT ☒ 28 │ 25 │ 28 │ VE

18, rue Troyon, 17ᵉ (Charles de Gaulle-Etoile/Ternes), 01 43 80 40 61; fax 46 22 43 09; www.guysavoy.com

■ For a "true Haute Cuisine experience" – "terrific, not terrifying" – the knowledgeable kneel in homage to Guy Savoy's table in the 17th; the "innovative" fare, including a "heaven-sent artichoke-truffle soup", "keeps getting better" ("the chef-owner is usually here, unlike some other places"), and it's served by a "flawless", "surprisingly unstuffy" staff amid "California"-like "modern decor"; even the "cost-conscious" confess this is "worth the splurge" for "a Beethoven symphony of taste and smell."

Hangar (Le) ◕☒⇥ ▽ 21 │ 8 │ 16 │ 36

12, impasse Berthaud, 3ᵉ (Rambuteau), 01 42 74 55 44

■ In a dead-end passage near the Pompidou Center, this "laid-back", "little hole-in-the-wall" is "full of culinary

surprises" in its Classic French "dishes that are simple"
but done with "delicacy", such as the "seared foie gras"
or "perfect poached salmon"; the room's rather "boring",
and the "cash-only [policy] is a drag, too" – but that's the
price you pay for "one of the best values to be had in Paris."

Hédiard ☒
21 | 18 | 16 | 40 |

21, pl de la Madeleine, 8ᵉ (Madeleine), 01 43 12 88 99;
fax 43 12 88 98; www.hediard.fr
■ Situated within the luxury grocer on the Place de la
Madeleine, this Contemporary French with a vaguely
Colonial atmosphere (parquet floors, wooden shutters)
offers "fantastic" fare that "you'll love" assuming that
"you can get served" by the staff; even so, it's certainly
"several cuts above a walk-in cafe", and of course there's
"wonderful shopping in the store" afterwards.

HÉLÈNE DARROZE ☒
24 | 22 | 20 | 96 |

4, rue d'Assas, 6ᵉ (Rennes/Sèvres-Babylone), 01 42 22 00 11;
fax 42 22 25 40; www.relaischateaux.com
◪ It may be "rare for a female chef to reach this level of
excellence in French restaurants", but Hélène Darroze has
made the ascent, serving up "cutting-edge" New French–
Southwestern "food from heaven" at her dining room with
"warm contemporary decor" in the 6th; a few pessimists
pout the place is "seriously pretentious", especially
the "erratic servers" who swing from "oblivious" to
"professional"; but most agree that if "it's not the best, it's
certainly in the running."

Hermitage (L') ☒
– | – | – | M |

5, bd de Denain, 10ᵉ (Gare du Nord), 01 48 78 77 09;
fax 42 85 17 27; www.restaurantlhermitage.com
Though situated close to the Gare du Nord, this Traditional
French is worth considering even if you're not traveling; its
warm parquet floors, ochre color scheme and low lighting
make for a relaxing atmosphere, which is heightened by
unusually friendly service, a well-chosen wine list and
bread baked on the premises.

Higuma
16 | 6 | 10 | 15 |

32 bis, rue Ste-Anne, 1ᵉʳ (Pyramides), 01 47 03 38 59; fax 47 03 38 52
◪ "Don't be put off by the rather dingy decor" at this
Nipponese near the Opéra Garnier – just concentrate on
the feed, which includes "finger-licking-good" gyozas and
"true Japanese curry"; it's "perfect for a quick lunch" or a
dinner, provided you "don't expect friendly service (they're
turning the tables over too fast to care)."

HIPPOPOTAMUS ●
10 | 10 | 10 | 25 |

29, rue Berger, 1ᵉʳ (Les Halles), 01 45 08 00 29; fax 40 41 98 63
1, bd des Capucines, 2ᵉ (Opéra), 01 47 42 75 70; fax 42 65 23 08
1, bd Beaumarchais, 4ᵉ (Bastille), 01 44 61 90 40; fax 48 87 84 67
(continued)

(continued)

HIPPOPOTAMUS

9, rue Lagrange, 5ᵉ (Maubert-Mutualité), 01 43 54 13 99; fax 44 07 18 20
119, bd du Montparnasse, 6ᵉ (Vavin), 01 43 20 37 04; fax 43 22 68 95
20, rue Quentin Bauchart, 8ᵉ (George V), 01 47 20 30 14; fax 47 20 95 31
8, bd St-Denis, 10ᵉ (Strasbourg-St-Denis), 01 53 38 80 28; fax 53 38 80 26
68, bd du Montparnasse, 14ᵉ (Montparnasse-Bienvenüe), 01 40 64 14 94; fax 43 21 46 10
12, avenue du Maine, 15ᵉ (Duroc/Montparnasse-Bienvenüe), 01 42 22 36 75; fax 45 44 46 18 ⊠
CNIT, 2, pl de la Défense, Puteaux (La Défense-Grande Arche), 01 46 92 13 75; fax 46 92 13 69
www.hippopotamus.fr
Additional locations throughout Paris
◪ "Pretty mediocre" is the prevailing opinion about this omnipresent steakhouse chain, whose branches are suffused by the "smell of grill smoke" and service that is at best "absent-minded"; but those undeterred note "in an expensive city, it's cheap and reliable", and works well as a "place to take the kids" or "for late at night."

HIRAMATSU ⊠   28 | – | 27 | VE

52, rue de Longchamp, 16ᵉ (Trocadéro), 01 56 81 08 80; www.hiramatsu.co.jp
■ At his new, more spacious setting in the 16th, "rising star" Hiroyuki Hiramatsu offers an "insanely creative", "intelligent interpretation of Haute Cuisine" in which "French and Japanese food meld seamlessly" and is brought to table by "energetic young servers" who are "attentive but not intrusive" as they negotiate the spare elegance of the dark wood and ivory-toned premises; "prices are terribly high", and "it's hard to get into", but for a "romantic splurge" most say it's "worth every euro."

Huîtrier (L')   ▽ 18 | 9 | 15 | 46

16, rue Saussier-Leroy, 17ᵉ (Ternes), 01 40 54 83 44; fax 40 54 83 86
■ It may be "off the beaten track" and the decor is dull, but mavens maintain this seafood bar in the 17th is worth it for "the mountains of" "marvelous oysters", along with a nice menu of "the freshest fish"; if a little expensive, it's "always dependable", which explains why "it can be crowded."

I Golosi ●⊠   18 | 12 | 16 | 46

6, rue de la Grange-Batelière, 9ᵉ (Richelieu-Drouot), 01 48 24 18 63; fax 45 23 18 96
◪ The "short but well designed menu" and "good selection of wines by the glass" have won this Italian with a "'70s decor" a solid following among the arts-and-antiques crowd who frequent the nearby Drouot auction rooms; however,

while the fare is "inventive", its quality can be "irregular", and "rather distant service" doesn't "compensate."

Il Baccello ⊠ `20` `18` `22` `46`
33, rue Cardinet, 17ᵉ (Monceau/Wagram), 01 43 80 63 60;
fax 43 80 63 65

■ "You won't find any pizza or pasta bolognaise" at this "well-hidden Italian-Med jewel" in the 17th, since young chef Raphael Bembaron proposes a "refined" and "highly original" menu that reflects his training at Joia, the famed Milanese meat-free restaurant; it's sometimes "smoky" in the small dining room with a "surprisingly Japanese-looking decor", but the "personal attention" from the staff creates a "highly agreeable atmosphere", and prices are "reasonable" for such "excellent" food.

Il Barone ●⊠ `19` `5` `13` `38`
5, rue Léopold Robert, 14ᵉ (Raspail/Vavin), 01 43 20 87 14;
fax 43 20 87 14

■ If you're after a "genuine trattoria in Paris", come to Montparnasse, where this *famiglia*-style place offers a "really good antipasti buffet" and "puntarella salad like you only find in Rome"; no one minds the "too-tight" digs, but "to be hip, make sure you sit in the back room" and not in the crowded one up front.

Il Carpaccio `-` `-` `-` `E`
Hôtel Royal Monceau, 37, av Hoche, 8ᵉ (Charles de Gaulle-Etoile/Ternes), 01 42 99 98 90; fax 42 99 89 94; www.royalmonceau.com

Known to only a few reviewers, this "refined", "real" Italian opening onto the courtyard garden of the Hôtel Royal Monceau wins raves for "the best risotto in Paris", among many other "inventive" and "authentic" dishes; the "service is impeccable", and the decor was recently remodelled by designer Jacques Garcia.

Il Cortile ⊠ `23` `21` `20` `70`
Hôtel Castille, 37, rue Cambon, 1ᵉʳ (Concorde/Madeleine), 01 44 58 45 67; fax 44 58 44 00

◪ Few know it, but the "excellent French interpretation of Italian cuisine" you'll find at this 1st arrondissement address is actually the work of a talented Dutchman, Tjaco Van Eijken; the "lovely courtyard" garden with a fountain and faience tiles is a midsummer's night dream, but views vary about the staff, which is generally "gracious" but sometimes "young and clumsy"; a few fuss it's "overrated", but to happier hearts, this hotel eatery is "heaven."

Ile (L') ● `15` `19` `11` `44`
170, quai de Stalingrad, Parc de l'Ile St-Germain, Issy-les-Moulineaux (RER Issy-Val de Seine), 01 41 09 99 99; fax 41 09 99 19

■ With a waterside location in Issy-les-Moulineaux ("the country only minutes from Paris"), this "trendy TV and show-biz place" is a "pretty factory", perfect for "out-of-towners or to celebrate a birthday" ("every five minutes, another cake is brought out"); it's "not very interesting from a culinary point of view", but the combo of Classic and Contemporary French dishes offers "something for every taste"; "disorganized service" is a problem though – "even in a fashion restaurant, you need professional service."

Il Etait une Oie dans le Sud-Ouest ☒
∇ 15 | 8 | 14 | 35

8, rue Gustave Flaubert, 17ᵉ (Ternes/Courcelles), 01 43 80 18 30; fax 43 80 99 50

☑ "One of the best deals" in solid Southwestern specialties is at this "pleasant" place near the Place des Ternes; perhaps "they could make a little [more] effort" when it comes to decor and service, but at "these prices, you don't hesitate", especially when the foie gras is so "succulent."

Il Punto ☒
– | – | – | M

2, rue du Général Henrion Bertier, Neuilly (Pont-de-Neuilly), 01 46 24 21 06; fax 47 47 46 71

Featuring a taupe-and-ivory interior – kind of a stylized take on a medieval castle – this well-mannered new Italian pulls in professionals (all well-dressed – this is Neuilly, after all) for lunch and dinner; the menu favors dishes from Sardinia, and many of its cheerful servers come from over the Alps as well.

Il Viccolo ☒
17 | 13 | 17 | 44

34, rue Mazarine, 6ᵉ (Odéon), 01 43 25 01 11

☑ In Saint-Germain, this "affable, trendy Italian" serves up "modern", "original" fare that most "enjoy immeasurably", even if some shrug it's sometimes "so-so"; with glassed-in sidewalk seating, the site may be "decorated like an airport hotel bar", but the "welcoming atmosphere" is definitely "first class", even if you're flying "solo."

Inagiku ☒
∇ 17 | 11 | 15 | 53

14, rue de Pontoise, 5ᵉ (Maubert-Mutualité), 01 43 54 70 07; fax 40 51 74 44

■ The seafood is "irreproachably fresh" at this quiet, "reliable Japanese" in the Latin Quarter, where it's "fun to watch the chef griddle and sizzle your shrimp", scallops and "other delicacies" "under your nose" "on a heated table"; "though it is, alas, expensive", it's "a good option on the Left Bank, where relatively few" teppanyaki places exist.

Indiana Café ◗
8 | 8 | 9 | 23

7, bd des Capucines, 2ᵉ (Opéra), 01 42 68 02 22
1, pl de la République, 3ᵉ (République), 01 48 87 82 35
130, bd St-Germain, 6ᵉ (Odéon), 01 46 34 66 31
235-237, rue du Faubourg St-Honoré, 8ᵉ (Ternes), 01 44 09 80 00
79, bd de Clichy, 9ᵉ (Place de Clichy), 01 48 74 42 61
14, pl de la Bastille, 11ᵉ (Bastille), 01 44 75 79 80

(continued)
Indiana Café
*72, bd du Montparnasse, 14ᵉ (Montparnasse-Bienvenüe),
01 43 35 36 28; fax 43 35 07 25*

☑ Yup, "Paris has it all – even" a "parody of American food" sneer cynics about this "touristy" chain serving "bad burgers" and a "sorry excuse for Tex-Mex eats" ("Tex-Mess would be more like it"); fans find it "practical for a rapid", "reasonable" snack, but more folks urge "avoid" the "poor service" and "dark", "strange Americana-style decor" that's so "generic you "might as well be in Indianapolis" – though come to think of it, "why call a Tex-Mex place Indiana?"

Indra ⌧
∇ 21 | 18 | 18 | 49

*10, rue du Commandant Rivière, 8ᵉ (St-Philippe-du-Roule),
01 43 59 46 40; fax 42 25 00 32*

■ Equipped with an "amusing theatrical decor", this thirtysomething has been "one of the best Indians in Paris" for nearly 40 years; though some speculate that "the cooking's been toned down for French tastes", most recommend you come here when you're in a hurry for curry, even if it is "a bit expensive" (after all, "they have to pay for their site" in the high-rent 8th).

Isami ⌧
24 | 12 | 16 | 52

4, quai d'Orléans, 4ᵉ (Pont-Marie), 01 40 46 06 97

☑ This tiny Japanese on the Ile Saint-Louis is "incontestably the best place in Paris for sushi and sashimi prepared by a real master" – which means, "dammit, it's always full when you want to go"; those who persevere proclaim the service and "atmosphere a little cold" and warn that while "prices are low" on the "limited menu", "the desire to eat more and more creates a big bill"; still, "the technique and exceptional quality of the fish" make all worthwhile.

JACQUES CAGNA ⌧
25 | 24 | 24 | VE

*14, rue des Grands-Augustins, 6ᵉ (Odéon/St-Michel),
01 43 26 49 39; fax 43 54 54 48; www.jacquescagna.com*

■ "It's always a treat to dine with Jacques" declare devotees of this "special-occasion" veteran in the 6th, which for nearly 40 years has been serving traditional, "rich" Haute Cuisine "as if nouvelle had never been invented"; it's an "elegant" "old-world" experience here throughout, from the "charming" 17th-century environs, adorned "with beautiful oil paintings", to the service that's "a little stuffy" but "pleasantly" "attentive"; "dated" or not, "this is one of the last truly romantic spots left."

JAMIN ⌧
25 | 20 | 24 | VE

*32, rue de Longchamp, 16ᵉ (Boissière/Trocadéro),
01 45 53 00 07; fax 45 53 00 15*

■ While "it's no longer the temple of Joël Robuchon", his protégé chef Benoît Guichard still insures "creative" Haute

Cuisine dining at this "discreet spot" in the 16th; sometimes the "service is initially cool, but it warms up" fast in the pastel-colored "pretty room", so most visitors "can't wait to go back" to experience its "enormous charm"; P.S. "lunch is a great value if you order the prix fixe."

Jardin (Le) ⊠   21 | 23 | 21 | 88

Hôtel Royal Monceau, 37, av Hoche, 8ᵉ (Charles de Gaulle-Etoile), 01 42 99 98 70; fax 42 99 89 94; www.royalmonceau.com
■ "One of the nicest settings in Paris" – a dining room "covered by a glass dome, in a garden" – imparts a "sense of calm" to this address near the Etoile; it's a "good place to slow down" and sample "nice Med" and New French specialties and a southern regional wine list, all the while being waited upon by "refined servers"; N.B. a recent decor re-do by Jacques Garcia, complete with his characteristic Napoleon-style tents, may outdate the Decor score.

Jardin des Cygnes   20 | 24 | 23 | 92

Hôtel Prince de Galles, 33, av George V, 8ᵉ (George V), 01 53 23 78 50; fax 53 23 78 82; www.luxurycollection.com
■ "The garden is absolute heaven on a nice night" say surveyors about this "oasis of calm" in the 8th; "attentive servers" proffer "a variety of pleasing dishes" in the Classic French mode three times a day; and while some joke "it only costs two arms and legs", the "prix fixes are great deals", especially on the "very good breakfast buffet."

Jardinier (Le)   – | – | – | M

5, rue Richer, 9ᵉ (Bonne Nouvelle/Poissonière), 01 48 24 79 79; fax 48 24 79 79; lejardinier.lesrestos.com
This tiny restaurant's fussy decor – think framed show posters, bright lighting and elaborate curtains – may not suggest a fine culinary touch, but the quality of the Traditional French menu has won it a steady crowd of regulars; located along Les Grands Boulevards, in an area dominated by fast-food shops, it draws businesspeople at noon and young locals and theatergoers in the evening.

Jardins de Bagatelle (Les)   18 | 22 | 15 | 67

Parc de Bagatelle, Route de Sèvres, 16ᵉ (Pont-de-Neuilly), 01 40 67 98 29; fax 40 67 93 04; www.restaurantbagatelle.com
◪ This Classic French is, "in the summer, a great place to have lunch" "or a romantic dinner", thanks to its "beautiful setting" in the Bois de Boulogne (they've even managed "to get rid of the mosquitoes"); pessimists posit it's "rather pricey" for "middling-quality" cuisine, but a "walk through the Bagatelle Gardens" "makes it all worthwhile."

Jarrasse   – | – | – | E

4, av de Madrid, Neuilly (Pont-de-Neuilly), 01 46 24 07 56; fax 40 88 35 60
A slick renovation – clean lines, minimal furnishings and fabric lanterns – imparts a Japanese-style lightness to this

Classic French, a Neuilly fixture since 1932; the revamp
also added more contemporary preparations to the seafood-
oriented menu, all the better to appeal to its affluent
and business clientele.

Jean-Paul Hévin 🖾 ▽ 22 | 20 | 19 | 26
*231, rue St-Honoré, 1er (Madeleine/Tuileries), 01 55 35 35 96;
fax 55 35 35 97; www.jphevin.com*
■ Bet you didn't know the 1st arrondissement branch of the
"earth's best chocolatier" also possessed a tearoom on
the second floor; those who did find its snacklike savories
such as quiches and salads "quite easy on the taste buds" –
though of course, others just "go for the pastries" and the
"most sumptuous gateaux in the world"; with its cocoa-
colored decor, some even believe it "a blessing for a [light]
business lunch", presumably with a sweet-toothed client.

Je Thé . . . Me 🖾 ▽ 21 | 22 | 20 | 38
*4, rue d'Alleray, 15e (Convention/Vaugirard), 01 48 42 48 30;
fax 48 42 70 66; www.jetheme.tk*
☑ In the 15th arrondissement, this tearoom suits many to a
'T' indeed, since the "extremely hospitable", "bilingual"
"family that runs this place inspires joy and happiness";
served in a fin-de-siècle setting "with cachet", the light
"simple plates" "will not let you down"; "you eat well and
the owner has a sense of humor, so what else do you want?"

J'Go ◗🖾 – | – | – | M
*4, rue Drouot, 9e (Richelieu-Drouot), 01 40 22 09 09;
fax 40 22 07 15; www.lejgo.com*
Chain-smoking Parisian yuppies love to go to this 9th
arrondissement outpost of a popular Bordeaux chain,
whose name is a Franglais pun on the *gigot* (roast leg of
lamb) – a signature dish on the Southwestern French menu;
other pluses are long hours, easy prices and smiling (if
somewhat chaotic) service.

Joe Allen ◗ 16 | 15 | 18 | 38
*30, rue Pierre Lescot, 1er (Etienne Marcel), 01 42 36 70 13;
fax 42 36 90 80; www.joeallenparis.com*
☑ "A little corner of America" in Les Halles, this "low-key"
branch of the NY theater district restaurant offers *"très
bon* côte de boeuf, a burger worthy of the name and
cheesecake" in "large portions (American-style)"; some
scold "why bother when you're in Paris, for God's sake",
especially since to them this joint is "past its prime"; but
expats parry that "it's a nice haven when you need a little
break from the whole Europe thing."

Jo Goldenberg ◗ 13 | 10 | 12 | 31
*7, rue des Rosiers, 4e (St-Paul), 01 48 87 20 16;
fax 42 78 15 29*
☑ "The nostalgia is almost as heavy as the chopped liver"
at this 1920 delicatessen "in the heart of the Marais"

(Paris' historic Hebrew quarter) that's "a standard" for the Jewish "specialties"; but "don't expect grandma's cooking" carp critics "disappointed" in the "overpriced", "tasteless" fare and staff that acts "as if they were doing you a service to allow you in"; "if you need a deli fix, this is the place"; otherwise, "don't bother."

Joséphine "Chez Dumonet" ⊠   19 | 16 | 17 | 53 |
117, rue du Cherche-Midi, 6ᵉ (Duroc/Falguière), 01 45 48 52 40; fax 42 84 06 83

■ Voilà, here's a "bistro-lover's bistro" on the Left Bank, "authentic" in everything from the "old-fashioned atmosphere" and "1900-style decor" to the "Traditional French food and service" (Grand Marnier soufflé, anyone?); one pleasantly modern touch: "you choose the size of your portions" – full-serving or "small-plate", the latter "a nice option for grazing."

JULES VERNE (LE)   24 | 27 | 24 | VE |
Tour Eiffel, 2nd level, 7ᵉ (Bir-Hakeim), 01 45 55 61 44; fax 47 05 29 41

■ The Classic French cooking may be "*magnifique*", but it's the "magical setting" atop the Eiffel Tower "that makes this place worthwhile", since you dine with all of Paris at your feet; not surprisingly, it's "chock-full of tourists", which may be why the maitre d' displays "a little too much attitude with the altitude", though the rest of the staff is "attentive and polished" as they negotiate the '70s-disco, "black-clad interior"; tabs, of course, are sky-high, but this is the "No. 1 impress-your-date place in town."

Jumeaux (Les) ⊠   – | – | – | M |
73, rue Amelot, 11ᵉ (Chemin Vert), 01 43 14 27 00; fax 43 14 27 00

Near the Cirque d'Hiver in the 11th, this small site run by "eponymous twins who are the maitre d' and the cook" is "just delightful" with "good service" and "amazing" food that offers an "imaginative" mixture of "Asian flavors and New French cuisine" on a "menu that changes all the time"; decorated with modern art, the "unpretentious" dining room has a "certain New York feel to it."

Juvéniles ⊠   16 | 12 | 18 | 32 |
47, rue de Richelieu, 1ᵉʳ (Bourse/Palais Royal-Musée du Louvre), 01 42 97 46 49; fax 42 60 31 52

☑ "Known for its amazing selection" of varietals, this *bar à vins* near the Palais Royal is "an inspired, wacky, friendly" joint with a "funky staff" led by owner "Tim Johnston, the irrepressible Scotsman", who some say is its "key selling point"; an Eclectic array of "well prepared, wine-friendly food" – this has got to be Paris' "only place with haggis regularly on the menu" – is on hand; only the "noisy", "unkempt" surroundings seem a bit juvenile.

Kaïten ◐⧄   – | – | – | M

*63, rue Pierre Charron, 8ᵉ (Franklin D. Roosevelt), 01 43 59 78 78;
fax 43 59 71 51*

At this "amusing", moderately priced Japanese just off the
Champs, the "conveyor belt could make you fear the worst,
but the sushi, sashimi and maki [revolving on it] are really
very good"; regulars might follow them up with a hot dish
or two, then finish with some "green-tea ice cream that
alone is worth elbowing up to the bar for."

Kambodgia ⧄   ▽ 20 | 20 | 19 | 45

*15, rue de Bassano, 16ᵉ (Charles de Gaulle-Etoile/George V),
01 47 23 31 80; fax 47 20 41 22*

■ "Don't be put off by the walk down to the basement"
room of this Asian in the 16th, since the bamboo-and-
tropical-woods interior is "exceptional", "the service is
irreproachable" and the Cambodian and Vietnamese
cuisine is "amazingly authentic"; all in all, it's a "refined"
experience that "transports you" to Southeast Asia.

Khun Akorn   ▽ 18 | 18 | 15 | 35

*8, av de Taillebourg, 11ᵉ (Nation), 01 43 56 20 03;
fax 40 09 18 44*

■ Even if you have to guide your elephant to an outlying
part of the 11th, it's worth it, since this "creative" Thai
table, though "one of the lesser-known in Paris, offers the
best bang for the buck" followers find; the regulars also
rave about the "beautiful" "rooftop terrace", which come
summer offers a "bucolic view" "for a lovers' dinner."

Kim Anh   ▽ 23 | 16 | 23 | 42

*51, av Emile Zola, 15ᵉ (Charles Michels), 01 45 79 40 96;
fax 40 59 49 78*

■ You "absolutely have to discover" this compact corner
in the 15th for "the best Vietnamese food outside of
Saigon"; Viet vets vaunt the "immensely subtle cooking",
including "perfect brochettes de boeuf with lemongrass",
"nems stuffed with more crab than you'd think they could
fit in the tiny kitchen" and "great sweet-corn pudding",
dished out by "helpful, charming servers"; small wonder
the adoring aver they've "been here at least 100 times and
never been disappointed."

Kinugawa ⧄   22 | 14 | 18 | 65

*9, rue du Mont Thabor, 1ᵉʳ (Tuileries), 01 42 60 65 07;
fax 42 60 57 36*
*4, rue St-Philippe-du-Roule, 8ᵉ (St-Philippe-du-Roule),
01 45 63 08 07*

◪ "Beautiful, delicate sushi" and Kyoto-style delicacies
rule at this duo in the 1st and 8th, "classic, consistent"
contenders for "the best Japanese in town"; but many
mutter their traditional decor falls "far from reaching
the cuisine's heights", and nearly all agree the pair's

"outrageously overpriced", with tabs that practically "justify a trip to Japan" instead.

Kiosque (Le)
17 | 16 | 15 | 44

1, pl de Mexico, 16ᵉ (Trocadéro), 01 47 27 96 98;
fax 45 53 89 79

☑ At this "lively" Classic French overlooking "a pretty square" in the 16th, "a different region stars on the menu every week – an amusing concept even if the cooking is uneven"; as its name suggests, "the inventive decor has a journalistic theme" ("they distribute a local newspaper" with the meal), and while the "service is slow", "the place is always busy" with well-heeled crowds craving "comfort food in a relaxed atmosphere."

Kong ◑
14 | 24 | 14 | 45

Pont Neuf Bldg., 1, rue du Pont Neuf, 1ᵉʳ (Pont-Neuf),
01 40 39 09 00; fax 40 39 09 10; www.kong.fr

■ This "cool place" offers "spectacular views" from the top floor of the Pont Neuf building, "enticing music" and "a nice bar area"; but while enthusiasts find the Eclectic "cuisine full of imagination", critics cry "Kong is the king of rip-offs": "entirely too expensive", and its "servers nowhere to be found"; at least Philippe Starck's Asiatique "renovation of the old Samaritaine building is superb" – though some wonder "how long do you want to see geisha holograms on the back of your chair?"

Lac-Hong ☒
21 | 12 | 15 | 49

67, rue Lauriston, 16ᵉ (Boissière/Victor Hugo),
01 47 55 87 17

■ "Worth finding on the streets of the 16th", this midsize site serves some of "the best Asian food in Paris" "short of Hanoi"; though the "waiters are helpful", many deem the decor kind of "kitschy" and sigh about "sky-rocketing prices", "but if you like genuine Vietnamese food" you'll be happy "even after seeing the bill."

LADURÉE
21 | 23 | 16 | 34

21, rue Bonaparte, 6ᵉ (St-Sulpice), 01 44 07 64 87;
fax 44 07 64 93
75, av des Champs-Elysées, 8ᵉ (George V), 01 40 75 08 75;
fax 40 75 06 75 ◑
16, rue Royale, 8ᵉ (Concorde/Madeleine), 01 42 60 21 79;
fax 49 27 01 95
Printemps, 64, bd Haussmann, 9ᵉ (Havre-Caumartin),
01 42 82 40 10; fax 42 82 62 00 ☒
www.laduree.fr

■ Others "may be more trendsetting, but this remains the classic patisserie" say the sweet-toothed about these "upscale tea salons" known for their "plush atmosphere" (especially the Champs address, with its "Napoleon III–style delirious decor"); "they can be noisy" and the "zippy" staff "impolite", but they're still "places to frequent from morning till night": "a must for breakfast", "lunch when shopping" or "wonderful teas"; no matter which meal, the "world-famous macaroons" "are not to be missed."

Languedoc (Le) 17 | 13 | 18 | 31
64, bd de Port-Royal, 5ᵉ (Les Gobelins/Port Royal), 01 47 07 24 47
☑ Time seems to have stopped at this long-running, "homey" "old-style bistro with mimeographed menus that never change" in the 5th; it serves "consistently good" Classic French food that "offers a glimpse of the flavorful region" of Languedoc; prices are "inexpensive", but there are a couple of complaints about "skimpy portions."

Lao Siam - | - | - | M
49, rue de Belleville, 19ᵉ (Belleville/Pyrénées), 01 40 40 09 68
It may be a bit of a trudge up to Belleville in the 19th, but most don't mind when there's this "excellent Thai" table at the end of the slog; both the service and "the decor are neutral", but that "lets you concentrate on the essential" – the "fresh dishes" on the "enormous, original menu"; "prices are a lot lower than at other places with the same level of quality."

Lao Tseu ▽ 16 | 12 | 17 | 34
209, bd St-Germain, 7ᵉ (Rue du Bac), 01 45 48 30 06; fax 40 59 91 21
☑ The worldly, well-heeled citizenry of the 7th come into (or take out from) this "good neighborhood Chinese" whose dishes are savored for their "subtle flavors", though malcontents mutter "even dishes classified as spicy are really not"; "the staff is terribly nice", which makes it easy to overlook the nonexistent decor.

Lapérouse ☒ 21 | 26 | 22 | 91
51, quai des Grands-Augustins, 6ᵉ (Pont-Neuf/St-Michel), 01 43 26 90 14; fax 43 26 99 39
■ "Spreading through several elegant rooms" "overlooking the Seine" and decorated with "18th-century antiques", this "institution" in the 6th is "one of Paris' most romantic restaurants", ideal "if you like to kiss between courses" or as a "place to propose" (legend has it that the scratched-up mirrors reflect ladies testing the diamonds before saying yes or no); happily, chef Alain Hacquard has "rejuvenated" the Haute Cuisine, which now is "lovely", if "traditional" – as are the "discreet, unhurried waiters."

LASSERRE ☒ 26 | 27 | 27 | VE
17, av Franklin D. Roosevelt, 8ᵉ (Franklin D. Roosevelt), 01 43 59 02 13; fax 45 63 72 23
■ A meal at this "magical place" in the 8th is "more like attending an elegant dinner party than being at a restaurant", though it'd have to be one fabulous fête to offer the level of Haute Cuisine of chef Jean-Louis Nomicos;

"a dream for food and wine, if a nightmare for your wallet", this "very romantic" "reminder of days gone by" is also memorable for "service that's impeccable without being stuffy" and the famous "ceiling that opens up" on summer nights; in sum, "it doesn't get better than this."

LAURENT ⊠   24 | 26 | 24 | VE |
41, av Gabriel, 8ᵉ (Champs-Elysées-Clémenceau), 01 42 25 00 39; fax 45 62 45 21; www.le-laurent.com

◪ Come to this "elegant", "extremely expensive" belle-epoque pavilion in the Champs-Elysées gardens "to meet the crème de la crème of French politics (there's always a minister or two in the dining room)" or just for the "sublime" Haute Cuisine, the "team of attentive waiters" and the "great garden patio for romantic summer dining"; snipers snip that the "classic" food needs "a restorative kick toward modernity" to "justify the outrageous prices", but most insist on the pleasure of this "fabulous piece of Paris theater."

Lavinia ⊠   15 | 17 | 15 | 39 |
3-5, bd de la Madeleine, 8ᵉ (Madeleine), 01 42 97 20 20; fax 42 97 54 50

◼ "A great address for a business lunch" (they don't serve in the evening), the dining room at this shop with reportedly "the largest selection of wines" in Paris – "any of which you can try with your meal" "at retail prices" – is a "sleeper" with "good", "intelligently conceived" Classic French dishes; and if it gets "a little noisy sometimes", most are too happy swirling the contents of their Reidel glasses to notice.

LEDOYEN ⊠   25 | 27 | 25 | VE |
1, av Dutuit, 8ᵉ (Champs-Elysées-Clémenceau/Concorde), 01 53 05 10 00; fax 47 42 55 01

◪ "Perched above the trees overlooking the Champs-Elysées" gardens is this pretty Second Empire pavilion with "elegant decor" that's "a fabulous place to have a special meal", aided by chef Christian Le Squer's "creative yet classical" Haute Cuisine and an "attentive" staff; pessimists find the "formality" of the food and service "somewhat impersonal", but scores support those who say it's "superb in every way" – even if you'll pay stratospheric prices.

Legrand Filles et Fils ⊠   – | – | – | M |
(fka Caves Legrand)
Galerie Vivienne, 1, rue de la Banque, 2ᵉ (Bourse/Palais Royal), 01 42 60 07 12; fax 42 61 25 51; www.caves-legrand.com

"Isn't life great?" exclaims the small but happy crew who've discovered this "pleasant, efficient" wine bar in the Galerie Vivienne; sit under the glass-roofed terrace out front, or amid the "warm atmosphere" inside, and enjoy light eats – salads, sandwiches, cold meat and cheese – made with "first-rate ingredients" and accompanied by a 5,000-label strong selection of "inexpensive, good" labels.

Lei   – | – | – | M

17, av de la Motte-Picquet, 7ᵉ (Ecole Militaire/La Tour-Maubourg),
01 47 05 07 37

Yes, this is "another Italian" address, from the owners
of the popular Les Cailloux and Sasso – and given that
pedigree, "it's a hit with the young fashion crowd of the
7th"; though "not vast, its menu" offers eats from all over
The Boot, served in minimalist decor of cement floors, bare
walls and unadorned "windows everywhere"; and if the
jaded jeer it's "neither better nor worse than all the others",
kinder hearts "hope it keeps going."

Léna et Mimile ☒   ▽ 16 | 20 | 19 | 36

32, rue Tournefort, 5ᵉ (Censier-Daubenton/Place Monge),
01 47 07 72 47; fax 45 35 41 94

☑ "The setting is lovely and the service is sincere" at this
recently enlarged 1937-vintage bistro with a "pretty"
perched terrace "in between the Panthéon" and "the busy
Rue Mouffetard"; maybe the food, "a mix of original and
Traditional" French dishes, "is not that special, but who
cares" when you've got such a "heavenly" location that it
"doesn't even feel like you're in Paris"?

Léon de Bruxelles   13 | 9 | 13 | 25

120, rue Rambuteau, 1ᵉʳ (Les Halles), 01 42 36 18 50;
fax 42 36 27 50
3, bd Beaumarchais, 4ᵉ (Bastille), 01 42 71 75 55;
fax 42 71 75 56 ☽
131, bd St-Germain, 6ᵉ (Mabillon/Odéon), 01 43 26 45 95;
fax 43 26 47 02 ☽
63, av des Champs-Elysées, 8ᵉ (Franklin D. Roosevelt/
George V), 01 42 25 96 16; fax 42 25 95 42 ☽
1-3, pl Pigalle, 9ᵉ (Pigalle), 01 42 80 28 33;
fax 42 80 27 72 ☽
8, pl de la République, 11ᵉ (République), 01 43 38 28 69;
fax 43 38 33 41 ☽
64, av des Gobelins, 13ᵉ (Les Gobelins/Place d'Italie),
01 47 07 51 07; fax 47 07 89 04 ☽
82 bis, bd du Montparnasse, 14ᵉ (Edgar Quinet/Montparnasse-
Bienvenüe), 01 43 21 66 62; fax 43 21 66 76 ☽
349, rue de Vaugirard, 15ᵉ (Convention), 01 55 76 99 72;
fax 55 76 99 71 ☽
95, bd Gouvion-St-Cyr, 17ᵉ (Porte Maillot), 01 55 37 95 30;
fax 55 37 95 35 ☽
www.leon-de-bruxelles.fr

☑ "Featuring huge bowls of moules" ("prepared a gazillion
ways"), "plates of frites and cold Belgian beer", "the
McDonald's of mussels" "hits the spot when you want a
quick, cheap meal"; you have to deal with "nondescript
chain-restaurant decor", and the "overly busy staff can
make obtaining service a challenge", but it's a more-or-
less "safe bet anytime of the day" (most serve until 1 AM),
if "nothing to get excited about."

Lescure ⊠
13 | 12 | 14 | 29

7, rue de Mondovi, 1er (Concorde), 01 42 60 18 91
☑ "They really cram the diners in", but that's actually part of the "enormously convivial" "charm" of this "boisterous" bistro "at the end of a small alley" in the 1st; the "old-fashioned Traditional" fare is no better than "standard", but there's "a lot of it for the money", and that's proved a working formula for this family-run "favorite" since 1919.

Libre Sens
– | – | – | M

33, rue Marbeuf, 8e (Franklin D. Roosevelt), 01 53 96 00 72
Occupying the space that housed the late Korova, this address off the Champs is attracting a young crowd that likes the prompt, attentive service, the low-lit dining room that feels like a nightclub and the diverse menu, which includes sandwiches and salads, along with more elaborate New French dishes.

Lina's ⊠
13 | 10 | 10 | 15

61, rue Charon, 8e (Franklin D. Roosevelt/George V), 01 42 25 34 24; fax 42 25 34 25
50, rue Etienne Marcel, 2e (Bourse/Etienne Marcel), 01 42 21 16 14; fax 42 33 78 03
22, rue des Saints-Pères, 7e (St-Germain-des-Prés), 01 40 20 42 78; fax 40 20 42 79
105, rue du Faubourg-St-Honoré, 8e (St-Phillipe du Roule), 01 42 56 42 57; fax 42 89 93 01
8, rue Marbeuf, 8e (Alma-Marceau), 01 46 23 04 63; fax 47 23 93 09
30, bd des Italiens, 9e (Opéra/Richelieu-Drouot), 01 42 46 02 06; fax 42 46 02 40
2, rue Henri Desgrange, 12e (Bercy), 01 43 40 42 42; fax 43 40 65 11
23, av de Wagram, 17e (Charles de Gaulle-Etoile/Ternes), 01 45 74 76 76; fax 45 74 76 77
156, av Charles de Gaulle, Neuilly (Pont-de-Neuilly), 01 47 45 60 60; fax 47 45 34 68
www.linascafe.com
☑ "Handy" for "healthy, dependable" "sandwiches on various breads, soups, salads and cookies", this string of shops with seating is ideal for "anyone who doesn't have time for a long lunch with red wine"; on the downside, the "disorganization and long lines" are a bore, the "decor's nothing special" and many lament it's "a little expensive for what it is (only sandwiches, after all)."

Loir dans la Théière (Le)
12 | 15 | 14 | 25

3, rue des Rosiers, 4e (St-Paul), 01 42 72 90 61
☑ The "*très* cool" atmosphere, "funky flea-market decor and communal seating" are part of the charm of this *salon de thé* in the Marais, patronized by "an interesting mix of people"; however, there's a general feeling that "it's gone downhill a bit" if you're hungry for anything more than one of their "excellent cakes", which gives it "less appeal to adults" than to twentysomethings.

Lô Sushi ● | 17 | 19 | 13 | 38 |
Pont Neuf Bldg., 1, rue du Pont Neuf, 1er (Pont-Neuf),
01 42 33 09 09; fax 42 33 09 20
8, rue de Berri, 8e (Franklin D. Roosevelt/George V),
01 45 62 01 00; fax 45 62 01 10
www.losushi.com

☑ At the Pont Neuf branch of this "sophisticated" self-
serve spot, it's "fun to play on the Internet stations" at
every seat, while the original in the 8th is "a perfect stop
before heading out to the bars"; both feature a "pretty
cool" "conveyor-belt system of presenting" the "fresh" fish;
most enjoy the "sushi-a-go-go" at "a steal of a price" –
until "you realize how many plates you've chosen."

Louchebem (Le) ●🗷   ∇ | 17 | 13 | 13 | 31 |
31, rue Berger, 1er (Châtelet), 01 42 33 12 99; fax 40 28 45 50;
www.le-louchebem.fr

☑ Steak lovers swear "some of the best meat in Paris" is
served at "one of the few remaining originals in Les Halles";
it's "rather noisy" and the service can be "cold", but why
beef when there are such good buys as an "an all-you-
can-eat rotisserie plate" that's "a must on a winter night."

Lozère (La) 🗷   ∇ | 21 | 11 | 17 | 30 |
4, rue Hautefeuille, 6e (St-Michel), 01 43 54 26 64; fax 43 54 55 66

■ Tucked away in a tiny street in the 6th, this funky place
is one of the longer-running regionals in Paris, specializing
in the "tasty" "homestyle cooking" of Lozère; "reservations
are essential" on Thursdays, aka 'aligot night', when special
menus feature the cheesy whipped potato dish served with
sausage, tripe or steak; "service is pleasant", too.

LUCAS CARTON 🗷 | 27 | 26 | 25 | VE |
9, pl de la Madeleine, 8e (Concorde/Madeleine), 01 42 65 22 90;
fax 42 65 06 23; www.lucascarton.com

■ Those who are "Haute to trot" set a course for this "bit
of French heaven" appropriately "right by the Madeleine";
its "magnificent art nouveau decor" is the backdrop for
"cutting-edge" "dishes you will taste in your dreams",
especially if you do the *dégustation* menu, which pairs
"a suitable glass of wine" with each course brought by
"approachable staffers who never hover"; prices are
enough to make "a mogul blanch", but you can always "go
for the prix fixe lunch if you don't want to go into hock."

Luna (La) 🗷 | 24 | 16 | 18 | 63 |
69, rue du Rocher, 8e (Villiers), 01 42 93 77 61; fax 40 08 02 44

■ The "exceptionally talented" kitchen team at this New
French seafooder stirs up culinary excitement in an
otherwise "ho-hum" locale behind the Gare Saint-Lazare;
some venture it's "one of the best fish restaurants in Paris",
making it a hot table for a deep-pocketed lunchtime crowd
as well as a smart bet for a dinner "date."

Lyonnais (Aux) 🖹   22 | 20 | 20 | 51
32, rue St-Marc, 2ᵉ (Bourse/Richelieu-Drouot), 01 42 96 65 04; fax 42 97 42 95

■ "What a difference a new owner can make" – especially one named Alain Ducasse – say those who've noticed a "quantum leap" in the Lyonnais fare (the "quenelles melt in your mouth!") as well as a stylish "tidying up" of the vintage-bistro decor at this Bourse oldie; while the change (undertaken with Thierry de la Brosse, of Chez L'Ami Louis) has made this table a "tough ticket", devotees dig the newfound "buzz in the room" and "pleasant" staff, calling prices "reasonable" "considering the quality of the cuisine."

Ma Bourgogne ●≠   17 | 16 | 16 | 39
19, pl des Vosges, 4ᵉ (Bastille/St-Paul), 01 42 78 44 64; fax 42 78 19 37

◩ It's the "privilege of dining on the Place des Vosges" that makes this "highly trafficked" cash-only bistro worth its salt, especially when fair weather permits "alfresco" seating; though the "decor and service have worn a little thin", the "quintessential" classics, like "steak tartare", "eggs poached in red wine" and "gigantic salads", plus an "appealing" wine list, offer fitting compensation.

Macéo 🖹   19 | 20 | 20 | 54
15, rue des Petits-Champs, 1ᵉʳ (Bourse/Palais Royal-Musée du Louvre), 01 42 97 53 85; fax 47 03 36 93; www.maceorestaurant.com

◩ Take a "wine suggestion from the skilled staff" and you're off to a flying start at oenophile Mark Williamson's (owner of nearby Willi's Wine Bar) eatery behind the Palais Royal; while some are more enthusiastic about the *vins*, "spacious" belle-epoque room and "casual vibe" than the New and Classic French food, others "delight" in what's on their plate and are thankful that there's always a "very good vegetarian option."

MAGNOLIAS (LES) 🖹   26 | 19 | 23 | 64
48, av de Bry, Perreux-sur-Marne (RER Nogent-le-Perreux), 01 48 72 47 43; fax 48 72 22 28

■ "Well-informed gastronomes" happily board the RER train to the eastern suburb of Perreux-sur-Marne to visit chef-owner Jean Chauvel's New French that's "wonderful in every way"; from the "highly innovative blends of flavors" woven into his edible "works of art" to the room overseen by Mme C. to the "astonishing bargain" at bill time, diners are in for a "incomparably" favorable experience.

Maharajah (Le) ●   ▽ 15 | 8 | 13 | 34
72, bd St-Germain, 5ᵉ (Maubert-Mutualité/St-Michel), 01 43 54 26 07; fax 40 46 08 18; www.maharajah.fr

◩ While the room might be a little "chilly" and in need of a decorative jump-start, the "spices will warm your blood" at this Saint-Michel Indian that's one of the oldest of its ilk in town; the staff is "friendly", the prices suit the Latin Quarter collegiate crowd and vegetarian options abound.

Main d'Or (La) ⊠   – | – | – | M
133, rue du Faubourg St-Antoine, 11ᵉ (Ledru-Rollin), 01 44 68 04 68; fax 44 68 04 68
"Terrific traditional Corsican food" ("the roast kid is a true delight") and wine "is worth the trek" out to this bastion near Bastille, where "the service is friendly, if a bit slow"; while the millstone-and-wrought-iron "setting is simple", management has "improved the place somewhat with the addition of ventilation to chase away the cigarette smoke."

Maison Blanche   20 | 24 | 17 | 85
15, av Montaigne, 8ᵉ (Alma-Marceau), 01 47 23 55 99; fax 47 20 09 56; www.maison-blanche.fr
◪ No one disputes the "sumptuous view" of "Paris rooftops" from a "movie set"–like "all-white" room ("don't spill your wine!") at this *atelier* atop the Théâtre des Champs-Elysées; but while some find the Haute French cuisine "creative", more counter it "doesn't live up to expectations", given that the Pourcel twins (from Montpellier's acclaimed Jardin des Sens) are consultants; many also fault the "amateurish" service and "high prices", but it nonetheless remains a "chic" place to "see and be seen."

Maison Courtine (La) ⊠   22 | 15 | 19 | 49
157, av du Maine, 14ᵉ (Mouton-Duvernet), 01 45 48 08 04; fax 45 45 91 35
◪ "Like eating in the provinces" profess fans of this Southwestern in Montparnasse who'd rather keep quiet "so it's still possible to get a table"; the modern dining room with "decorative birds" isn't everyone's bag, but the "diverse wine list" and "bargain" tabs are universally pleasing.

Maison de l'Amérique Latine ⊠   ▽ 14 | 24 | 13 | 57
217, bd St-Germain, 7ᵉ (Rue du Bac/Solférino), 01 49 54 75 10; fax 40 49 03 94; www.mal217.org
◪ In summer, the "divine" garden terrace of this Latin-American cultural center housed in an elegant 18th-century mansion in Saint-Germain's diplomatic quarter is a "splendid" backdrop for a "peaceful" lunch or dinner, particularly when one "anticipates a proposal"; alas, the Classic French food can't quite compete with the surrounds, and prices are scaled to an expense-account clientele.

Maison du Caviar (La) ◐   19 | 12 | 21 | 95
21, rue Quentin Bauchart, 8ᵉ (George V), 01 47 23 53 43; fax 47 22 21 76
◼ The "name says it all", as this longtime haunt for "caviar lovers and socialites" aptly situated in the posh 8th is *the* place for "flawlessly" fresh fish eggs, plus salmon, the "best borsch" and, of course, Russian vodka; while time

hasn't been kind to the decor, the "great" service and "animated" atmosphere remain, making this splurge "ideal for a quick lunch or a late supper after the movies or theater."

Maison du Jardin (La) 🗷 ∇ | 24 | 17 | 22 | 43 |
27, rue de Vaugirard, 6ᵉ (Rennes/St-Placide), 01 45 48 22 31; fax 45 48 22 31

■ From the owners of La Ferme St-Simon, this "charming" Left Bank bistro across from the Luxembourg Gardens is still a bit confidential, but those who've been say "the kitchen works with care" to create "delicious" New French results; a room that's like a "civilized jewel box for grown-ups" and a "good value" prix fixe help make it a "favorite" "find."

Maison Prunier 🗷 | 22 | 25 | 22 | 70 |
16, av Victor Hugo, 16ᵉ (Charles de Gaulle-Etoile), 01 44 17 35 85; fax 44 17 90 10; www.prunier.com

■ The "gorgeous, admirably restored art deco interior" featuring mosaics of sea creatures mirrors the fish and caviar served at this 16th-arrondissement seafooder owned by Pierre Bergé, co-founder of Yves Saint Laurent; though not the temple of Haute gastronomy it was in its previous life, it remains a "magnificent", and "pricey", reminder of "les Années Folles."

Maison Rouge (La) ◑ | 12 | 19 | 13 | 45 |
13, rue des Archives, 4ᵉ (Hôtel-de-Ville), 01 42 71 69 69; fax 42 71 04 08

▨ The seductively baroque (black-and-silver wallpaper, red velvet upholstery and a Murano glass chandelier) at this Marais *maison* sets the perfect stage for a good-looking crowd intent on "being seen"; with respect to the Contemporary French cooking, however, this house is in need of some serious repair, as most politely describe their meal as "unmemorable", adding that the staff could renovate its "attitude" as well.

Mandalay (Le) 🗷 | – | – | – | M |
35, rue Carnot, Levallois (Anatole France/Louise Michel), 01 45 57 68 69

Chef Guy Guenego (ex L'Orénoc) goes out on his own with this tremendously popular suburbanite in Levallois-Perret whose Eclectic menu visits all points of the compass, from Brittany to Japan; the small dining room is dominated by brown and mauve tones and furnished with metal chairs and miscellaneous ethnic art, and the service is well-informed – a good thing, since dishes like shellfish ravioli 'blanquette style' need explanation.

Mandarin de Neuilly 🗷 | – | – | – | M |
148, av Charles de Gaulle, Neuilly (Pont-de-Neuilly), 01 46 24 11 80

"This little Chinese in Neuilly has a good reputation" for serving "consistently" "high-quality" Szechuan dishes, including "excellent chef specials", at "prices that are reasonable for the neighborhood"; true, the decor's drab, but it's "comfortable" and come summer, the outdoor deck is fit for a mandarin's repose.

Man Ray ◑ — | 23 | 13 | 59 |
34, rue Marbeuf, 8ᵉ (Franklin D. Roosevelt), 01 56 88 36 36; fax 42 25 36 36; www.manray.fr
◪ "Go for a drink to see what the hoopla is about" – i.e. the "impressive" transporting decor and people-watching potential that keep this celebrity-backed club/restaurant off the Champs perennially on the radar; critics who kvetch that the "glitz can't hide" that the service is "shaky" and the fare is "nothing special" and "overpriced" for what it is, may be appeased by the arrival of a new chef's New French menu post-*Survey*; whatever, it's a still a "scene", particularly once the "DJ pumps" up the house music.

Mansouria ⌧ 22 | 17 | 18 | 41 |
11, rue Faidherbe, 11ᵉ (Faidherbe-Chaligny), 01 43 71 00 16; fax 40 24 21 97
■ It's "always a treat" to "feast" on the "extremely large portions" of "flavorful" couscous and "excellent tagines" at this "tastefully" decorated Moroccan; near Place de la Nation, it's "worth the detour if you like to travel" without loading up your caravan for the Dark Continent.

Manufacture (La) ⌧ ▽ 23 | 21 | 16 | 38 |
20, esplanade de la Manufacture, Issy-les-Moulineaux (Corentin-Celton/Porte de Versailles), 01 40 93 08 98; fax 40 93 57 22
■ The "exceptional setting" of this "trendy" retrofitted tobacco factory in Issy-les-Moulineaux makes it popular with an aesthetically sensitive clientele, who likewise appreciate the "lusty" Bistro cooking off "a menu that changes with the seasons" – and for which, given its quality, "you'd pay twice as much for in Paris" itself.

Marée (La) ⌧ 24 | 17 | 23 | VE |
1, rue Daru, 8ᵉ (Ternes), 01 43 80 20 00; fax 48 88 04 04
■ This "impeccably in-the-swim" Traditional French *poissonerie* near the Place des Ternes serves "spectacular and titanic fish" accompanied by a "great wine list"; although prices could send you scrambling for a lifeboat, most among the heavily local crowd feel it's "worth" it for such a "pleasant dining experience" that's nurtured by "heartwarming management and staff."

Marée de Versailles ⌧ 21 | 21 | 19 | 46 |
22, rue au Pain, Versailles (RER Versailles-Rive Droite), 01 30 21 73 73; fax 39 49 98 29
■ Versailles may be landlocked, but this midsize seafood specialist reels in fish fans with luxury specimens, including lots of lobster; the nautical decor helps set the mood, and there's a "delightful terrace" for deck-inclined diners.

Maresco ⊠   _ | _ | _ | M

5, rue de Pontoise, 5ᵉ (Maubert-Mutualité), 01 43 25 56 81
Occupying the space of the venerable Chez Toutoune, this
slick seven-day-a-week spot in the Latin Quarter targets
a well-heeled thirtysomething crowd that wants a one-
stop night on the town with Provençal-accented, homey
traditional cooking and live jazz (Thursdays and Fridays);
its predecessor's zealously floral decor has been retired in
favor of a cleaner, more contemporary look with wicker
chairs and a contrasting red-and-cream color scheme.

Mariage Frères   19 | 20 | 19 | 30

*30, rue du Bourg-Tibourg, 4ᵉ (Hôtel-de-Ville), 01 42 72 28 11;
fax 42 74 51 68*
*13, rue des Grands-Augustins, 6ᵉ (St-Michel), 01 40 51 82 50;
fax 44 07 07 52*
*260, rue du Faubourg St-Honoré, 8ᵉ (Ternes), 01 46 22 18 54;
fax 42 67 18 54*
www.mariagefreres.com
■ "Forget London – the best afternoon tea" some swear is
served at this chainlet of "posh" importers/salons with an
"overwhelming" selection of blends as well as "sublime"
pastries, "inventive sandwiches and salads"; "waiters
clad in linen suits" contribute to the "elegant" "Colonial"
atmosphere, as they impart their knowledge on the basics of
brewing; P.S. try to "go early" for weekend brunch, lest the
queues cause you to steep your "golden leaves" at home.

Marius ⊠   22 | 15 | 17 | 53

*82, bd Murat, 16ᵉ (Porte de St-Cloud), 01 46 51 67 80;
fax 40 71 83 75*
■ In the 16th, this "handsome" oceanic address is "never
empty because the fish are prepared to perfection", with
some finding their way into a justly famous bouillabaisse;
most concede it's a "solid value" relative to the first-rate
catch, and the "attentive" service ensures smooth sailing.

Marius et Janette   21 | 17 | 18 | 75

4, av George V, 8ᵉ (Alma-Marceau), 01 47 23 84 36; fax 47 23 07 19
☑ This Neptunian lair by the Seine in the 8th has built a
reputation on "delicious seafood" and "personality"
sightings amid a "goofy" nautical decor of portholes and
knotty-pine paneling; mutineers claim "it's overrated",
citing "perfunctory" service and elevated prices, and with
"high noise and table density", it's not a place for intimate
conversation; but such energy, along with a side of
"wonderful oysters", is sure to "raise your spirits."

MARKET ◐   22 | 23 | 19 | 70

*15, av Matignon, 8ᵉ (Champs-Elysées-Clemenceau),
01 56 43 40 90; fax 43 59 10 87; www.jean-georges.com*
☑ Housed in the Christie's building in the 8th, "his majesty
Jean-Georges Vongerichten's" first eatery in his homeland

channels "NYC-cool" via its "sleek", "minimalist" decor and "imaginative", "Asian-influenced" Eclectic eats that allow diners to "discover new flavors"; as at his stateside restaurants, the clientele counts many "cool dudes and beautiful chicks" who turn a blind eye toward "inconsistent" bumps in the kitchen and blips in the service, heralding it as a "hip" place that's also handy "for Sundays."

Marlotte (La) 🖾   17 | 15 | 17 | 40

55, rue du Cherche-Midi, 6ᵉ (Sèvres-Babylone/St-Placide), 01 45 48 86 79; fax 45 44 34 80; www.lamarlotte.com

■ "Quintessentially Parisian" and ever "reliable", this Classic French near the Bon Marché is a "busy place" thanks to its "high-quality" cooking (including "excellent lamb"), "appealingly rustic" decor and the "charming family that runs it"; though you may hear "more English than French" at the tables on some days, the prices are decent in any language.

Marsangy (Le) 🖾   – | – | – | M

73, av Parmentier, 11ᵉ (Parmentier), 01 47 00 94 25; fax 47 00 94 25

With its ox-blood-colored interior, dangling ceiling lamps, reasonable prices and daily changing chalkboard menus that sweetly showcase both Classic and Contemporary French dishes – plus a nice array of wines – this bustling newcomer in the 11th is the very definition of what a neighborhood bistro should be; friendly servers help foster a relaxed atmosphere.

Martel (Le) ◑   – | – | – | M

3, rue Martel, 10ᵉ (Château d'Eau), 01 47 70 67 56

"Owner Mehdi Gana" maintains the "sweet ambiance" at this "trendy", if buzzingly "noisy", low-lit spot in the increasingly hip 10th that specializes in "copious portions" of "simple" North African dishes like couscous, tagines and grilled meats, plus some Classic French offerings, at gentle prices.

Marty ◑   17 | 19 | 15 | 46

20, av des Gobelins, 5ᵉ (Les Gobelins), 01 43 31 39 51; fax 43 37 63 70; www.marty-restaurant.com

◪ The "beautiful" art deco decor is the "best part of the experience" at this circa-1913 and still independently owned brasserie at Les Gobelins; but while the "shellfish stand outside is inviting" and there are some "old classics" to be had, most lament that the food is merely "fair" with service that's equally "lackluster."

Mascotte (La) 🖾   – | – | – | E

270, rue du Faubourg St-Honoré, 8ᵉ (Ternes), 01 42 27 75 26; fax 45 72 20 44

Regulars tick off several "reasons why it's increasingly difficult to find a table" at this "reliable old bistro" in a "nice area" near the Place des Ternes: "well-prepared Classic French food" (based on "great meat"), "good wine and friendly service" overseen by a "professional boss."

Mascotte (La) ◗ — | — | — | M
52, rue des Abbesses, 18ᵉ (Abbesses/Blanche), 01 46 06 28 15; fax 42 23 93 83

"Decorating is not a concept that crossed the door" here, but that doesn't deter Montmartre denizens from seeking "a refuge against the increasing trendiness of the *quartier*" at this Auvergnat brasserie that traffics in "great, little wines by the glass" and "solid, authentic traditional food from the Massif Central"; it also boasts "the only shellfish stand" on the Rue des Abbesses.

Mathusalem (Le) ⌧ 18 | 12 | 15 | 41
5 bis, bd Exelmans, 16ᵉ (Exelmans), 01 42 88 10 73; fax 42 88 42 43; www.mathusalem.fr

■ Situated "in a lost corner of the 16th", this "amiable" bistro is a "typical" "neighborhood place", dishing up consistently "solid" Classic French fare like a "tempting tête de veau" from time to time; a "friendly owner who greets everyone" and "correct prices for what you get" make it the kind of place you "return to with pleasure."

Matsuri 15 | 16 | 13 | 31
36, rue de Richelieu, 1ᵉʳ (Pyramides), 01 42 61 05 73; fax 42 96 60 64 ⌧
2, rue de Passy, 16ᵉ (Passy), 01 42 24 96 85; fax 42 24 14 54 ◗

◪ A "dark-wood-and-mauve decor" lends an upscale air to this pair of sushi sisters in the 1st and the 16th that converts call standbys for "good, basic meals" of maki; but malcontents mutter that the little morsels' emergence on an "automatic conveyor belt", while "entertaining", "perfectly represents their industrial taste."

Maupertu (Le) ⌧ 19 | 14 | 22 | 42
94, bd de La Tour-Maubourg, 7ᵉ (Ecole Militaire/ La Tour-Maubourg), 01 45 51 37 96; fax 53 59 94 83; www.restaurant-maupertu-paris.com

■ "Delightful owners" Sophie and Alain de Guest offer "good-humored" "personal service" at their "quiet place" known for its highly "tasty" "Traditional French cuisine at reasonable prices"; the interior itself "isn't much to look at", but it does boast "a lovely view of the dome of Les Invalides", especially when "reflecting the rays of the setting sun"; so most praise their "pleasant" time here as "worth every penny."

Mauzac (Le) ⌧ ▽ 15 | 11 | 12 | 30
7, rue de l'Abbé de l'Epée, 5ᵉ (Luxembourg), 01 46 33 75 22

◪ A change in ownership left many regulars railing that this wine bar/bistro near the Luxembourg Gardens has "lost its charm" and now serves "only average" "Traditional

French cuisine"; but more short-memoried supporters find the combination of "private labels" and "generous portions" a recipe for "total relaxation."

Mavrommatis ☒   19 | 14 | 16 | 42

42, rue Daubenton, 5ᵉ (Censier-Daubenton), 01 43 31 17 17; fax 43 36 13 08; www.mavrommatis.fr

■ The "authentic old-world charm" of this Greek in the Latin Quarter comes from its "understated decor of crocheted curtains, ficus trees" and sepia photos, plus some "superb" cooking that "updates the classics with real verve" ("you have to try the zucchini and eggplant moussaka"); "owned by a well-known Cypriot caterer", it's "a little expensive", but "probably the best [of its ilk] in town."

MAXIM'S ☒   20 | 22 | 21 | 84

3, rue Royale, 8ᵉ (Concorde/Madeleine), 01 42 65 27 94; fax 42 65 30 26

◪ Even if she's "past her prime" – after all, she is 112 – this "famous" grande dame off the Place de la Concorde remains "a special place", not just "for nostalgia" but also for "surprisingly" "quite good" Classic French fare fans find; the irreverent retort "everything here seems worn, even the friendly service" and the "art nouveau decor, lovely" as it may be; still, it remains "a must, at least once" – perhaps on "Friday nights, when it transforms into an exotic club" frequented by *le tout* Paris.

Méditerranée (La)   20 | 20 | 19 | 63

2, pl de l'Odéon, 6ᵉ (Odéon), 01 43 26 02 30; fax 43 26 18 44; www.la-mediterranee.com

■ "The light Cocteau-esque decor" ("Cocteau actually designed the tableware and menus") lends a *la-vie-en-rose* atmosphere to this "specialist in fish dishes" "overlooking the Place de l'Odéon"; while "it's worth it for the refreshingly elegant decor" alone, the cuisine "has improved in the last few years" and is now "very nice", especially the signature "superb bouillabaisse" proffered by a "proud staff."

Mesturet (Le) ☒   – | – | – | M

77, rue de Richelieu, 2ᵉ (Bourse), 01 42 97 40 68; fax 42 97 40 68

Located in the heart of town not far from the Bourse, the old Paris stock exchange, and featuring modest prices on Traditional French dishes, this cafe/bistro has quickly become a hit with bankers and brokers at noon, and locals seeking supper at night; despite lots of hustle and bustle, the service is good-natured and the atmosphere friendly.

MEURICE (LE) ☒   25 | 28 | 26 | VE

Hôtel Meurice, 228, rue de Rivoli, 1ᵉʳ (Concorde/Tuileries), 01 44 58 10 55; fax 44 58 10 76; www.meuricehotel.com

■ This "regal" Right Bank dining room, with a mélange of mirrors, marble, crystal chandeliers, painted ceilings and ormolu ("could this be Versailles?"), "comes very close to perfection" as does the "impeccable service"; in addition, chef Yannick Alléno has made this Haute Cuisine table "a must-try for foodies" as he dazzles with dishes that display culinary "creativity" in "picture-perfect presentations"; so if the tabs are "eye-popping", they're "worth every euro."

MICHEL ROSTANG ⊠   27 | 23 | 26 | VE

20, rue Rennequin, 17ᵉ (Péreire/Ternes), 01 47 63 40 77; fax 47 63 82 75; www.michelrostang.com

■ "From start to finish, a first-class experience" is the consensus on Michel Rostang's New French in the 17th, where "big flavors and complex sauces" – "especially fine when game or truffles are in season" – reign in a "luxurious setting" of paneling, porcelains and paintings; the servers are all "polished professionals", especially the "superb sommeliers", who act "friendly even if you're not a regular" – though it's certainly worth becoming one, "if you can afford it."

Mirama   20 | 5 | 11 | 23

17, rue St-Jacques, 5ᵉ (Maubert-Mutualité/St-Michel), 01 43 54 71 77; fax 43 25 37 63

☑ Ok, "the decor is nonexistent" and the "waiters surly, but just try and get a table" at this "old and known" Latin Quarter Chinese; the secret is in the "amazing food" "that's not like anywhere else – it's better" – and at bargain-basement prices too; just remember, if the service seems "pressed", it's to "clear spaces for those in the long line", "drooling outside the window."

Moissonnier ⊠   21 | 15 | 20 | 42

28, rue des Fossés St-Bernard, 5ᵉ (Cardinal Lemoine/ Jussieu), 01 43 29 87 65; fax 43 29 87 65

■ "Year after year, the menu remains true to" "hearty Lyonnais cooking" – "oeufs en meurette (poached eggs in red-wine-and-bacon sauce)", "real quenelles" and a whole heaping table of "traditional hors d'oeuvres" – which explains the enduring popularity of this "old standard" bistro in the 5th; its "simple decor makes you feel like you're in the provinces" circa 1962 (as does the "smoky atmosphere"), and with its moderate prices, it's perfect for those craving a "culinary cocooning" in "heavy cream and sauces."

Monsieur Lapin   21 | 20 | 20 | 40

11, rue Raymond Losserand, 14ᵉ (Gaîté/Pernety), 01 43 20 21 39; fax 43 21 84 86

■ "There are bunnies everywhere" decorating the walls and the plates at this veteran Traditional French "jewel in Montparnasse"; happy hares hop over for the "charming service" and the "delectable food, even for non-rabbit eaters", topped off by "very reasonable prices."

Montalembert (Le) 15 | 21 | 18 | 54
Hôtel Montalembert, 3, rue de Montalembert, 7ᵉ (Rue du Bac),
01 45 49 68 03; fax 45 49 69 49; www.montalembert.com
☑ Mainstay of Saint-Germain's publishers, antique dealers
and fashionistas, this "chic but expensive" ground-floor
dining room is known for providing an "excellent hotel
lunch" of French fare with an innovative touch; but while
most appreciate the "minimalist charm" of Christian
Liaigre's decor (and the "pretty patio"), malcontents
mutter the designer's "magic no longer works" to overcome
only "ok food."

Mont Liban (Le) – | – | – | I
42, bd des Batignolles, 17ᵉ (Rome), 01 45 22 35 01; fax 43 87 04 59
In a bustling part of the 17th, this ethnic watering hole is "a
real steal for great Lebanese food" ("the falafel sandwich
is so inexpensive they practically give it away") and native
wines, served in a smiling, familial atmosphere; the deals
are so good, devotees disregard the nondescript digs.

Montparnasse 25 (Le) ⌧ ▽ 23 | 21 | 23 | 67
Le Méridien-Montparnasse, 19, rue du Cdt. René Mouchotte,
14ᵉ (Montparnasse-Bienvenüe), 01 44 36 44 25; fax 44 36 49 03;
www.lemeridien-montparnasse.com
■ For a "luxurious experience", sink "into the comfort of
deep chairs and the silence of well-spaced tables" that
characterize the Méridien-Montparnasse's second-floor,
'20s-style (hence the name) dining room; the Haute Cuisine
hits some as "a little expensive", but everyone raves about
the "memorable cheese platter", accompanied by "a
surprisingly rich commentary."

Mon Vieil Ami – | – | – | M
69, rue St-Louis-en-l'Ile, 4ᵉ (Hôtel-de-Ville/St-Michel),
01 40 46 01 35; fax 40 46 01 36
In a handsome setting of glass-paneled walls trimmed
with black mock timbering – a reference to the original
construction of this ancient Ile Saint-Louis home – this
contemporary bistro has become everyone's favorite
ami, thanks to a chef who trained under owner Antoine
Westermann, of Strasbourg's Buerehiesel; under a beamed
ceiling, diners can choose to sit at either a long, ebony-
stained *table d'hôte* or at regular tables to feast on follow-
the-market, moderately priced prix fixes and *plats du jour*.

MOULIN À VENT 25 | 17 | 22 | E
"CHEZ HENRI" (AU) ⌧
20, rue des Fossés St-Bernard, 5ᵉ (Cardinal Lemoine/Jussieu),
01 43 54 99 37; fax 40 46 92 23
■ The "decor hasn't changed in decades – and it shouldn't"
in this "oh-so-French" vet that offers "everything you
want in a classic bistro" (including a typical "Parisian
staff"); "always reserve ahead", because it's "filled with

meat-eating locals" of the arty 5th, devouring "the best entrecôte in town."

Moulin de la Galette (Le)   – | – | – | M |
83, rue Lepic, 18ᵉ (Abbesses/Lamarck-Caulaincourt), 01 46 06 84 77; fax 46 06 84 78
With a "great location at the top of Montmartre", this Classic French has undergone "a renaissance", thanks to a revamp a while back; the combination of a fresh modern interior and "nice garden patio" in the shadow of a landmarked mill makes for "stunning atmosphere"; it's an ideal place for a "reasonably priced" "romantic dinner" or a "pleasurable Sunday brunch."

Mum Sabai ◑   – | – | – | E |
5, rue Bernard Palissy, 6ᵉ (St-Germain-des-Prés), 01 42 22 14 40
Brightly colored silk cushions on a white-upholstered banquette that runs the length of one wall gives this snug new Thai in Saint-Germain its visual personality, while the careful, authentically fiery cooking, plus equally precise service, explains its immediate popularity; N.B. as in Bangkok, the seating is low to the ground.

Murano (Le) ◑   – | – | – | E |
Murano Urban Resort, 13, bd du Temple, 3ᵉ (Filles-du-Calvaire/ République), 01 42 71 20 00; fax 42 71 21 01; www.muranoresort.com
This sleek white dining room in the new Murano hotel has become an instant fashionista address (sometimes the only people not wearing sunglasses are the waiters), thanks to its location on the trendy northern edge of the Marais; the menu offers an equally stylish hit list of expensively turned-out New French eats in slimming portions.

Murat (Le) ◑   13 | 16 | 13 | 52 |
1, bd Murat, 16ᵉ (Porte d'Auteuil), 01 46 51 33 17; fax 53 17 88 54
◪ Yes, this is "one more Costes place [geared] for small appetites and showing off", but still its "kitschy" digs are "always filled" with the "air-kissing" "16th arrondissement 'in'-crowd", which claims the Classic French cuisine (with some Asian touches) is "good despite the malicious gossip"; the unmollified mutter over the "mediocre food" and "itchy service", but on the plus side, it's "kid-tolerant" and for those "who have no problem forking out the euros, valet parking is available."

Muscade   – | – | – | M |
36, rue Montpensier, 1ᵉʳ (Palais Royal-Musée du Louvre/ Pyramides), 01 42 97 51 36; fax 42 97 51 36
The wonderful setting at the Palais Royal makes this "cozy" eatery/tearoom definitely "worth the trek"; its classic Bistro fare, "well-prepared seafood" and "big salads" can easily make it a "lunch staple in the summertime" especially if

you can "score a table outside" amid the historical gardens where the writer Colette lived for many years.

Muses (Les) 🗷   27 | 16 | 23 | 96

Hôtel Scribe, 1, rue Scribe, 9ᵉ (Opéra), 01 44 71 24 26;
fax 44 71 24 64; www.sofitel.com

■ Despite a "basement location" that's "a little oppressive", this "quiet, high-quality" "restaurant in the Hôtel Scribe" near the Opéra Garnier "does not disappoint", thanks to its "enchanting", "creative" Haute Cuisine and "wonderful staff", including an "outstanding sommelier"; it's "a bit expensive", though connoisseurs commend the (relative) "bargain four-course lunch."

Musichall ●🗷   – | – | – | E

63, av Franklin Roosevelt, 8ᵉ (St-Philippe-du-Roule),
01 45 61 03 63; fax 45 61 03 88; www.music-hallparis.com
Theater producer Valério Berkovics' sprawling newcomer just off the Champs-Elysées is quite the showpiece, what with 600 computerized projectors that change the lighting, as well as live DJ music and a pianist in an adjacent lounge/bar; aimed at the young, international crowd that's made the area the epicenter of Paris nightlife, the New French menu mixes grandmotherly comfort food with racier creations like duck breast roasted in cocoa, plus some Asian-inspired fare.

Natacha ●🗷   17 | 15 | 17 | 53

17 bis, rue Campagne-Première, 14ᵉ (Raspail), 01 43 20 79 27;
fax 43 22 93 97

■ Even though namesake-owner Natacha is no longer there, this dual-level Montparnasse hangout "with a history as a celebrity hot spot" continues to exhibit "more attitude than a drag queen with a broken heel"; but while devotees dig the "deep, dark and sexy" decor and "typical Classic French cuisine", the jaded jeer "oh, how the trendy have fallen": these days, it's all "average food" and "people looking at people looking for stars."

Nemrod (Le) 🗷   15 | 9 | 14 | 26

51, rue du Cherche-Midi, 6ᵉ (Sèvres-Babylone/St-Placide),
01 45 48 17 05; fax 45 48 17 83; www.lenemrod.com

■ "Great for lunch when shopping" around the Bon Marché store, this "fun" "neighborhood favorite" offers "lots of choice" to "refill you", from "good Auvergnat products" like "gigantic steaks" to "copious salads", all at "cheap" prices and slung by "friendly servers"; just "stay away if you're hard of hearing" 'cuz it gets "very crowded and noisy" at noontime.

New Jawad ●   ∇ 17 | 13 | 18 | 38

12, av Rapp, 7ᵉ (Alma-Marceau), 01 47 05 91 37; fax 45 50 31 27

■ Perhaps the decor's a bit bland, but don't worry – the place is "better than it looks" promise patrons of this

Pakistani-Indian in the 7th that serves "surprisingly good" food "365 days a year"; the "staff's very friendly" and the check's "extremely reasonable", so go ahead and shoot the ja-wad on the "authentic" eats.

New Nioullaville ◐   ▽ 17 | 8 | 11 | 31

32-34, rue de l'Orillon, 11ᵉ (Belleville), 01 40 21 96 18; fax 40 21 96 58

■ With "trolleys of dim sum rolling around the tables", this "huge", funky Belleville space is "one of the most authentic" "carnivals of Chinese cuisine" (plus some Thai and Vietnamese) in Paris; some dis the digs, claiming it's "better to block out the decor", but most find that "for the price, this is a welcome, exotic outing."

Noces de Jeannette (Les)   – | – | – | M

14, rue Favart, 2ᵉ (Richelieu-Drouot), 01 42 96 36 89; fax 47 03 97 31; www.lesnocesdejeannette.com

"Tourists come by the busload" to this century-old standby, since it's situated conveniently near 2nd-arrondissement theaters and its several "pleasant" salons are decorated in different florid styles; featuring well-priced classics like duck à l'orange, the classic Bistro cuisine is quite "correct, if nothing more."

No Stress Café ◐   – | – | – | E

2, pl Gustave Toudouze, 9ᵉ (St-Georges), 01 48 78 00 27

A touch of Tangiers in the 9th's theater district, this late-night watering hole (bar closes 2 AM) also serves "nice" Eclectic fare earlier in the eve – from Chinese stir-fries to burgers, "delicious salads" to Traditional French dishes – in a Moroccan-inspired setting; stressed-out surveyors who sigh it's "way overpriced" can relax with an in-house, in-chair shiatsu massage and tarot-card readings (several times a week), or get fresh air on the large terrace.

Noura   19 | 13 | 15 | 34

29, bd des Italiens, 2ᵉ (Opéra/Richelieu-Drouot), 01 53 43 00 53; fax 53 43 83 53
121, bd du Montparnasse, 6ᵉ (Vavin), 01 43 20 19 19; fax 43 20 05 40 ◐
21, av Marceau, 16ᵉ (Alma-Marceau/George V), 01 47 20 33 33; fax 47 20 60 31 ◐
27, av Marceau, 16ᵉ (Alma-Marceau/George V), 01 47 03 02 20; fax 47 23 99 80
www.noura.fr

◪ "Some of the best Lebanese fare in Paris" is the buzz about these "authentic" Middle Eastern enclaves issuing "exquisite" eats to an often "packed" and "noisy" crowd (leaving the "servers to do what they can"); the more "upscale" experience at the 21 Avenue Marceau original (Noura Pavillon) "comes at a higher price" than at its informal offshoots; P.S. "great takeout, too."

Nouveau Village Tao-Tao ● ▽ | 18 | 12 | 15 | 39 |
159, bd Vincent Auriol, 13ᵉ (Nationale), 01 45 86 40 08; fax 45 86 46 21

☑ Tucked deep in the 13th, this Thai-tinged Chinese offers a "wide choice" of "agreeable" dishes; satisfied villagers Tao-t the "cheaply priced Peking duck" and choose "not to be put off" by the "rather unsophisticated" digs.

O à la Bouche (L') ☒ | 18 | 12 | 12 | 43 |
124, bd du Montparnasse, 14ᵉ (Vavin), 01 56 54 01 55; fax 43 21 07 87

☑ "As neighborhood bistros go, this is wonderful" vow voters who make "the long trek" down Montparnasse's eponymous boulevard for chef Franck Paquier's "creative" New French cooking that's a "very good value"; on the down side, word of mouth is that service is so-so and decor "remains a little sad."

Obélisque (L') | 23 | 20 | 24 | 71 |
Hôtel de Crillon, 10, pl de la Concorde, 8ᵉ (Concorde), 01 44 71 15 15; fax 44 71 15 02; www.crillon.com

■ "An excellent alternative to its stratospherically priced peers", this "elegant" but "comfortable setting" located "discreetly" within the posh Hôtel de Crillon offers "a first-class meal" in the New French style; the "superb service" adds to the "luxuriously Parisian" experience, so much so that "it's hard to leave"; N.B. the Food score may not reflect the arrival of chef Jean-Francois Piège (ex Plaza-Athénée).

Oeillade (L') ☒ | 16 | 12 | 14 | 43 |
10, rue de St-Simon, 7ᵉ (Rue du Bac/Solférino), 01 42 22 01 60

☑ Though "low on decor", this "friendly neighborhood" classic bistro is a pleasant "place to unwind" say followers who favor its fresh flower arrangements and "authentic, old-fashioned" cuisine; sure, it may be a bit "boring", but being a "bang for the buck" makes it "worth going back to."

Oenothèque (L') ☒ | – | – | – | M |
20, rue St-Lazare, 9ᵉ (Notre-Dame-de-Lorette), 01 48 78 08 76; fax 40 16 10 27

Eager oenophiles enjoy this small wine bar in the 9th, where the "chatty owner" showcases his sensibly priced sipping selections (available by the bottle or glass) with Traditional French food considered "ok but nothing special"; while some have been "disappointed" by "iffy service", more-wine and less-whine types insist "don't miss the place."

Olivades (Les) ☒ | 21 | 15 | 17 | 48 |
(aka Bruno Deligne-Les Olivades)
41, av de Ségur, 7ᵉ (Ségur/St-François-Xavier), 01 47 83 70 09; fax 42 73 04 75; www.deligne-lesolivades.fr.tc

■ This "tiny" Traditional French presents tempting "tastes of Provence" in a "posh residential neighborhood" near the

Ecole Militaire; the "accommodating" staff tends the "well-heeled Americans" and "chic" locals who happily squeeze into "tight tables" for a "truly delightful" experience.

Opportun (L') ●Ⓢ — | — | — | M

64, bd Edgar Quinet, 14ᵉ (Edgar Quinet), 01 43 20 26 89; fax 43 21 61 88

"Authentic cooking" and "fresh products" characterize this small, wallet-friendly Lyonnais bistro just behind the Tour Montparnasse, which serves regional specialties like sweetbreads fricassee and Royan ravioli; all in all, an "excellent" address for "Beaujolais, meat, cognac and a cigar with pals."

Orangerie (L') ● 22 | 23 | 22 | 84

28, rue St-Louis-en-l'Ile, 4ᵉ (Pont-Marie), 01 46 33 93 98; fax 43 29 25 52

✔ A "great find" in the "quaint neighborhood" of the Ile Saint-Louis, this once "very in", "old-style" Classic French has lost some of its star sizzle (now actor-owner Jean-Claude Brialy only hosts "film people from time to time"); but it remains "one of the most romantic restaurants in Paris", complete with "gorgeous flowers", "wonderful" food and "personal" service; claustrophobic critics caution that the "cozy" space is really "too cramped": "I wanted a tête-à-tête with my husband, not the guy at the next table."

Orenoc (L') Ⓢ 21 | 22 | 18 | 57

Le Méridien Etoile, 81, bd Gouvion St-Cyr, 17ᵉ (Porte Maillot), 01 40 68 30 40; fax 40 68 30 81; www.lemeridien-etoile.com

■ On the ground floor of the refurbished Méridien Etoile near the Porte Maillot, this "beautiful" dining room serves "incredible" Classic French cuisine with "innovative" international influences in a "lovely" room crafted in "exotic wood"; all told, it's a "pleasant surprise" and an ideal place for a "business lunch" – especially if you can write it off.

Orient-Extrême ●Ⓢ 19 | 16 | 15 | 48

4, rue Bernard Palissy, 6ᵉ (St-Germain-des-Prés), 01 45 48 92 27; fax 45 48 20 94

✔ This "hip" Japanese in the center of Saint-Germain-des-Prés is often filled with "show-biz stars" who come for "refined", "fresh fish" dishes and "very good sushi" that's "better than most" admirers insist; however, those oriented toward negativity say the "rather expensive" tabs are too extrême for what they maintain is "mediocre" fare.

Ormes (Les) Ⓢ — | — | — | M

22, rue Surcouf, 7ᵉ (La Tour-Maubourg), 01 45 51 46 93; fax 45 50 30 11

There's a "chef to watch" at this "real discovery", which recently moved from the remote 16th to a somewhat formal, stylish new site in the 7th (the departed Bellecour's address); the "shy but extremely gifted" Stéphane Molé creates "superb" contemporary Haute Cuisine at reasonable rates, presented by a "warm, hospitable" staff.

Os à Moëlle (L') ●⬚ | 23 | 13 | 19 | 44 |
3, rue Vasco de Gama, 15ᵉ (Lourmel), 01 45 57 27 27; fax 45 57 28 00
■ This "diamond in the rough" (aka "hole-in-the-wall") is "always packed" with "lots of buzz from the many locals" who trek deep into the distant 15th for chef-owner Thierry Faucher's "fabulous" Traditional French fare that's "on the inventive side" thanks to a daily changing menu; ok, it's "out of the way" and "tables are tight", but the "service makes you feel like a regular" and gentle prices translate to "one of the greatest bangs for the buck in Paris."

Ostéria (L') ⬚ | 23 | 12 | 17 | 49 |
10, rue de Sévigné, 4ᵉ (St-Paul), 01 42 71 37 08; fax 48 06 27 71
◪ "Don't be discouraged by the decor or the wait" when you march to the Marais for this Italian "treasure", considered one of the "best-kept secrets in Paris"; the staff can be "aloof", but the "fresh and delicious" food (the "daily risotto is a must") is ever-present.

Osteria Ascolani ●⊄ | – | – | – | I |
98, rue des Martyrs, 18ᵉ (Abbesses/Pigalle), 01 42 62 43 94
This simply decorated Italian on a fashionable street in increasingly trendy Montmartre draws an arty, young crowd that appreciates the value prices; while the menu does not provide any choices, what leisurely comes to the table usually appeals to a wide array of appetites; book early to avoid the smoky atmosphere that develops as the night goes on.

Oulette (L') ⬚ | 21 | 16 | 20 | 48 |
15, pl Lachambeaudie, 12ᵉ (Cour St-Emilion/Dugommier), 01 40 02 02 12; fax 40 02 04 77; www.l-oulette.com
■ A "fantastic" find turning out "tasty" Southwestern specialties at "reasonable prices", this "snug little place" is "worth the trip off the beaten path" to the increasingly trendy 12th; the owners' "warm welcome" adds a personal touch that offsets the sometimes "slow service."

Oum el Banine ⬚ | – | – | – | E |
16 bis, rue Dufrenoy, 16ᵉ (Porte Dauphine/Rue de la Pompe), 01 45 04 91 22; fax 45 03 46 26
Creating "colorful zest" in the 16th, this "authentic" Moroccan is known for its "cozy" space, "friendly welcome" from the owner and "delicious cuisine", including couscous *mechoui* (roasted lamb) and classic tagines; P.S. if you feel like staying at home, "you can even have it delivered" (if it's a large order) – something that's not run of the mill in the City of Lights.

Ourcine (L') ⌧   _| _| _| M
92, rue Broca, 13ᵉ (Les Gobelins/Glacière), 01 47 07 13 65;
fax 47 07 18 48
Located near Gobelins, the famous tapestry manufacturing
atelier, this simple, snug contemporary bistro specializes
in home-cooked Basque and Bearnais classics, such as
piperade (scrambled eggs with peppers and onions) and
piquillos (red peppers) stuffed with *brandade* (whipped
salt cod) that constitute an edible tour of the region – from
the Bay of Biscay to the peaks of the Pyrénées.

Palanquin (Le) ⌧   ▽ 13 | 14 | 16 | 32
12, rue Princesse, 6ᵉ (Mabillon/St-Germain-des-Prés),
01 43 29 77 66; www.lepalanquin.com
◪ "For something completely different" amid the bustle
of Saint-Germain, try this "oasis of calm" that offers
"authentic Vietnamese" victuals at "reasonable prices",
though also in "paltry portions"; "gracious servers" add to
the relaxing experience.

Pamphlet (Le) ⌧   21 | 18 | 20 | 42
38, rue Debelleyme, 3ᵉ (Filles-du-Calvaire), 01 42 72 39 24
◼ The innlike "dining room's attractive and the service
good, but the star is the food" at this "savory" Basque in the
trendy Marais; it "gets much press" for its "novel takes on
traditional Southwestern dishes", and folks are also willing
"to write home about" the fact that "the price is right."

Paolo Petrini ⌧   20 | 6 | 15 | 60
6, rue du Débarcadère, 17ᵉ (Argentine/Porte Maillot),
01 45 74 25 95; fax 45 74 12 95; www.paolo-petrini.fr
◪ Behind the Porte Maillot, this "calm, classy" vintage
Italian is one of "the best on the Right Bank", offering
"terrific" eats ("don't miss the truffle menu at the end of
the year") and "attentive" service, which alleviates the
"expensive" tab; the ratings don't reflect that the once-
"depressing decor" was redone, post-*Survey.*

Papilles (Les) ⌧   _| _| _| M
30, rue Gay Lussac, 5ᵉ (RER Luxembourg), 01 43 25 20 79;
fax 43 25 24 35
Decorated like an old-fashioned grocery store, with open
shelves stocked with various canned and bottled foodstuffs,
this new bistro specializes in Southwestern cuisine; seated
at bare wood tables dressed with Basque napkins, its hip,
young Latin Quarter customers find their *papilles* (tastebuds)
tickled by the generous portions of homemade terrines,
soups and casseroles, served by a smugly trendy staff.

Papinou ⌧   _| _| _| M
26, rue du Château, Neuilly (Pont de Neuilly), 01 55 24 90 40
This Neuilly outpost is a "super address for good, down-to-
earth" classic Bistro cuisine, served in a "typical Gallic

ambiance" – either on the ground floor decorated with wooden beams and a bar, or in the darker wine cellar where you can pick among a "large choice of reasonably priced" labels; whichever you choose, the "endearing service" "warrants a return visit."

Paradis Thai ◗   – | – | – | M
132, rue de Tolbiac, 13ᵉ (Tolbiac), 01 45 83 22 26; fax 45 83 22 26
Equipped with golden Buddhas and native decorations, this two-story Thai temple serves up "spicy" Siamese savories near Chinatown; as a "reliable" source for something "different", certainly "it's a good idea for the area", even if, some sniff, the cuisine itself is "not very distinctive."

Parc aux Cerfs (Le)   ▽ 15 | 13 | 17 | 42
50, rue Vavin, 6ᵉ (Notre-Dame-des-Champs/Vavin), 01 43 54 87 83; fax 43 26 42 86
■ Behind the Luxembourg gardens, this Montparnasse "favorite" is a "good choice for a well-prepared", if "rather Traditional" French "neighborhood meal"; "service that is always friendly" ensures a "pleasant, relaxed" atmosphere, especially if in summer you "get a table in the back" – the "little patio is a haven of peace."

Paris (Le) 🖾   – | – | – | E
Hôtel Lutétia, 23, rue de Sèvres, 6ᵉ (Sèvres-Babylone), 01 49 54 46 90; fax 49 54 46 00; www.lutetia-paris.com
"First-rate in all respects" proclaim passengers of this "uncrowded" Haute Cuisine haven with an "understated" ocean-liner decor by designer Sonia Rykiel for the very chic Hotel Lutétia; the "solid", classically oriented food and "realistically priced, well-chosen wine list" is offered by "service that is attentive, without hovering or rushing", resulting in a "calm, luxurious" atmosphere that is "worth every penny."

Paris Seize (Le) 🖾   15 | 11 | 14 | 37
18, rue des Belles Feuilles, 16ᵉ (Trocadéro), 01 47 04 56 33
■ Run by the Dumant brothers, Jérôme and Stéphane, this "easygoing", easy-on-the-wallet bistro near the Place Victor Hugo offers "solid" Italian fare "without pretension" in a sports-themed setting; survey seize the ambiance is "lively", thanks to a "young crowd" that doesn't mind cramming into the "tight, smoky" quarters.

Passage des   – | – | – | I
Carmagnoles (Le) ◗🖾
18, passage de la Bonne Graine, 11ᵉ (Ledru Rollin), 01 47 00 73 30; fax 47 00 65 68
Famous for its *andouillettes* (tripe sausage) and lengthy wine list, this cozy spot tucked away in a dead-end street near the Bastille also serves other Traditional French dishes

and a vegetarian option or two, all at gentle prices; the wood tables, jazz soundtrack and cheerful service make it popular with arty locals, who also appreciate the philosophy debates held once a month here.

Passiflore ⊠ 24 | 20 | 20 | E

33, rue de Longchamp, 16ᵉ (Boissière/Trocadéro), 01 47 04 96 81; fax 47 04 32 27

■ On a residential street in the 16th, this Classic French "real find" with "exotic" Asian accents is the passion of the "inventive" Roland Durand (ex Pré Catelan), a "friendly" chef-owner who blossoms as he "works the room"; service is "attentive" and the dining room "pleasant and spacious", so even if "prices have crawled up recently", it's an "excellent address."

Passy Mandarin 22 | 19 | 22 | 42

6, rue Bois-le-Vent, 16ᵉ (La Muette), 01 42 88 12 18; fax 45 24 58 54

■ This "well-hidden" Asian in Passy serves consistently "superb" cuisine ("the Peking duck is incredible") in a "beautifully wood-carved" space complemented by "accommodating, efficient" service; tightwads wonder "why prices are so high", but still appreciate it as "one of the better Chinese" choices around; N.B. the popular Opéra location has closed, alas.

Patrick Goldenberg – | – | – | M

69, av de Wagram, 17ᵉ (Ternes), 01 42 27 34 79; fax 42 27 98 85

Ask your "Ashkenazi grandmother" where to go for "hearty portions of traditional Eastern European food" or a pastrami sandwich, and she'll likely laud this Jewish standby near the Place des Ternes serving "good, cheap" noshes; if a bit low on decor, it's as close as you'll get to a deli around here – and it's even open Saturdays.

Paul Chêne ⊠ 25 | 16 | 26 | 57

123, rue Lauriston, 16ᵉ (Trocadéro/Victor Hugo), 01 47 27 63 17; fax 47 27 53 18

■ Sending you back to Paris of the 1950s, this old-school Traditional French offering "excellent" eats with "super service" is a "favorite" "neighborhood spot" in the 16th; perhaps while not cheap, it's less expensive "than those more famous, fancy" establishments, and those who found the "intimate" setting a tad "reminiscent of an old-world bordello" should note the decor's been refreshed, post-*Survey*.

Paul, Restaurant ∇ 15 | 15 | 18 | 40

15, pl Dauphine, 1ᵉʳ (Pont-Neuf), 01 43 54 21 48; fax 56 24 94 09

■ It's a "treat to settle down" at the sidewalk tables of this "Classic" French old-timer (circa 1900) on the Ile de la Cité for views of the Seine and "men playing boule under the trees"; the proximity to the Palais de Justice lures lawyer types who advocate its "reliable food and friendly service", and the verdict is: "it's still nice after all these years."

Pavillon Montsouris

| 20 | 24 | 18 | 54 |

20, rue Gazan, 14ᵉ (Porte d'Orleans), 01 43 13 29 00;
fax 43 12 29 02; www.pavillon-montsouris.fr

■ "An ideal spot in summer" thanks to an "unbelievable setting" overlooking the Parc Montsouris ("you feel like you're in the country"), this "charming" belle-epoque "greenhouse" with a colonial interior is also "quite nice in winter"; the Classic French menu offers "good quality" for the price, and service is almost up to the scenic snuff, too.

Pearl

| – | – | – | M |

53 bis bd Arago, 13ᵉ (Les Gobelins/Glacière), 01 47 07 58 57;
fax 47 07 46 09

It's hard to believe this aggressively fashionable newcomer is located in such a quiet, residential part of town (the 13th), but it is, drawing a hip young crowd with its baroque decor of Louis-something armchairs, huge erotic-themed oil paintings and alabaster-white finish; the Eclectic menu is equally cutting-edge, following all the latest food fashions – from hibiscus flowers to quinoa to star anise – in its global and Gallic dishes.

Père Claude (Le)

| – | – | – | M |

51, av de La Motte-Picquet, 15ᵉ (La Motte-Picquet-Grenelle), 01 47 34 03 05; fax 40 56 97 84

This family-run Classic French rotisserie near the Ecole Militaire is a steady standby offering "adequate bistro food" and "good grilled meat" in modern surroundings; patrons particularly appreciate when Papa Claude Perraudin, the eponymous owner, is around to add a parental touch.

Pères et Filles

| – | – | – | M |

81, rue de Seine, 6ᵉ (Odéon/Mabillon), 01 43 25 00 28;
fax 43 25 69 21

Since it sometimes seems easier to find an Italian restaurant in Saint-Germain-des-Prés than a French one, this easygoing entry (from the owners of Bistrot Vivienne) is a welcome addition; while framed antique posters, globe lights, tile floors and wooden tables constitute a vaguely Hollywood-style take on a Paris bistro, the menu runs to the classics, brought to the international crowd by young waiters in white shirts and black aprons.

Pergolèse (Le) ●🖾

| ▽ | 22 | 16 | 21 | 85 |

40, rue Pergolèse, 16ᵉ (Porte Dauphine/Porte Maillot), 01 45 00 21 40; fax 45 00 81 31

■ Porte Maillot locals have uncovered a "neighborhood jewel" in this "small" Traditional French with an "innovative" menu (think langoustine ravioli and lamb carpaccio) that's "ideal for a business dinner or an intimate celebration."

Perraudin 🔒   _ | _ | _ | M

*157, rue St-Jacques, 5ᵉ (Cluny-La Sorbonne/Luxembourg),
01 46 33 15 75*

Just behind the Panthéon "is the real deal" for a Traditional French meal: "homey, warm, simple, good food" at unbeatable prices in a mirror-and-tile decorated room that's typical turn-of-the-century Latin Quarter (1903, to be exact); it's quite popular, so "don't go without a reservation."

Perron (Le) 🔒   ▽ 21 | 14 | 18 | 56

*6, rue Perronet, 7ᵉ (St-Germain-des-Prés), 01 45 44 71 51;
fax 45 44 71 51*

■ "A pleasant welcome" always awaits pasta aficionados at this "very good Italian" whose "aromas titillate the taste buds" (but whose bills burn wallets a bit); the place is generally "hopping at lunch" with a "local crowd" of Saint-Germain dwellers, and more "quiet at dinner", creating the "ideal ambiance for romance."

Pershing, Restaurant ◑   12 | 24 | 11 | 65

*Hotel Pershing Hall, 49, rue Pierre Charron, 8ᵉ
(Charles de Gaulle-Etoile), 01 58 36 58 36; fax 58 36 58 01;
www.pershinghall.com*

◪ It's "all in the looks" at this "smart" hotel eatery near the Champs-Elysées with "very modern" decor by Andrée Putman and an "impressive vertical garden" covering one wall of an "agreeable patio"; however, neither the setting nor the "well-proportioned" (but "badly trained") waitresses can make up for the food, "uninteresting" Asian-inspired Eclectic–Contemporary French cuisine "out of sync with the pretentious prices."

Petit Bofinger   16 | 15 | 18 | 34

*1, pl Dome, La Défense (La Grande Arche); fax 46 92 46 47 🔒
2, av de Paris, Vincennes (Chateau de Vincennes); fax 49 57 02 79
6, rue de la Bastille, 4ᵉ (Bastille), 01 42 72 05 23; fax 42 72 04 94 ◑
20, bd Montmartre, 9ᵉ (Richelieu-Drouot), 01 47 70 91 35;
fax 42 47 08 99 ◑
10, pl Maréchal Juin, 17ᵉ (Péreire), 01 56 79 56 20;
fax 56 79 56 21 ◑*

◪ While "nothing outstanding", this Flo Group chain of traditional bistros is "good in a franchise sort of way" – i.e. handy "post-opera or if you're alone" for a "quick snack" of "honestly prepared", though sometimes "uneven" eats; alas, they have "none of the charm of the original Bofinger", but at least the service is reassuringly "crisp."

Petit Colombier (Le) 🔒   ▽ 22 | 17 | 21 | 83

*42, rue des Acacias, 17ᵉ (Argentine/Charles de Gaulle-Etoile),
01 43 80 28 54; fax 44 40 04 29*

■ Loyalists of this Classic French in the Etoile area are happy to announce that the owner extends an "excellent welcome" at the door, and that once *à table,* the "cooking merits special consideration", in particular the "game" offerings; be sure to "pay attention to the wine list", which features some "good bottles" at moderate prices.

Petit Colombier Côté Mer ⧄ — — — M
40, rue des Acacias, 17ᵉ (Argentine/Charles de Gaulle-Etoile), 01 40 55 06 63; fax 44 40 04 29
In the 17th, this annex of the neighboring Petit Colombier has a seafood vocation, as seen in its appealingly varied and modestly priced catch-of-the-day menu, which specializes in shellfish; cozy, friendly and open daily, it's immediately become popular with oyster-loving locals, especially since prices are moderate compared to other belly-up-to-the-counter bivalve veterans in Paris.

Petite Chaise (A la) ◐ 17 15 17 39
36, rue de Grenelle, 7ᵉ (Rue du Bac), 01 42 22 13 35; fax 42 22 33 84
▐ For "old-fashioned" "country French" fare in a "cozy setting", locals and tourists ("too many", some add) "rely" on this circa-1680 address in the 7th; though its pint-size digs have some dining on their "neighbor's lap" and exacerbates the "noise", the staff is ever "accommodating" and the tab *toujours* a "bargain."

Petite Cour (La) ◐ 20 18 19 49
8, rue Mabillon, 6ᵉ (Mabillon/St-Germain-des-Prés), 01 43 26 52 26; fax 44 07 11 53; www.la-petitecour.com
■ An "international clientele" lauds the "very good" classic Bistro offerings, "helpful service" and "intimate setting" at this Mabillon site whose "lovely terrace" permits a "peaceful" meal in fair weather; factor in the "good-value prix fixe" and "interesting" wines and you have a "favorite."

Petite Sirène de Copenhague (La) ⧄ ▽ 23 16 23 46
47, rue Notre-Dame-de-Lorette, 9ᵉ (St-Georges), 01 45 26 66 66
■ Sea-starved sirens sing nothing but praises for this "Danish delight" in the 9th, where pedigreed chef-owner Peter Thulstrup (ex Crillon and Tour d'Argent) and staff "warmly greet" guests and serve "refined" fish-centric cuisine based on "high-quality ingredients" in a "laid-back" atmosphere; although it's "not cheap", all concede it's "one of the best tables in the neighborhood."

Petites Sorcières (Les) ⧄ — — — M
12, rue Liancourt, 14ᵉ (Denfert Rochereau), 01 43 21 95 68; fax 43 21 95 68
The witch-themed decor (*sorcière* means witch) may be a bit hokey (witchy puppets are suspended from the ceiling and there's a fair amount of Halloween paraphernalia around), but no sorcery is needed to attract admirers to this Montparnasse lair, where the traditional Bistro cooking of chef Christian Teule casts a convivial spell.

Petite Tour (La) 🛇
_ _ _ E

11, rue de la Tour, 16ᵉ (Passy), 01 45 20 09 31; fax 45 20 09 97
"Nestled in the upscale 16th", this Passy "classic" takes its cue from the local crowd ("no trendy types here") that appreciates the "Traditional French cuisine" and "attentive" service in a recently refreshed, "restful" raspberry-colored environment; while it can be costly, some note more "reasonable prices" of late.

Petit Laurent (Le) 🛇
∇ 21 18 22 55

38, rue de Varenne, 7ᵉ (Rue du Bac), 01 45 48 79 64; fax 45 44 15 95
■ A "favorite" among politicos seeking a "tranquil" respite from ministerial machinations in the 7th, this "friendly" "neighborhood" Classic French may be "unexciting" but it also "never disappoints" with "quality" fare, "classy" ambiance and "unpretentious" service.

Petit Lutétia (Le) ☾
∇ 14 17 18 36

107, rue de Sèvres, 6ᵉ (Vaneau), 01 45 48 33 53; fax 45 48 74 59
☑ "Step back into old Paris" at this circa-1915 brasserie that lures loads of "American tourists" and Rue de Sèvres shoppers with its "romantic" air and "not special, but solid" traditional offerings at "reasonable" prices; however, some scoff that it's "not worth the detour."

Petit Marché (Le) ☾
_ _ _ I

9, rue de Béarn, 3ᵉ (Bastille/Chemin Vert), 01 42 72 06 67; fax 42 76 00 03
"Hip" in a very "Parisian" way, this New French just a "stone's throw from the Place des Vosges" is an "excellent place to lunch with the locals", who agree the "good food" and "friendly" service makes this quite a "decent value."

Petit Marguery (Le) 🛇
23 18 22 47

9, bd de Port-Royal, 13ᵉ (Les Gobelins), 01 43 31 58 59; fax 43 36 73 34
■ Though this Port Royal mainstay recently changed ownership, the "superb" "menu and quality remain" report delighted devotees of "bistro classics" ("if you like *cèpes* and game, this is your place"); in addition, "veteran" waiters still attend to your needs and the decor is forever "old-fashioned"; some words of advice: order the dessert soufflé or "you'll regret it to the end of your days."

Petit Niçois (Le)
∇ 16 12 15 38

10, rue Amélie, 7ᵉ (La Tour-Maubourg), 01 45 51 83 65; fax 47 05 77 46; www.lepetitnicois.com
■ This "lively" bistro in the residential 7th trawls the waters of Nice to present an "authentic bouillabaisse" and other Southern-style dishes that match the "Provençal decor"; it's a "simple place", but "pleasant" enough for a Sunday supper.

Petit Pergolèse (Le) ☒   _ | _ | _ | M
38, rue Pergolèse, 16ᵉ (Argentine/Porte Maillot), 01 45 00 23 66; fax 45 00 44 03

Imbued with "the advantages of the mother ship next door", this young Porte Maillot adjunct of Le Pergolèse offers a "rather original" New French menu "without the prices" of its parent (but "with more noise", alas); though the "decor is simple", most remember it as a "pretty little" address.

Petit Pontoise (Le)   _ | _ | _ | M
9 rue de Pontoise, 5ᵉ (Maubert-Mutualité), 01 43 29 25 20

"Close to the Seine on the Left Bank", this "tiny" "joint" is "not fancy" – you order from "blackboards [scattered] all around" the environs – but it's a "great place to indulge in good" classic Bistro cooking, served by a "helpful, efficient staff"; relaxed prices ensure that those who've discovered it "will definitely go back."

Petit Poucet (Le)   17 | 19 | 15 | 43
4, rd-pt Claude Monet, Levallois (Pont de Levallois), 01 47 38 61 85; fax 47 38 20 49; www.le-petitpoucet.net

■ Owing to an "exceptional setting" on the Ile de la Jatte, this multilevel Contemporary French is "still trendy" – ergo "always packed" – especially "when it's warm enough to sit on the terrace" "overlooking the Seine"; because "the cuisine is simple", technically moderate tabs can seem "a little expensive", but it's a really "fun place to go, plus you can get your car washed (and parked) while you eat."

Petit Prince de Paris (Le) ◐   21 | 19 | 22 | 39
12, rue de Lanneau, 5ᵉ (Maubert-Mutualité), 01 43 54 77 26

■ "All are welcome" – "gay, straight", "English-speaking" – at this "slightly campy establishment" in the 5th that's a "must for *The Little Prince* lovers" and "smoochy couples" everywhere; certainly the "old-school" French menu is "delicious", but to many the "attractive", "entertaining staff is the reason to keep coming back."

Petit Rétro (Le) ☒   20 | 20 | 20 | 37
5, rue Mesnil, 16ᵉ (Victor Hugo), 01 44 05 06 05; www.petitretro.fr

■ "What we imagine a Parisian bistro to be" sigh *amants* of this "gem" off the Place Victor Hugo; the "classic" dishes can be "delicious", service is usually "gracious" and the glazed art nouveau tile walls and an old bar are "charming"; plus, the *prix* are "reasonable" for the neighborhood; P.S. it's also a hospitable place to dine alone "with a book."

Petit Riche (Au) ◐☒   15 | 20 | 15 | 46
25, rue Le Peletier, 9ᵉ (Le Peletier/Richelieu-Drouot), 01 47 70 68 68; fax 48 24 10 79; www.aupetitriche.com

■ At this "old-style brasserie" in the 9th, "nothing seems to have changed for years", starting with the "satisfactory" "post-war"–era Classic French menu and the "lovely" turn-

of-the-century decor featuring mirrors and banquettes –
all of which make it a smart bet "to bring foreigners to"; an
Opéra Garnier and "theater crowd" pops in late at night
when perchance you can spy "a well-known face."

Petits Marseillais (Les) ◖ ▽ 15 | 15 | 17 | 38
*72, rue Vieille-du-Temple, 3ᵉ (Hôtel-de-Ville), 01 42 78 91 59;
fax 42 78 91 59*

☑ This tiny Provençal enclave in the Marais tries to make
things "comfy" with an "intimate space and subdued
lighting"; but while its defenders find the fare "decent",
Marseilles expats are sometimes "disappointed" by a lack
of care in the kitchen.

Petit St. Benoît (Le) ⌧⍢ 16 | 12 | 17 | 37
4, rue St-Benoît, 6ᵉ (St-Germain-des-Prés), 01 42 60 27 92

☑ "Everyone is packed in tight" at this "fun", "noisy"
"student canteen" behind the Saint-Germain-des-Prés
church, whose authentic 1901-bistro decor draws many
retro-oriented tourists (even though "you can't make a
reservation"); the Traditional French menu is "passable",
but critics claim that, despite its "cheap prices", it's not
necessarily "a good value."

Petit Victor Hugo (Le) ◖⌧ 14 | 14 | 14 | 41
*143, av Victor Hugo, 16ᵉ (Victor Hugo/Rue de la Pompe),
01 45 53 02 68; fax 44 05 13 46*

☑ This Traditional French in the 16th is popular with
"classy locals" who receive a "golden welcome" when
they slip in for a "fairly priced", "honest" meal of "salad,
frites and a glass of wine"; unknowns, however, tell a
different story, citing "cranky" service and inconsistency
in the kitchen.

Petit Zinc (Le) ◖ 16 | 20 | 16 | 49
*11, rue St-Benoît, 6ᵉ (St-Germain-des-Prés/Mabillon),
01 42 86 61 00; fax 42 86 61 09; www.petitzinc.com*

☑ While the "wonderful belle-epoque interior" is the main
asset of this venerable Saint-Germain brasserie, it doesn't
prevent the Frères Blanc property from exuding a "franchise
feel" – not that this deters the multitudes of "touristy"
types, who stick to such "simple" choices as "a shellfish
platter that's a treat"; still, a vocal handful huffs that, given
the "wandering service", this "old standby" is "better for
people-watching than for eating."

Petrossian ⌧ 24 | 18 | 20 | 85
*18, bd de La Tour-Maubourg, 7ᵉ (La Tour-Maubourg/Invalides),
01 44 11 32 32; fax 44 11 32 35; www.petrossian.fr*

■ If "luscious smoked salmon" and "caviar is your pleasure,
this is the spot" say seduced surveyors of this *de luxe*
seafooder/shop in the 7th; it's a top "address to invite a
client" to as the "adventurous mixes" and "magnificent
desserts" "always get people talking", even if the "chic

gray decor" leaves warm-water species feeling a trifle "cold"; while a "full wallet" is indeed a prerequisite, the prix fixe lunch is a tantalizing lure.

Pharamond ⌧ 15 23 15 60
24, rue de la Grande Truanderie, 1er (Etienne Marcel/Les Halles), 01 40 28 45 18; fax 40 28 45 87; www.le-pharamond.com
■ Exhaling a whiff of the bygone Les Halles market, this "splendid old standby" of the 1st seems the "last of an era", with its "beautiful" belle-epoque decor; "if you're in the mood for tripes" and other classic Bistro favorites, this is "an offal place" (and we mean that nicely).

Pichet de Paris (Le) ⌧ ∇ 18 13 17 62
68, rue Pierre Charron, 8e (Franklin D. Roosevelt), 01 43 59 50 34; fax 42 89 68 91
☑ The "fresh" "seafood classics" are "sole good" at this "typical brasserie" in the 8th; however, some say that "unless you're a regular" (as was the late President Mitterrand) "the service is on the cooler side"; but whether you lean left or right, your oysters come straight from the "shellfish shucker" stationed out front.

Pied de Chameau (Au) ● ∇ 15 18 12 35
20, rue Quincampoix, 4e (Hôtel-de-Ville), 01 42 78 35 00; fax 42 78 00 50; www.aupieddechameau.fr
☑ For "fun with a group of friends", those missing Morocco head toward this North African address behind the Centre Beaubourg that's best known for its "kitschy", fantasy decor and nightly "entertainment"; though it's of "good quality", the fare "lacks pep" foes fume; perhaps they should just fixate on the "delights of the belly dancer" or snake charmer.

Pied de Cochon (Au) ● 17 18 16 45
6, rue Coquillière, 1er (Châtelet-Les Halles), 01 40 13 77 00; fax 40 13 77 09; www.pieddecochon.com
☑ "For onion soup at the break of dawn", revelers trot down to this 24/7 "touristy", "lively" "leftover from the Les Halles market glory days" in the 1st; some say the balance of the brasserie standards is "disappointingly" "ordinary", but the namesake pig's feet, accompanied by a chilled Brouilly from the Beaujolais-heavy wine list, hits a weak spot for happy hogs who dream of "gnawing on the bone till they roll me out."

Pierre au Palais Royal ⌧ 16 13 15 61
10, rue Richelieu, 1er (Palais Royal-Musée du Louvre), 01 42 96 09 17; fax 42 96 26 40
☑ Now under different ownership, this Traditional French has been "enlarged" and "renovated" along ancient lines after a fire (which may not be reflected in the Decor score); it's a "good place for lunch" if you're breezing through the Palais Royal supporters say, even if a rebellious contingent

finds it "too fussy" and the loss of the charming flower shop in front "a pity."

PIERRE GAGNAIRE   28 | 25 | 27 | VE

Hôtel Balzac, 6, rue Balzac, 8ᵉ (Charles de Gaulle-Etoile/ George V), 01 58 36 12 50; fax 58 36 12 51; www.pierre-gagnaire.com

■ A hands-down "must-try for any real foodie", this Haute Cuisine "extravaganza" located in the Hôtel Balzac portends an "unforgettable" experience that "blows away" diners with a "dazzling", "endless parade" of "edible art", "exquisitely served" in an "elegant" sycamore setting; admittedly, some of the "strange combinations" are "not for the faint of heart – or wallet", but to those up for a multi-hour meal, chef-owner Pierre Gagnaire, aka the "Picasso of the palate", "is worthy of a special trip to Paris."

Pinxo ◐   – | – | – | M

Plaza Vendôme Hotel, 9, rue d'Alger, 1ᵉʳ (Tuileries), 01 40 20 72 00; fax 40 20 72 02

'*Pinxo*' means 'to pinch' in Basque, and the concept at this handsome, moderately priced site in the Place Vendôme Hotel is to pinch whatever tasty morsels or little plates you fancy from the updated Southwestern and New French menu, then watch them being assembled in the open kitchen by a staff trained by chef Alain Dutournier of Carré des Feuillants and Thierry de la Brosse, owner of Chez L'Ami Louis.

Pitchi Poï   – | – | – | M

7, rue Caron, 4ᵉ (St-Paul), 01 42 77 46 15; fax 42 77 75 49; www.pitchipoi.com

In the Marais, this "cute" Eastern European enclave serves kosher food with a Polish flair in a "pleasantly" classic setting brightened by mosaics and an endearing terrace; the "large choice of vodkas" is perfect for washing down the homemade salmon blini or the signature apple strudel.

Pizzeria d'Auteuil   ▽ 20 | 16 | 18 | 38

(fka Le Petit Marguery)
81, rue la Fontaine, 16ᵉ (Michel Ange-Auteuil), 01 42 88 00 86

■ While nostalgists miss the "old iconoclastic Petit Marguery", this Franco-Italian current incarnation entices "budget-conscious students" and office workers at lunch, and Porte d'Auteuil locals in the evening, with its "pretty darn good" food, including a "delicious pizza."

Place (La) ⌺   – | – | – | M

Hôtel Radisson Champs-Elysées, 78, av Marceau, 8ᵉ (Charles de Gaulle-Etoile), 01 53 23 43 63; fax 53 23 43 44; www.radissonsas.com

This intimate hotel address, with a clean, contemporary decor, well-spaced tables and a garden courtyard, is the place to be for high-flying media and luxury-business executives; well-drilled waiters dish up the New French menu with global inspirations and present bills that are actually reasonable for such a pricey part of town (the 8th).

Planet Hollywood ●   8 | 12 | 10 | 31
78, av des Champs-Elysées, 8ᵉ (Franklin D. Roosevelt/George V), 01 53 83 78 27; fax 45 63 02 84; www.planethollywood.com
■ As an ambassador of "Yankee" cuisine, this "noise" "factory" serves "industrial" "chain" fare on the Champs-Elysées that has Americans fretting over "what the Europeans think of us"; it's "fun with the kids" or "if you're homesick for burgers and fries"; otherwise, "you're better off with a candy bar."

Ploum 🅢   – | – | – | M
20, rue Alibert, 10ᵉ (Goncourt), 01 42 00 11 90
The New French menu speaks with a Japanese accent at this loft-like space near the Canal Saint-Martin in the 10th; dark wood furniture, white walls and a few plants sum up the Zen-like interior, with the animation coming from an arty young crowd that's pleased to find such a chic site in a rather nondescript part of town.

Point Bar 🅢⊘   – | – | – | M
40, pl du Marché St-Honoré, 1ᵉʳ (Pyramides), 01 42 61 76 28; fax 42 96 46 90
Alice Bardet, daughter of Tours chef Jean Bardet, makes a point of her own with this stylish new table overlooking the Ricardo Bofil–designed Marché Saint-Honoré; the servers are relaxed and smiling, the art gallery–like decor is streamlined, and while the inventive menu takes inspiration from a variety of kitchens – Indian, Mauritian, North African – it remains decidedly French with a contemporary attitude.

Polidor ●⊘   14 | 14 | 14 | 24
41, rue Monsieur-le-Prince, 6ᵉ (Luxembourg/Odéon), 01 43 26 95 34; fax 43 26 22 79
■ "Everyone should go" once to this 150-plus-year-old "authentic bistro" near the Luxembourg Gardens, if only to "step back in time" to Vieux Paris and experience the "communal tables" that have tourists sitting cheek-by-jowl with "Sorbonne students" and local "characters"; yes, the Classic French cuisine "is pretty basic" and the service "hasty", but at least the prices "leave you with lots of pocket change."

Pomponette (A la) 🅢   – | – | – | M
42, rue Lepic, 18ᵉ (Abbesses/Blanche), 01 46 06 08 36; fax 42 52 95 44
Those trolling for a "typical" classic-bistro experience won't be disappointed by this "friendly" Montmartre locale run by the same family since 1909; serving well-prepared standards and "affordable wines" in an "authentic" turn-

of-the-century decor, it also hosts musical soirées with
traditional Parisian songs one evening per month.

Pomze ⌧   – – – M

109, bd Haussmann, 8ᵉ (Miromesnil/St-Augustin), 01 42 65 65 83;
fax 42 65 30 03; www.pomze.com

With the Vergers d'Anjou (an association of orchards
from the Anjou region) as one of its main backers, this
handsome, white-walled new place in the banking quarter
of the 8th near Miromesnil is all about apples; not only is
the New French menu dominated by them (anyone for
artichokes stuffed with crawfish and Granny Smiths?), but
a small, stylish ground-floor grocery sells byproducts like
cider and Calvados.

Poquelin (Le) ⌧   ▽ 20 17 18 51

17, rue Molière, 1ᵉʳ (Palais Royal-Musée du Louvre/Pyramides),
01 42 96 22 19; fax 42 96 05 72

■ "Dark and cozy", with a "theatrically themed" interior that
recalls the nearby Comédie Française, this "*petit*" place
"off the beaten path" "is as charming as it gets" – thanks
to its proprietors, a "delightfully attentive couple" and
their chef son, who serve up "very good", market-oriented
Traditional French food and "specialties from the Auvergne."

Port Alma ⌧   20 15 19 73

10, av de New York, 16ᵉ (Alma-Marceau), 01 47 23 75 11;
fax 47 20 42 92

◪ "Fish and nothing but" "delicious" fish is featured at this
"quiet", contemporary seafooder with a maritime-influenced
decor on the quay near the Place de l'Alma; some scoff at
the "pricey" menu and "slightly rigid" service typical of
this "high-rent neighborhood", but all's "redeemed by the
view of the Eiffel Tower" from a large picture window –
and a signature "chocolate soufflé that's a sin."

Potager du Roy (Le) ⌧   21 18 21 56

1, rue du Maréchal-Joffre, Versailles (RER Versailles-
Rive Gauche), 01 39 50 35 34; fax 30 21 69 30

◪ Named for the nearby kitchen garden that once furnished
France's royalty with fruit and vegetables, this "old-
fashioned", "tiny place" in Versailles serves Traditional
French food and a reasonable weekday lunch menu,
"including a good glass of wine" admirers attest; but a few
revolutionaries decree this "so-so" spot wouldn't measure
up to the Sun King's standards.

Pouilly Reuilly ⌧   ▽ 23 19 17 38

68, rue André Joineau, Le Pré-St-Gervais (Hoche),
01 48 45 14 59; fax 48 45 93 93

■ It's easy to "feel like one of the locals" at this authentic,
early-20th-century bistro, "certainly the best table" in the
villagelike suburb of Pré-St-Gervais; the menu of "very-
good cuisine" highlights down-to-earth classics such as

blood sausage, sweetbreads and baba au rhum, delivered by "fast service."

Poulbot Gourmet
– | – | – | M

39, rue Lamarck, 18ᵉ, 01 46 06 86 00; fax 46 06 63 14

In a quiet, residential part of Montmartre, this formal, old-fashioned address pulls a crowd of older regulars with the quality and precision of its Traditional French cooking, cozy ambiance (globe lamps light the dining room) and serious service that believes in the ceremony of a restaurant meal.

Poule au Pot (La) ●
– | – | – | M

9, rue Vauvilliers, 1ᵉʳ (Châtelet-Les Halles/Louvre-Rivoli), 01 42 36 32 96; fax 40 91 90 64; www.lapouleaupot.com

Night-owls who hanker for the "definitive" onion soup, eponymous chicken in a pot or "lots of" other Traditional French favorites flock to this "fun, relaxed classic bistro" (an institution since 1935) in Les Halles; it's a taste of "authentic Paris at its lusty, straight-ahead best", served up – along with prime "people-watching" – until 5 AM.

PRÉ CATELAN (LE) 🗷
26 | 27 | 24 | VE

Bois de Boulogne, route de Suresnes, 16ᵉ, 01 44 14 41 14; fax 45 24 43 25; www.lenotre.fr

■ There's something "magical" about this "dreamlike" veteran in the Bois de Boulogne, "far from the noise of the city": "in the summer, the garden is the most beautiful spot in Paris to dine" (or better yet, lunch), while in the winter, a fireplace warms the 1900 interior; of course, all this, plus chef Frédéric Anton's "world-class" Haute Cuisine "creations", "comes with a high price", but the Tuesday–Saturday noontime "prix fixe is a true bargain", so "don't miss" the chance to "celebrate a special occasion" here.

Press Café 🗷
– | – | – | I

89, rue Montmartre, 2ᵉ (Sentier), 01 40 26 07 30

Its name inspired by the nearby offices of Le Figaro and press agencies, this intimate, exposed-stone bistro in the 2nd naturally draws hard-driving journalists at lunch, while stylish young locals dine to a hip soundtrack in the evening; the daily changing blackboard makes a few feints at originality, but mostly stays within a traditional register (steak frites, steak tartare, etc.).

Pressoir (Au) 🗷
– | – | – | E

257, av Daumesnil, 12ᵉ (Michel Bizot), 01 43 44 38 21; fax 43 43 81 77

Year in, year out, chef Henri Séguin forges on as a standard-bearer of the tried-and-true classics (seasonal game and a warm seafood platter) at his refined table with leather armchairs and oak paneling deep in the 12th; both business folk and bourgeois couples come here for "Traditional French cuisine that's top quality", though – weight-watchers beware – "not light."

Pré Verre (Le) ☒ — — — M
8, rue Thénard, 5ᵉ (Maubert-Mutualité), 01 43 54 59 47
"Everything is tremendous" in this casual, bustling New French addition to the Latin Quarter (from the "charming people" behind Clos Morillons), which serves "highly ambitious" dishes made with "exotic spices" and an "imaginative list of cheap wines"; there are jazz album covers on the walls and jazz music on the sound system – just "don't get seated in the basement."

Procope (Le) ◑ 16 21 17 51
13, rue de l'Ancienne Comédie, 6ᵉ (Odéon), 01 40 46 79 00; fax 40 46 79 09; www.procope.com
◣ In the heart of Saint-Germain, the city's oldest cafe is a "history buff's delight", attracting those who come to "experience the ghosts" of Voltaire, Diderot and Robespierre in a "gorgeous" setting of salons and old portraits; but while traditionalists are "happily surprised" by the Classic French cuisine and "helpful" staff, modernists mutter "don't bother" with this "tired old" "tourist trap" ("should be made into a museum and put out of its misery").

Prosper — — — M
89, rue du Rocher, 8ᵉ (Villiers), 01 43 87 55 03; fax 43 87 55 03
Set in the up-and-coming Les Batignolles area, this restaurant "à la mode" draws a prosper-ous business clientele with its "soigné decor" including "very comfortable armchairs" in red leather and picture windows that open wide in the summer; culinary director Guy Legay (ex Ritz) oversees a menu of inventive, "very New French cuisine", but some sniff prices, though relatively modest, seem "steep for what's on the plate."

P'Tit Panisse (Le) ☒ — — — I
35, rue de Montreuil, 11ᵉ (Faidherbe-Chaligny), 01 43 71 37 90
This tiny 11th-arrondissement bistro's gorgeous retro decor – complete with ceiling fan, a beautiful zinc-framed chalkboard listing daily specials and lots of old-fashioned enameled plaques – brightens the scene; the hearty, old-fashioned menu is low-priced, so be sure to book ahead; just don't expect a lot of elbow room or smoke-free air.

P'tit Troquet (Le) ☒ 22 18 23 36
28, rue de l'Exposition, 7ᵉ (Ecole Militaire), 01 47 05 80 39; fax 47 05 80 39
■ "What you envision a Paris neighborhood restaurant to be" profess fans of this "down-to-earth" family-run eatery near the Eiffel Tower – from the "well-prepared", "no-nonsense classic Bistro grub" to the "authentic" 1930s decor and zinc bar; a "warm welcome" pervades an atmosphere that's "intimate", both figuratively and literally: the "tables are so close together they're almost communal."

Publicis Drugstore ◑

— | — | — | M

133, av des Champs Elysées, 8ᵉ (Charles de Gaulle-Etoile/George V), 01 44 43 77 64; fax 44 43 79 02; www.publicisdrugstore.com

Le Drugstore, one of the great institutions along the Champs, has been redone with an undulating glass facade by American architect Michele Saee; foodwise, it now offers two adjacent venues for a meal, both with menus conceived by Alain Ducasse and Thierry de la Brosse (the owner of Chez L'Ami Louis): the Brasserie, where diners can expect the likes of macaroni with ham and truffles, and the modernistic, red-and-ivory–hued Marcel, where more ambitious and expensive New French dishes are on offer.

Pure Café ◑

— | — | — | I

14, rue Jean-Macé, 11ᵉ (Faidherbe-Chaligny), 01 43 71 47 22; fax 43 71 47 22

This young bistro with its horseshoe-shaped bar on the corner of a tiny street in the 11th serves inexpensive, "inventive cuisine that's hit-or-miss depending on the day"; what's more dependable is the "warm welcome" and, in summer, a small but "charming patio" on the sidewalk.

Purple ▨

— | — | — | M

35, rue Faidherbe, 11ᵉ (Charonne/Faidherbe Chaligny), 01 43 71 65 30; fax 40 09 79 75

Located on the site of the late, lamented A Sousceyrac, in a wonderfully old-fashioned neighborhood of the 11th, this newcomer reflects the area's recent influx of ambitious young residents, who appreciate its stylish Downtown attitude and lush decor dominated by oversized, dark fabric lamp shades; the Contemporary French menu focuses on salads, grills and other low-calorie options.

Quai Ouest ◑

15 | 17 | 13 | 38

1200, quai Marcel Dassault, St-Cloud (Pont-de-St-Cloud), 01 46 02 35 54; fax 46 02 33 02

■ "French TV stars", business-lunch types and cool courting couples hit the scene on the Seine in this "hip", "gigantesque" and "consistently fun" loftlike barge with a "superb terrace" overlooking the river in Saint-Cloud; it dishes up a "pretty diverse" array of Eclectic eats and on Sundays, a popular "brunch and clown" ("to be avoided if you don't like kids"); just steer clear of this ship if you're "afraid of noise" or in a hurry, since "service is rather slow."

404 (Le) ◑

21 | 25 | 18 | 42

69, rue des Gravilliers, 3ᵉ (Arts et Métiers), 01 42 74 57 81; fax 42 74 03 41

■ As long as you're ready for the noise and "clowns-in-a-Volkswagen seating", you'll have "an absolutely transporting experience" at this "unique", "sexy Moroccan" in the "hard-to-find" Sentier; "delicious food" ("fabulous tagines", "terrific couscous and stuffed sardines"), plus a "festive" atmosphere created by "fashionably loud music", "friendly staff" and "super-funky" North African decor mean "reservations are necessary" if you want to join the crowd "dancing on the tables."

Quinson (Le)   ⏤ | ⏤ | ⏤ | M

5, pl Etienne Pernet, 15ᵉ (Commerce/Félix Faure), 01 45 32 48 54; fax 44 19 73 18

A taste of Marseille in the heart of the 15th, this circa-1945 bistro has earned a reputation for its "excellent bouillabaisse" and fish dishes ranging from salt cod brandade to sea bass; adorned with model boats, its simple bistro setting is "calm", if perhaps "a little sad."

R. ◖   11 | 19 | 13 | 49

6-8, rue de la Cavalerie, 15ᵉ (La Motte-Picquet-Grenelle), 01 45 67 06 85; fax 45 67 55 72

■ Though "hard to find" – it's atop a "nondescript apartment building" in the 15th – it's "worth the effort" to visit this penthouse proffering a "sublime view" of the Eiffel Tower from the recently revamped Asian interior or – "even more enjoyable – the 22-seat terrace in summer"; served by "slightly amateurish but sweet staffers", the "simple", "imaginative" New French cuisine matches the minimalist setting, except for the big-basin loos ("am I here to wash my hands or baptize a baby?").

Radis Roses Restaurant ⌧   ⏤ | ⏤ | ⏤ | M

68, rue Rodier, 9ᵉ (Anvers), 01 48 78 03 20; fax 48 78 03 20; www.radis-roses.com

With stylish modern decor accented by potted orchids and white laminate, this new bistro in the 9th appeals to the bohemian-bourgeois types who are gentrifying quiet, run-down parts of central Paris; complementing the fashionable setting and relaxed service are lots of vegetable offerings and dishes that reflect a strong regional pedigree – in this case, that of the Drôme area of the French Alps.

R'Aliment ⌧   ⏤ | ⏤ | ⏤ | I

57, rue Charlot, 3ᵉ (Temple), 01 48 04 88 28; www.resodesign.com

In the quiet end of the Marais, this New French from the Reso Design firm is right in step with trends both culinary and decorative; the daily changing menu features light, healthy fare that's heavy on organic pasta and vegetarian dishes, served in a stainless-steel interior whose cool whites are punctuated with long, tall lime-green tables.

Ravi   ∇ 23 | 21 | 18 | 56

50, rue de Verneuil, 7ᵉ (Rue du Bac), 01 42 61 17 28; fax 42 61 12 18

◪ Regulars rave this small spot in the 7th serves "the best Indian food in Paris" that's well worth the "fairly expensive" prices – especially considering the "warm welcome" and "lovely" traditional setting that accompany it; some do get ravi-nous waiting on the one "overtaxed" server (just "consider it an opportunity to enjoy every moment of an excellent meal").

Rech (Le) 🖻   ▽ 20 | 16 | 17 | 55 |
62, av des Ternes, 17ᵉ (Charles de Gaulle-Etoile/Ternes), 01 45 72 29 47; fax 45 72 41 60

■ Locals have been coming to this brasserie in the 17th since 1925, knowing they can count on "delicious" "pre-nouvelle cuisine" classics: "fine fish", top-notch Gillardeau oysters and a house-ripened "Camembert to die for"; although the decor seemingly hasn't changed since its opening, the tables are "spaced well apart" and there's a sidewalk terrace that's a real "refuge in summer."

Réconfort (Le)   – | – | – | M |
37, rue de Poitou, 3ᵉ (St-Sébastien Froissart), 01 49 96 09 60; fax 49 96 09 62

Housed in a 16th-century stone building on a "charming" street in the 3rd, this quaint table is decorated like a private home – one so chock-full of knickknacks it's almost "baroque"; however, dis-conforted critics come here "more for the ambiance" and "good-natured service" than the standard New French fare.

RÉGALADE (LA) 🖻   25 | 14 | 17 | M |
49, av Jean Moulin, 14ᵉ (Alésia), 01 45 45 68 58; fax 45 40 96 74

◪ It's "a schlep" to the "southern 14th", but even after a change of owners – founding chef Yves Camdeborde has left to pursue other projects – it's still "worth it" for "rich" Classic French "gourmet food on a budget"; the dining room remains "loud and cramped," suggesting that for many, this remains "the best bistro in Paris, hands down."

RELAIS D'AUTEUIL   26 | 21 | 25 | VE |
"PATRICK PIGNOL" 🖻
31, bd Murat, 16ᵉ (Michel Ange-Molitor/Porte d'Auteuil), 01 46 51 09 54; fax 40 71 05 03

■ In the high-end district near the Porte d'Auteuil, this "*grand petit* restaurant" may be "small" in size but it belongs in the big leagues insist enthusiasts enamored of chef-owner Patrick Pignol's "imaginatively prepared" Haute Cuisine and extensive wine list; completing the picture is a simple yet "beautiful dining room", all paneled and pastels, and "amicable service" overseen by Madame P.

Relais de l'Entrecôte (Le) ◑   23 | 14 | 17 | 35 |
20, rue St-Benoit, 6ᵉ (St-Germain-des-Prés), 01 45 49 16 00; fax 45 49 29 75
15, rue Marbeuf, 8ᵉ (Franklin D. Roosevelt), 01 49 52 07 17; fax 47 23 34 98

■ Addicts of a "mythic entrecôte", "crisp, hot frites" and "secret-magic sauce" "stand in line" (no reservations taken) and sit "on top of each other" at these "outstanding" steakhouse "staples" in Saint-Germain and near the Champs; when ordering from the "friendly but no-nonsense servers", "rare, medium or well done are the only words you need to know" because the "reasonably priced" beef's the only game in town here; but "when they have perfected this so well, why serve anything else?"

Relais de Venise (Le) ● | 20 | 13 | 17 | 36 |
271, bd Péreire, 17ᵉ (Porte Maillot), 01 45 74 27 97
◪ "Rain or shine, there's always a line at the door" of this "simple, consistent" "food factory" close to Porte Maillot, where carnivores satisfy their craving with a one-choice menu: "exceptional entrecôte and inimitable fries" (plus the "best profiteroles"); you'll wait for a seat but not for your food, given the "sometimes too efficient" waitresses.

RELAIS LOUIS XIII ⌧ | 26 | 24 | 24 | VE |
8, rue des Grands-Augustins, 6ᵉ (Odéon/St-Michel), 01 43 26 75 96; fax 44 07 07 80; www.relaislouis13.com
■ You "feel like you were just crowned king" at this Haute Cuisine table in the 6th owned by chef Manuel Martinez, who honed his "conservative but perfectly done cooking" at La Tour d'Argent; catered to by "courteous staffers", a "not very *nouvelle* crowd" comes for a "classic" "taste of *Vieux* Paris", from the "signature duck" to the "intimate" 16th-century interior complete with "timbered walls."

Relais Plaza (Le) ● | 21 | 21 | 23 | 69 |
Hôtel Plaza-Athénée, 21, av Montaigne, 8ᵉ (Alma-Marceau/Franklin D. Roosevelt), 01 53 67 64 00; fax 53 67 66 66; www.plaza-athenee-paris.com
■ That "Hermès scarf won't be out of place" in the "chic" "art deco" digs of this Plaza-Athénée site whose brasserie bites and "excellent" Eclectic eats are, like its more famous Haute Cuisine sibling, under the "influence of Ducasse"; an "international clientele" agrees that it's a "great place for lunch" as well as "after the opera or symphony."

⚹Réminet | 24 | 15 | 21 | E |
3, rue des Grands Degrés, 5ᵉ (Maubert-Mutualité/St-Michel), 01 44 07 04 24; fax 44 07 17 37
■ Run by a "husband-and-wife duo", this "charming little bistro" is having trouble remaining "happily undiscovered" in its Latin Quarter neighborhood; thanks to the "lovely, memorable" New French cuisine, candlelit, "quaint atmosphere" and "highly personal service from Madame", the place is "getting more and more crowded", but respondents shrug "oh, well, can't keep it a secret forever."

Rendez-vous des Camionneurs (Au) ⌧ | – | – | – | M |
34, rue des Plantes, 14ᵉ (Alésia/Plaisance), 01 45 40 43 36
A "throwback" to another era, this "real neighborhood bistro" in the unpretentious 14th near Place d'Alésia –

whose name means 'truck drivers' hangout' – has long been a great place to fill up your tank with "simple but flavorful cooking", featuring robust classics in an "easygoing" ambiance and at unbeatable prices.

Rendez-vous des Chauffeurs (Au)   _ _ _ I
11, rue des Portes Blanches, 18e (Marcadet-Poissonniers), 01 42 64 04 17
"Like your dream of a neighborhood bistro" off the beaten track in the humble part of the 18th, this 100-year-old standby is named for the cab drivers who once ate here between round-the-clock shifts; it still cooks copious amounts of dirt-cheap traditional fare for local "regulars."

Repaire de Cartouche (Le) ⊠   20 13 17 40
99, rue Amelot, 11e (St-Sébastien Froissart), 01 47 00 25 86; fax 43 38 85 91
◪ Chef-owner Rodolphe Paquin has made a name for himself with his "great value" of a classic bistro in the increasingly gentrified 11th; but while converts cheer his "remarkable" "regional" cuisine and "inventive" take on earthy dishes, skeptics snipe the "service is scattered" and the country-inn interior both "dreary" and "dated."

RESTAURANT ALAIN DUCASSE   27 26 26 VE
AU PLAZA-ATHÉNÉE ⊠
Hôtel Plaza-Athénée, 25, av de Montaigne, 8e (Alma-Marceau/ Franklin D. Roosevelt), 01 53 67 65 00; fax 53 67 65 12; www.alain-ducasse.com
◼ Chef "Alain Ducasse is king", but it's the diners who get "treated like royalty" gush guests at his "pinnacle-of-elegance" Plaza-Athénée outpost where "sumptuous", "imaginative" Haute Cuisine is presented by "service so discreet you won't realize when your roll is replenished"; the room's "draped crystal chandeliers and bold design make a grand" statement and prices are pretty "stunning" as well, but "if you're able to get a reservation", this is a ticket to "true happiness."

Restaurant de la Tour ⊠   _ _ _ M
6, rue Desaix, 15e (Dupleix/La Motte-Picquet-Grenelle), 01 43 06 04 24; fax 44 49 05 66
Located just steps from the Eiffel Tower, this Classic French run by a "pleasant" couple attracts a (not surprisingly) "very touristy" clientele, which finds that "after a day of sightseeing, this is the perfect place to relax with a good bottle of wine and great food" in a contemporary yellow-and-rust-colored, Provençal-inspired decor.

Restaurant du Marché ⊠   _ _ _ M
59, rue de Dantzig, 15e (Porte de Versailles/Porte de Vanves), 01 48 28 31 55; fax 48 28 18 31
At this veteran 15th-arrondissement classic bistro with red-leather benches and a pewter bar, chef-owner Francis

Lévêque (ex the late Dame Jeanne) cooks up an "excellent value" of a menu that includes duck *hachis Parmentier* (minced bird with mashed potatoes) and warm madeleines; disciples delight in it being "different every day", but detractors decree it "a bit disappointing."

Restaurant du Musée d'Orsay   15 | 23 | 14 | 35
Musée d'Orsay, 1, rue de Légion d'Honneur, 7ᵉ (Solférino), 01 45 49 47 03; fax 42 22 34 12
☑ "After seeing the Impressionists", go and be impressed by the "spectacular setting" of this "elegant, old" Musée d'Orsay eatery, "a perfect respite from the bustling crowds" with "gilding and chandeliers" throughout; as for the Classic French food, some describe it as "artful" while others say it's "so-so", sunk further by sometimes "surly service."

Restaurant du Palais Royal ☒   19 | 22 | 19 | 65
110, Galerie de Valois, 1ᵉʳ (Bourse/Palais Royal-Musée du Louvre), 01 40 20 00 27; fax 40 20 00 82
■ When the warm weather hits, this "elegant" table is a royal "treat" thanks to its "exceptional terrace" that "overlooks the Palais Royal" (a "convivial" contemporary room welcomes cold-weather clients); Med-influenced, "trustworthy Classic French cuisine" and a "good wine list" mean this garden getaway "never disappoints"; "sure, you pay for eating [here] – but it's worth paying for."

Restaurant GR5   – | – | – | I
19, rue Gustave Courbet, 16ᵉ (Rue de la Pompe), 01 47 27 09 84
14, rue Saussier Leroy, 17ᵉ (Ternes), 01 47 66 15 11 ☒
Though the decor of rough-wood paneling, vintage skis and mountain posters still invokes the Alps, the menu at these celebrated Savoyard specialists has had a major updating: salads and grills have been added to the Traditional French menu renowned for its raclette, fondue and other cheesy glories; named for a footpath that runs from the Jura to the Alps, they're popular with a 16th- and 17th-arrondissement crowd making tracks for a relaxed, inexpensive meal.

Riad (Le) ☒   – | – | – | E
42, av Charles de Gaulle, Neuilly (Les Sablons/Porte Maillot), 01 46 24 42 61; fax 46 40 19 91
It's a quick jaunt from Neuilly to North Africa at this Moroccan establishment just west of Porte Maillot offering "delicious" couscous, tagines, pastillas and imported wines along with "pleasant service", all in an "exotic decor" composed of cozy nooks and cushioned banquettes.

River Café   17 | 20 | 14 | 46
146, quai de Stalingrad, Issy-les-Moulineaux (RER Issy-Val de Seine), 01 40 93 50 20; fax 41 46 19 45; www.lerivercafe.net
☑ The river is the reason to dine on this houseboat in Issy-les-Moulineaux – but only if you "insist" on a table with a

F | D | S | €C

"pretty little view of the Seine" (as opposed to the industrial wharf on the other side); with such engaging surrounds, the "simple" New French eats and sometimes "absent" service tend to fade into the background.

Robe et le Palais (La) 🗷 — | — | — | M
13, rue des Lavandières-Ste-Opportune, 1er (Châtelet-Les Halles), 01 45 08 07 41; fax 45 08 07 41
Select one of the "mouthwatering" vintages, including 40 "by the glass" choices, and soak up the "jovial ambiance" in this little *bistrot à vins* just steps from the Place du Châtelet that features a changing blackboard menu of "sound" food, with roots in the Southwest and Corsica, and "convivial service."

Robert et Louise 🗷⌿ — | — | — | M
64, rue Vieille-du-Temple, 3e (Rambuteau), 01 42 78 55 89
Fancy yourself dining "in a couple's home" when you sit at the "long communal tables" at this Marais mainstay and partake of the "basic hearth-cooked" classic Bistro food that's heavy on roasted meats but also includes such wild cards as "escargot thrown into the fire"; while it's nothing short of "atmospheric", some find the rustic setting a little "rundown."

Roi du Pot-au-Feu (Le) 🗷 ▽ 18 | 15 | 18 | 36
34, rue Vignon, 9e (Havre-Caumartin/Madeleine), 01 47 42 37 10
■ "Bring on the beef and marrow" say subjects of this meat-stew sovereign, a "good-humored" 1930s classic bistro that's a "perfect retreat" on a "cold wintery day" or "after shopping" at the nearby Grands Boulevards department stores; just be sure to also "bring an appetite, as the portions are large."

Romantica (La) 🗷 21 | 19 | 18 | 62
73, bd Jean Jaurès, Clichy (Mairie-de-Clichy), 01 47 37 29 71; fax 47 37 76 32; www.claudiopuglia.com
■ "An address to keep under wraps at all costs", this Clichy Italian lives up to its name thanks to a setting that encompasses an "idyllic" garden for warm-weather dining; the kitchen turns out "pastas with pizzazz", like those spectacularly "flambéed in a Parmesan wheel"; though tabs are a bit "pricey", most admit "the experience is worth it."

Rosimar 🗷 ▽ 23 | 8 | 21 | 41
26, rue Poussin, 16e (Michel Ange Auteuil/Porte d'Auteuil), 01 45 27 74 91; fax 45 20 75 05
"You feel you're in Catalonia" at this "small, out-of-the-way" Spaniard near the Porte d'Auteuil; savvy surveyors say *sí* to "the best paella in France" (that must be ordered when you reserve) and the "very friendly" husband-and-wife owners; the kitchen and their service far outscores the "love-it-or-hate-it" multi-mirrored decor that sends some reaching for supplemental sangria.

Rôtisserie de Neuilly (La)   _ | _ | _ | M

12, av de Madrid, Neuilly (Pont-de-Neuilly), 01 46 24 14 80;
fax 40 88 35 60

Owned by the folks behind Jarrasse, this traditional
rôtisserie in Neuilly, which also serves grilled meat and fowl,
has become popular for business lunches thanks to its
high-quality ingredients and prompt service; in the evening,
a stylish local crowd takes over the relaxing, contemporary
interior of white walls and wood banquettes.

RÔTISSERIE D'EN FACE (LA) ⌫   22 | 17 | 20 | 48

2, rue Christine, 6ᵉ (Odéon/St-Michel), 01 43 26 40 98;
fax 43 54 22 71; www.jacques-cagna.com

■ "Comfortable as a favorite pair of shoes" say regulars of
Jacques Cagna's "cheerful" "baby bistro" in the 6th; that
it's more "Californian" than Classic French sits well with
the crowds of Americans who "rely" on its "simple" roast
meat–heavy menu that may lack a few "fireworks" but has
"no duds either."

Rôtisserie du Beaujolais (La)   21 | 16 | 18 | 44

19, quai de la Tournelle, 5ᵉ (Jussieu/Pont-Marie),
01 43 54 17 47; fax 56 24 43 71

◪ This quai-side, casual and "less-expensive offshoot of the
Tour d'Argent" fills up with tables of "gossiping neighbors"
from the 5th and tourists who "depend" on it for "finger-
licking", if "not very exciting", classic Bistro and "country
French food"; the "cramped, noisy" room fades away if
you "sit by the window" where "the only thing holier than
the rôtisserie chicken is a view of Notre Dame."

Rotonde ◗   13 | 15 | 15 | 43

105, bd du Montparnasse, 6ᵉ (Vavin), 01 43 26 48 26; fax 46 34 52 40

◪ Regulars find it "comforting" that this "Montparnasse old-
time boulevardier" is "always the same": nothing "special"
but a "good enough brasserie" that's "open late" everyday;
if some complain it has become "overpriced", at least it's
a treat for "a drink to watch the passing crowd."

Rouge Tomate   _ | _ | _ | M

34, pl du Marché St-Honoré, 1ᵉʳ (Pyramides/Tuileries),
01 42 61 16 09; fax 42 61 17 01

Overlooking the square surrounding the Marché Saint-
Honoré, this Eclectic newcomer has a menu constructed
around a single product – the tomato, in as many different
fresh varieties as the market permits (plus dishes made from
preserves); photos of the namesake fruit and groceries-
laden shelves accent the white-painted interior.

Rouge Vif (Le) ⌫   ∇ 15 | 12 | 15 | 35

48, rue de Verneuil, 7ᵉ (Musée d'Orsay/Solférino), 01 42 86 81 87

◪ The "charming" staff "provides the fun" at this "local
haunt" "close to the Musée d'Orsay" that's not the place "for

a romantic date but is excellent with loud friends"; if some are unimpressed by the "unpretentious" Southwestern–classic Bistro food, they rave over the "reasonable" tabs.

Rubis (Le) 🈂️   ▽ 13 | 8 | 13 | 24
10, rue du Marché St Honoré, 1ᵉʳ (Tuileries), 01 42 61 03 34
◪ This 100-year-old Place du Marché Saint-Honoré–area wine bistro is postcard Paris, specializing in "respectably priced" Beaujolais by the glass and a simple Classic French lunch menu, though some confide "you can do better for the money in the neighborhood"; in the evening when the kitchen's closed, it's "ideal for a pre-dinner bottle of wine and charcuterie plate."

Rucola (La) 🈂️   – | – | – | M
198, bd Malesherbes, 17ᵉ (Wagram), 01 44 40 04 50; fax 47 63 13 20
Latin-lovers are trekking from afar to this "excellent" Italian trattoria near Place de Wagram that's painted in warm Mediterranean colors and run "by a young, attentive crew" under the direction of two former Sormani employees; "fresh products" and "truly al dente pasta" are two constants on a menu that changes regions every two weeks.

Rue Balzac ●   18 | 19 | 19 | 59
3-5, rue Balzac, 8ᵉ (George V), 01 53 89 90 91; fax 53 89 90 94
▪ Fans croon about this "à la mode" address off the Champs-Elysées, not just for the "chance to catch a glimpse of [rocker and part-owner] Johnny Hallyday", but also for "accommodating" service, "interesting" New French cuisine by a Michel Rostang protégé and a modern decor that includes frescoes, red-velvet banquettes and a bar designed by the singer himself; it's unabashedly "pricey" and may "try too hard to be trendy", but that's show biz.

Rughetta (La) ●   15 | 11 | 13 | 29
41, rue Lepic, 18ᵉ (Abbesses/Blanche), 01 42 23 41 70
◪ Perched on a winding Montmartre street, this "friendly" Italian gets "crowded" with a local "show-biz clientele" and tourists craving "quick" pastas and "Roman-style pizzas"; though decor and service won't win awards, it's nonetheless "difficult to get a table" on weekends and in the summer, when the small terrace is a treat.

Safran (Le) 🈂️   – | – | – | M
29, rue d'Argenteuil, 1ᵉʳ (Pyramides), 01 42 61 25 30; fax 42 61 25 30
Followers of chef Caroll Sinclair who formerly frequented her eponymous address at the Bastille have to seek out her latest venture, a "pretty" saffron-colored bistro, on a little-trafficked street in the 1st; but while some applaud her "good organic" Mediterranean-inspired cooking, the more stringent say it's "hit-or-miss", citing "small portions" and "long delays" in service.

Saint Vincent (Le) ⑤
–|–|–| M

26, rue de la Croix-Nivert, 15ᵉ (Cambronne), 01 47 34 14 94
It's "far from nouvelle" at this classic bistro in the 15th that serves "hearty traditional" Lyonnais fare – think coq au vin, andouillette – along with Beaujolais wines; though the regular crowd is quite international thanks to the nearby UNESCO headquarters, the ambiance is pure French.

Sale e Pepe ⑤
–|–|–| I

30, rue Ramey, 18ᵉ (Château Rouge/Jules Joffrin), 01 46 06 08 01
It's like dining "at home" – albeit a spirited Sicilian one – at this small, casual address in the 18th that's known for its "convivial" ambiance and family-style formula: "you can't choose your dish because there's only one kind of pizza and pasta" – but at these prices, nobody's complaining.

Salon d'Hélène ⑤
19 | 18 | 16 | 57

4, rue d'Assas, 6ᵉ (Sèvres-Babylone), 01 42 22 00 11; fax 42 22 25 40
☑ A "less-expensive alternative" to Hélène Darroze's "exquisite restaurant upstairs" in the 6th, this *salon* is the place to graze on "tapas"-size portions of her signature riffs on Southwestern cooking; the praise isn't universal, as some find her offerings a little too "strange", and the overall experience "a let-down after the high expectations" garnered by "such a well-known chef."

Sardegna a Tavola ⑤
–|–|–| M

1, rue de Cotte, 12ᵉ (Ledru-Rollin), 01 44 75 03 28; fax 44 75 03 02
Ignoring the "uneven service", Italophiles willingly traverse the town for the "generous" portions of "exceptional" regional cuisine at this unofficial "embassy of Sardegna" – it's even decorated in native style, with lots of carved wood – hidden away in the 12th; P.S. "reservations obligatory."

Sarladais (Le) ⑤
–|–|–| M

2, rue de Vienne, 8ᵉ (St-Augustin), 01 45 22 23 62; fax 45 22 23 62; www.lesarladais.com
Bring an appetite to this "very good Southwestern table", a "real sleeper off the beaten track" near the Gare Saint-Lazare, where the "hearty", "non–lean cuisine" – lots of "duck-based dishes and a large variety of foie gras" – is a "fantastic value"; the region's warmth is reflected in the "friendly, unobtrusive service."

Saudade ⑤
–|–|–| M

34, rue des Bourdonnais, 1ᵉʳ (Châtelet-Les Halles), 01 42 36 03 65; fax 42 36 27 77; www.restaurantsaudade.com
'Saudade' means nostalgia, and Lisbon lovers longing for authentic "Portuguese chic" find it at this table near Châtelet cooking up the country's classics, such as grilled

cod and roast suckling pig, accompanied by a "fabulous wine list" that boasts a "good choice of Portos and Vinho Verde"; the service is "elegant" and so is the live fado music the first Tuesday of every month.

Sauvignon (Au) ⊠   ▽ | 16 | 14 | 13 | 19 |
80, rue des Saints-Pères, 7ᵉ (Sèvres-Babylone), 01 45 48 49 02; fax 45 49 41 00
■ A "great place to go for lunch after shopping" if all you want is "a glass of inexpensive wine and an open-faced sandwich" on "famous Poîlane bread", this "quintessential Parisian wine bar" is an oasis in the 7th (a neighborhood not known for cheap and cheerful choices); in the summer "grab an outside table" and "watch *le tout* Paris pass by."

Saveurs de Claude (Aux) ⊠ | – | – | – | M |
12, rue Stanislas, 6ᵉ (Notre-Dame-des-Champs/Vavin), 01 45 44 41 74; fax 45 44 41 95; www.auxsaveursdeclaude.fr
After doing the rounds of Guy Savoy's bistros, chef Claude Lamain now has his own place in Montparnasse, with a minimalist art deco decor and open kitchen where clients can watch him bring original touches to "delicious", affordably priced Traditional French dishes with lots of vegetables, "well presented" by "knowledgeable" servers.

Saveurs du Marché (Aux) ⊠ | – | – | – | M |
4, rue de l'Eglise, Neuilly (Pont de Neuilly), 01 47 45 72 11; fax 46 37 72 13
An open market just steps away means that freshness is guaranteed at this tiny table in the well-heeled suburb of Neuilly, where the young chef-owner offers skillfully prepared Traditional French food (including a sinful caramel French toast dessert) and simple seasonal dishes to a local clientele.

Sawadee ⊠ | 19 | 11 | 15 | 32 |
53, av Emile Zola, 15ᵉ (Charles Michels), 01 45 77 68 90; fax 45 77 57 78; www.sawadee-paris.com
◪ Believers in Bangkok make a beeline for this site in the 15th, where the menu of "good westernized Thai is a gentle introduction" to Southeast Asian classics in an aquarium-dominated decor; some "disappointed" curry connoisseurs deem the cuisine bereft of "zest", but to many it's still the "best" Siamese in town.

Scheffer (Le) ⊠ | 22 | 15 | 18 | 37 |
22, rue Scheffer, 16ᵉ (Trocadéro), 01 47 27 81 11
■ "You can't go wrong" at this "truly old-style bistro", the sort of "neighborhood eatery" "that is rare in the 16th"; its popularity means "you have to squeeze between all the other locals to get to your chair" (and be prepared for "too many smokers") before digging into the "ideal" "classic dishes" that are "excellent value", especially for this well-heeled neighborhood.

Scoop — | — | — | I
154, rue St-Honoré, 1er (Louvre-Rivoli/Palais Royale),
01 42 60 31 84; fax 42 36 01 81; www.scoopcafe.com
A quirky, modern interior – a long counter lined with low-
back ergonomic chairs and an open kitchen set behind a red
Plexiglas partition – has helped make this newcomer steps
from the Louvre popular for an upmarket quick eat; the
Eclectic menu runs from imaginative soups, salads and
sandwiches, many made with organic produce, to inventive
dishes like millefeuille of spice bread and marinated salmon.

Sébillon ● 16 | 16 | 16 | 52
66, rue Pierre Charron, 8e (Franklin Roosevelt), 01 43 59 28 15;
fax 43 59 30 00
20, av Charles de Gaulle, Neuilly (Les Sablons/Porte Maillot),
01 46 24 71 31; fax 46 24 43 50
www.rest-gj.com
☑ "Known for its all-you-can-eat leg of lamb and beans"
sliced at the table, these "classic" brasseries just off the
Champs and in Neuilly are "always a hit with out-of-towners
who say 'how French!'"; alas, that "traditional" "*Vieille*
France" image also means it's "*sans* surprise" some sneer.

16 Haussmann (Le) ☒ 15 | 16 | 15 | 48
*Hôtel Ambassador, 16, bd Haussmann, 9e (Chaussée d'Antin/
Richelieu-Drouot), 01 44 83 40 58; fax 44 83 40 57;*
www.hotelambassador-paris.com
☑ Just up the street from the Galeries Lafayette and Au
Printemps, this hotel dining room with a colorfully "modern",
"pleasantly cold" interior by Philippe Starck offers an
"interesting formula", especially for lunch, with its
"consistently good" combination of Classic French–Med
fare, fans feel; but foes profess the food's "without passion."

Senso ☒ 17 | 20 | 17 | 56
*Hôtel de la Trémoille, 14, rue de la Trémoille, 8e (Alma-Marceau/
Franklin D. Roosevelt), 01 56 52 14 14; fax 56 52 14 13;*
www.hotel-tremoille.com
■ Terence Conran's "stylish" establishment in the 8th
manages to be simultaneously "trendy" and "grown-up",
"without ridiculous attributes like model waitresses and
tiring lounge music"; the sober gray-and-ivory interior
provides "agreeable and relaxing decor far from the tumult
of the Champs" nearby, while the "excellent bar" offers a
cheaper bite and "a chic drink"; at press time, a new Med
menu was pending, outdating the Food score.

7ème Sud ● 16 | 16 | 15 | 37
159, rue de Grenelle, 7e (La Tour-Maubourg), 01 44 18 30 30;
fax 44 18 07 42
56 rue de Boulainvillers, 16e (La Muette), 01 45 20 18 32
☑ A "young, trendy" crowd gets "noisy" over "good
Mediterranean and North African food" ("solid, if not

spectacular") at this rare outpost of hip in a quiet corner near the Ecole Militaire; some say the service can be "a little slow", but for "a neighborhood place" it's "pleasant" and "original", especially for relatively moderate prices; P.S. "there's one in the 16th too."

Sept Quinze (Le) 🖾   22 | 14 | 20 | 35

29, av Lowendal, 15ᵉ (Cambronne/Ségur), 01 43 06 23 06; fax 45 67 14 11

■ Its name refers to its location straddling the 7th and 15th, and regulars from both arrondissements flock to this "lively neighborhood" eatery for its "inventive, even audacious cuisine" (Med-Provençal, with some California-like "tasty twists"), "cool ambiance", "young, charming staff" and "nifty wine selection"; the only drawback is the noise that comes from cramming "too many tables into the room."

Si 🖾   – | – | – | M

14, rue Charlot, 3ᵉ (Arts et Métiers/Filles-du-Calvaire), 01 42 78 02 31; fax 40 76 34 37

It's hard to say no to the "original" Med meals in this "convivial" corner near the Musée Picasso, where the 1970s-style "decor is minimalist but the cuisine is not" (e.g. raw red mullet with tapenade, or preserved duck with potatoes); a particularly inexpensive lunchtime menu is another reason supporters smile *sí*.

Sinago (Le) 🖾   – | – | – | I

17, rue de Maubeuge, 9ᵉ (Cadet/Notre-Dame-de-Lorette), 01 48 78 11 14

Asian-food aficionados in-the-know make tracks to this tiny place in the Gare du Nord neighborhood for "refined, traditional" Cambodian dishes such as pork-filled crêpes and fish with ginger; prices are as modest as the boatlike decor (the fixings, like the name, are from an actual ship).

6 New York 🖾   20 | 19 | 19 | 62

6, av de New York, 16ᵉ (Alma-Marceau), 01 40 70 03 30; fax 40 70 04 77

🗹 Overlooking the Seine near the Place de l'Alma, with an "incredible view of the Eiffel Tower", this New French "aspires to being discreetly fashionable", but "unlike other trendy places, the cooking has real quality" (no surprise, since it's done by "a student of [chef/co-owner] Jean-Pierre Vigato"); however, dissenters deep-six the "noisy" digs and generically "chic" atmosphere – it could be "in New York or California, and I don't go to Paris for U.S. ambiance."

Sizin 🖾   – | – | – | I

47, rue St-Georges, 9ᵉ (St-Georges), 01 44 63 02 28

Ceramic tiles and old postcards of Istanbul help create an authentic ambiance at this family-run traditional Turkish table in the 9th, where the menu includes hummus, skewered lamb brochettes with tomatoes and homemade baklava – all helped down by native potables, such as Kavaklidere wine and strong anise-flavored raki.

Soleil (Le) ▽ 23 | 18 | 23 | 49
109, av Michelet, St-Ouen (Porte de Clignancourt), 01 40 10 08 08; fax 40 10 16 85

■ Antiques hunters with an appetite claim this classic bistro is "a great find", "a refuge from the fray of the flea market" at Saint-Ouen, where hitting upon a good meal used to be a bigger challenge than unearthing a Louis XVI commode; here, the "hospitable", "multilingual patron is justly proud of his product" and its "terrific", "authentic flavors", served in a "congenial setting."

Sologne (La) ☒ – | – | – | M
164, av Daumesnil, 12ᵉ (Daumesnil), 01 43 07 68 97; fax 43 44 66 23

When hunting season hits, locals are wild about the "very good game" on the menu at this pleasant bourgeois address with exposed stone walls in the 12th; the rest of the year, chef-owner Didier Maillet's affordable Traditional French "daily specials" are much appreciated.

Sora Lena ☒ – | – | – | M
18, rue Bayen, 17ᵉ (Ternes), 01 45 74 73 73; fax 45 74 73 52

Sporting a restful taupe-colored decor accented by Japanese lanterns and Vietnamese light fixtures, as well as a '70s vintage disco soundtrack that animates the room without overwhelming it, this spot near the Place des Ternes has immediately started pulling in a glamorous, young crowd, including a lot of recognizable film and show-biz folks; the young, Italy-reared Cambodian chef previously worked at Sormani, a pedigree that appears in his deft Mediterranean cooking, brought by men in black.

SORMANI ☒ 25 | 18 | 22 | VE
4, rue du Général Lanrezac, 17ᵉ (Charles de Gaulle-Etoile), 01 43 80 13 91; fax 40 55 07 37

■ Considered by many the "best Italian in Paris", this "small" star near the Etoile "always offers a wonderful time", maybe because "the amount of truffles used" in the "*cuisine de luxe*" here is "almost obscene"; if prices are a tad tough, the "service is gentle."

Sot l'y Laisse (Le) ☒ – | – | – | M
70, rue Alexandre Dumas, 11ᵉ (Alexandre Dumas), 01 40 09 79 20; fax 40 09 79 20

Tucked away in a quiet corner of the 11th, this bistro is a textbook example of the genre: a convivial neighborhood place with chalkboard specials, grandmotherly old-fashioned dishes and stenciled bunches of grapes covering its yellow walls, hinting at the owner's wine-friendly ways – the extensive list highlights bottles from up-and-coming regions, like the Languedoc-Roussillon, as well as overlooked corners of the country.

Soufflé (Le) ☒   21 | 16 | 20 | 44
36, rue du Mont-Thabor, 1er (Concorde), 01 42 60 27 19; fax 42 60 54 98

■ "If you love" those rising egg whites, "this is the place" say surveyors who blow hot over this "old standby" in a "superb location" near the Place de la Concorde – a veritable "soufflé central" with an "incredible variety" of "cloudlike" sweet and savory versions served by "old-fashioned" waiters who seem part of the slightly "frayed-around-the-edges" decor; some are deflated by it being a "big American hangout", and the rest of the Classic French menu is pretty "narrow", but still, it's a "must, at least once."

Soupière (La) ☒   – | – | – | M
154, av de Wagram, 17e (Wagram), 01 46 22 80 10; fax 46 22 27 09

A "local crowd" ignores the "dull" trompe l'oeil decor in favor of the forest floor – specifically, the wild mushrooms that chef-owner and fungi fanatic Christian Thuillart makes the centerpiece of his "satisfyingly good" Traditional French menu; regulars from the Place de Wagram neighborhood also appreciate this "genteel mom-and-pop kind of place" for its "very-nice service" and reasonable prix fixes.

Spaghetti Bar Le Curieux ◗   – | – | – | M
14, rue St-Merri, 4e (St-Paul/Châtelet), 01 42 72 75 97; fax 40 13 87 58; www.curieuxspag.com

With its crystal chandeliers and long red Chinese lacquer counter, this new hot spot between Les Halles and the Marais would seem fated to serve a Franco-Asian fusion menu; instead, the concept is reasonably priced pasta, especially spaghetti, offered with a variety of garnishes to a clientele of young, high-energy types seated in the long, narrow room.

Spicy ◗   18 | 17 | 17 | 38
8, av Franklin D. Roosevelt, 8e (Franklin D. Roosevelt/ St-Philippe-du-Roule), 01 56 59 62 59; fax 56 59 62 50; www.spicyrestaurant.com

■ White-collar types working in the 8th make this "casual" corner a convenient "canteen" for "business lunches" or "a quick meal before the movies"; the Asian-Med–influenced New French "food is good, though not extraordinary" ("tartare lovers take note" – this is a house specialty); still, the "warm" brick-and-wood "setting is agreeable" and a rise in the Service score confirms that the young staff's "welcoming" efforts have "improved."

Spoon, Food & Wine ☒   22 | 20 | 19 | 72
Sofitel Hôtel Marignan, 14, rue de Marignan, 8e (Franklin D. Roosevelt), 01 40 76 34 44; www.spoon.tm.fr

■ Alain Ducasse devotees adore his "sophisticated" world-food bistro off the Champs-Elysées with its "casual", tightly spaced "Zen decor", "incredible wine list" and "interesting menu concept" that allows you to mix and match the elements to create "fresh, imaginative and surprising" Eclectic dishes; but the worn-out wail "if I wanted to think that much about a meal, I'd cook for myself" and carp that the service at this "chichi money machine" is "good but not as efficient as you'd expect at these prices."

Square (Le) 🗷 | 10 | 14 | 11 | 37 |

31, rue St-Dominique, 7ᵉ (Invalides/Solférino), 01 45 51 09 03
🔲 Squares abstain from this "lively", very "en vogue" site that's "good for a younger set" interested more in the scene than in the "mediocre" "Classic" French food (at least, it's a "good value" for the high-toned 7th); habitués head for the outside tables, which offer a view of a "nice little park" and respite when the place gets too "smoky and loud."

Square Trousseau (Le) ◗🗷 | 17 | 17 | 13 | 39 |

1, rue Antoine Vollon, 12ᵉ (Bastille/Ledru-Rollin), 01 43 43 06 00; fax 43 43 00 66
🔲 A "chic clientele" says "it's worth the trip" east of the Bastille to this "timeless classic" Bistro for its original "1900 decor", "creative take on traditional fare" and eagerly sought tables overlooking a "lovely little square"; alas, the place's popularity means the service can be "poor", and pessimists protest that it "takes itself a little too seriously."

Stella (Le) ◗ | – | – | – | M |

133, av Victor Hugo, 16ᵉ (Rue de la Pompe/Victor Hugo), 01 56 90 56 00; fax 56 90 56 01
This venerable brasserie with a winsome '50s-vintage interior has returned under different ownership, and is being frequented by almost exactly the same tweed-wearing, bourgeois 16th-arrondissement clientele it always had; its allure includes shellfish trays, solid Classic French favorites, swift service and reasonable prices for this expensive part of town.

Stella Maris 🗷 | 23 | 15 | 21 | 78 |

4, rue Arsène Houssaye, 8ᵉ (Charles de Gaulle-Etoile), 01 42 89 16 22; fax 42 89 16 01
⬛ "Wow" exclaim enthusiasts of this "hidden pearl" near the Etoile in the 8th, where chef Tateru Yoshino brings an "inventive" deft hand and Japanese perfectionism to "excellent" French Classic cuisine (including "very good game in season"); "the service is warm and welcoming.", and a sleek new decor of ivory walls, contemporary art and Italian lighting fixtures (done post-*Survey*) may answer critics who rated the old setting "a trifle soulless."

Stéphane Martin 🗷 | ▽ 22 | 17 | 22 | 48 |

67, rue des Entrepreneurs, 15ᵉ (Charles Michels/Commerce), 01 45 79 03 31; fax 45 79 44 69
⬛ "As charming as can be" say supporters of this "out-of-the-way locale" in the 15th, where the namesake chef-

owner exhibits "perfect mastery" of "refined" dishes that are "inventive (but not wildly so) riffs on Traditional" French fare as well as an "excellent value"; his wife, Marie-Lucille, oversees both the "good wine list" and "attentive service"; N.B. a renovation pending at press time may outdate the Decor score.

Strapontins (Les)   – | – | – | M
16, av Richerand, 10ᵉ (Bonsergent/République), 01 42 41 94 79; fax 42 41 74 49
Hipsters in the funky Canal Saint-Martin area rub elbows with hospital workers from down the street at this "neo-bistro" with its long gray-and-white banquettes, saying it's "a decent place to grab a bite" of Classic French cuisine from an oft-changing menu without breaking the bank.

Stresa (Le) 🖾   19 | 13 | 14 | 83
7, rue Chambiges, 8ᵉ (Alma-Marceau), 01 47 23 51 62
■ A "chic" clientele of stars and supermodels makes it "hard to get a table" at this gastronomic Italian, an 8th arrondissement institution that always attracts an 'in' crowd – not for the 1950s decor, but "for the fun, the atmosphere and the owners"; there's no denying "it is expensive" ("watch out for those wines") but "the whole scene is worth the pricey tag."

Studio (The) ◑   ▽ 11 | 17 | 14 | 29
41, rue du Temple, 4ᵉ (Hôtel-de-Ville/Rambuteau), 01 42 74 10 38; fax 42 41 50 34; www.the-studio.fr
◧ 'Salsa night' means both dipping and dancing at this Tex-Mex located in a "lovely big courtyard" with "a view of the classes at the Marais Dance Center"; it's an ideal destination on a "summer evening or for a drink" though nobody's bending over backward for the "mediocre food"; then again, "with a few margaritas, who cares?"

Suave 🖾   – | – | – | I
20, rue de la Providence, 13ᵉ (Corvisart/Tolbiac), 01 45 89 99 27; fax 45 81 34 60
This Vietnamese blazes new ground in the funky Butte-aux-Cailles neighborhood: it's calm and chic (elegant place mats, ceramic chopstick rests shaped like chile peppers), and the dishes are prepared with more finesse than the competition's; in addition, the kitchen's lavish use of fresh herbs smacks of authentic Saigon eateries, which is why it's attracting followers from Paris' substantial Indo-Chinese community.

Sud (Le) 🖾   16 | 23 | 15 | 49
91, bd Gouvion-St-Cyr, 17ᵉ (Porte Maillot), 01 45 74 02 77; fax 45 74 35 36
◪ "Escape to Provence without leaving Paris" profess patrons of this regional retreat – "just off the heavy traffic of Porte Maillot" – that's "guaranteed to transport you"

with its "fabulous decor" including an interior patio, olive trees and "singing crickets" ("be sure to be seated upstairs"); the Mediterranean-Provençal cuisine ranges from "pretty good to passable", but the "warm ambiance" "makes it worthwhile."

Suite (La) 14 | 18 | 11 | 66
40, av George V, 8ᵉ (George V), 01 53 57 49 49; fax 53 57 49 48
◪ "Make sure to wear your new Gucci stilettos" to this "slightly decadent" restaurant/nightspot in the 8th run by the Guettas, king and queen of Paris nightlife; it's a "clublike" space with a fresh pink-toned decor (not reflected in the above score) where "the most jet-set crowd in Paris" flocks "to see and be seen" despite the "average" New French food and "absolutely unprofessional service" provided by "hostesses who look and dress like models."

Table d'Anvers (La) 23 | 15 | 21 | 80
2, pl d'Anvers, 9ᵉ (Anvers), 01 48 78 35 21; fax 45 26 66 67; www.latabledanvers.com
◪ Decorated with pink and purple chairs and light-colored wood walls, this "delightful" Traditional French at the foot of Montmartre wins praise as "an absolute treat in an out-of-the-way location" for its "sublime" cooking and "highly courteous service"; the only thing that gives wallet-watchers pause is the "somewhat pricey" check.

Table de Joël Robuchon (La) – | – | – | M
16, av Bugeaud, 16ᵉ (Victor Hugo), 01 56 28 16 16; fax 56 28 16 78
In the 16th, chef-owner Joël Robuchon's follow-up to his first-come, first-counter-served Atelier gives fans of his classic Haute Cuisine the chance to reserve and sit at a real table (albeit one with plastic flower arrangements); the patrons, whose attire ranges from T-shirts to suits, can expect a bevy of waiters dressed in black tunics to serve a menu divided in half between tapas-sized tasting plates and proper appetizers, main courses and desserts.

Table de la Fontaine (La) ◐ ⊠ – | – | – | M
5, rue Henri Monnier, 9ᵉ (St-Georges), 01 45 26 26 30; fax 40 23 90 69
"One of the nicer, less touristy places in the area" around Pigalle, this table with its theatrical red-and-gold decor is "perfect for dinner with friends", serving "quite good" Med meals – veal kidneys *à l'orange,* chicken with olives and chile peppers – at "prices that can't be beat."

Table de Lucullus (La) ⊠ – | – | – | E
129, rue Legendre, 17ᵉ (Brochant/La Fourche), 01 40 25 02 68; fax 40 25 02 68
Not new, but "still to be discovered", is this "funky", tiny table up in the 17th run by "young, talented" Nicolas Vagnon, a "brilliant culinary mad scientist" whose seafood menu (written on oversized blackboard menus) is "fresh-

fresh-fresh", all wild, and remarkably "original"; P.S. "there is a nonsmoking policy."

Table du Baltimore (La) 🖅 — | — | — | E
Sofitel Demeure Hôtel Baltimore, 88, bis av Kléber, 16ᵉ (Boissiere), 01 44 34 54 34; fax 44 34 54 44
"Wish more people would find this place" profess fans of chef Jean-Philippe Pérol, whose talent for "imaginative" Haute Cuisine – perfected during his tenure as second-in-command at Pré Catelan – remains "confidential" while he is hidden in this upscale hotel restaurant in the 16th; for now, it's primarily business folk who commandeer this "calm" space, perhaps to indulge in a seven-course champagne menu that includes a bottle of bubbly.

Table du Lancaster (La) — | — | — | E
Hôtel Lancaster, 7, rue de Berri, 8ᵉ (George V), 01 40 76 40 18; fax 40 76 40 00; www.hotel-lancaster.fr
Now open to the public, with Rhône Valley chef Michel Troisgros as a consultant, the revamped dining room of the Hôtel Lancaster has become the talk of the town for nervy, Asian-influenced Haute Cuisine (frogs' legs in tamarind sauce, lassi-marinated lamb chops); in a further break with its former grand-hotel style, the redo has replaced the waiters' uniforms with well-cut black suits, and added hand painted Chinese wallpaper and Zen floral arrangements.

Tadoussac 🖅 — | — | — | M
396, rue St-Honoré, 2nd fl., 1ᵉʳ (Madeleine/Concorde), 01 42 60 12 77; fax 42 60 30 89
The sturdy cooking of Quebec, which favors fatback, game and maple syrup, stars at this relaxing, rustic auberge steps from the Place de la Concorde in the heart of town; a working fireplace and beamed ceiling add to the old-fashioned atmosphere, warming a crowd that includes Canadian ex pats looking for a taste of home.

TAILLEVENT 🖅 28 | 27 | 28 | VE
15, rue Lamennais, 8ᵉ (Charles de Gaulle-Etoile/George V), 01 44 95 15 01; fax 42 25 95 18; www.taillevent.com
■ "Reserve far ahead for your own slice of heaven" (minutes from l'Etoile) at "the grandest establishment on Earth" where "genius" chef Alain Solivérès' "epitome of Classic French" Haute Cuisine is voted No. 1 for Food in the city; "come here to be cosseted" (for "the staff to be any better they'd have to spoon-feed you"), knowing that owner "Jean-Claude Vrinat sets the standard for elegance" in a "beautifully decorated townhouse" whose cellar "makes wine lovers drool."

Taïra 🖅 — | — | — | E
10, rue des Acacias, 17ᵉ (Argentine), 01 47 66 74 14; fax 47 66 74 14
East meets West in this small, modern room in the 17th, where chef-owner Taïra Kurihara's "unique New French–

Japanese fusion cooking" results in "superb fish dishes" that seem "moderately priced", given their "inventive" nature (and also the three-course prix fixe).

Taka ⬛   ▽ 24 | 14 | 21 | 34
1, rue Véron, 18ᵉ (Abbesses), 01 42 23 74 16

■ Open only at night, this "miniscule establishment" is a "haunt known by the locals" of Montmartre as a "real Japanese" (right down to "the bill, calculated on an abacus"); it was one of the first to provide Parisians with authentically "savory" dishes, including "super-fresh" sushi and what raw-fish fans call the "best sashimi in Paris"; if the Nipponese-style decor is a little "simple", the service is "personalized" and "sweet."

Tan Dinh ⬛⌀   22 | 13 | 21 | 60
60, rue de Verneuil, 7ᵉ (Rue du Bac/Solférino), 01 45 44 04 84; fax 45 44 36 93

■ The "best Vietnamese outside of Saigon" fawn fans of this family-run place in the 7th, as famed for its "fabulous", even "intimidating" wine list (including a spectacular selection of Pomerols) and "charming" staff as for the "subtle flavors and spices" of its cuisine; "forget the decor", which is "nothing to write home about", and bring along a wad of cash ("how can they get by without taking credit cards?") to cover a bill that some find "a tad excessive."

Tang ⬛   21 | 14 | 19 | 62
125, rue de la Tour, 16ᵉ (Rue de la Pompe), 01 45 04 35 35; fax 45 04 58 19

◩ If there's one point upon which all surveyors agree, it's that this 16th arrondissement Asian is "*cher*" – and though admirers argue the "well-prepared" Cantonese food and "professional service" are worth the price, skeptics snap this "pretentious" place has lost its tang, asking sarcastically "does it taste better if it's expensive?"

Tanjia ●⬛   – | – | – | E
23, rue de Ponthieu, 8ᵉ (Franklin D. Roosevelt), 01 42 25 95 00; fax 42 25 95 02

A "young, cosmopolitan Euro crowd with money to spend" turns out for this trendy lounge/eatery near the Champs, which has metamorphosized under new management: the old "Marrakesh-in-Paris ambiance" has been replaced by an eye-catching, modern decor (velour and raw silk furnishings, red and burgundy hues) and the menu is now Eclectic, with a few "vaguely Moroccan" dishes; no news on whether the servers still "tend to forget you are there."

Tante Jeanne ⬛   – | – | – | E
116, bd Péreire, 17ᵉ (Péreire), 01 43 80 88 68; fax 47 66 53 02; www.bernard-loiseau.com

"This is a place to recommend, even after the loss of Bernard Loiseau", the late, esteemed Burgundian chef; the last of his three Paris establishments to open, this address in the 17th offers "delicious" Classic French fare, accompanied by an interesting selection of Burgundy wines, in an "agreeable" chandeliered-and-mirrored setting.

Tante Louise ⌧   22 | 16 | 21 | 60
41, rue Boissy-d'Anglas, 8ᵉ (Concorde/Madeleine), 01 42 65 06 85; fax 42 65 28 19; www.bernard-loiseau.com
■ "Long live the aunt" (*tante*) say faithful followers of "deceased chef Bernard Loiseau's" 8th arrondissement bistro, who continue to come for the "overall high quality" of the "simple" "Traditional" French dishes with a Burgundy accent, "cordial service" and an "elegant" '30s-style decor.

Tante Marguerite ⌧   21 | 16 | 22 | 58
5, rue de Bourgogne, 7ᵉ (Assemblée Nationale/Invalides), 01 45 51 79 42; fax 47 53 79 56; www.bernard-loiseau.com
■ "Go just to see the politicians" who lunch at this comfortable annex near the Assemblée Nationale on "good" Classic French "rural dishes" that "neither disappoint nor surprise"; the "sophisticated, smooth service" is just what one would expect in this bourgeois part of town.

Tastevin   25 | 21 | 21 | 58
9, av Eglé, Maisons-Laffitte (RER Maisons-Laffitte), 01 39 62 11 67; fax 39 62 73 09
■ "The walk into the park, the rooms and the meal are all delightful" at this bucolic yet "chic" Classic French with "a Napoleon III–style atmosphere" in the gardens at Maisons-Laffitte; "pleasant", "traditional cooking" by chef-owner Michel Blanchet combines with the warm reception of his wife Amélia to make this country outing "a marvelous experience", especially if you sit outside in summer.

Taverna de Gli Amici ◑⌧   – | – | – | M
16, rue du Bac, 7ᵉ (Rue du Bac), 01 42 60 37 74; fax 42 60 37 74
Popular with editors and politicos by day and chic Italophiles at night, this duplex not far from the Musée d'Orsay successfully re-creates the warm, busy atmosphere of a Roman taverna thanks to earth-toned walls, antique wooden hutches and a staff from The Boot; the kitchen follows a rustic bent, turning out honest country food, including grilled sausages and roasts.

Taverne de Maître Kanter ◑   ▽ 13 | 10 | 12 | 33
16, rue Coquillière, 1ᵉʳ (Châtelet-Les Halles/Louvre-Rivoli), 01 42 36 74 24; fax 43 42 19 75
☑ With its "beer-hall atmosphere and the convenience of being open 24/7", this "Alsatian venue" close to Les Halles is "practical for nighttime hunger pangs", and also offers "a safe bet for large appetites" in need of a choucroute or seafood platter anytime of the day; however, pickier palates would rather "run away" from what they deem "pedestrian" brasserie fare.

Taverne Henri IV (La) 🖼 — — — M
13, pl du Pont-Neuf, 1ᵉʳ (Pont-Neuf), 01 43 54 27 90; fax 43 54 27 90

Tucked away in a handsome 16th-century building on the Ile-de-la-Cité, one of Paris' oldest wine bars has reopened as a *bistrot à vins* following a sensitive renovation of the vaulted-brick-and-stone interior; known to fans of the mystery writer Georges Simenon – it often figured in his novels – the room is also popular with legal types from the nearby courthouse and local antique dealers munching on an assortment of old-fashioned open-faced sandwiches, plates of cheese and cold cuts, and a changing assortment of Bistro dishes.

Taverne "L'Esprit Boulevard" ◐ — — — M
24, bd des Italiens, 9ᵉ (Opéra/Richelieu-Drouot), 01 55 33 10 00; fax 55 33 10 09; www.taverne.com

Ballet-goers who crave oysters and beer after the show can bound over to this immense, "upbeat", baroque-style restaurant near the Opéra Garnier; belonging to one of the city's brasserie dynasties, it's a "classic Blanc Brothers" joint, serving simple fare from choucroute to shellfish seven days a week and late into the night.

Télégraphe (Le) ◐ — 15 22 17 57
41, rue de Lille, 7ᵉ (Rue du Bac/Solférino), 01 42 92 03 04; fax 42 92 02 77

■ "You'll feel like you entered a Klimt painting" when you see the "gorgeous art nouveau decor" at this "cool space" with a courtyard garden near the Musée d'Orsay; a dormitory for telegraph operators a century ago, it now serves "good" kosher Classic French fare and, though not as "trendy" as in the past, it's "still crowded and noisy", and "a good bet for first-time Paris visitors."

Temps au Temps (Le) 🖼 — — — M
13, rue Paul Bert, 11ᵉ (Faidherbe-Chaligny), 01 43 79 63 40

Amusing stenciled profiles of famous chefs (Bocuse, et al.) line the walls of this friendly traditional bistro in the 11th, whose homey found-at-the-flea-market look (lots of old clocks) puts its arty young patrons at ease; the chalkboard menu changes regularly but runs to slow-braised or pan-roasted preparations such as veal kidneys, and there's a fairly priced wine list with some unusual bottles.

Temps des Cerises (Le) ◐🖼 ▽ 15 15 15 27
18, rue de la Butte-aux-Cailles, 13ᵉ (Place d'Italie), 01 45 89 69 48; fax 45 88 18 53

■ Working-class stiffs appreciate the "proletarian meals at proletarian prices" at this "very-well-known Butte-aux-Cailles" classic run by an employees' cooperative, where "strangers" share "long communal tables" and tuck into "copious" portions of "basic grub in a laid-back fun atmosphere"; the whole experience is so "typically French" that the crowd even "breaks out into song sometimes."

Terminus Nord ◗

17	21	16	41

23, rue de Dunkerque, 10ᵉ (Gare du Nord), 01 42 85 05 15; fax 40 16 13 98

■ A "perfect welcome to Paris after the Chunnel" (or conversely, the "last chance for a decent meal if you're using Eurostar"), this "big, bustling brasserie" "convenient to the Gare du Nord" "brings back *la belle époque*" with its "polished wood, beveled glass" and "acrobatic waiters carrying silver plates of shellfish"; the "reliable", "tasty" seafood is "typical of the Flo Group", its owner.

Terrasse (La)

–	–	–	E

Hôtel Terrass, 12, rue Joseph de Maistre, 18ᵉ (Abbesses/ Place de Clichy), 01 44 92 34 00; fax 42 52 29 11; www.terrass-hotel.com

The name says it all, since most people come to "this secret hideaway" in a Montmartre hotel for (and, some say, "only for") the "beautiful view over all Paris" offered by the seventh-floor "terrace when the weather is fine"; surveyors are more mum when it comes to the Med-Provençal menu, but at least the prices, while elevated, aren't sky-high.

Terrasse Mirabeau (La) ⊠

–	–	–	M

5, pl de Barcelone, 16ᵉ (Mirabeau/Javel), 01 42 24 41 51; fax 42 24 43 48

The smart, earth-toned decor – think leather-upholstered armchairs, dark-wood tables and tan linens – makes a perfect backdrop for business lunching or amorous dining at this upmarket newcomer in the 17th; the fashionably contemporary Bistro fare is the work of young, up-and-coming chef-owner Pierre Négrevergne, who trained at Michel Rostang's Bistrot d'à Côté.

Terres de Truffes ⊠

–	–	–	VE

21, rue Vignon, 8ᵉ (Madeleine), 01 53 43 80 44; fax 42 66 18 20

Truffle mavens will want to dig their way to this new Classic French near the Madeleine, where fresh specimens of fragrant fungi figure in almost every dish – even desserts – and the formal, dark wood-paneled atmosphere seems just right for the clientele of bankers at noon and well-heeled foreigners in the evening; an adjacent boutique offers preserved, canned and packaged goodies for those who want a taste to take home.

Terroir (Le) ⊠

18	11	18	53

11, bd Arago, 13ᵉ (Les Gobelins), 01 47 07 36 99; fax 42 72 52 20

◩ "A must when you're in the mood for *la France profonde*" rave reviewers of this "rustic" bistro in the 13th, where "huge portions" of "down-home" cuisine are made from "ingredients that taste like they were in the garden this morning"; "the owner, Michel Chavanon, knows everyone and treats all his clients like friends"; however, a few find the prices as "overwhelming" as the welcome and the servings.

Tête Ailleurs (La) 🖂

‾ | ‾ | ‾ | M

20, rue Beautreillis, 4ᵉ (St-Paul/Sully Morland), 01 42 72 47 80; fax 42 74 66 85

The imaginative Southern French menu at this new spot on the edge of the Marais reflects the fact that the owner formerly worked at the famous Voile Rouge beach club in Saint-Tropez; it's not only Provence and the Côte d'Azur that inspire the kitchen, though, since dishes from the Basque country and the Languedoc-Roussillon make an appearance as well; a well-drilled staff, quietly fashionable atmosphere and attractive location on one of the oldest streets in Paris also draw in the arty locals.

Thaï

‾ | ‾ | ‾ | M

39, rue St-Roch, 1ᵉʳ (Pyramides/Tuileries), 01 42 96 28 24

Located not far from the Tuileries, this intimate newcomer invokes the best of Bangkok (as well as regions all over Thailand) with a diverse assortment of fresh but conservatively spiced salads, satays and curries; an upscale setting – soft lighting, silk fabrics, light wood-paneled walls and orchids – attracts a stylish crowd.

Thanksgiving

▽ 15 | 10 | 14 | 32

20, rue St-Paul, 4ᵉ (St-Paul), 01 42 77 68 28; fax 42 77 70 83; www.thanksgivingparis.com

■ "Homesick Americans" get their fix of gumbo and pecan pie at this "quaint, small" restaurant in the Marais specializing in "big portions" (U.S.-style) of "surprisingly good" Cajun-Creole cuisine and a "copious brunch" on weekends at "moderate" prices; pining pilgrims "suffering from peanut-butter withdrawal" can stock up on such "much-needed staples" at the adjacent store.

Thierry Burlot 🖂

‾ | ‾ | ‾ | E

(aka Le Quinze)

8, rue Nicolas Charlet, 15ᵉ (Pasteur), 01 42 19 08 59; fax 45 67 09 13

After knocking around several institutions, Crillon-trained chef Thierry Burlot is at last on his own, running this small table in the15th; his technical dexterity comes through in his "wonderfully creative", monthly changing New French menu, served in "casually elegant", subdued-toned digs.

Thiou 🖂

22 | 21 | 17 | 52

49, quai d'Orsay, 7ᵉ (Invalides), 01 40 62 96 70; fax 40 62 97 30
3, rue Surcouf, 7ᵉ (Invalides), 01 40 62 96 50
12, av George V, 8ᵉ (Alma-Marceau), 01 47 20 89 56

■ Mme. Thiou's fashionable fan club has considered her "a star" since her days cooking at the old Les Bains Douches, and they now trek happily to her "refined" establishment on the Quai d'Orsay for "authentic, flavorful" and "original Thai cuisine" "that's among the best in Paris"; the budget-conscious boogie to the nearby annex on the Rue Surcouf, which is "cheaper and as nice, though you won't be able to people-watch"; N.B. the branch in the 8th is unrated.

Thoumieux
16 | 17 | 15 | 40 |

Hôtel Thoumieux, 79, rue St-Dominique, 7ᵉ (Invalides/ La Tour-Maubourg), 01 47 05 49 75; fax 47 05 36 96; www.thoumieux.com

☑ Those wondering "what it must have been like in Paris 40 years ago" get a taste at this "quintessential" brasserie with "mirrored walls and crisp, white table linens" that's been open since 1923 near Les Invalides; tourists and "local regulars" crowd together "elbow to elbow" for "solid and consistent" "comfort" food from the Southwest that's "edible" if not excellent, served by authentically "arrogant waiters" seven days a week.

Timbre (Le) ☒
∇ 18 | 11 | 19 | 35 |

3, rue St-Beuve, 6ᵉ (Vavin), 01 45 49 10 40; fax 45 78 20 35

■ Barely bigger than the postage stamp it's named for, this "nice spot" with "no decor" is easy to miss, but those who discover it behind the Luxembourg gardens give their stamp of approval to the "tasty" classic Bistro "food, prepared without pretension", and the British cheese platter, at prices worth writing home about.

Timgad (Le)
23 | 23 | 18 | 50 |

21, rue Brunel, 17ᵉ (Argentine), 01 45 74 23 70; fax 40 68 76 46

■ Adventurers looking for a "transporting evening" are not disappointed by this "fabulous Moroccan", "the best in Paris", that's open every day in the 17th; the ornate Moorish interior (which has "nothing Parisian" about it) makes an exotic backdrop for "always-perfect" tagines and all-you-can-eat couscous, accompanied by North African wines.

Tire-Bouchon (Le) ☒
22 | 13 | 22 | 37 |

62, rue des Entrepreneurs, 15ᵉ (Charles Michels), 01 40 59 09 27; fax 40 59 09 27

■ There's "all the charm of a mom-and-pop" at this "small", "convivial" corner in the 15th, where the "chef-owner and his wife know what the word welcome means"; the "original" New French cuisine is enhanced by a "good wine list" ('tire-bouchon' means corkscrew in French) and "interesting tasting menu", resulting in an experience that "verges on fine dining without the high prices"; N.B. a recent decor re-do may outdate the above score.

Toi ◑ ☒
− | − | − | M |

27, rue du Colisée, 8ᵉ (Franklin D. Roosevelt/St-Philippe-du-Roule), 01 42 56 56 58; fax 42 56 09 60; www.restaurant-toi.com

Admirers of Austin Powers will feel right at home at this hip lounge/eatery near the Champs-Elysées, whose "fun psychedelic decor" conjures up the swinging '70s; it's already a playground for Paris' golden youth, pre- or post-clubbing, with an "original" New French menu that ranges from sandwiches to more substantial eats.

Tokyo Eat ◐
– | – | – | M

Palais de Tokyo, 13, av du President Wilson, 16ᵉ (Iéna), 01 47 20 00 29; fax 47 20 05 62; www.palaisdetokyo.com
Contemporary culture vultures with a taste for fusion food can sate their appetites at the cavernous Palais de Tokyo museum in the 16th, where this spacious site offers a futuristic feast for the eyes; though officially New French, the offerings from the open kitchen at the Eat cafe are also "good for a sushi fix" between installations, while a quicker bite can be had downstairs at the Idem cafeteria.

Tong Yen ◐
21 | 9 | 17 | 58

1 bis, rue Jean Mermoz, 8ᵉ (Franklin D. Roosevelt), 01 42 25 04 23; fax 45 63 51 57
◼ For four decades, owner Thérèse Luong has greeted the town's movers and shakers at her 8th-arrondissement institution for "remarkable" Chinese and Southeast Asian classics that some call "the best in Paris"; the "expensive" prices and "dusty", "dated" interior lead some to suggest she "spend a bit of money renewing the decor", but stalwart patrons profess "if the President of the Republic dines here, it's good enough for me."

Tonkinoise (La) ⌀
– | – | – | I

20, rue Philibert Lucot, 13ᵉ (Maison Blanche), 01 45 85 98 98; fax 45 77 88 86
Aficionados of authentic Vietnamese food are willing to make the pilgrimage to this *petite* pay-no-mind address in the 13th for real family-style cooking, from shrimp cakes to "soups that are all worth trying" – and there's no reason not to when the prices are so low.

Tonnelle Saintongeaise (La) ☒
– | – | – | M

32, bd Vital Bouhot, Neuilly (Pont-de-Levallois), 01 46 24 43 15; fax 46 24 36 33
Chic island dwellers make this homey restaurant on the Ile de la Jatte in Neuilly their weekday warm-weather hangout, noting it's "very nice in summer, especially with its covered courtyard for rainy weather"; when it turns cold outside they take refuge in a glass-enclosed winter garden, over plates of Classic French fare like steamed mussels and steak tartare.

Toque (La) ☒
– | – | – | E

16, rue de Tocqueville, 17ᵉ (Villiers), 01 42 27 97 75; fax 47 63 97 69
Clients take their toques off to this "very small" (30 seats) site in the 17th with its "charming" painted trompe l'oeil sky, where chef-owner Jacky Joubert has offered an

inventive and "excellent" take on Classic French cooking for over 25 years; the "service is friendly and attentive", and the prices "attractive" for the quality of the cuisine.

Toupary (Le) ⌧   13 | 24 | 15 | 47
La Samaritaine, 2, quai du Louvre, 1ᵉʳ (Pont-Neuf), 01 40 41 29 29; fax 42 33 96 79
▧ "Tourists aren't the only ones blown away" by the "magnificent vista" this restaurant offers from its perch atop the Samaritaine department store ("reserve early for a window seat"); but Parisians and visitors alike grumble that "it's all about the view", since the "service is efficient if unfriendly" and the "disappointing" Traditional French cuisine falls flat.

TOUR D'ARGENT (LA)   25 | 28 | 26 | VE
15-17, quai de la Tournelle, 5ᵉ (Cardinal Lemoine/Pont Marie), 01 43 54 23 31; fax 44 07 12 04; www.latourdargent.com
▧ "The grande dame of Paris Haute Cuisine restaurants" is "a mythical place" "packed with" patrons who gasp at the "fairy-tale" view of Notre Dame and order the "exquisite numbered duck" while gushing over "gracious service" and the "vertiginous" wine list ("500,000 bottles"); if critics knock this tower down as an "overpriced" ("am I paying for the lighting of the cathedral by myself?") "museum" "living on its glory", it's still a "gotta-go once" address; P.S. do note that at lunch "the prices are easier to handle."

Tourelle (La) ⌧   – | – | – | I
43, rue Croix des Petits Champs, 1ᵉʳ (Bourse/Louvre-Rivoli), 01 42 61 35 41; fax 42 61 35 41
Mainly open for lunch, this cozy little *bistrot à vins* is a big hit with employees from the adjacent Banque de France as well as with boutique owners, antique dealers and shoppers drawn to the fashion stores lining the Place des Victoires nearby; one or two old-fashioned dishes are offered daily to complement a menu that runs to cheese, charcuterie, salads and excellent wines from the nearby Caves Augé.

Tournesol (Le)   14 | 17 | 16 | 47
2, av de Lamballe, 16ᵉ (Passy), 01 45 25 95 94; fax 45 25 43 09
■ The "excellent ambiance" of this "cool" "neighborhood" hang means it's "always full" with Passy's "privileged youth", who crowd in for the "party" atmosphere created by "good", "basic Bistro cuisine" and summer terrace "facing the Seine."

TRAIN BLEU (LE)   17 | 28 | 18 | 58
Gare de Lyon, 12ᵉ (Gare de Lyon), 01 43 43 09 06; fax 43 43 97 96; www.le-train-bleu.com
▧ "May the train never come" sigh fans of the "awesome belle-epoque interior" in this brasserie at the Gare de Lyon, where the "frescoed ceilings" and "fabulous murals" "take one back to days of yore"; a year under "a new chef" has

some convinced that the Classic French "food is improving", while others say it's simply "competent"; but "the real star" is the setting, "perfect for a glass of champagne" "even if you don't need" to travel anywhere.

Tricotin — | — | — | I

15, av de Choisy, 13ᵉ (Porte de Choisy), 01 45 84 74 44; fax 41 55 51 52

"Lines out the door" attest to the fact that "this large, loud, bustling restaurant is the real deal", a "reference" for "authentic Chinese food" and other Southeast Asian specialties in the 13th arrondissement's Chinatown; nobody's raving about the "canteen setting" or dour service, but the "extremely reasonable" prices make those easier to swallow.

Triporteur (Le) 🖾 — | — | — | M

4, rue de Dantzig, 15ᵉ (Convention), 01 45 32 82 40

A loyal clientele of "regulars" brings a "joyous, noisy atmosphere" to this "charming" "neighborhood" address deep in the 15th, with its "young, dynamic staff" that "takes real pleasure in receiving" you; the "blackboard menu" proposes Basque-inspired cuisine that is "mouthwatering", "straightforward and unpretentious", but do note that "reservations are imperative."

TROIS MARCHES (LES) 🖾 25 | 24 | 23 | 85

Hôtel Trianon Palace, 1, bd de la Reine, Versailles (RER Versailles-Rive Droite), 01 39 50 13 21; fax 30 21 01 25; www.trianonpalace.fr

■ "How charming" coo customers of this Haute Cuisine table, "only a five-minute walk to the Palais" of Versailles; the scene is all "elegance in a small-village environment", from the "exquisite food" to "multitiered cheese carts", from a "staff falling all over you" to a lovely "summer terrace" overlooking what were once Louis XIV's gardens; P.S. "don't deprive yourself of the Hôtel Trianon's charms" afterwards.

TROQUET (LE) 🖾 25 | 15 | 19 | M

21, rue François Bonvin, 15ᵉ (Sèvres-Lecourbe/Volontaire), 01 45 66 89 00; fax 45 66 89 83

■ An "enthusiastic welcome awaits" at this "neighborhood find" in the 15th, a "justly popular little bistro that packs them in for an extraordinary four-course prix fixe" of moderately priced New French fare ("throw in a few more euros and get a fifth course of cheese") "rich with creative flavors"; the menu may be "brief", but "the daily changes keep you coming back for more."

Trou Gascon (Au) 🖾 24 | 17 | 22 | E

40, rue Taine, 12ᵉ (Daumesnil), 01 43 44 34 26; fax 43 07 80 55

■ "Foie gras, confit, cassoulet": bring on the "great Gascon food" cry fans of this "longtime favorite" belonging to chef Alain Dutournier, a "homey", though contemporary, site with "cordial" "old-timey waiters" located a bit "off the beaten path" in the 12th; while some huff it's "hugely expensive", most others call it a "bargain" for "the best Southwestern in Paris."

Truffe Noire (La) ⓢ   19 | 13 | 16 | 62
2, pl Parmentier, Neuilly (Les Sablons/Porte Maillot),
01 46 24 94 14; fax 46 24 94 60
■ Black-gold diggers strike it rich at this Neuilly address specializing in "truffles, elegantly prepared in a variety of forms"; although the "slightly formal" setting is "a bit old-fashioned", it's a "charming" outpost for "consistently good quality" Classic French cuisine, and a new, hipper decor (not reflected in the score above).

TRUFFIÈRE (LA) ⓢ   25 | 22 | 24 | E
4, rue Blainville, 5ᵉ (Cardinal Lemoine/Place Monge),
01 46 33 29 82; fax 46 33 64 74; www.latruffiere.com
■ "Time stops when you're seated by the fireplace" in the vaulted cellar of this "cozy, welcoming" 17th-century house in the 5th; the "refined" menu, a combo of New and Classic French dishes, is "laced with gorgeous truffles", "the wine list is phenomenal" and the "cheese cart is huge", so no one minds that "it's a bit of a tourist trap" where "your money disappears without even waving good-bye."

Trumilou (Le)   16 | 9 | 17 | 31
84, quai de l'Hôtel-de-Ville, 4ᵉ (Hôtel-de-Ville/Pont-Marie),
01 42 77 63 98; fax 48 04 91 89
■ "When you don't want to dress up", this "old-style" family-run bistro "steps from the Hôtel de Ville" is ideal for a "convenient and casual" Classic meal that "tastes like what your French mom would make"; the environs may look "a little worn around the edges", but all agree it's a "great value" nonetheless.

Tsé-Yang   18 | 20 | 19 | 67
25, av Pierre 1er de Serbie, 16ᵉ (Alma-Marceau/Iéna),
01 47 20 70 22; fax 49 52 03 68
■ Beijing goes bourgeois at this "classy" Chinese in the 16th that boasts a "classic" imperial setting, "attentive service" and "extensive" wine list; its "excellent" menu from all over the mainland omits the Vietnamese or Thai dishes found at other Sino sites in Paris; regulars tout the Peking duck as "the best" – but warn, "you pay for it."

Tsukizi ⓢ   – | – | – | M
2 bis, rue des Ciseaux, 6ᵉ (Mabillon/St-Germain-des-Prés),
01 43 54 65 19
Nipponphiles note that "if you miss Tokyo" this "tiny place" "is closest to the real thing", bringing "Japanese charm" to Saint-Germain with an assortment of "delicate" sushis and sashimis served at the bar or a few tables; but your yen for raw fish should match the yen in your wallet, for

while it's moderate overall, "expensive" extras mean it's easy to "inadvertently run up the tab."

Uitr | – | – | – | M |

1, pl Falguière, 15ᵉ (Pasteur/Pernety), 01 47 34 12 24; fax 47 34 12 34
Spacious and relaxed and decked out with a nautical theme, this seafooder conjures up a sense of the big blue sea, even though it's actually behind the Gare Montparnasse; even more evocative are its super-fresh shellfish platters and simple fish preparations, whose moderate prices attract schools of hungry sharks – er, suits – and couples.

Va et Vient (Le) ⊠ | – | – | – | M |

8, rue des Batignolles, 17ᵉ (Place de Clichy/Rome), 01 45 22 54 22; www.vaetvient.fr
Clients come and come again to this family-run hole-in-the-wall bistro in the increasingly trendy Batignolles neighborhood; its "pleasant" ambiance, replete with copper pots hanging from the wall, is the backdrop for "huge, tasty portions" of Traditional French and Alsatian-style cooking (onion tart, pork shank) just like *grand-mère* used to make.

Vagenende ● | 15 | 23 | 15 | 45 |

142, bd St-Germain, 6ᵉ (Odéon), 01 43 26 68 18; fax 40 51 73 38
■ Serving late seven days a week, this "historic" Left Bank brasserie is "busy all the time", mainly with travelers who come to "feast the eyes" on the "great 1900-era decor"; while the setting's authentically "belle epoque, the food is less than belle" – though it remains "reliable" and "reasonably priced"; but even if the "old warhorse" seems "a little tired", it keeps charging, and that – like the "personnel, who have been around for ages" – is "part of the charm."

Vaudeville (Le) ● | 16 | 21 | 17 | 48 |

29, rue Vivienne, 2ᵉ (Bourse), 01 40 20 04 62; www.vaudevilleparis.com
■ When "near the Bourse, drown your stock-market sorrows" at this "cheerful", "classic" brasserie that seems "less of a factory than others [owned by] the Flo Group" with its "pretty" "art deco surroundings" and raw bar that's "heaven for oyster and shellfish lovers"; if the rest of the traditional menu "can be uneven", this trouper still offers a "bustling" good show "for a Sunday night out."

Verre Bouteille (Le) ● | – | – | – | M |

85, av des Ternes, 17ᵉ (Porte Maillot), 01 45 74 01 02; fax 47 63 07 02
5, bd Gouvion-St-Cyr, 17ᵉ (Porte de Champerret), 01 47 63 39 99; fax 47 63 07 02
www.leverrebouteille.com
A low-key bite and a tipple are on the menu at this pair of "agreeably" relaxed neighborhood wine bars in the 17th offering an identical selection of classic Bistro "simple

dishes" that are somewhat "inconsistant – good one day, bad the next" – and a couple of dozen wines by the glass; at the more casual Ternes location, night-owls can wet their beaks until 4:30 AM.

Verre Volé (Le) _ _ _ I
67, rue de Lancry, 10ᵉ (République), 01 48 03 17 34; fax 68 03 17 34
This "walk-in closet–size" wine bar/boutique is as offbeat as the Canal Saint-Martin neighborhood it calls home; locals quickly "snag the 20 or so seats" in the funky space where the walls are lined with young vintages for sale, and accompany their selections with such classic Bistro fare as "excellent charcuterie, oysters and a butter from Bretagne that's so good you'll eat it like cheese."

Viaduc Café (Le) ● 12 15 14 30
43, av Daumesnil, 12ᵉ (Bastille/Gare de Lyon), 01 44 74 70 70; fax 44 74 70 71
☑ Weekend strollers appreciate this "pit stop on the promenade" "under the arcades" of a renovated railway viaduct in the 12th for its "pretty", "airy" decor and "nice but noisy terrace"; but most mutter that the mixture of "basic" Classic and New French cuisine, delivered by "indifferent" servers, is "terribly uneven", so stick to "salads and fresh foods", "a drink with friends" or the "crowded" Sunday jazz brunch.

Vieille Fontaine Rôtisserie (La) ∇ 20 22 19 46
8, av Grétry, Maisons-Laffitte (RER Maisons-Laffitte), 01 39 62 01 78; fax 39 62 13 43; www.lesbouchonsdefrancoisclerc.com
■ There's a "great feel" to this "sublime setting" in Maisons-Laffitte, a "beautiful house" with authentic Napoleon III decor offering "better-than-average" New and Classic French cuisine (especially rotisseried meats) at lower-than-average prices; its "summer terrace" overlooking a park makes it especially welcoming in warm weather.

Vieux Bistro (Le) 20 15 17 44
14, rue du Cloître Notre-Dame, 4ᵉ (Cité), 01 43 54 18 95; fax 44 07 35 63
☑ "The name fits to a 'T'" at this "old-time bistro in the shadow of Notre Dame", where the faithful feed on "solid French fare" that's "some of the most classic and best Lyonnais cuisine" in the city; "it hasn't lost a step, despite" an influx of tourists (though visitors remark that "the back room seems to be reserved for English-speakers"), but natives and foreigners alike are struck by the offhand service "that lacks grace, even after Sunday mass."

Vieux Chêne (Au) ⌧ _ _ _ M
7, rue du Dahomey, 11ᵉ (Faidherbe Chaligny), 01 43 71 67 69
Near the Bastille, this newcomer feels like it's been around for at least a century, thanks to vanilla walls, wooden coat

trees and frosted-glass lighting fixtures that are the essence
of the bistro style; the menu embraces tradition as well,
with such genre favorites as pigeon with cabbage and
fresh strawberries with rhubarb compote; it's popular with
an edgy young crowd, so be sure to reserve.

Villa (La)   – | – | – | M

17-19, rue St-Blaise, 20ᵉ (Porte de Bagnolet), 01 30 09 92 36
In a quiet, almost rural, part of the 20th, this cozy, little
bistro is making a reputation for itself with generous, high-
quality Spanish-Argentinean cooking, including beef
imported from the Pampas; the young clientele also enjoys
the relaxed atmosphere, friendly service and good selection
of Iberian and South American wines.

Villa Corse (La) ◑☒   18 | 19 | 13 | 40

164, bd de Grenelle, 15ᵉ (Cambronne/La Motte-Picquet-Grenelle),
01 53 86 70 81; fax 53 86 90 73
■ Corsicans adrift in Paris seize an "invitation to travel"
home without leaving the 15th at this "villa" where the
"cozy" setting, complete with a library, is as "warm" as the
climate on the actual Ile de Beauté; the "real regional
products" include a tempting charcuterie platter and a
"good wine cellar" featuring robust reds from the island.

Village d'Ung et Li Lam ◑   – | – | – | M

10, rue Jean Mermoz, 8ᵉ (Franklin D. Roosevelt), 01 42 25 99 79;
fax 42 25 12 06
Ung is in the glass-walled kitchen, Li Lam is at the door and
there's a surprising six-ton aquarium on the ceiling at this
"convivial space" steps from the Champs, where for two
decades fans of Thai and Chinese cuisine have "satisfied
their appetite" over plates of shrimp dumplings, Peking
duck and chocolate nems (fried stuffed pastries).

Village Kabyle ☒   – | – | – | M

4, rue Aimé Lavy, 18ᵉ (Jules Joffrin), 01 42 55 03 34;
fax 45 86 68 35
The inimitable Wally le Saharien's second (smaller, plainer)
address, in the northern reaches of the 18th, is an oasis for
"out-of-the-ordinary couscous" (including one variety
with tripe) and other Kabyle specialties from the Algerian
desert, along with North African wines for parched palates.

Villa Mauresque (La) ☒   – | – | – | M

5-7, rue du Cdt-Rivière, 8ᵉ (St-Philippe-du-Roule), 01 42 25 16 69;
fax 42 56 37 05; www.villamauresque.com
This North African table in the chic 8th "has a certain
exoticism" with its three rooms replicating the different
ambiances of Marrakesh, Fez and Casablanca; patrons
praise the "refined presentation" but pan the "more
good-looking than effective staff" and "small portions" of
"trendy" Franco-Moroccan cuisine that have some diners
asking for moor.

F | D | S | €C

Villaret (Le) ●🔲   27 | 16 | 19 | 44
13, rue Ternaux, 11ᵉ (Oberkampf/Parmentier), 01 43 57 89 76
■ Delighted diners say this "brick-and-stone-walled",
"unpretentious setting" "off the beaten track" in the 11th
is a "jewel" offering "one of best values in Paris": "abundant
portions" of "incredible, true Classic French cuisine" with
modern, "inventive" touches and "subtle combinations" of
flavors, along with a list of "exceptional but affordable
wines"; what's more, the "gastronomic adventure" changes
with the menu every day.

Vinci (Le) 🔲   - | - | - | E
23, rue Paul Valéry, 16ᵉ (Victor Hugo), 01 45 01 68 18;
fax 45 01 60 37
This "chic" "neighborhood Italian" near the Place Victor
Hugo may be "small" but it turns out "*grande* cuisine" thanks
to a chef who worked with Joël Robuchon and so brings
fine French technique to "very good" imported products,
with "excellent service" to boot.

Vin dans les voiles (Le) 🔲   - | - | - | M
8, rue Chapu, 16ᵉ (Exelmans), 01 46 47 83 98;
fax 46 47 83 98
On the old site of the relocated Les Ormes, this small dining
room in a quiet corner of the 16th has kept the same
provincial look but is reborn as a relaxed *bistrot à vins*
where the amiable owner proffers an impressive selection
of quaffs by the glass as well as by the bottle, accompanied
by a regularly changing chalkboard menu of modestly
priced Bistro dishes.

Vinea Café (Le) ●   - | - | - | M
26-28, Cour St-Emilion, 12ᵉ (Cour St-Emilion), 01 44 74 09 09;
fax 44 74 06 66
Shoppers browsing the "trendy Bercy district" and the
Cour Saint-Emilion (old home to the city's wine storehouses)
can stop for a bite of Med-influenced French cuisine at
this wood-and-stone café with two terraces, open daily
and for Sunday brunch.

Vin et Marée   16 | 11 | 15 | 43
165, rue St-Honoré, 1ᵉʳ (Palais Royal-Musée du Louvre),
01 42 86 06 96; fax 42 86 06 97
71, av de Suffren, 7ᵉ (La Motte-Picquet-Grenelle), 01 47 83 27 12;
fax 43 06 62 35
276, bd Voltaire, 11ᵉ (Nation), 01 43 72 31 23;
fax 40 09 05 24
108, av du Maine, 14ᵉ (Gaîté), 01 43 20 29 50;
fax 43 27 84 11
183, bd Murat, 16ᵉ (Porte de St-Cloud), 01 46 47 91 39;
fax 46 47 69 07
☑ Fin fanatics flock to this chain for seafood (and nothing
but) that, while "simply prepared" ("you could do the same

at home"), is "consistently good" and "always fresh", since the chalkboard menu follows the "offerings at Rungis market"; the "reasonable prices" make up for the "sad decor" and "a welcome that can be as cold as the fish" at some sites; but everywhere, sweet tooths swoon over the "famous baba au rhum" they say is "as big as your head."

20 de Bellechasse (Le) ●🅵   _–_ | _–_ | _–_ | M

20, rue de Bellechasse, 7ᵉ (Solférino), 01 47 05 11 11
Just a few steps from the Musée d'Orsay in the stylish 7th, this casual, friendly traditional bistro offers generous portions, easy prices and cheerful young servers; very popular at noon with a crowd from the many government ministries in the area, it's quieter at night when frequented by a mix of locals and tourists; the decor is highlighted by the many framed caricatures of various celebrities.

Vin sur Vin 🅵   21 | 17 | 24 | 53

20, rue de Monttessuy, 7ᵉ (Alma-Marceau/Ecole Militaire), 01 47 05 14 20
■ Surveyors toast this "quiet", "intimate" place just a couple "blocks from the *Tour Eiffel*" for its "wonderful wine" cellar – 600 different vintages that constitute not a "list but a book" – complemented by "elegant", "inventive" New French cuisine and "exceptional, personalized service" by the oenophile owner and his wife.

VIOLON D'INGRES (LE) 🅵   24 | 19 | 22 | VE

135, rue St-Dominique, 7ᵉ (Ecole Militaire), 01 45 55 15 05; fax 45 55 48 42; www.leviolondingres.com
☑ Like the painter Ingres himself, chef-owner Christian Constant is "technically impeccable" and his loyal supporters are "never disappointed" by his "exquisite", "rather classic" Haute Cuisine and the "unobtrusive" service overseen by his wife, Catherine, in their narrowly proportioned and "conservatively decorated" establishment near the Eiffel Tower; the only constant regret for some is that it's been "taken over by tourists" – but hey, they have the right to "a harmonious indulgence" too.

Virgin Café ●   ▽ 9 | 7 | 8 | 22

Virgin Megastore, 52-60, av Champs-Elysées, 8ᵉ (Franklin D. Roosevelt), 01 42 56 15 96; fax 49 53 03 76
☑ "Music fans" hungry from trolling the aisles at the Virgin Megastore can grab a "basic" Classic French snack at this pit stop whose upper-level perch offers a "view over the Champs-Elysées"; it's hardly Haute Cuisine, but it's "cheap" and "handy for meeting up with friends."

Voltaire (Le) 🅵   23 | 20 | 21 | 64

27, quai Voltaire, 7ᵉ (Rue du Bac), 01 42 61 17 49
■ In the "same family for three generations", this clubby classic bistro facing the Louvre in Saint-Germain has a roster that's "just elaborate enough" to accommodate all

tastes and remain "enjoyable from beginning to end"; service "in the grand tradition" and "classy ambiance" attract "wealthy Americans", "literary" bigwigs and the district's antique dealers, with "a bit expensive" prices helping to "keep out the riffraff."

Wadja ☒
18 | 14 | 17 | 32

10, rue de la Grande Chaumière, 6ᵉ (Vavin), 01 46 33 02 02

■ Local artists won't be starving if they alight upon this "imaginative" Montparnasse bistro that's a "good value" for classic "comfort food" (think "excellent leg of lamb cooked for seven hours"), an "impressive" wine list that includes some organic vintages and "lively" service.

Waknine ☒
▽ 18 | 17 | 21 | 43

9, av Pierre-1er de Serbie, 16ᵉ (Iéna), 01 47 23 48 18; fax 47 23 87 33

■ Patrons settle into "comfy" brown velvet armchairs and order off a "solid" Contemporary French menu at this "noisy" but "inviting" address with a 1940s-inspired decor; additional pluses include a "kind" staff and its location in an area – the affluent 16th – that tends to be short on "warm" "neighborhood places."

Wally Le Saharien ☒
– | – | – | M

36, rue Rodier, 9ᵉ (Anvers/Notre-Dame-de-Lorette), 01 42 85 51 90; fax 42 85 81 90

Berber-cuisine buffs trek from all points to this atmospheric Algerian in a shabby part of the 9th for "superb" "classics" like an "airy" pigeon pastilla, "delicious" stuffed sardines and the signature desert-style "dry couscous", to be drunk with a "limited" North African wine selection; N.B dinner is exclusively a set menu.

Water Bar Colette (Le) ☒
17 | 19 | 17 | 31

213, rue St-Honoré, 1ᵉʳ (Tuileries), 01 55 35 33 93; fax 55 35 33 99; www.colette.fr

☑ Located in the basement of Colette, Paris' perennially hot boutique, this "hip lunch hangout" has "healthy" New French–Italian "great salads and a water bar", with a choice of the wet stuff from all over the world ("a bit has-been" some sniff); it's "perfect for a quick stop while shopping", but as light meals go, damn if it isn't "expensive to be trendy."

Wepler ☽
16 | 17 | 17 | 42

14, pl Clichy, 18ᵉ (Place de Clichy), 01 45 22 53 24; fax 44 70 07 50; www.wepler.com

■ Oyster lovers find a pearl on the Place Clichy at this oldtime (and still independently owned) "brasserie par excellence" where "everybody is having" "sparkling" "fresh, delicious seafood" platters (the other stuff's "just average") in a slightly "shabby" yet endearingly "nostalgic"

1930s setting that somehow feels more "cozy" when it's "crowded and noisy."

Willi's Wine Bar ☒

| 19 | 16 | 19 | 43 |

13, rue des Petits-Champs, 1ᵉʳ (Palais Royal-Musée du Louvre/Pyramides), 01 42 61 05 09; fax 47 03 36 93; www.williswinebar.com

■ This "delightful watering hole" near the Palais Royal is "a must for wine geeks" who "squeeze" into the narrow space decorated with posters to sample "outstanding", "reasonably priced" international vintages along with "tasty" Bistro food; owned by Brit Mark Williamson and staffed by "cheery" compatriots, it's a "second home" for "anglo"- and "oenophiles" who wish the kitchen didn't close "so early" (the bar beats on until midnight).

Wok Cooking ●

| – | – | – | I |

25, rue des Taillandiers, 11ᵉ (Bastille), 01 55 28 88 77

"Choose your ingredients" along with your preferred sauces "and they're stir-fried in front of you" at this Asian "concept" restaurant near the Bastille; it's "fun with a group", as the "antiseptic" setting provides little diversion for solo diners.

W, Restaurant ☒

| – | – | – | E |

Hôtel Warwick, 5, rue de Berri, 8ᵉ (George V), 01 45 61 82 08; fax 45 63 75 81; www.warwickhotels.com

"Excellent" eats and "very nice service" are the draw at this "discreet" dining room in the Hôtel Warwick, steps from the Champs-Elysées; chef Franck Charpentier turns out "inventive" Haute Cuisine with a Provençal accent that possesses much more dash than the beige-colored, somewhat "sterile environment"; however, sampling one of the 150 *eaux de vie* that they offer can ensure "a wonderful" time here.

Yen

| 20 | 22 | 19 | 45 |

22, rue St-Benoît, 6ᵉ (St-Germain-des-Prés), 01 45 44 11 18; fax 45 44 19 48

■ Soba and tempura, not sushi, are the stars at this "unpretentious" little Saint-Germain noodle house where a largely Japanese clientele and occasional "celebrities" are drawn by the "soothing" "Zen" ambiance, "pleasant" staff and "light, healthy" cuisine.

Yvan ☒

| ∇ 17 | 14 | 18 | 66 |

1 bis, rue Jean Mermoz, 8ᵉ (Franklin D. Roosevelt), 01 43 59 18 40; fax 42 89 30 95

■ Although he "remains an absentee chef", owner Yvan Zaplatilek's "intimate and well-run" place near the Champs-Elysées reflects his Belgian roots with a "rustic menu" of "tasty" "classics such as waterzooi" (a creamy fish stew), served in a "snazzy" setting of red velvet and fresh flowers.

Zebra Square ◐ 11 16 11 48
*3, pl Clément-Ader, 16ᵉ (Passy/RER Kennedy-Radio France),
01 44 14 91 91; fax 45 20 46 41; www.zebrasquare.com*
◪ On-air personalities from "the nearby Maison de la Radio"
make this New French with a "zebra motif" their station of
choice for breakfast or a "convenient" lunch despite merely
"adequate" eats, "pricey" tabs and "servers too cool to
actually do any serving"; it's more "fun for drinks" when a
"loud" crowd heats up the sleekly "bohemian" room.

Ze Kitchen Galerie ⌧ 23 20 21 53
*4, rue des Grands-Augustins, 6ᵉ (St-Michel), 01 44 32 00 32;
fax 44 32 00 33*
◪ The open kitchen invites diners to watch chef-owner
William Ledeuil (ex Les Bouquinistes) and his "young team"
inject their culinary "verve" into the "exciting", "fusiony"
Eclectic fare (like "soups that redefine the category") at
this "snazzy", "art-filled" "piece of NY" in Saint-Germain;
ze only main debate is over decor – "cool" "if you like the
pared-down, minimalist look", "cold" if you don't.

Zéphyr (Le) ◐ 19 21 23 35
*1, rue du Jourdain, 20ᵉ (Jourdain), 01 46 36 65 81;
fax 40 33 10 89*
■ An original art-deco interior provides a "typically
Parisian" setting for "refined" contemporary Bistro cuisine
prepared by the "sure hand" of chef-owner Ludovic Enée
at this "animated" "real find" in the "out-of-the-way" 20th;
open every day, it offers a prix fixe menu that's hard to beat.

Zeyer (Le) ◐ ▽ 17 15 17 36
62, rue d'Alésia, 14ᵉ (Alésia), 01 45 40 43 88; fax 45 40 64 51
■ This "authentic" brasserie "à l'ancienne" in the 14th
uses fresh products as the basis for its "quality cuisine"
like the "reputable fish dishes" and "good choucroute
and tartare"; service is "amiable" and the "interestingly
ugly" interior is the designer Slavik's 1970s update of the
original 1930s decor.

Zinc-Zinc – – – E
*209 ter, av Charles de Gaulle, Neuilly (Pont de Neuilly),
01 40 88 36 06; fax 47 38 16 21*
"Just what we need" quips the Neuilly party pack that's
happy to find this "young and somewhat trendy" bistro
with its "simple food" ranging from "tasty" tapas to such
staples as farm-raised chicken; all's served in "light-filled",
"lively surroundings" dominated by a central bar.

Zo ◐⌧ ▽ 18 18 20 40
*13, rue Montalivet, 8ᵉ (Champs-Elysées-Clémenceau),
01 42 65 18 18; fax 42 65 10 91; www.restaurantzo.com*
■ Globally minded suits and style-mongers inhabiting the
8th call this "funky" address their local "canteen" thanks

to an "interesting", "decently priced" menu that mingles Mediterranean and Japanese flavors; the most "daring" of them also wet their whistles with "homemade" fruit-flavored vodka shots.

Zygomates (Les) 🈯 ∇ 24 | 18 | 23 | 42
7, rue de Capri, 12ᵉ (Daumesnil/Michel Bizot), 01 40 19 93 04
■ "The name means the muscles that you grin with, and this friendly place indeed elicits smiles" for its "enjoyable", "excellent" Traditional French "cuisine with a flair" and its "youthful enthusiastic staff"; it's "well worth" going "off the beaten track" in the evolving 12th for this "miniscule" "treasure" set in a former butcher shop.

Indexes

FRENCH CUISINES

(Restaurant Names, Food Ratings and
Arrondissements)

Bistros

Absinthe/*19* (1er)
A et M Le Bistrot/*15* (16e)
Affiche/– (8e)
Affriolé/*21* (7e)
Allobroges/– (20e)
Ami Marcel/– (15e)
Ami Pierre/– (11e)
Amognes/*19* (11e)
Ampère/– (17e)
AOC/– (5e)
Ardoise/*22* (1er)
Assiette/*26* (14e)
Astier/*21* (11e)
Astuce/– (15e)
Atelier Maître Albert/– (5e)
Aub. Nicolas Flamel/*16* (3e)
Authenti©/– (15e)
Babylone/– (7e)
Bar des Théâtres/*14* (8e)
Bath's/*27* (8e)
Benoît/*23* (4e)
Beurre Noisette/*23* (15e)
Bistro 121/– (15e)
Bistro de Breteuil/*14* (7e)
Bistro de Gala/*18* (9e)
Bistro du 17ème/*16* (17e)
Bistro Melrose/– (17e)
Bistro St. Ferdinand/*15* (17e)
Bistrot Baracane/*22* (4e)
Bistrot d'à Côté/*21* (multi. loc.)
Bistrot d'Alex/*14* (6e)
Bistrot d'André/*15* (15e)
Bistrot de l'Etoile Niel/*21* (17e)
Bistrot de l'Université/– (7e)
Bistrot de Marius/*17* (8e)
Bistrot de Paris/*17* (7e)
Bistrot des Capucins/– (20e)
Bistrot des Dames/– (17e)
Bistrot des Vignes/*17* (16e)
Bistrot d'Henri/*20* (6e)
Bistrot du Cap/– (15e)
Bistrot du Dôme/*19* (multi. loc.)
Bistrot du Peintre/*15* (11e)
Bistrot du Sommelier/*19* (8e)

Bistrot Papillon/*20* (9e)
Bistrot Paul Bert/*19* (11e)
Bistrot Vivienne/*17* (1er)
Bon Accueil/*23* (7e)
Bouche à Oreille/– (14e)
Boulangerie/*15* (20e)
Bourguignon du Marais/*21* (4e)
Buisson Ardent/– (5e)
Butte Chaillot/*20* (16e)
Café Burq/– (18e)
Café Charbon/*14* (11e)
Café Constant/– (7e)
Café d'Angel/*18* (17e)
Café de l'Industrie/*11* (11e)
Café de Mars/*17* (7e)
Café des Délices/*21* (6e)
Café des Lettres/– (7e)
Café du Commerce/*10* (15e)
Café la Jatte/*15* (Neuilly)
Café Max/– (7e)
Café Moderne/– (2e)
Café Ruc/*13* (1er)
C'Amelot/*21* (11e)
Camille/*19* (3e)
Carpe Diem/– (Neuilly)
Cave de l'Os à Moëlle/*18* (15e)
Cave Gourmande/*25* (19e)
Chardenoux/*16* (11e)
Charpentiers/*16* (6e)
Chateaubriand/– (11e)
Chez André/*18* (8e)
Chez Arthur/– (10e)
Chez Catherine/*21* (8e)
Chez Denise/*22* (1er)
Chez Diane/*19* (6e)
Chez Fred/*18* (17e)
Chez Georges/*23* (2e)
Chez Gérard/*18* (Neuilly)
Chez Janou/*20* (3e)
Chez L'Ami Louis/*26* (3e)
Chez la Vieille/– (1er)
Chez Léon/– (17e)
Chez Maître Paul/*21* (6e)
Chez Marcel/– (6e)
Chez Nénesse/– (3e)

Chez Paul/*20* (11e)
Chez Paul/*21* (13e)
Chez Ramulaud/*18* (11e)
Chez René/*20* (5e)
Chez Savy/– (8e)
Christine/*23* (6e)
Coconnas/*17* (4e)
Comédiens/– (9e)
. . . Comme Cochon/– (12e)
Contre-Allée/*18* (14e)
Coupe Gorge/– (4e)
Crus de Bourgogne/– (2e)
D'Chez Eux/*21* (7e)
Dix Vins/*17* (15e)
Dos de la Baleine/*14* (4e)
Duc de Richelieu/– (12e)
Ebauchoir/– (12e)
Ecailler du Bistrot/– (11e)
Entracte/– (18e)
Entredgeu/– (17e)
Epi d'Or/*21* (1er)
Epi Dupin/*24* (6e)
Escargot Montorgueil/*18* (1er)
Ferme des Mathurins/– (8e)
Florimond/*22* (7e)
Fontaine de Mars/*19* (7e)
Fontaines/*20* (5e)
Fous d'en Face/*12* (4e)
Frugier/– (16e)
Gauloise/*17* (15e)
Gavroche/*21* (2e)
Gourmand/– (6e)
Gourmets des Ternes/*21* (8e)
Grille/– (10e)
Grille St-Germain/*16* (6e)
Joséphine Ch. Dumonet/*19* (6e)
Languedoc/*17* (5e)
Lescure/*13* (1er)
Ma Bourgogne/*17* (4e)
Maison du Jardin/*24* (6e)
Manufacture/*23* (Issy-les-Moul.)
Mascotte/– (8e)
Mesturet/– (2e)
Moissonnier/*21* (5e)
Mon Vieil Ami/– (4e)
Moulin à Vent/*25* (5e)
Muscade/– (1er)
Noces de Jeannette/– (2e)
Oeillade/*16* (7e)
Ourcine/– (13e)
Papinou/– (Neuilly)

Pères et Filles/– (6e)
Petit Bofinger/*16* (multi. loc.)
Petite Cour/*20* (6e)
Petites Sorcières/– (14e)
Petit Marguery/*23* (13e)
Petit Pontoise/– (5e)
Petit Rétro/*20* (16e)
Pharamond/*15* (1er)
Polidor/*14* (6e)
Pomponette/– (18e)
Pouilly Reuilly/*23* (Le Pré-St-
   Gervais)
Poule au Pot/– (1er)
Press Café/– (2e)
P'Tit Panisse/– (11e)
P'tit Troquet/*22* (7e)
Pure Café/– (11e)
Quinson/– (15e)
Radis Roses/– (9e)
Régalade/*25* (14e)
Rendez-vous/Camion./– (14e)
Rendez-vous/Chauff./– (18e)
Repaire de Cartouche/*20* (11e)
Rest. du Marché/– (15e)
Robert et Louise/– (3e)
Roi du Pot-au-Feu/*18* (9e)
Rôtiss. d'en Face/*22* (6e)
Rôtiss. du Beaujolais/*21* (5e)
Rouge Vif/*15* (7e)
Saint Vincent/– (15e)
Scheffer/*22* (16e)
Soleil/*23* (St-Ouen)
Sot l'y Laisse/– (11e)
Square Trousseau/*17* (12e)
Temps au Temps/– (11e)
Terrasse Mirabeau/– (16e)
Terroir/*18* (13e)
Timbre/*18* (6e)
Tournesol/*14* (16e)
Troquet/*25* (15e)
Trumilou/*16* (4e)
Va et Vient/– (17e)
Verre Bouteille/– (17e)
Verre Volé/– (10e)
Vieux Bistro/*20* (4e)
Vieux Chêne/– (11e)
20 de Bellechasse/– (7e)
Voltaire/*23* (7e)
Zéphyr/*19* (20e)
Zinc-Zinc/– (Neuilly)

Brasseries
Arbuci/*13* (6e)
Aub. Dab/*16* (16e)
Ballon des Ternes/*15* (17e)
Boeuf sur le Toit/*17* (8e)
Bofinger/*18* (4e)
Brass. Balzar/*18* (5e)
Brass. de la Poste/*14* (16e)
Brass. de l'Ile St. Louis/*19* (4e)
Brass. du Louvre/*20* (1er)
Brass. Flo/*17* (10e)
Brass. Julien/*18* (10e)
Brass. La Lorraine/– (8e)
Brass. Lipp/*17* (6e)
Brass. Lutétia/*15* (6e)
Brass. Mollard/*18* (8e)
Café de Flore/*14* (6e)
Café de la Musique/*14* (19e)
Café Terminus/*19* (8e)
Charlot - Roi des Coq./*16* (9e)
Chez Francis/*15* (8e)
Chez Georges-Maillot/*18* (17e)
Chez Jenny/*18* (3e)
Chien qui Fume/*18* (1er)
Closerie des Lilas/*17* (6e)
Congrès Maillot/*12* (17e)
Costes/*18* (1er)
Coupole/*17* (14e)
Editeurs/*13* (6e)
Flandrin/*13* (16e)
Garnier/*18* (8e)
Grand Café/*16* (9e)
Grand Colbert/*16* (2e)
Grandes Marches/*17* (12e)
Léon de Bruxelles/*13* (multi.)
Marty/*17* (5e)
Petit Lutétia/*14* (6e)
Petit Riche/*15* (9e)
Petit Zinc/*16* (6e)
Pichet de Paris/*18* (8e)
Pied de Cochon/*17* (1er)
Publicis Drugstore/– (8e)
Rech/*20* (17e)
Relais Plaza/*21* (8e)
Rotonde/*13* (6e)
Sébillon/*16* (multi. loc.)
Stella/– (16e)
Tav. Maître Kanter/*13* (1er)
Tav. L'Esprit Blvd./– (9e)
Terminus Nord/*17* (10e)
Thoumieux/*16* (7e)

Vagenende/*15* (6e)
Vaudeville/*16* (2e)
Wepler/*16* (18e)
Zeyer/*17* (14e)

Classic
Aiguière/– (11e)
Allard/*22* (6e)
Altitude 95/*15* (7e)
Anacréon/*17* (13e)
Appart'/*14* (8e)
Aristide/– (17e)
Armand, Palais Royal/*21* (1er)
Aub. Bressane/*21* (7e)
Aub. du Champ de Mars/*19* (7e)
Auguste/– (7e)
Bacchantes/– (9e)
Bar des Théâtres/*14* (8e)
Bar Vendôme/*20* (1er)
Basilic/*13* (7e)
Beaujolais d'Auteuil/*17* (16e)
BE Boulangépicier/*19* (17e)
Bélier/– (6e)
Beudant/– (17e)
Biche au Bois/*21* (12e)
Bistro de Breteuil/*14* (7e)
Bistro des Deux Th./*16* (9e)
Bistro St. Ferdinand/*15* (17e)
Bistrot d'à Côté/*21* (multi. loc.)
Bistrot d'André/*15* (15e)
Bistrot d'Henri/*20* (6e)
Bistrot du Sommelier/*19* (8e)
Boeuf Couronné/*23* (19e)
Bon Accueil/*23* (7e)
Bon Saint Pourçain/*19* (6e)
Café Beaubourg/*14* (4e)
Café de la Paix/*17* (9e)
Café de la Poste/– (4e)
Café de l'Esplanade/*14* (7e)
Café Faubourg/*18* (8e)
Café Flo/*14* (9e)
Café Guitry/– (9e)
Café Les Deux Magots/*14* (6e)
Café Marly/*15* (1er)
Café Very/Dame Tart./*11* (multi.)
Caméléon/*17* (6e)
Cap Seguin/*16* (Boulogne)
Caveau du Palais/*21* (1er)
Caves Pétrissans/*18* (17e)
Céladon/*22* (2e)
Chai 33/*13* (12e)
Chalet de Neuilly/– (Neuilly)

Chalet des Iles/*13*(16e)
Chartier/*12*(9e)
Chez Clément/*13*(multi. loc.)
Chez Denise/*22*(1er)
Chez Françoise/*15*(7e)
Chez Gégène/*15*(Joinville)
Chez Georges/*23*(2e)
Chez L'Ami Louis/*26*(3e)
Chez la Vieille/–(1er)
Chez Nénesse/–(3e)
Chez Pauline/*18*(1er)
Chien qui Fume/*18*(1er)
Christine/*23*(6e)
Closerie des Lilas/*17*(6e)
Clos Saint-Honoré/–(1er)
Coconnas/*17*(4e)
Cordonnerie/–(1er)
Côté Coulisses/–(2e)
Coupe-Chou/*21*(5e)
Crus de Bourgogne/–(2e)
Dagorno/–(19e)
Dauphin/*19*(1er)
De Lagarde/–(15e)
Deux Canards/*21*(10e)
Djoon/–(13e)
Dôme du Marais/*18*(4e)
Dominique Bouchet/–(8e)
Drouant/*21*(2e)
Ecluse/*14*(multi. loc.)
Espadon/*25*(1er)
Etoile/*17*(16e)
Ferme des Mathurins/–(8e)
Ferme St-Simon/*23*(7e)
Fermette Marbeuf 1900/*17*(8e)
Flora Danica/*18*(8e)
Flore en l'Ile/*17*(4e)
Florimond/*22*(7e)
Fontaine Gaillon/*17*(2e)
Fouquet's/*16*(8e)
Gallopin/*15*(2e)
Gare/*13*(16e)
Gastroquet/–(15e)
Gérard Besson/*27*(1er)
Gitane/*18*(15e)
Grande Armée/*12*(16e)
Grande Rue/–(15e)
Grand Louvre/*16*(1er)
Grill/–(2e)
Grille/–(10e)
Guinguette/Neuilly/*12*(Neuilly)
Hangar/*21*(3e)

Hermitage/–(10e)
Huîtrier/*18*(17e)
Ile/*15*(Issy-les-Moulineaux)
Jardin des Cygnes/*20*(8e)
Jardinier/–(9e)
Jardins de Bagatelle/*18*(16e)
Joséphine Ch. Dumonet/*19*(6e)
Jules Verne/*24*(7e)
Kiosque/*17*(16e)
Languedoc/*17*(5e)
Lavinia/*15*(8e)
Léna et Mimile/*16*(5e)
Ma Bourgogne/*17*(4e)
Macéo/*19*(1er)
Maison de l'Amér. Lat./*14*(7e)
Marée/*24*(8e)
Marlotte/*17*(6e)
Marsangy/–(11e)
Martel/–(10e)
Mathusalem/*18*(16e)
Maupertu/*19*(7e)
Maxim's/*20*(8e)
Méditerranée/*20*(6e)
Monsieur Lapin/*21*(14e)
Moulin de la Galette/–(18e)
Murat/*13*(16e)
Natacha/*17*(14e)
Obélisque/*23*(8e)
Orangerie/*22*(4e)
Orenoc/*21*(17e)
Os à Moëlle/*23*(15e)
Parc aux Cerfs/*15*(6e)
Passage/Carm./–(11e)
Passiflore/*24*(16e)
Paul Chêne/*25*(16e)
Paul, Restaurant/*15*(1er)
Pavillon Montsouris/*20*(14e)
Père Claude/–(15e)
Pergolèse/*22*(16e)
Perraudin/–(5e)
Petit Colombier/*22*(17e)
Petite Chaise/*17*(7e)
Petite Tour/–(16e)
Petit Laurent/*21*(7e)
Petit Prince de Paris/*21*(5e)
Petit Rétro/*20*(16e)
Petit Riche/*15*(9e)
Petit St. Benoît/*16*(6e)
Petit Victor Hugo/*14*(16e)
Pierre au Palais Royal/*16*(1er)
Polidor/*14*(6e)

Poquelin/*20* (1er)
Potager du Roy/*21* (Versailles)
Poulbot Gourmet/– (18e)
Pressoir/– (12e)
Procope/*16* (6e)
Rest. de la Tour/– (15e)
Rest./Musée d'Orsay/*15* (7e)
Rest./Palais Royal/*19* (1er)
Restaurant GR5/– (multi. loc.)
Rôtiss. de Neuilly/– (Neuilly)
Rubis/*13* (1er)
Saveurs de Claude/– (6e)
Saveurs du Marché/– (Neuilly)
16 Haussmann/*15* (9e)
Sologne/– (12e)
Soufflé/*21* (1er)
Soupière/– (17e)
Square/*10* (7e)
Stella/– (16e)
Stella Maris/*23* (8e)
Stéphane Martin/*22* (15e)
Strapontins/– (10e)
Table d'Anvers/*23* (9e)
Taillevent/*28* (8e)
Tante Jeanne/– (17e)
Tante Louise/*22* (8e)
Tante Marguerite/*21* (7e)
Tastevin/*25* (Maisons-Laffitte)
Télégraphe/*15* (7e)
Temps des Cerises/*15* (13e)
Terres de Truffes/– (8e)
Tonnelle Saintong./– (Neuilly)
Toque/– (17e)
Toupary/*13* (1er)
Train Bleu/*17* (12e)
Triporteur/– (15e)
Truffe Noire/*19* (Neuilly)
Truffière/*25* (5e)
Viaduc Café/*12* (12e)
Vieille Fontaine Rôtiss./*20*
  (Maisons-Laffitte)
Villaret/*27* (11e)
Vinea Café/– (12e)
Virgin Café/*9* (8e)
Wadja/*18* (6e)
Zebra Square/*11* (16e)
Zygomates/*24* (12e)

Contemporary
Aiguière/– (11e)
Alcazar/*16* (6e)
Ambassadeurs/*26* (8e)

Amphyclès/*24* (17e)
Amuse Bouche/*17* (14e)
Angle du Faubourg/*24* (8e)
Angl'Opera/– (2e)
Apollo/*10* (14e)
Argenteuil/*23* (1er)
Astor/*22* (8e)
Astrance/*26* (16e)
Astrée/– (17e)
Atelier Berger/*21* (1er)
Atelier Gourmand/– (17e)
Aub. du Clou/– (9e)
Avant Goût/*22* (13e)
Avenue/*16* (8e)
Bains/*9* (3e)
Baptiste/– (17e)
Béatilles/– (17e)
Berkeley/*10* (8e)
BIOArt/– (13e)
Bistro d'Hubert/*20* (15e)
Bistrot de l'Etoile Laur./*20* (16e)
Bon/– (16e)
Bon 2/*14* (2e)
Bouchons/Fr. Clerc/*17* (multi.)
Boulangerie/Odéon/– (6e)
Bouquinistes/*22* (6e)
Braisière/– (17e)
Bristol/*27* (8e)
Café Beaubourg/*14* (4e)
Café de l'Esplanade/*14* (7e)
Café Lenôtre/*19* (8e)
Café M/*19* (8e)
Café Marly/*15* (1er)
Caïus/– (17e)
Camélia/*23* (Bougival)
Cap Vernet/*16* (8e)
Cartes Postales/*20* (1er)
Cazaudehore La For./*18* (St-
  Germain-en-Laye)
182 Rive Droite/– (16e)
123/– (17e)
Chamarré/*21* (7e)
Chez Catherine/*21* (8e)
Chez Jean/*23* (9e)
Chez Michel/*21* (10e)
Chiberta/– (8e)
59 Poincaré/*21* (16e)
Clos des Gourmets/*22* (7e)
Clos Morillons/*17* (15e)
Clovis/*26* (8e)
Cottage Marcadet/*24* (18e)

Cristal Room/– (16ᵉ)
Cuisine/– (7ᵉ)
1728/*18* (8ᵉ)
Dôme du Marais/*18* (4ᵉ)
Doobie's/*11* (8ᵉ)
En Vue/– (8ᵉ)
Excuse/*22* (4ᵉ)
Feuilles/Entrées Libres/– (Neuilly)
Flora/*23* (8ᵉ)
Grande Rue/– (15ᵉ)
Hédiard/*21* (8ᵉ)
Hélène Darroze/*24* (6ᵉ)
Hiramatsu/*28* (16ᵉ)
Ile/*15* (Issy-les-Moulineaux)
Jardin/*21* (8ᵉ)
Jumeaux/– (11ᵉ)
Libre Sens/– (8ᵉ)
Luna/*24* (8ᵉ)
Macéo/*19* (1ᵉʳ)
Magnolias/*26* (Perreux-sur-Marne)
Maison du Jardin/*24* (6ᵉ)
Maison Rouge/*12* (4ᵉ)
Man Ray/– (8ᵉ)
Marsangy/– (11ᵉ)
Michel Rostang/*27* (17ᵉ)
Montalembert/*15* (7ᵉ)
Murano/– (3ᵉ)
Musichall/– (8ᵉ)
O à la Bouche/*18* (14ᵉ)
Ourcine/– (13ᵉ)
Pershing/*12* (8ᵉ)
Petit Marché/– (3ᵉ)
Petit Pergolèse/– (16ᵉ)
Petit Poucet/*17* (Levallois)
Pinxo/– (1ᵉʳ)
Place/– (8ᵉ)
Ploum/– (10ᵉ)
Point Bar/– (1ᵉʳ)
Pomze/– (8ᵉ)
Pré Verre/– (5ᵉ)
Prosper/– (8ᵉ)
Publicis Drugstore/– (8ᵉ)
Purple/– (11ᵉ)
R./*11* (15ᵉ)
R'Aliment/– (3ᵉ)
Réminet/*24* (5ᵉ)
River Café/*17* (Issy-les-Moul.)
Rue Balzac/*18* (8ᵉ)
Senso/*17* (8ᵉ)
6 New York/*20* (16ᵉ)
Spicy/*18* (8ᵉ)

Spoon, Food/Wine/*22* (8ᵉ)
Suite/*14* (8ᵉ)
Thierry Burlot/– (15ᵉ)
Tire-Bouchon/*22* (15ᵉ)
Toi/– (8ᵉ)
Tokyo Eat/– (16ᵉ)
Troquet/*25* (15ᵉ)
Truffière/*25* (5ᵉ)
Viaduc Café/*12* (12ᵉ)
Vieille Fontaine Rôtiss./*20* (Maisons-Laffitte)
Villa Mauresque/– (8ᵉ)
Vin sur Vin/*21* (7ᵉ)
Waknine/*18* (16ᵉ)
Water Bar Colette/*17* (1ᵉʳ)
Zebra Square/*11* (16ᵉ)

Haute Cuisine
Ambroisie/*26* (4ᵉ)
Apicius/*27* (8ᵉ)
Arpège/*26* (7ᵉ)
Astor/*22* (8ᵉ)
Atelier Joël Robuchon/*26* (7ᵉ)
Bristol/*27* (8ᵉ)
Carré des Feuillants/*25* (1ᵉʳ)
Cazaudehore La For./*18* (St-Germain-en-Laye)
Cinq/*28* (8ᵉ)
Clovis/*26* (8ᵉ)
Dominique Bouchet/– (8ᵉ)
Elysées/*26* (8ᵉ)
Etoile/*17* (16ᵉ)
Grande Cascade/*25* (16ᵉ)
Grand Véfour/*28* (1ᵉʳ)
Guy Savoy/*28* (17ᵉ)
Hiramatsu/*28* (16ᵉ)
Jacques Cagna/*25* (6ᵉ)
Jamin/*25* (16ᵉ)
Lapérouse/*21* (6ᵉ)
Lasserre/*26* (8ᵉ)
Laurent/*24* (8ᵉ)
Ledoyen/*25* (8ᵉ)
Lucas Carton/*27* (8ᵉ)
Maison Blanche/*20* (8ᵉ)
Meurice/*25* (1ᵉʳ)
Montparnasse 25/*23* (14ᵉ)
Muses/*27* (9ᵉ)
Ormes/– (7ᵉ)
Paris/– (6ᵉ)
Pierre Gagnaire/*28* (8ᵉ)
Pré Catelan/*26* (16ᵉ)
Relais d'Auteuil/Pignol/*26* (16ᵉ)
Relais Louis XIII/*26* (6ᵉ)

Rest. Alain Ducasse/*27* (8e)
Table/Joël Robuchon/– (16e)
Table du Baltimore/– (16e)
Table du Lancaster/– (8e)
Taillevent/*28* (8e)
Tour d'Argent/*25* (5e)
Trois Marches/*25* (Versailles)
Violon d'Ingres/*24* (7^e)
W, Restaurant/– (8^e)

Regional
Alpine
Chalet de Neuilly/– (Neuilly)
Radis Roses/– (9e)
Restaurant GR5/– (multi. loc.)

Alsace/Jura
Alsace/*16* (8e)
Alsaco/*18* (9e)
Bofinger/*18* (4e)
Chez Jenny/*18* (3e)
Chez Maître Paul/*21* (6e)

Auvergne
Ambassade d'Auv./*20* (3e)
Auvergne Gourmande/– (7e)
Bath's/*27* (8e)
Bistrot à Vins Mélac/*16* (11e)
Chantairelle/– (5e)
Chez Gérard/*18* (Neuilly)
Lozère/*21* (6e)
Mascotte/– (18e)
Nemrod/*15* (6e)

Aveyron
Aub. Aveyronnaise/– (12e)
Chez Savy/– (8e)

Basque
Bascou/*20* (3e)
Bistro d'Hubert/*20* (15e)
Ourcine/– (13e)
Pamphlet/*21* (3e)

Brittany
Crêperie de Josselin/*19* (14e)

Corsican
Alivi/*19* (4e)
Cafetière Corse/*19* (6e)
Cosi (Le)/– (5e)
Main d'Or/– (11e)
Villa Corse/*18* (15e)

Gascony
Braisière/– (17e)
Comte de Gascogne/*21*
   (Boulogne)

Lyon
Assiette Lyonnaise/*16* (8e)
Aub. Pyrénées Cévennes/*20* (11e)
Benoît/*23* (4e)
Bons Crus/– (1er)
Chez Marcel/– (6e)
Chez René/*20* (5e)
Duc de Richelieu/– (12e)
Lyonnais/*22* (2e)
Moissonnier/*21* (5e)
Opportun/– (14e)
Saint Vincent/– (15e)
Vieux Bistro/*20* (4e)

Northern France
Ch'Ti Catalan/– (9e)
Fernandises/– (11e)
Graindorge/*21* (17e)

Provence
Aimant du Sud/– (13e)
Bastide Odéon/*21* (6e)
Bistro de l'Olivier/*20* (8e)
Bistrot d'Alex/*14* (6e)
Bon 2/*14* (2e)
B4/– (1er)
Casa Olympe/*19* (9e)
182 Rive Droite/– (16e)
Chez Janou/*20* (3e)
Fish La Boissonnerie/*21* (6e)
Jardin/*21* (8e)
Maresco/– (5e)
Olivades/*21* (7e)
Petit Niçois/*16* (7e)
Petits Marseillais/*15* (3e)
Réconfort/– (3e)
Safran/– (1er)
Sept Quinze/*22* (15e)
Si/– (3e)
Sud/*16* (17e)
Table de la Fontaine/– (9e)
Terrasse/– (18e)
Tête Ailleurs/– (4e)

Southwest
Ami Pierre/– (11e)
Aub. Etchégorry/– (13e)
Aub. et Cie/– (9e)
Aub. Pyrénées Cévennes/*20* (11e)
Bistrot Baracane/*22* (4e)
Bistrot des Capucins/– (20e)
Café Faubourg/*18* (8e)
Chez L'Ami Jean/*16* (7e)
Chez Papa/*12* (multi. loc.)

Dauphin/*19* (1ᵉʳ)
D'Chez Eux/*21* (7ᵉ)
Domaine de Lintillac/*18* (9ᵉ)
Fins Gourmets/*16* (7ᵉ)
Fontaine de Mars/*19* (7ᵉ)
Gamin de Paris/*19* (4ᵉ)
Gitane/*18* (15ᵉ)
Hélène Darroze/*24* (6ᵉ)
Il Etait une Oie/*15* (17ᵉ)
J'Go/– (9ᵉ)
Maison Courtine/*22* (14ᵉ)
Mesturet/– (2ᵉ)
Oulette/*21* (12ᵉ)
Papilles/– (5ᵉ)
Pinxo/– (1ᵉʳ)
Rouge Vif/*15* (7ᵉ)
Salon d'Hélène/*19* (6ᵉ)
Sarladais/– (8ᵉ)
Thoumieux/*16* (7ᵉ)
Triporteur/– (15ᵉ)
Trou Gascon/*24* (12ᵉ)

Seafood

Bar à Huîtres/*17* (multi. loc.)
Beudant/– (17ᵉ)
Bistro de l'Olivier/*20* (8ᵉ)
Bistrot Bigorneau/– (16ᵉ)
Bistrot de Marius/*17* (8ᵉ)
Bistrot du Dôme/*19* (multi. loc.)
Bouchons/Fr. Clerc/*17* (8ᵉ)
Brass. Lutétia/*15* (6ᵉ)
Cagouille/*24* (14ᵉ)
Cap Vernet/*16* (8ᵉ)
Charlot - Roi des Coq./*16* (9ᵉ)
Comptoir/Saumon/– (multi. loc.)
Dessirier/*22* (17ᵉ)
Divellec/*23* (7ᵉ)
Dôme/*22* (14ᵉ)
Duc/*25* (14ᵉ)
Écaille de la Fontaine/– (2ᵉ)
Ecailler du Bistrot/– (11ᵉ)
Espadon Bleu/*21* (6ᵉ)
Estaminet Gaya/– (1ᵉʳ)
Fables de La Fontaine/– (7ᵉ)
Fish La Boissonnerie/*21* (6ᵉ)
Garnier/*18* (8ᵉ)
Gaya Rive Gauche/*22* (7ᵉ)
Goumard/*24* (1ᵉʳ)
Huîtrier/*18* (17ᵉ)
Jarrasse/– (Neuilly)
Luna/*24* (8ᵉ)
Maison Prunier/*22* (16ᵉ)

Marée/*24* (8ᵉ)
Marée de Versailles/*21*
  (Versailles)
Marius/*22* (16ᵉ)
Marius et Janette/*21* (8ᵉ)
Méditerranée/*20* (6ᵉ)
Petit Colombier Mer/– (17ᵉ)
Petrossian/*24* (7ᵉ)
Pichet de Paris/*18* (8ᵉ)
Port Alma/*20* (16ᵉ)
Quinson/– (15ᵉ)
Rech/*20* (17ᵉ)
Table de Lucullus/– (17ᵉ)
Uitr/– (15ᵉ)
Vin et Marée/*16* (multi. loc.)

Shellfish

Ballon des Ternes/*15* (17ᵉ)
Ballon et Coquillages/– (17ᵉ)
Bar à Huîtres/*17* (multi. loc.)
Bistrot Bigorneau/– (16ᵉ)
Brass. Lutétia/*15* (6ᵉ)
Brass. Mollard/*18* (8ᵉ)
Charlot - Roi des Coq./*16* (9ᵉ)
Congrès Maillot/*12* (17ᵉ)
Coupole/*17* (14ᵉ)
Dessirier/*22* (17ᵉ)
Dôme/*22* (14ᵉ)
Ecailler du Bistrot/– (11ᵉ)
Garnier/*18* (8ᵉ)
Huîtrier/*18* (17ᵉ)
Maison Prunier/*22* (16ᵉ)
Marée de Versailles/*21*
  (Versailles)
Marius/*22* (16ᵉ)
Marius et Janette/*21* (8ᵉ)
Petit Colombier Mer/– (17ᵉ)
Stella/– (16ᵉ)
Tav. L'Esprit Blvd./– (9ᵉ)
Terminus Nord/*17* (10ᵉ)
Uitr/– (15ᵉ)

Steakhouses

Boeuf Couronné/*23* (19ᵉ)
Dagorno/– (19ᵉ)
Devez/*12* (8ᵉ)
Gavroche/*21* (2ᵉ)
Gourmets des Ternes/*21* (8ᵉ)
Hippopotamus/*10* (multi. loc.)
Louchebem/*17* (1ᵉʳ)
Relais/l'Entrecôte/*23* (multi.)
Relais de Venise/*20* (17ᵉ)

Tearooms

Angelina/*18* (1er)
A Priori Thé/*17* (2e)
Dalloyau/*22* (multi. loc.)
Deux Abeilles/*14* (7e)
Fauchon/– (8e)
Jean-Paul Hévin/*22* (1er)
Je Thé . . . Me/*21* (15e)
Ladurée/*21* (multi. loc.)
Loir dans la Théière/*12* (4e)
Mariage Frères/*19* (multi. loc.)
Muscade/– (1er)

Wine Bars/Bistros

Bacchantes/– (9e)
Baron Bouge/*13* (12e)
Bar Rouge/– (9e)
Bistrot à Vins Mélac/*16* (11e)
Bons Crus/– (1er)
Bouchons/Fr. Clerc/*17* (multi.)
Bourguignon du Marais/*21* (4e)
Café Burq/– (18e)
Café du Passage/– (11e)
Cave de l'Os à Moëlle/*18* (15e)
Caves Pétrissans/*18* (17e)

Cloche des Halles/– (1er)
Clown Bar/*17* (11e)
. . . Comme Cochon/– (12e)
Coude Fou/*16* (4e)
Couleurs de Vigne/– (15e)
Dix Vins/*17* (15e)
Ecluse/*14* (multi. loc.)
Enoteca/*18* (4e)
Juvéniles/*16* (1er)
Lavinia/*15* (8e)
Legrand Filles et Fils/– (2e)
Mauzac/*15* (5e)
Mesturet/– (2e)
Oenothèque/– (9e)
Robe et le Palais/– (1er)
Rubis/*13* (1er)
Sauvignon/*16* (7e)
Taverne Henri IV/– (1er)
Tourelle/– (1er)
Verre Bouteille/– (17e)
Verre Volé/– (10e)
Vin dans les voiles/– (16e)
Vin sur Vin/*21* (7e)
Willi's Wine Bar/*19* (1er)

OTHER CUISINES

(Restaurant Names, Food Ratings and
Arrondissements)

American
Breakfast in America/– (5e)
Buffalo Grill/7 (multi. loc.)
Chicago Pizza/9 (8e)
Coffee Parisien/14 (multi. loc.)
Joe Allen/16 (1er)
Planet Hollywood/8 (8^e)

Argentinean
Anahï/19 (3^e)
El Palenque/18 (5^e)
Villa/– (20^e)

Armenian
Diamantaires/– (9^e)

Asian
Asian/14 (8^e)
Buddha Bar/16 (8^e)
Wok Cooking/– (11^e)

Belgian
Bouillon Racine/13 (6^e)
Graindorge/21 (17^e)
Yvan/17 (8^e)

Cajun
Thanksgiving/15 (4^e)

Cambodian
Kambodgia/20 (16^e)
Sinago/– (9^e)

Canadian
Tadoussac/– (1er)

Caviar
Maison du Caviar/19 (8e)
Maison Prunier/22 (16e)
Petrossian/24 (7e)

Central European
Pitchi Poï/– (4e)

Chinese
(* dim sum specialist)
Chen Soleil d'Est/20 (15e)
Chez Ngo/19 (16e)

Chez Vong/21 (1er)*
China Club/17 (12e)
China Town Olymp./– (13e)
Davé/19 (1er)
Délices de Szechuen/18 (7e)
Diep/18 (8e)
Elysées Hong Kong/– (16e)
Lao Tseu/16 (7e)
Mandarin/Neuilly/– (Neuilly)
Mirama/20 (5e)
New Nioullaville/17 (11e)
Nouveau Village Tao/18 (13e)
Passy Mandarin/22 (16e)
Tang/21 (16e)
Tong Yen/21 (8e)
Tricotin/– (13e)
Tsé-Yang/18 (16e)
Village d'Ung et Li Lam/– (8e)

Creole
Thanksgiving/15 (4e)

Danish
Copenhague/21 (8e)
Flora Danica/18 (8e)
Petite Sirène Copenh./23 (9e)

Dessert
Angelina/18 (1er)
A Priori Thé/17 (2e)
Café Lenôtre/19 (8e)
Dalloyau/22 (multi. loc.)
Deux Abeilles/14 (7e)
Hédiard/21 (8e)
Je Thé . . . Me/21 (15e)
Ladurée/21 (multi. loc.)
Loir dans la Théière/12 (4e)
Mariage Frères/19 (multi. loc.)
Soufflé/21 (1er)

Eclectic
Ailleurs/11 (8e)
Ampère/– (17e)
Aub. du Clou/– (9e)
B*fly/13 (8e)
Barramundi/– (9e)
Berkeley/10 (8e)

Brass. La Lorraine/– (8ᵉ)
Café de Mars/*17* (7ᵉ)
Café Etienne Marcel/*17* (2ᵉ)
Café Fusion/– (13ᵉ)
Café Moderne/– (2ᵉ)
Chamarré/*21* (7ᵉ)
Chez Prune/*14* (10ᵉ)
Comptoir/Saumon/– (multi. loc.)
Cook Book/– (7ᵉ)
Cosi/*20* (6ᵉ)
Costes/*18* (1ᵉʳ)
Djoon/– (13ᵉ)
Doobie's/*11* (8ᵉ)
Durand Dupont/*9* (Neuilly)
Epicure 108/– (17ᵉ)
Famille/– (18ᵉ)
Fumoir/*15* (1ᵉʳ)
Georges/*17* (4ᵉ)
Juvéniles/*16* (1ᵉʳ)
Kong/*14* (1ᵉʳ)
Mandalay/– (Levallois)
Man Ray/– (8ᵉ)
Market/*22* (8ᵉ)
No Stress Café/– (9ᵉ)
Pearl/– (13ᵉ)
Pershing/*12* (8ᵉ)
Pomze/– (8ᵉ)
Quai Ouest/*15* (St-Cloud)
Relais Plaza/*21* (8ᵉ)
Rouge Tomate/– (1ᵉʳ)
Scoop/– (1ᵉʳ)
Spoon, Food/Wine/*22* (8ᵉ)
Taïra/– (17ᵉ)
Ze Kitchen Galerie/*23* (6ᵉ)
Zo/*18* (8ᵉ)

Ethiopian
Entoto/– (13ᵉ)

Greek
Délices d'Aphrodite/*20* (5ᵉ)
Mavrommatis/*19* (5ᵉ)

Hamburgers
Coffee Parisien/*14* (multi. loc.)
Indiana Café/*8* (multi. loc.)
Joe Allen/*16* (1ᵉʳ)
Planet Hollywood/*8* (8ᵉ)

Health Food
Bon/– (16ᵉ)
R'Aliment/– (3ᵉ)

Indian
Annapurna/*18* (8ᵉ)
Indra/*21* (8ᵉ)
Maharajah/*15* (5ᵉ)
New Jawad/*17* (7ᵉ)
Ravi/*23* (7ᵉ)

Indonesian
Djakarta/– (1ᵉʳ)

Irish
Carr's/– (1ᵉʳ)

Italian
(N=Northern; S=Southern)
Al Caratello/– (18ᵉ)
Amici Miei/– (3ᵉ)
Appennino/– (13ᵉ) (N)
Bartolo/*17* (6ᵉ)
Bauta/– (6ᵉ)
Beato/*15* (7ᵉ)
Bel Canto/*14* (multi. loc.)
Bellini/*19* (16ᵉ)
Bocconi/– (8ᵉ)
Ca d'Oro/*16* (1ᵉʳ) (N)
Caffe del Gattopardo/– (18ᵉ) (S)
Caffé Toscano/– (7ᵉ)
Cailloux/– (13ᵉ)
Cantinella/– (14ᵉ)
Casa Bini/*20* (6ᵉ) (N)
Casa Vigata/– (11ᵉ)
Caves Miard/– (6ᵉ)
Cherche Midi/*18* (6ᵉ)
Chez Gildo/*18* (7ᵉ)
Chez Livio/*12* (Neuilly)
Chez Vincent/*22* (19ᵉ)
Da Mimmo/*19* (10ᵉ)
Dell 'Angelo/– (7ᵉ)
Dell Orto/– (9ᵉ)
Emporio Armani/*19* (6ᵉ)
Enoteca/*18* (4ᵉ)
Fellini/*21* (multi. loc.)
Filo Delle Stagioni/– (3ᵉ) (S)
Findi/*17* (8ᵉ)
Finzi/*16* (8ᵉ)
Fontanarosa/*21* (15ᵉ)
Giulio Rebellato/*20* (16ᵉ)
Gli Angeli/*17* (3ᵉ)
Grand Venise/*24* (15ᵉ)
I Golosi/*18* (9ᵉ)
Il Baccello/*20* (17ᵉ)
Il Barone/*19* (14ᵉ)

Il Carpaccio/– (8e)
Il Cortile/23 (1er)
Il Punto/– (Neuilly)
Il Viccolo/17 (6e)
Lei/– (7e)
Ostéria/23 (4e)
Osteria Ascolani/– (18e)
Paolo Petrini/20 (17e)
Paris Seize/15 (16e)
Perron/21 (7e) (S)
Pizzeria d'Auteuil/20 (16e)
Romantica/21 (Clichy)
Rucola/– (17e)
Rughetta/15 (18e)
Sale e Pepe/– (18e)
Sardegna a Tavola/– (12e)
Sormani/25 (17e)
Spaghetti Bar/Curieux/– (4e)
Stresa/19 (8e)
Taverna de Gli Amici/– (7e)
Vinci/– (16e)
Water Bar Colette/17 (1er)

Japanese
(* sushi specialist)
Azabu/– (6e)
Benkay/23 (15e)
Foujita/16 (1er)*
Higuma/16 (1er)
Inagiku/17 (5e)
Isami/24 (4e)
Kaïten/– (8e)
Kinugawa/22 (multi. loc.)
Lô Sushi/17 (multi. loc.)
Matsuri/15 (multi. loc.)
Orient-Extrême/19 (6e)
Ploum/– (10e)
Taka/24 (18e)
Tsukizi/– (6e)
Yen/20 (6e)

Jewish
Jo Goldenberg/13 (4e)
Patrick Goldenberg/– (17e)
Pitchi Poï/– (4e)

Kosher
Patrick Goldenberg/– (17e)
Télégraphe/15 (7e)

Lebanese
Al Dar/20 (multi. loc.)
Al Diwan/20 (8e)

B-Café/21 (16e)
Escale du Liban/– (4e)
Fakhr el Dine/16 (multi. loc.)
Mont Liban/– (17e)
Noura/19 (multi. loc.)

Mediterranean
Chateaubriand/– (11e)
Il Baccello/20 (17e)
16 Haussmann/15 (9e)
7ème Sud/16 (multi. loc.)
Sora Lena/– (17e)

Mexican
Anahuacalli/24 (5e)

Middle Eastern
Chez Marianne/15 (4e)

Moroccan
Al Mounia/19 (16e)
Andy Whaloo/– (3e)
Atlas/21 (5e)
Chez Omar/20 (3e)
Comptoir Paris-Marrak./15 (1er)
El Mansour/21 (8e)
Etoile Marocaine/21 (8e)
Mansouria/22 (11e)
Martel/– (10e)
Oum el Banine/– (16e)
Pied de Chameau/15 (4e)
404/21 (3e)
Riad/– (Neuilly)
Tanjia/– (8e)
Timgad/23 (17e)
Villa Mauresque/– (8e)

North African
7ème Sud/16 (multi. loc.)
Village Kabyle/– (18e)
Wally Le Saharien/– (9e)

Nuevo Latino
Barroco/– (6e)

Pan-Latin
Barrio Latino/8 (12e)

Pizza
Amici Miei/– (3e)
Bartolo/17 (6e)
Chicago Pizza/9 (8e)
Da Mimmo/19 (10e)

Portuguese
Chez Albert/– (6ᵉ)
Saudade/– (1ᵉʳ)

Russian
Caviar Kaspia/*22* (8ᵉ)
Daru/– (8ᵉ)
Dominique/– (6ᵉ)

Sandwiches
BE Boulangépicier/*19* (17ᵉ)
Boulangerie/Odéon/– (6ᵉ)
Café Very/Dame Tart./*11* (multi.)
Cosi/*20* (6ᵉ)
Ferme/– (1ᵉʳ)
Lina's/*13* (multi. loc.)
Sauvignon/*16* (7ᵉ)

Seychelles
Coco de Mer/– (5ᵉ)

Southeast Asian
Tong Yen/*21* (8ᵉ)
Tricotin/– (13ᵉ)

Spanish
(* tapas specialist)
Bar Rouge/– (9ᵉ)*
Bellotta-Bellotta/– (7ᵉ)
Bistrot La Catalogne/*13* (6ᵉ)
Casa Alcalde/*16* (15ᵉ)
Casa Hidalgo/– (11ᵉ)
Casa Tina/*12* (16ᵉ)
Ch'Ti Catalan/– (9ᵉ)
Fogón Saint Julien/*23* (5ᵉ)
Rosimar/*23* (16ᵉ)
Villa/– (20ᵉ)

Swedish
Café des Lettres/– (7ᵉ)

Tex-Mex
Indiana Café/*8* (multi. loc.)
Studio/*11* (4ᵉ)

Thai
Baan-Boran/*20* (1ᵉʳ)
Bains/*9* (3ᵉ)
Banyan/– (15ᵉ)
Blue Elephant/*20* (11ᵉ)
Chez Ngo/*19* (16ᵉ)
Chieng Mai/*18* (5ᵉ)
Erawan/*21* (15ᵉ)
Khun Akorn/*18* (11ᵉ)
Lao Siam/– (19ᵉ)
Mum Sabai/– (6ᵉ)
Paradis Thai/– (13ᵉ)
Sawadee/*19* (15ᵉ)
Thaï/– (1ᵉʳ)
Thiou/*22* (multi. loc.)
Village d'Ung et Li Lam/– (8ᵉ)

Turkish
Sizin/– (9ᵉ)

Vegetarian
Macéo/*19* (1ᵉʳ)
R'Aliment/– (3ᵉ)

Vietnamese
Baie d'Ha Long/– (16ᵉ)
Can Tin'h/– (Boulogne)
Cô Ba Saigon/– (8ᵉ)
Coin des Gourmets/*24* (5ᵉ)
Dan Bau/– (18ᵉ)
Davé/*19* (1ᵉʳ)
Diep/*18* (8ᵉ)
Kambodgia/*20* (16ᵉ)
Kim Anh/*23* (15ᵉ)
Lac-Hong/*21* (16ᵉ)
Palanquin/*13* (6ᵉ)
Suave/– (13ᵉ)
Tan Dinh/*22* (7ᵉ)
Tonkinoise/– (13ᵉ)

LOCATIONS

PARIS

1st arrondissement
Absinthe
Angelina
Ardoise
Argenteuil
Armand, Palais Royal
Atelier Berger
Baan-Boran
Bar Vendôme
Bistrot Vivienne
Bons Crus
B4
Brass. du Louvre
Ca d'Oro
Café Marly
Café Ruc
Café Very/Dame Tart.
Carré des Feuillants
Carr's
Cartes Postales
Caveau du Palais
Chez Denise
Chez la Vieille
Chez Pauline
Chez Vong
Chien qui Fume
Cloche des Halles
Clos Saint-Honoré
Comptoir Paris-Marrak.
Cordonnerie
Costes
Dauphin
Davé
Djakarta
Ecluse
Epi d'Or
Escargot Montorgueil
Espadon
Estaminet Gaya
Fellini
Ferme
Foujita
Fumoir
Gérard Besson
Goumard
Grand Louvre
Grand Véfour

Higuma
Hippopotamus
Il Cortile
Jean-Paul Hévin
Joe Allen
Juvéniles
Kinugawa
Kong
Léon de Bruxelles
Lescure
Lô Sushi
Louchebem
Macéo
Matsuri
Meurice
Muscade
Paul, Restaurant
Pharamond
Pied de Cochon
Pierre au Palais Royal
Pinxo
Point Bar
Poquelin
Poule au Pot
Rest./Palais Royal
Robe et le Palais
Rouge Tomate
Rubis
Safran
Saudade
Scoop
Soufflé
Tadoussac
Tav. Maître Kanter
Taverne Henri IV
Thaï
Toupary
Tourelle
Vin et Marée
Water Bar Colette
Willi's Wine Bar

2nd arrondissement
Angl'Opera
A Priori Thé
Bon 2
Café Etienne Marcel

Locations

Café Moderne
Céladon
Chez Clément
Chez Georges
Côté Coulisses
Crus de Bourgogne
Drouant
Écaille de la Fontaine
Fontaine Gaillon
Gallopin
Gavroche
Grand Colbert
Grill
Hippopotamus
Indiana Café
Legrand Filles et Fils
Lina's
Lyonnais
Mesturet
Noces de Jeannette
Noura
Press Café
Vaudeville

3rd arrondissement
Ambassade d'Auv.
Amici Miei
Anahï
Andy Whaloo
Aub. Nicolas Flamel
Bains
Bar à Huîtres
Bascou
Buffalo Grill
Camille
Chez Janou
Chez Jenny
Chez L'Ami Louis
Chez Nénesse
Chez Omar
Filo Delle Stagioni
Gli Angeli
Hangar
Indiana Café
Murano
Pamphlet
Petit Marché
Petits Marseillais
404
R'Aliment
Réconfort

Robert et Louise
Si

4th arrondissement
Alivi
Ambroisie
Bel Canto
Benoît
Bistrot Baracane
Bistrot du Dôme
Bofinger
Bourguignon du Marais
Brass. de l'Ile St. Louis
Café Beaubourg
Café de la Poste
Café Very/Dame Tart.
Chez Clément
Chez Marianne
Coconnas
Comptoir/Saumon
Coude Fou
Coupe Gorge
Dalloyau
Dôme du Marais
Dos de la Baleine
Enoteca
Escale du Liban
Excuse
Flore en l'Ile
Fous d'en Face
Gamin de Paris
Georges
Hippopotamus
Isami
Jo Goldenberg
Léon de Bruxelles
Loir dans la Théière
Ma Bourgogne
Maison Rouge
Mariage Frères
Mon Vieil Ami
Orangerie
Ostéria
Petit Bofinger
Pied de Chameau
Pitchi Poï
Spaghetti Bar/Curieux
Studio
Tête Ailleurs
Thanksgiving
Trumilou
Vieux Bistro

Locations

5th arrondissement
Al Dar
Anahuacalli
AOC
Atelier Maître Albert
Atlas
Bar à Huîtres
Bouchons/Fr. Clerc
Brass. Balzar
Breakfast in America
Buffalo Grill
Buisson Ardent
Chantairelle
Chez René
Chieng Mai
Coco de Mer
Coin des Gourmets
Cosi (Le)
Coupe-Chou
Délices d'Aphrodite
El Palenque
Fogón Saint Julien
Fontaines
Hippopotamus
Inagiku
Languedoc
Léna et Mimile
Maharajah
Maresco
Marty
Mauzac
Mavrommatis
Mirama
Moissonnier
Moulin à Vent
Papilles
Perraudin
Petit Pontoise
Petit Prince de Paris
Pré Verre
Réminet
Rôtiss. du Beaujolais
Tour d'Argent
Truffière

6th arrondissement
Alcazar
Allard
Arbuci
Azabu
Barroco

Bartolo
Bastide Odéon
Bauta
Bélier
Bistrot d'Alex
Bistrot d'Henri
Bistrot La Catalogne
Bon Saint Pourçain
Bouillon Racine
Boulangerie/Odéon
Bouquinistes
Brass. Lipp
Brass. Lutétia
Café de Flore
Café des Délices
Café Les Deux Magots
Cafetière Corse
Caméléon
Casa Bini
Caves Miard
Charpentiers
Cherche Midi
Chez Albert
Chez Clément
Chez Diane
Chez Maître Paul
Chez Marcel
Christine
Closerie des Lilas
Coffee Parisien
Comptoir/Saumon
Cosi
Dalloyau
Dominique
Ecluse
Editeurs
Emporio Armani
Epi Dupin
Espadon Bleu
Fish La Boissonnerie
Gourmand
Grille St-Germain
Hélène Darroze
Hippopotamus
Il Viccolo
Indiana Café
Jacques Cagna
Joséphine Ch. Dumonet
Ladurée
Lapérouse
Léon de Bruxelles

Lozère
Maison du Jardin
Mariage Frères
Marlotte
Méditerranée
Mum Sabai
Nemrod
Noura
Orient-Extrême
Palanquin
Parc aux Cerfs
Paris
Pères et Filles
Petite Cour
Petit Lutétia
Petit St. Benoît
Petit Zinc
Polidor
Procope
Relais/l'Entrecôte
Relais Louis XIII
Rôtiss. d'en Face
Rotonde
Salon d'Hélène
Saveurs de Claude
Timbre
Tsukizi
Vagenende
Wadja
Yen
Ze Kitchen Galerie

7th arrondissement
Affriolé
Altitude 95
Arpège
Atelier Joël Robuchon
Aub. Bressane
Aub. du Champ de Mars
Auguste
Auvergne Gourmande
Babylone
Basilic
Beato
Bellotta-Bellotta
Bistro de Breteuil
Bistrot de l'Université
Bistrot de Paris
Bon Accueil
Café Constant
Café de l'Esplanade
Café de Mars

Café des Lettres
Café Max
Caffé Toscano
Chamarré
Chez Françoise
Chez Gildo
Chez L'Ami Jean
Clos des Gourmets
Cook Book
Cuisine
D'Chez Eux
Délices de Szechuen
Dell 'Angelo
Deux Abeilles
Divellec
Fables de La Fontaine
Ferme St-Simon
Fins Gourmets
Florimond
Fontaine de Mars
Gaya Rive Gauche
Jules Verne
Lao Tseu
Lei
Lina's
Maison de l'Amér. Lat.
Maupertu
Montalembert
New Jawad
Oeillade
Olivades
Ormes
Perron
Petite Chaise
Petit Laurent
Petit Niçois
Petrossian
P'tit Troquet
Ravi
Rest./Musée d'Orsay
Rouge Vif
Sauvignon
7ème Sud
Square
Tan Dinh
Tante Marguerite
Taverna de Gli Amici
Télégraphe
Thiou
Thoumieux
Vin et Marée

20 de Bellechasse
Vin sur Vin
Violon d'Ingres
Voltaire

8th arrondissement

Affiche
Ailleurs
Al Diwan
Alsace
Ambassadeurs
Angle du Faubourg
Annapurna
Apicius
Appart'
Asian
Assiette Lyonnaise
Astor
Avenue
B*fly
Bar des Théâtres
Bath's
Berkeley
Bistro de l'Olivier
Bistrot de Marius
Bistrot du Sommelier
Bocconi
Boeuf sur le Toit
Bouchons/Fr. Clerc
Brass. La Lorraine
Brass. Mollard
Bristol
Buddha Bar
Café Faubourg
Café Lenôtre
Café M
Café Terminus
Cap Vernet
Caviar Kaspia
Chez André
Chez Catherine
Chez Clément
Chez Francis
Chez Papa
Chez Savy
Chiberta
Chicago Pizza
Cinq
Clovis
Cô Ba Saigon
Copenhague
Dalloyau

Daru
Devez
Diep
1728
Dominique Bouchet
Doobie's
Ecluse
El Mansour
Elysées
En Vue
Etoile Marocaine
Fakhr el Dine
Fauchon
Ferme des Mathurins
Fermette Marbeuf 1900
Findi
Finzi
Flora
Flora Danica
Fouquet's
Garnier
Gourmets des Ternes
Hédiard
Hippopotamus
Il Carpaccio
Indiana Café
Indra
Jardin
Jardin des Cygnes
Kaïten
Kinugawa
Ladurée
Lasserre
Laurent
Lavinia
Ledoyen
Léon de Bruxelles
Libre Sens
Lina's
Lô Sushi
Lucas Carton
Luna
Maison Blanche
Maison du Caviar
Man Ray
Marée
Mariage Frères
Marius et Janette
Market
Mascotte
Maxim's

Musichall
Obélisque
Pershing
Pichet de Paris
Pierre Gagnaire
Place
Planet Hollywood
Pomze
Prosper
Publicis Drugstore
Relais/l'Entrecôte
Relais Plaza
Rest. Alain Ducasse
Rue Balzac
Sarladais
Sébillon
Senso
Spicy
Spoon, Food/Wine
Stella Maris
Stresa
Suite
Table du Lancaster
Taillevent
Tanjia
Tante Louise
Terres de Truffes
Thiou
Toi
Tong Yen
Village d'Ung et Li Lam
Villa Mauresque
Virgin Café
W, Restaurant
Yvan
Zo

9th arrondissement
Alsaco
Aub. du Clou
Aub. et Cie
Bacchantes
Barramundi
Bar Rouge
Bistro de Gala
Bistro des Deux Th.
Bistrot Papillon
Buffalo Grill
Café de la Paix
Café Flo
Café Guitry

Casa Olympe
Charlot - Roi des Coq.
Chartier
Chez Jean
Ch'Ti Catalan
Comédiens
Dell Orto
Diamantaires
Domaine de Lintillac
Grand Café
I Golosi
Indiana Café
Jardinier
J'Go
Ladurée
Léon de Bruxelles
Lina's
Muses
No Stress Café
Oenothèque
Petit Bofinger
Petite Sirène Copenh.
Petit Riche
Radis Roses
Roi du Pot-au-Feu
16 Haussmann
Sinago
Sizin
Table d'Anvers
Table de la Fontaine
Tav. L'Esprit Blvd.
Wally Le Saharien

10th arrondissement
Brass. Flo
Brass. Julien
Buffalo Grill
Chez Arthur
Chez Michel
Chez Papa
Chez Prune
Da Mimmo
Deux Canards
Grille
Hermitage
Hippopotamus
Martel
Ploum
Strapontins
Terminus Nord
Verre Volé

11th arrondissement
Aiguière
Ami Pierre
Amognes
Astier
Aub. Pyrénées Cévennes
Bistrot à Vins Mélac
Bistrot du Peintre
Bistrot Paul Bert
Blue Elephant
Café Charbon
Café de l'Industrie
Café du Passage
C'Amelot
Casa Hidalgo
Casa Vigata
Chardenoux
Chateaubriand
Chez Paul
Chez Ramulaud
Clown Bar
Ecailler du Bistrot
Ecluse
Fernandises
Indiana Café
Jumeaux
Khun Akorn
Léon de Bruxelles
Main d'Or
Mansouria
Marsangy
New Nioullaville
Passage/Carm.
P'Tit Panisse
Pure Café
Purple
Repaire de Cartouche
Sot l'y Laisse
Temps au Temps
Vieux Chêne
Villaret
Vin et Marée
Wok Cooking

12th arrondissement
Aub. Aveyronnaise
Baron Bouge
Barrio Latino
Biche au Bois
Chai 33
China Club

. . . Comme Cochon
Duc de Richelieu
Ebauchoir
Grandes Marches
Lina's
Oulette
Pressoir
Sardegna a Tavola
Sologne
Square Trousseau
Train Bleu
Trou Gascon
Viaduc Café
Vinea Café
Zygomates

13th arrondissement
Aimant du Sud
Anacréon
Appennino
Aub. Etchégorry
Avant Goût
BIOArt
Buffalo Grill
Café Fusion
Cailloux
Chez Paul
China Town Olymp.
Djoon
Entoto
Léon de Bruxelles
Nouveau Village Tao
Ourcine
Paradis Thai
Pearl
Petit Marguery
Suave
Temps des Cerises
Terroir
Tonkinoise
Tricotin

14th arrondissement
Amuse Bouche
Apollo
Assiette
Bar à Huîtres
Bel Canto
Bistrot du Dôme
Bouche à Oreille
Buffalo Grill
Cagouille

Cantinella
Chez Clément
Chez Papa
Contre-Allée
Coupole
Crêperie de Josselin
Dôme
Duc
Hippopotamus
Il Barone
Indiana Café
Léon de Bruxelles
Maison Courtine
Monsieur Lapin
Montparnasse 25
Natacha
O à la Bouche
Opportun
Pavillon Montsouris
Petites Sorcières
Régalade
Rendez-vous/Camion.
Vin et Marée
Zeyer

15th arrondissement
Ami Marcel
Astuce
Authenti©
Banyan
Benkay
Beurre Noisette
Bistro 121
Bistro d'Hubert
Bistrot d'André
Bistrot du Cap
Buffalo Grill
Café du Commerce
Casa Alcalde
Cave de l'Os à Moëlle
Chen Soleil d'Est
Chez Clément
Chez Papa
Clos Morillons
Comptoir/Saumon.
Couleurs de Vigne
Dalloyau
De Lagarde
Dix Vins
Erawan
Fellini
Fontanarosa

Gastroquet
Gauloise
Gitane
Grande Rue
Grand Venise
Hippopotamus
Je Thé . . . Me
Kim Anh
Léon de Bruxelles
Os à Moëlle
Père Claude
Quinson
R.
Rest. de la Tour
Rest. du Marché
Saint Vincent
Sawadee
Sept Quinze
Stéphane Martin
Thierry Burlot
Tire-Bouchon
Triporteur
Troquet
Uitr
Villa Corse

16th arrondissement
A et M Le Bistrot
Al Dar
Al Mounia
Astrance
Aub. Dab
Baie d'Ha Long
B-Café
Beaujolais d'Auteuil
Bellini
Bistrot Bigorneau
Bistrot de l'Etoile Laur.
Bistrot des Vignes
Bon
Brass. de la Poste
Butte Chaillot
Casa Tina
182 Rive Droite
Chalet des Iles
Chez Ngo
59 Poincaré
Coffee Parisien
Cristal Room
Elysées Hong Kong
Etoile
Fakhr el Dine

Flandrin
Frugier
Gare
Giulio Rebellato
Grande Armée
Grande Cascade
Hiramatsu
Jamin
Jardins de Bagatelle
Kambodgia
Kiosque
Lac-Hong
Maison Prunier
Marius
Mathusalem
Matsuri
Murat
Noura
Oum el Banine
Paris Seize
Passiflore
Passy Mandarin
Paul Chêne
Pergolèse
Petite Tour
Petit Pergolèse
Petit Rétro
Petit Victor Hugo
Pizzeria d'Auteuil
Port Alma
Pré Catelan
Relais d'Auteuil/Pignol
Restaurant GR5
Rosimar
Scheffer
7ème Sud
6 New York
Stella
Table/Joël Robuchon
Table du Baltimore
Tang
Terrasse Mirabeau
Tokyo Eat
Tournesol
Tsé-Yang
Vinci
Vin dans les voiles
Vin et Marée
Waknine
Zebra Square

17th arrondissement
Ampère
Amphyclès
Aristide
Astrée
Atelier Gourmand
Ballon des Ternes
Ballon et Coquillages
Baptiste
Béatilles
BE Boulangépicier
Beudant
Bistro du 17ème
Bistro Melrose
Bistro St. Ferdinand
Bistrot d'à Côté
Bistrot de l'Etoile Niel
Bistrot des Dames
Bouchons/Fr. Clerc
Braisière
Buffalo Grill
Café d'Angel
Caïus
Caves Pétrissans
123
Chez Clément
Chez Fred
Chez Georges-Maillot
Chez Léon
Comptoir/Saumon
Congrès Maillot
Dessirier
Ecluse
Entredgeu
Epicure 108
Graindorge
Guy Savoy
Huîtrier
Il Baccello
Il Etait une Oie
Léon de Bruxelles
Lina's
Michel Rostang
Mont Liban
Orenoc
Paolo Petrini
Patrick Goldenberg
Petit Bofinger
Petit Colombier
Petit Colombier Mer
Rech

Relais de Venise
Restaurant GR5
Rucola
Sora Lena
Sormani
Soupière
Sud
Table de Lucullus
Taïra
Tante Jeanne
Timgad
Toque
Va et Vient
Verre Bouteille

18th arrondissement
Al Caratello
Café Burq
Caffe del Gattopardo
Cottage Marcadet
Dan Bau
Entracte
Famille
Mascotte
Moulin de la Galette
Osteria Ascolani

Pomponette
Poulbot Gourmet
Rendez-vous/Chauff.
Rughetta
Sale e Pepe
Taka
Terrasse
Village Kabyle
Wepler

19th arrondissement
Boeuf Couronné
Buffalo Grill
Café de la Musique
Cave Gourmande
Chez Vincent
Dagorno
Lao Siam

20th arrondissement
Allobroges
Bistrot des Capucins
Boulangerie
Villa
Zéphyr

OUTLYING AREAS

Bougival
Camélia

Boulogne-Billancourt
Can Tin'h
Cap Seguin
Chez Clément
Comte de Gascogne
Dalloyau

Clichy
Romantica

Issy-les-Moulineaux
Ile
Manufacture
River Café

Joinville-le-Pont
Chez Gégène

La Défense
Petit Bofinger

Le Pré-St-Gervais
Pouilly Reuilly

Levallois-Perret
Mandalay
Petit Poucet

Maisons-Laffitte
Tastevin
Vieille Fontaine Rôtiss.

Neuilly-sur-Seine
Bel Canto
Bistrot d'à Côté
Café la Jatte
Carpe Diem
Chalet de Neuilly
Chez Gérard
Chez Livio
Coffee Parisien
Durand Dupont
Feuilles/Entrées Libres
Guinguette/Neuilly
Il Punto

Locations

Jarrasse
Lina's
Mandarin/Neuilly
Papinou
Riad
Rôtiss. de Neuilly
Saveurs du Marché
Sébillon
Tonnelle Saintong.
Truffe Noire
Zinc-Zinc

Perreux-sur-Marne
Magnolias

Puteaux
Hippopotamus

Saint-Cloud
Quai Ouest

Saint-Germain-en-Laye
Cazaudehore La For.

Saint-Ouen
Soleil

Versailles
Marée de Versailles
Potager du Roy
Trois Marches

Vincennes
Petit Bofinger

SPECIAL FEATURES

(Indexes list the best in each category. Multi-location restaurants' features may vary by branch.)

Additions
(Properties added since the last edition of the book)
Ami Marcel (15ᵉ)
Angl'Opera (2ᵉ)
Astrée (17ᵉ)
Aub. et Cie (9ᵉ)
Auguste (7ᵉ)
Authenti© (15ᵉ)
BIOArt (13ᵉ)
Boulangerie/Odéon (6ᵉ)
Café de la Poste (4ᵉ)
Café Guitry (9ᵉ)
Caffe del Gattopardo (18ᵉ)
Cantinella (14ᵉ)
Can Tin'h (Boulogne)
Caves Miard (6ᵉ)
Chalet de Neuilly (Neuilly)
Chateaubriand (11ᵉ)
Chez Arthur (10ᵉ)
Ch'Ti Catalan (9ᵉ)
Cô Ba Saigon (8ᵉ)
Cook Book (7ᵉ)
Cordonnerie (1ᵉʳ)
Coupe Gorge (4ᵉ)
Cuisine (7ᵉ)
Dan Bau (18ᵉ)
Dell 'Angelo (7ᵉ)
Djoon (13ᵉ)
Dominique Bouchet (8ᵉ)
Duc de Richelieu (12ᵉ)
Écaille de la Fontaine (2ᵉ)
Escale du Liban (4ᵉ)
Filo Delle Stagioni (3ᵉ)
Frugier (16ᵉ)
Hermitage (10ᵉ)
Il Punto (Neuilly)
Jardinier (9ᵉ)
Maresco (5ᵉ)
Marsangy (11ᵉ)
Mum Sabai (6ᵉ)
Murano (3ᵉ)
Musichall (8ᵉ)
Ourcine (13ᵉ)

Papilles (5ᵉ)
Passage/Carm. (11ᵉ)
Pearl (13ᵉ)
Pères et Filles (6ᵉ)
Petites Sorcières (14ᵉ)
Place (8ᵉ)
Ploum (10ᵉ)
Point Bar (1ᵉʳ)
Pomze (8ᵉ)
Poulbot Gourmet (18ᵉ)
Press Café (2ᵉ)
P'Tit Panisse (11ᵉ)
Publicis Drugstore (8ᵉ)
Purple (11ᵉ)
Radis Roses (9ᵉ)
Restaurant GR5 (multi. loc.)
Rôtiss. de Neuilly (Neuilly)
Rouge Tomate (1ᵉʳ)
Scoop (1ᵉʳ)
Sot l'y Laisse (11ᵉ)
Spaghetti Bar/Curieux (4ᵉ)
Suave (13ᵉ)
Table/Joël Robuchon (16ᵉ)
Table du Lancaster (8ᵉ)
Tadoussac (1ᵉʳ)
Taverna de Gli Amici (7ᵉ)
Taverne Henri IV (1ᵉʳ)
Temps au Temps (11ᵉ)
Terrasse Mirabeau (16ᵉ)
Terres de Truffes (8ᵉ)
Tête Ailleurs (4ᵉ)
Thaï (1ᵉʳ)
Uitr (15ᵉ)
Vieux Chêne (11ᵉ)
Vin dans les voiles (16ᵉ)

Breakfast
(See also Hotel Dining)
Alsace (8ᵉ)
Angelina (1ᵉʳ)
Angl'Opera (2ᵉ)
A Priori Thé (2ᵉ)
Avenue (8ᵉ)
Bar des Théâtres (8ᵉ)
Berkeley (8ᵉ)
Bon 2 (2ᵉ)

Special Features

Boulangerie/Odéon (6e)
Brass. Balzar (5e)
Brass. La Lorraine (8e)
Brass. Mollard (8e)
Breakfast in America (5e)
Café Beaubourg (4e)
Café de Flore (6e)
Café de la Musique (19e)
Café de l'Esplanade (7e)
Café de l'Industrie (11e)
Café Flo (9e)
Café Lenôtre (8e)
Café Les Deux Magots (6e)
Café Marly (1er)
Café Ruc (1er)
Camille (3e)
Cazaudehore La For. (St-
    Germain-en-Laye)
Chalet des Iles (16e)
Chez Clément (multi. loc.)
Chien qui Fume (1er)
Cloche des Halles (1er)
Closerie des Lilas (6e)
Congrès Maillot (17e)
Coupole (14e)
Cristal Room (16e)
Dalloyau (multi. loc.)
Dôme (14e)
Duc de Richelieu (12e)
Editeurs (6e)
En Vue (8e)
Fauchon (8e)
Ferme (1er)
Flandrin (16e)
Flore en l'Ile (4e)
Fontaines (5e)
Fouquet's (8e)
Gavroche (2e)
Grand Café (9e)
Grande Armée (16e)
Hédiard (8e)
Jardins de Bagatelle (16e)
Jo Goldenberg (4e)
Ladurée (multi. loc.)
Lina's (multi. loc.)
Loir dans la Théière (4e)
Ma Bourgogne (4e)
Main d'Or (11e)
Mascotte (8e)
Mascotte (18e)
Murano (3e)
Murat (16e)
Nemrod (6e)
Point Bar (1er)
Pomze (8e)
Procope (6e)
Publicis Drugstore (8e)
Purple (11e)
R'Aliment (3e)
Rotonde (6e)
Rue Balzac (8e)
Stella (16e)
Tav. Maître Kanter (1er)
Tav. L'Esprit Blvd. (9e)
Terminus Nord (10e)
Tricotin (13e)
Vaudeville (2e)
Viaduc Café (12e)
Wepler (18e)
Zebra Square (16e)
Zeyer (14e)
Zinc-Zinc (Neuilly)

Brunch

Alcazar (6e)
Angelina (1er)
Appart' (8e)
A Priori Thé (2e)
Asian (8e)
B*fly (8e)
Barrio Latino (12e)
Barroco (6e)
Berkeley (8e)
Blue Elephant (11e)
B4 (1er)
Brass. Lutétia (6e)
Breakfast in America (5e)
Café Beaubourg (4e)
Café Charbon (11e)
Café de Flore (6e)
Café de la Musique (19e)
Café de l'Esplanade (7e)
Café de l'Industrie (11e)
Café de Mars (7e)
Café des Lettres (7e)
Café la Jatte (Neuilly)
Carr's (1er)
Chai 33 (12e)
Chez Prune (10e)
Comptoir Paris-Marrak. (1er)
Dalloyau (multi. loc.)
Doobie's (8e)
Durand Dupont (Neuilly)

Editeurs (6e)
Ferme (1er)
Findi (8e)
Flore en l'Ile (4e)
Fouquet's (8e)
Fumoir (1er)
Jardin des Cygnes (8e)
Joe Allen (1er)
Jo Goldenberg (4e)
Kiosque (16e)
Ladurée (multi. loc.)
Libre Sens (8e)
Lina's (7e)
Loir dans la Théière (4e)
Maison Rouge (4e)
Mariage Frères (multi. loc.)
Market (8e)
Moulin de la Galette (18e)
Murano (3e)
Nemrod (6e)
No Stress Café (9e)
Pershing (8e)
Pied de Chameau (4e)
Pitchi Poï (4e)
Point Bar (1er)
Publicis Drugstore (8e)
Quai Ouest (St-Cloud)
404 (3e)
R. (15e)
Rouge Tomate (1er)
Scoop (1er)
7ème Sud (multi. loc.)
Spaghetti Bar/Curieux (4e)
Spicy (8e)
Studio (4e)
Télégraphe (7e)
Thanksgiving (4e)
Viaduc Café (12e)
Vinea Café (12e)
Wepler (18e)
W, Restaurant (8e)
Zebra Square (16e)

Business Dining

Affiche (8e)
Amphyclès (17e)
Angle du Faubourg (8e)
Angl'Opera (2e)
Argenteuil (1er)
Armand, Palais Royal (1er)
Astrance (16e)
Astrée (17e)

Auguste (7e)
Bistro St. Ferdinand (17e)
Bistrot de l'Etoile Laur. (16e)
Bistrot de l'Etoile Niel (17e)
Boeuf Couronné (19e)
Boeuf sur le Toit (8e)
Bon 2 (2e)
Buisson Ardent (5e)
Café de l'Esplanade (7e)
Café Faubourg (8e)
Cap Vernet (8e)
Caves Pétrissans (17e)
Céladon (2e)
Chez André (8e)
Chez L'Ami Louis (3e)
Chez Pauline (1er)
Chez Savy (8e)
Chiberta (8e)
Clos des Gourmets (7e)
Copenhague (8e)
Costes (1er)
Cuisine (7e)
Dessirier (17e)
Divellec (7e)
Dôme (14e)
Dôme du Marais (4e)
Dominique Bouchet (8e)
Drouant (2e)
Duc (14e)
Estaminet Gaya (1er)
Flora (8e)
Flora Danica (8e)
Fouquet's (8e)
Frugier (16e)
Gaya Rive Gauche (7e)
Gérard Besson (1er)
Goumard (1er)
Graindorge (17e)
Grandes Marches (12e)
Grill (2e)
Guy Savoy (17e)
Hélène Darroze (6e)
Il Baccello (17e)
Il Cortile (1er)
Jules Verne (7e)
Lapérouse (6e)
Macéo (1er)
Maison Blanche (8e)
Mansouria (11e)
Marée (8e)
Marius (16e)

Special Features

Marty (5ᵉ)
Meurice (1ᵉʳ)
Montalembert (7ᵉ)
Paris (6ᵉ)
Paris Seize (16ᵉ)
Petit Bofinger (4ᵉ)
Petit Marguery (13ᵉ)
Petit Pergolèse (16ᵉ)
Petrossian (7ᵉ)
Pichet de Paris (8ᵉ)
Pierre au Palais Royal (1ᵉʳ)
Pierre Gagnaire (8ᵉ)
Place (8ᵉ)
Pomze (8ᵉ)
Relais Louis XIII (6ᵉ)
Salon d'Hélène (6ᵉ)
Sébillon (multi. loc.)
16 Haussmann (9ᵉ)
Senso (8ᵉ)
Sormani (17ᵉ)
Stella Maris (8ᵉ)
Stresa (8ᵉ)
Table/Joël Robuchon (16ᵉ)
Table du Lancaster (8ᵉ)
Tan Dinh (7ᵉ)
Tante Louise (8ᵉ)
Terrasse Mirabeau (16ᵉ)
Thierry Burlot (15ᵉ)
Train Bleu (12ᵉ)
Trou Gascon (12ᵉ)
Vagenende (6ᵉ)
Vaudeville (2ᵉ)
Vin et Marée (multi. loc.)
Voltaire (7ᵉ)
W, Restaurant (8ᵉ)

Catering

Al Dar (16ᵉ)
Al Diwan (8ᵉ)
Astuce (15ᵉ)
Atelier Gourmand (17ᵉ)
Atlas (5ᵉ)
Avant Goût (13ᵉ)
Baan-Boran (1ᵉʳ)
Baie d'Ha Long (16ᵉ)
Banyan (15ᵉ)
B-Café (16ᵉ)
BE Boulangépicier (17ᵉ)
Bellotta-Bellotta (7ᵉ)
Blue Elephant (11ᵉ)
Caffe del Gattopardo (18ᵉ)
Caffé Toscano (7ᵉ)

Caïus (17ᵉ)
Cantinella (14ᵉ)
Casa Tina (16ᵉ)
Chez Fred (17ᵉ)
Chez Livio (Neuilly)
Chez Marianne (4ᵉ)
Chez Vong (1ᵉʳ)
China Town Olymp. (13ᵉ)
Coco de Mer (5ᵉ)
Comptoir/Saumon (multi. loc.)
Cook Book (7ᵉ)
Cosi (6ᵉ)
Dalloyau (multi. loc.)
Daru (8ᵉ)
Délices d'Aphrodite (5ᵉ)
Deux Abeilles (7ᵉ)
Dominique (6ᵉ)
Escale du Liban (4ᵉ)
Etoile Marocaine (8ᵉ)
Fakhr el Dine (multi. loc.)
Fauchon (8ᵉ)
Feuilles/Entrées Libres (Neuilly)
Filo Delle Stagioni (3ᵉ)
Findi (8ᵉ)
Flora Danica (8ᵉ)
Hédiard (8ᵉ)
Higuma (1ᵉʳ)
Il Punto (Neuilly)
Inagiku (5ᵉ)
Jardinier (9ᵉ)
Jarrasse (Neuilly)
Jo Goldenberg (4ᵉ)
Khun Akorn (11ᵉ)
Kim Anh (15ᵉ)
Kinugawa (multi. loc.)
Lac-Hong (16ᵉ)
Lao Siam (19ᵉ)
Lao Tseu (7ᵉ)
Lina's (multi. loc.)
Maison du Caviar (8ᵉ)
Matsuri (multi. loc.)
Mavrommatis (5ᵉ)
Musichall (8ᵉ)
New Jawad (7ᵉ)
New Nioullaville (11ᵉ)
Noura (multi. loc.)
Oum el Banine (16ᵉ)
Pamphlet (3ᵉ)
Passy Mandarin (16ᵉ)
Patrick Goldenberg (17ᵉ)
Petrossian (7ᵉ)

Pitchi Poï (4e)
Point Bar (1er)
Pomze (8e)
404 (3e)
Riad (Neuilly)
Roi du Pot-au-Feu (9e)
Rosimar (16e)
Sauvignon (7e)
Scoop (1er)
Terrasse Mirabeau (16e)
Terres de Truffes (8e)
Timgad (17e)
Tong Yen (8e)
Tsé-Yang (16e)
Villa (20e)
Village d'Ung et Li Lam (8e)
Village Kabyle (18e)
Wally Le Saharien (9e)

Celebrity Chefs

Ambroisie (4e), *Bernard Pacaud*
Ampère (17e), *Philippe Detourbe*
Angl'Opera (2e), *Gilles Choukroun*
Apicius (8e), *Jean-Pierre Vigato*
Arpège (7e), *Alain Passard*
Astrance (16e), *Pascal Barbot*
Atelier Joël Robuchon (7e), *Joël Robuchon*
Bistrot d'à Côté (multi. loc.), *Michel Rostang*
Bouquinistes (6e), *Guy Savoy*
Bristol (8e), *Eric Frechon*
Butte Chaillot (16e), *Guy Savoy*
Carré des Feuillants (1er), *Alain Dutournier*
Chiberta (8e), *Guy Savoy*
Cinq (8e), *Philippe Legendre*
Elysées (8e), *Eric Briffard*
Espadon (1er), *Michel Roth*
Fables de La Fontaine (7e), *Christian Constant*
Grand Véfour (1er), *Guy Martin*
Guy Savoy (17e), *Guy Savoy*
Hélène Darroze (6e), *Hélène Darroze*
Hiramatsu (16e), *Hiroyuki Hiramatsu*
Jacques Cagna (6e), *Jacques Cagna*
Jamin (16e), *Benoît Guichard*

Lasserre (8e), *Jean-Louis Nomicos*
Ledoyen (8e), *Christian Le Squer*
Lucas Carton (8e), *Alain Senderens*
Lyonnais (2e), *Alain Ducasse*
Market (8e), *Jean-Georges Vongerichten*
Michel Rostang (17e), *Michel Rostang*
Mon Vieil Ami (4e), *Antoine Westermann*
Pierre Gagnaire (8e), *Pierre Gagnaire*
Pinxo (1er), *Alain Dutournier*
Publicis Drugstore (8e), *Alain Ducasse*
Rest. Alain Ducasse (8e), *Alain Ducasse*
Salon d'Hélène (6e), *Hélène Darroze*
Spoon, Food/Wine (8e), *Alain Ducasse*
Table/Joël Robuchon (16e), *Joël Robuchon*
Table du Lancaster (8e), *Michel Troisgros*
Taillevent (8e), *Alain Solivérès*
Trou Gascon (12e), *Alain Dutournier*
Violon d'Ingres (7e), *Christian Constant*
Ze Kitchen Galerie (6e), *William Ledeuil*

Cheese Trays

Ambroisie (4e)
Ami Marcel (15e)
Ampère (17e)
Amphyclès (17e)
Arpège (7e)
Astier (11e)
Astor (8e)
Atelier Joël Robuchon (7e)
Atelier Gourmand (17e)
Aub. et Cie (9e)
Béatilles (17e)
Benoît (4e)
BIOArt (13e)
Bistro de Gala (9e)
Bistrot à Vins Mélac (11e)
Bistrot du Sommelier (8e)

Special Features

Boeuf Couronné (19e)
Bon Accueil (7e)
Bouchons/Fr. Clerc (multi. loc.)
Bourguignon du Marais (4e)
Braisière (17e)
Café Constant (7e)
Café de Flore (6e)
Caffe del Gattopardo (18e)
Camélia (Bougival)
Carré des Feuillants (1er)
Caves Miard (6e)
Céladon (2e)
123 (17e)
Chez Catherine (8e)
Chez Fred (17e)
Chez Gildo (7e)
Chez Jean (9e)
Chez Maître Paul (6e)
Chez René (5e)
Cloche des Halles (1er)
Cook Book (7e)
Cordonnerie (1er)
Divellec (7e)
Dôme (14e)
Dôme du Marais (4e)
Elysées (8e)
Epicure 108 (17e)
Epi d'Or (1er)
Espadon (1er)
Estaminet Gaya (1er)
Ferme St-Simon (7e)
Fernandises (11e)
Fins Gourmets (7e)
Flora (8e)
Fontaine Gaillon (2e)
Fontaines (5e)
Fouquet's (8e)
Frugier (16e)
Garnier (8e)
Goumard (1er)
Graindorge (17e)
Grande Cascade (16e)
Grand Véfour (1er)
Guy Savoy (17e)
Hélène Darroze (6e)
Hermitage (10e)
Il Punto (Neuilly)
Jamin (16e)
Jarrasse (Neuilly)
J'Go (9e)
Jules Verne (7e)

Lasserre (8e)
Laurent (8e)
Lavinia (8e)
Ledoyen (8e)
Maison Courtine (14e)
Marée (8e)
Maresco (5e)
Marsangy (11e)
Mesturet (2e)
Meurice (1er)
Michel Rostang (17e)
Moissonnier (5e)
Montparnasse 25 (14e)
Murano (3e)
Oenothèque (9e)
Papilles (5e)
Papinou (Neuilly)
Paris (6e)
Passage/Carm. (11e)
Passiflore (16e)
Pères et Filles (6e)
Pergolèse (16e)
Petit Colombier (17e)
Petit Laurent (7e)
Pierre Gagnaire (8e)
Point Bar (1er)
Pomze (8e)
Port Alma (16e)
Press Café (2e)
Pressoir (12e)
P'Tit Panisse (11e)
Purple (11e)
Relais d'Auteuil/Pignol (16e)
Relais Louis XIII (6e)
Rest. Alain Ducasse (8e)
Rôtiss. du Beaujolais (5e)
Sébillon (multi. loc.)
Sot l'y Laisse (11e)
Soufflé (1er)
Stella (16e)
Table/Joël Robuchon (16e)
Table du Baltimore (16e)
Table du Lancaster (8e)
Tante Jeanne (17e)
Tante Louise (8e)
Taverna de Gli Amici (7e)
Taverne Henri IV (1er)
Terrasse (18e)
Terroir (13e)
Tête Ailleurs (4e)
Thoumieux (7e)

Tour d'Argent (5ᵉ)
Train Bleu (12ᵉ)
Trois Marches (Versailles)
Trou Gascon (12ᵉ)
Truffe Noire (Neuilly)
Truffière (5ᵉ)
Vaudeville (2ᵉ)
Vieux Chêne (11ᵉ)
Villaret (11ᵉ)
Vin dans les voiles (16ᵉ)
W, Restaurant (8ᵉ)

Child-Friendly

Affiche (8ᵉ)
Aiguière (11ᵉ)
Alcazar (6ᵉ)
Altitude 95 (7ᵉ)
Ampère (17ᵉ)
Amuse Bouche (14ᵉ)
Anahuacalli (5ᵉ)
A Priori Thé (2ᵉ)
Asian (8ᵉ)
Atelier Joël Robuchon (7ᵉ)
Atlas (5ᵉ)
Aub. Dab (16ᵉ)
Aub. et Cie (9ᵉ)
Bar à Huîtres (multi. loc.)
Bar Vendôme (1ᵉʳ)
BE Boulangépicier (17ᵉ)
BIOArt (13ᵉ)
Bistro 121 (15ᵉ)
Bistro de Breteuil (7ᵉ)
Bistro d'Hubert (15ᵉ)
Bistrot d'André (15ᵉ)
Bistrot du Dôme (4ᵉ)
Boeuf sur le Toit (8ᵉ)
Bofinger (4ᵉ)
Bouillon Racine (6ᵉ)
Brass. de la Poste (16ᵉ)
Brass. du Louvre (1ᵉʳ)
Brass. Julien (10ᵉ)
Brass. Lutétia (6ᵉ)
Brass. Mollard (8ᵉ)
Buffalo Grill (multi. loc.)
Café de la Musique (19ᵉ)
Café de la Paix (9ᵉ)
Café Very/Dame Tart. (multi.)
Chai 33 (12ᵉ)
Chalet de Neuilly (Neuilly)
Chalet des Iles (16ᵉ)
Chez Clément (multi. loc.)

Chez Jenny (3ᵉ)
Chez Livio (Neuilly)
Chicago Pizza (8ᵉ)
Comptoir/Saumon (15ᵉ)
Congrès Maillot (17ᵉ)
Cook Book (7ᵉ)
Coupole (14ᵉ)
Fouquet's (8ᵉ)
Gare (16ᵉ)
Gauloise (15ᵉ)
Gitane (15ᵉ)
Grandes Marches (12ᵉ)
Hippopotamus (multi. loc.)
Indiana Café (multi. loc.)
Jardinier (9ᵉ)
J'Go (9ᵉ)
Kiosque (16ᵉ)
Ladurée (8ᵉ)
Languedoc (5ᵉ)
Léon de Bruxelles (multi. loc.)
Monsieur Lapin (14ᵉ)
Noura (6ᵉ)
Orenoc (17ᵉ)
Pavillon Montsouris (14ᵉ)
Pearl (13ᵉ)
Petit Bofinger (multi. loc.)
Petite Cour (6ᵉ)
Petite Sirène Copenh. (9ᵉ)
Petite Tour (16ᵉ)
Petit Lutétia (6ᵉ)
Petit Poucet (Levallois)
Pied de Cochon (1ᵉʳ)
Planet Hollywood (8ᵉ)
Point Bar (1ᵉʳ)
Port Alma (16ᵉ)
Procope (6ᵉ)
Publicis Drugstore (8ᵉ)
Quai Ouest (St-Cloud)
Relais/l'Entrecôte (multi. loc.)
Rendez-vous/Camion. (14ᵉ)
Rest./Musée d'Orsay (7ᵉ)
Rest./Palais Royal (1ᵉʳ)
River Café (Issy-les-Moul.)
Rôtiss. d'en Face (6ᵉ)
Rôtiss. du Beaujolais (5ᵉ)
Rotonde (6ᵉ)
Saint Vincent (15ᵉ)
Sardegna a Tavola (12ᵉ)
Sébillon (multi. loc.)
Spicy (8ᵉ)
Studio (4ᵉ)

Tadoussac (1er)
Tang (16e)
Tav. Maître Kanter (1er)
Terminus Nord (10e)
Terrasse (18e)
Terroir (13e)
Toupary (1er)
Train Bleu (12e)
Trumilou (4e)
Vagenende (6e)
Vaudeville (2e)
Viaduc Café (12e)
Vieux Bistro (4e)
Village d'Ung et Li Lam (8e)
Virgin Café (8e)
Wepler (18e)

Closed in August

(Call ahead to confirm)
Absinthe (1er)
A et M Le Bistrot (16e)
Affriolé (7e)
Ailleurs (8e)
Aimant du Sud (13e)
Allard (6e)
Allobroges (20e)
Alsaco (9e)
Ambroisie (4e)
Amici Miei (3e)
Amognes (11e)
Ampère (17e)
Amphyclès (17e)
Amuse Bouche (14e)
Anacréon (13e)
Angle du Faubourg (8e)
Apicius (8e)
Ardoise (1er)
Armand, Palais Royal (1er)
Assiette (14e)
Astier (11e)
Astor (8e)
Astrance (16e)
Atelier Gourmand (17e)
Aub. du Champ de Mars (7e)
Aub. Etchégorry (13e)
Aub. Pyrénées Cévennes (11e)
Auvergne Gourmande (7e)
Avant Goût (13e)
Azabu (6e)
Babylone (7e)
Baie d'Ha Long (16e)

Ballon des Ternes (17e)
Baptiste (17e)
Barroco (6e)
Bartolo (6e)
Bascou (3e)
Bath's (8e)
Béatilles (17e)
BE Boulangépicier (17e)
Bel Canto (multi. loc.)
Bélier (6e)
Bellini (16e)
Bellotta-Bellotta (7e)
Benoît (4e)
Beudant (17e)
Beurre Noisette (15e)
Biche au Bois (12e)
Bistrot à Vins Mélac (11e)
Bistrot de l'Université (7e)
Bistrot de Paris (7e)
Bistrot des Capucins (20e)
Bistrot du Sommelier (8e)
Bistrot La Catalogne (6e)
Bistrot Papillon (9e)
Bistrot Paul Bert (11e)
Braisière (17e)
Brass. de l'Ile St. Louis (4e)
Buisson Ardent (5e)
Butte Chaillot (16e)
Café d'Angel (17e)
Café de Mars (7e)
Café des Délices (6e)
Café Lenôtre (8e)
Café Max (7e)
Cafetière Corse (6e)
Cailloux (13e)
Caméléon (6e)
Camélia (Bougival)
C'Amelot (11e)
Carré des Feuillants (1er)
Casa Olympe (9e)
Cave de l'Os à Moëlle (15e)
Cave Gourmande (19e)
Caves Pétrissans (17e)
Céladon (2e)
Chen Soleil d'Est (15e)
Chez Albert (6e)
Chez Catherine (8e)
Chez Diane (6e)
Chez Georges (2e)
Chez Gildo (7e)
Chez Jean (9e)

Chez L'Ami Jean (7ᵉ)
Chez L'Ami Louis (3ᵉ)
Chez la Vieille (1ᵉʳ)
Chez Léon (17ᵉ)
Chez Marcel (6ᵉ)
Chez Nénesse (3ᵉ)
Chez René (5ᵉ)
Chez Savy (8ᵉ)
Chiberta (8ᵉ)
Cloche des Halles (1ᵉʳ)
Clos Morillons (15ᵉ)
Clovis (8ᵉ)
Coco de Mer (5ᵉ)
Copenhague (8ᵉ)
Cosi (Le) (5ᵉ)
Cottage Marcadet (18ᵉ)
Da Mimmo (10ᵉ)
Daru (8ᵉ)
D'Chez Eux (7ᵉ)
De Lagarde (15ᵉ)
Délices de Szechuen (7ᵉ)
Dell Orto (9ᵉ)
Deux Canards (10ᵉ)
Dix Vins (15ᵉ)
Domaine de Lintillac (9ᵉ)
Dôme du Marais (4ᵉ)
Dominique (6ᵉ)
Doobie's (8ᵉ)
Drouant (2ᵉ)
Duc (14ᵉ)
Ecailler du Bistrot (11ᵉ)
Elysées (8ᵉ)
Entoto (13ᵉ)
Entracte (18ᵉ)
Entredgeu (17ᵉ)
Epi d'Or (1ᵉʳ)
Epi Dupin (6ᵉ)
Espadon Bleu (6ᵉ)
Estaminet Gaya (1ᵉʳ)
Excuse (4ᵉ)
Fellini (15ᵉ)
Ferme des Mathurins (8ᵉ)
Fernandises (11ᵉ)
Fins Gourmets (7ᵉ)
Florimond (7ᵉ)
Garnier (8ᵉ)
Gavroche (2ᵉ)
Gaya Rive Gauche (7ᵉ)
Gérard Besson (1ᵉʳ)
Giulio Rebellato (16ᵉ)
Gli Angeli (3ᵉ)

Gourmets des Ternes (8ᵉ)
Grande Rue (15ᵉ)
Grandes Marches (12ᵉ)
Grand Véfour (1ᵉʳ)
Grand Venise (15ᵉ)
Grill (2ᵉ)
Grille (10ᵉ)
Hangar (3ᵉ)
Hédiard (8ᵉ)
Hiramatsu (16ᵉ)
Huîtrier (17ᵉ)
Il Carpaccio (8ᵉ)
Il Viccolo (6ᵉ)
Inagiku (5ᵉ)
Isami (4ᵉ)
Jacques Cagna (6ᵉ)
Jamin (16ᵉ)
Je Thé . . . Me (15ᵉ)
Joe Allen (1ᵉʳ)
Joséphine Ch. Dumonet (6ᵉ)
Jumeaux (11ᵉ)
Kambodgia (16ᵉ)
Lac-Hong (16ᵉ)
Languedoc (5ᵉ)
Lapérouse (6ᵉ)
Lasserre (8ᵉ)
Ledoyen (8ᵉ)
Lescure (1ᵉʳ)
Lucas Carton (8ᵉ)
Luna (8ᵉ)
Lyonnais (2ᵉ)
Magnolias (Perreux-sur-Marne)
Maison Courtine (14ᵉ)
Maison du Jardin (6ᵉ)
Mandarin/Neuilly (Neuilly)
Marée (8ᵉ)
Marius (16ᵉ)
Marlotte (6ᵉ)
Mascotte (8ᵉ)
Mavrommatis (5ᵉ)
Meurice (1ᵉʳ)
Michel Rostang (17ᵉ)
Moissonnier (5ᵉ)
Monsieur Lapin (14ᵉ)
Montparnasse 25 (14ᵉ)
Moulin à Vent (5ᵉ)
Muses (9ᵉ)
O à la Bouche (14ᵉ)
Obélisque (8ᵉ)
Oenothèque (9ᵉ)
Olivades (7ᵉ)

Special Features

Orangerie (4e)
Orenoc (17e)
Orient-Extrême (6e)
Ormes (7e)
Os à Moëlle (15e)
Ostéria (4e)
Pamphlet (3e)
Paolo Petrini (17e)
Parc aux Cerfs (6e)
Paris (6e)
Passiflore (16e)
Passy Mandarin (16e)
Paul Chêne (16e)
Pergolèse (16e)
Perraudin (5e)
Perron (7e)
Petite Sirène Copenh. (9e)
Petite Tour (16e)
Petit Laurent (7e)
Petit Marguery (13e)
Petit Niçois (7e)
Petit Pergolèse (16e)
Petrossian (7e)
Pharamond (1er)
Pierre au Palais Royal (1er)
Pomponette (18e)
Poquelin (1er)
Port Alma (16e)
Pressoir (12e)
P'tit Troquet (7e)
Quinson (15e)
R'Aliment (3e)
Régalade (14e)
Relais d'Auteuil/Pignol (16e)
Relais/l'Entrecôte (8e)
Relais Louis XIII (6e)
Relais Plaza (8e)
Réminet (5e)
Rendez-vous/Camion. (14e)
Repaire de Cartouche (11e)
Rest. de la Tour (15e)
Rest. du Marché (15e)
Riad (Neuilly)
Robert et Louise (3e)
Rosimar (16e)
Rouge Vif (7e)
Rucola (17e)
Sardegna a Tavola (12e)
Sarladais (8e)
Sauvignon (7e)
16 Haussmann (9e)

7ème Sud (multi. loc.)
Sept Quinze (15e)
Sinago (9e)
6 New York (16e)
Sormani (17e)
Soufflé (1er)
Soupière (17e)
Spoon, Food/Wine (8e)
Square Trousseau (12e)
Stéphane Martin (15e)
Stresa (8e)
Sud (17e)
Table de Lucullus (17e)
Table du Baltimore (16e)
Taillevent (8e)
Tan Dinh (7e)
Tang (16e)
Tante Jeanne (17e)
Tante Louise (8e)
Tante Marguerite (7e)
Tastevin (Maisons-Laffitte)
Terroir (13e)
Thiou (multi. loc.)
Timbre (6e)
Tire-Bouchon (15e)
Tong Yen (8e)
Tonkinoise (13e)
Tonnelle Saintong. (Neuilly)
Toque (17e)
Trois Marches (Versailles)
Troquet (15e)
Trou Gascon (12e)
Truffe Noire (Neuilly)
Vagenende (6e)
Villa Mauresque (8e)
Villaret (11e)
Vinci (16e)
Vin sur Vin (7e)
Wally Le Saharien (9e)
Zygomates (12e)

Critic-Proof
(Get lots of business despite so-so food)
Café Marly (1er)
Chez Clément (multi. loc.)
Hippopotamus (multi. loc.)
Léon de Bruxelles (multi. loc.)

Dancing
Arbuci (6e)
B*fly (8e)

Bains (3e)
Barramundi (9e)
Barrio Latino (12e)
Brass. de la Poste (16e)
Café de Mars (7e)
Chez Clément (17e)
Chez Gégène (Joinville)
Coupole (14e)
Djoon (13e)
Etoile (16e)
Musichall (8e)
Planet Hollywood (8e)
Suite (8e)
Tanjia (8e)
Vinea Café (12e)

Dining Alone

(Other than hotels and places
with counter service)
Affiche (8e)
Aimant du Sud (13e)
Alcazar (6e)
Alsace (8e)
Ami Marcel (15e)
Ampère (17e)
Amuse Bouche (14e)
Astrée (17e)
Ballon des Ternes (17e)
Bar des Théâtres (8e)
Bar Rouge (9e)
BIOArt (13e)
Bistrot à Vins Mélac (11e)
Bistrot d'Alex (6e)
Bistrot de Marius (8e)
Bistrot du Peintre (11e)
Boeuf sur le Toit (8e)
Bouchons/Fr. Clerc (multi. loc.)
Bouillon Racine (6e)
Boulangerie/Odéon (6e)
Bourguignon du Marais (4e)
Brass. de l'Ile St. Louis (4e)
Breakfast in America (5e)
Buffalo Grill (multi. loc.)
Buisson Ardent (5e)
Café Beaubourg (4e)
Café de Flore (6e)
Café de la Poste (4e)
Café des Lettres (7e)
Café du Commerce (15e)
Café du Passage (11e)
Café Lenôtre (8e)

Café Les Deux Magots (6e)
Café Marly (1er)
Carr's (1er)
Charlot - Roi des Coq. (9e)
Chez Jenny (3e)
Chez Marcel (6e)
Chez Marianne (4e)
Closerie des Lilas (6e)
Cô Ba Saigon (8e)
Congrès Maillot (17e)
Coupole (14e)
Duc de Richelieu (12e)
Ecluse (multi. loc.)
Ferme des Mathurins (8e)
Fernandises (11e)
Fins Gourmets (7e)
Fish La Boissonnerie (6e)
Fumoir (1er)
Gauloise (15e)
Hippopotamus (multi. loc.)
Indiana Café (multi. loc.)
Isami (4e)
Jarrasse (Neuilly)
Je Thé . . . Me (15e)
Joe Allen (1er)
Joséphine Ch. Dumonet (6e)
Ladurée (multi. loc.)
Languedoc (5e)
Legrand Filles et Fils (2e)
Lina's (multi. loc.)
Marsangy (11e)
Marty (5e)
Nemrod (6e)
Oenothèque (9e)
Papilles (5e)
Paradis Thai (13e)
Pères et Filles (6e)
Petit Colombier (17e)
Petite Chaise (7e)
Petite Sirène Copenh. (9e)
Petit Lutétia (6e)
Petit Marguery (13e)
Petit Pergolèse (16e)
Petit Rétro (16e)
Petit Riche (9e)
Polidor (6e)
Poule au Pot (1er)
Publicis Drugstore (8e)
Rubis (1er)
Sologne (12e)
Spaghetti Bar/Curieux (4e)

Special Features

Taverne Henri IV (1er)
Terminus Nord (10e)
Vagenende (6e)
Viaduc Café (12e)
Vieux Chêne (11e)
Vin et Marée (multi. loc.)
Virgin Café (8e)
Wepler (18e)
Wok Cooking (11e)
Zéphyr (20e)

Quai Ouest (St-Cloud) (clown)
Réconfort (3e) (jazz)
Relais Plaza (8e) (jazz)
Saudade (1er) (fado music)
Spicy (8e) (musicians)
Tanjia (8e) (DJ/dancers)
Viaduc Café (12e) (jazz)
Vinea Café (12e) (DJ)
Zebra Square (16e) (DJ)
Zo (8e) (DJ)

Entertainment

(Call for days and times of
performances)
Alivi (4e) (Corsican)
Annapurna (8e) (sitar)
Arbuci (6e) (DJ/jazz)
Asian (8e) (DJ)
B*fly (8e) (DJ)
Bains (3e) (DJ)
Barrio Latino (12e) (salsa)
Barroco (6e) (Brazilian orchestra)
Bar Vendôme (1er) (piano)
Bel Canto (multi. loc.) (opera)
Berkeley (8e) (DJ)
Ca d'Oro (1er) (Italian)
Café Charbon (11e) (concerts)
Café de la Mus. (19e) (jazz/world)
Café de l'Industrie (11e) (jazz)
Café Faubourg (8e) (piano)
Carr's (1er) (Irish)
Chez Françoise (7e) (piano)
Chez Ramulaud (11e) (Guinguette)
Chicago Pizza (8e) (DJ/dancers)
China Club (12e) (concerts)
China Town Olymp. (13e) (karaoke)
Cô Ba Saigon (8e) (sitar)
Diamantaires (9e) (orchestra)
Djakarta (1er) (Balinese dancing)
Jardin (8^e) (harp)
Jardin des Cygnes (8^e) (piano)
Jo Goldenberg (4^e) (Yiddish)
Jules Verne (7e) (piano)
Lasserre (8e) (piano)
Man Ray (8e) (DJ)
Maresco (5e) (jazz)
Maxim's (8e) (piano)
Musichall (8e) (varies)
Passage/Carm. (11e) (debates)
Petit Riche (9e) (theater)
Pied de Chameau (4e) (varies)

Family-Style

Aimant du Sud (13e)
Allard (6e)
Allobroges (20e)
Ampère (17e)
Ardoise (1er)
Aristide (17e)
Babylone (7e)
Bartolo (6e)
Bistrot d'Alex (6e)
Bon Accueil (7e)
Cafetière Corse (6e)
Chez Papa (multi. loc.)
Closerie des Lilas (6e)
Flore en l'Île (4e)
Fontaine de Mars (7e)
Marty (5e)
Mon Vieil Ami (4e)
Repaire de Cartouche (11e)
Toupary (1er)
Wok Cooking (11e)

Fireplaces

Atelier Maître Albert (5e)
Aub. du Clou (9e)
Bon (16e)
Caffe del Gattopardo (18e)
Carr's (1er)
Cazaudehore La For. (St-
  Germain-en-Laye)
Chalet des Iles (16e)
China Club (12e)
Costes (1er)
Coupe-Chou (5e)
Cristal Room (16e)
Diamantaires (9e)
1728 (8e)
Fontaine Gaillon (2e)
Grande Cascade (16e)
Je Thé . . . Me (15e)
Montalembert (7e)

Murano (3ᵉ)
Orangerie (4ᵉ)
Paradis Thai (13ᵉ)
Pavillon Montsouris (14ᵉ)
Petit Colombier (17ᵉ)
Petit Poucet (Levallois)
Petit Victor Hugo (16ᵉ)
Pré Catelan (16ᵉ)
Quai Ouest (St-Cloud)
River Café (Issy-les-Moul.)
Robert et Louise (3ᵉ)
Romantica (Clichy)
Sud (17ᵉ)
Tastevin (Maisons-Laffitte)
Truffière (5ᵉ)

Historic Places

(Year opened; * building)
1582 Tour d'Argent (5ᵉ)
1640 Cordonnerie (1ᵉʳ)*
1650 Aiguière (11ᵉ)*
1680 Petite Chaise (7ᵉ)
1686 Procope (6ᵉ)
1728 1728 (8ᵉ)*
1758 Ambassadeurs (8ᵉ)*
1760 Grand Véfour (1ᵉʳ)
1766 Lapérouse (6ᵉ)
1800 Andy Whaloo (3ᵉ)*
1823 A Priori Thé (2ᵉ)*
1832 Escargot Montorgueil (1ᵉʳ)
1845 Polidor (6ᵉ)
1855 Brass. du Louvre (1ᵉʳ)
1856 Charpentiers (6ᵉ)
1862 Café de la Paix (9ᵉ)
1864 Bofinger (4ᵉ)
1865 Dagorno (19ᵉ)
1867 Brass. Mollard (8ᵉ)
1868 Ladurée (multi. loc.)
1870 Boeuf Couronné (19ᵉ)
1872 Goumard (1ᵉʳ)
1876 Gallopin (2ᵉ)
1880 Aub. du Clou (9ᵉ)*
1880 Brass. Lipp (6ᵉ)
1880 Drouant (2ᵉ)
1880 Petit Riche (9ᵉ)
1881 Café Terminus (8ᵉ)
1885 Café Les Deux Magots (6ᵉ)
1886 Brass. Balzar (5ᵉ)
1890 Amphyclès (17ᵉ)*
1890 Brass. Julien (10ᵉ)
1890 Passage/Carm. (11ᵉ)
1892 Wepler (18ᵉ)
1893 Aristide (17ᵉ)
1893 Maxim's (8ᵉ)
1895 Caves Pétrissans (17ᵉ)
1896 Chartier (9ᵉ)
1898 Espadon (1ᵉʳ)
1899 Fouquet's (8ᵉ)
1900 Brass. de l'Ile St. Louis (4ᵉ)
1900 Café Lenôtre (8ᵉ)*
1900 Chez Gégène (Joinville)
1900 Chez Pauline (1ᵉʳ)
1900 Filo Delle Stagioni (3ᵉ)*
1900 Gauloise (15ᵉ)
1900 Grande Cascade (16ᵉ)
1900 Ledoyen (8ᵉ)
1900 Noces de Jeannette (2ᵉ)
1900 Paul, Restaurant (1ᵉʳ)
1900 Pré Catelan (16ᵉ)
1900 Vieux Chêne (11ᵉ)*
1901 Petit St. Benoît (6ᵉ)
1901 Train Bleu (12ᵉ)
1903 Angelina (1ᵉʳ)
1903 Bistrot de Paris (7ᵉ)
1903 Perraudin (5ᵉ)
1904 Vagenende (6ᵉ)
1905 Bons Crus (1ᵉʳ)
1906 Rendez-vous/Chauff. (18ᵉ)
1908 Chardenoux (11ᵉ)
1909 Bistrot d'André (15ᵉ)
1909 Pomponette (18ᵉ)
1910 Brass. Lutétia (6ᵉ)
1910 Fontaine de Mars (7ᵉ)
1910 Il Punto (Neuilly)*
1910 Pouilly Reuilly (Le Pré-St-Gervais)
1912 Benoît (4ᵉ)
1913 Marty (5ᵉ)
1913 Zeyer (14ᵉ)
1914 Sébillon (Neuilly)
1918 Daru (8ᵉ)
1919 Chez Marcel (6ᵉ)
1919 Lescure (1ᵉʳ)
1920 Closerie des Lilas (6ᵉ)
1920 Jo Goldenberg (4ᵉ)
1920 59 Poincaré (16ᵉ)*
1922 Café du Commerce (15ᵉ)
1923 Thoumieux (7ᵉ)
1924 Bristol (8ᵉ)
1924 Chez L'Ami Louis (3ᵉ)
1925 Biche au Bois (12ᵉ)
1925 Grand Venise (15ᵉ)

1925 Guinguette/Neuilly (Neuilly)
1925 Rech (17ᵉ)
1925 Terminus Nord (10ᵉ)
1926 Chez Georges-Maillot (17ᵉ)
1927 Caviar Kaspia (8ᵉ)
1927 Coupole (14ᵉ)
1928 Cazaudehore La For. (St-Germain-en-Laye)
1928 Dominique (6ᵉ)
1929 Diamantaires (9ᵉ)
1929 Jardin des Cygnes (8ᵉ)
1929 Petit Colombier (17ᵉ)
1929 Tante Louise (8ᵉ)
1929 Zéphyr (20ᵉ)
1930 Allard (6ᵉ)
1930 Garnier (8ᵉ)
1930 Trumilou (4ᵉ)
1931 Chez L'Ami Jean (7ᵉ)
1932 Chiberta (8ᵉ)
1932 Crus de Bourgogne (2ᵉ)
1935 Epi d'Or (1ᵉʳ)
1935 Poule au Pot (1ᵉʳ)
1936 Relais Plaza (8ᵉ)
1937 Chez André (8ᵉ)
1937 Léna et Mimile (5ᵉ)
1939 Voltaire (7ᵉ)
1940 Flandrin (16ᵉ)
1940 Rôtiss. de Neuilly (Neuilly)*
1942 Lasserre (8ᵉ)
1942 Méditerranée (6ᵉ)
1945 Aub. Bressane (7ᵉ)
1945 Chez Fred (17ᵉ)
1945 Ferme des Mathurins (8ᵉ)
1945 Pied de Cochon (1ᵉʳ)
1945 Quinson (15ᵉ)
1946 Chez Maître Paul (6ᵉ)
1946 Taillevent (8ᵉ)
1947 Moulin à Vent (5ᵉ)
1948 Rubis (1ᵉʳ)
1949 Chez Françoise (7ᵉ)
1950 Chez Arthur (10ᵉ)
1950 Maresco (5ᵉ)*
1950 Terrasse (18ᵉ)
1950 Terrasse Mirabeau (16ᵉ)*
1950 Va et Vient (17ᵉ)
1951 Bartolo (6ᵉ)
1951 Deux Canards (10ᵉ)
1952 Bistro 121 (15ᵉ)
1954 Coconnas (4ᵉ)
1954 Sauvignon (7ᵉ)

Holiday Meals

(Special prix fixe meals offered at major holidays)

Ambassadeurs (8ᵉ)
Ambroisie (4ᵉ)
Amognes (11ᵉ)
Amphyclès (17ᵉ)
Apicius (8ᵉ)
Arpège (7ᵉ)
Astor (8ᵉ)
Atelier Joël Robuchon (7ᵉ)
Benoît (4ᵉ)
Bristol (8ᵉ)
Café Les Deux Magots (6ᵉ)
123 (17ᵉ)
Chen Soleil d'Est (15ᵉ)
Chiberta (8ᵉ)
Cinq (8ᵉ)
Coupole (14ᵉ)
Daru (8ᵉ)
Divellec (7ᵉ)
Espadon (1ᵉʳ)
Goumard (1ᵉʳ)
Grande Cascade (16ᵉ)
Guy Savoy (17ᵉ)
Huîtrier (17ᵉ)
Jardins de Bagatelle (16ᵉ)
Jules Verne (7ᵉ)
Lapérouse (6ᵉ)
Lasserre (8ᵉ)
Ledoyen (8ᵉ)
Lucas Carton (8ᵉ)
Marée (8ᵉ)
Maxim's (8ᵉ)
Montparnasse 25 (14ᵉ)
Paris (6ᵉ)
Petrossian (7ᵉ)
Pierre Gagnaire (8ᵉ)
Potager du Roy (Versailles)
Pré Catelan (16ᵉ)
Relais Louis XIII (6ᵉ)
Romantica (Clichy)
Rue Balzac (8ᵉ)
Salon d'Hélène (6ᵉ)
Sormani (17ᵉ)
Table d'Anvers (9ᵉ)
Taillevent (8ᵉ)
Tan Dinh (7ᵉ)
Terrasse (18ᵉ)
Tour d'Argent (5ᵉ)
Trou Gascon (12ᵉ)
Wally Le Saharien (9ᵉ)

Special Features

Hotel Dining

Four Seasons George V
  Cinq (8e)
Grand Hôtel Inter-Continental
  Café de la Paix (9e)
Hôtel Ambassador
  16 Haussmann (9e)
Hôtel Astor
  Astor (8e)
Hôtel Balzac
  Pierre Gagnaire (8e)
Hôtel Castille
  Il Cortile (1er)
Hôtel Concorde St-Lazare
  Café Terminus (8e)
Hôtel Costes
  Costes (1er)
Hôtel de Crillon
  Ambassadeurs (8e)
  Obélisque (8e)
Hôtel de la Trémoille
  Senso (8e)
Hôtel du Louvre
  Brass. du Louvre (1er)
Hotel Edouard VII
  Angl'Opera (2e)
Hôtel El Dorado
  Bistrot des Dames (17e)
Hôtel Hyatt
  Café M (8e)
Hôtel Lancaster
  Table du Lancaster (8e)
Hôtel Le Bristol
  Bristol (8e)
Hôtel Le Parc
  59 Poincaré (16e)
Hôtel Lutétia
  Brass. Lutétia (6e)
  Paris (6e)
Hôtel Meurice
  Meurice (1er)
Hôtel Montalembert
  Montalembert (7e)
Hôtel Novotel Tour Eiffel
  Benkay (15e)
Hotel Pershing Hall
  Pershing (8e)
Hôtel Plaza-Athénée
  Relais Plaza (8e)
  Rest. Alain Ducasse (8e)

Hôtel Prince de Galles
  Jardin des Cygnes (8e)
Hotel Radisson Champs-Elysées
  Place (8e)
Hôtel Ritz
  Bar Vendôme (1er)
  Espadon (1er)
Hôtel Royal Monceau
  Il Carpaccio (8e)
  Jardin (8e)
Hôtel Scribe
  Muses (9e)
Hôtel Terrass
  Terrasse (18e)
Hôtel Thoumieux
  Thoumieux (7e)
Hôtel Trianon Palace
  Trois Marches (Versailles)
Hôtel Vernet
  Elysées (8e)
Hôtel Warwick
  W, Restaurant (8e)
Hôtel Westminster
  Céladon (2e)
Hyatt Paris Vendôme
  Grill (2e)
Le Méridien Etoile
  Orenoc (17e)
Le Méridien-Montparnasse
  Montparnasse 25 (14e)
L'Hôtel
  Bélier (6e)
Murano Urban Resort
  Murano (3e)
Plaza Vendôme Hotel
  Pinxo (1er)
Sofitel Arc de Triomphe
  Clovis (8e)
Sofitel Demeure Hôtel
  Baltimore
  Table du Baltimore (16e)
Sofitel Hôtel Marignan
  Spoon, Food/Wine (8e)
Sofitel Le Faubourg
  Café Faubourg (8e)

Jacket Required
(* Tie also required)
Ambroisie (4e)*
Arpège (7e)
Astrance (16e)

subscribe to zagat.com

Carré des Feuillants (1er)*
Cinq (8e)
Espadon (1er)*
Grande Cascade (16e)*
Grand Véfour (1er)
Jules Verne (7e)*
Lasserre (8e)*
Ledoyen (8e)*
Lucas Carton (8e)*
Maxim's (8e)*
Meurice (1er)*
Michel Rostang (17e)*
Orangerie (4e)
Pré Catelan (16e)*
Relais d'Auteuil/Pignol (16e)*
Relais Plaza (8e)
Rest. Alain Ducasse (8e)*
Salon d'Hélène (6e)
Sarladais (8e)
Taillevent (8e)
Tour d'Argent (5e)*

Late Dining
(Weekday closing hour)
Alcazar (6e) (1 AM)
Al Diwan (8e) (1 AM)
Alsace (8e) (24 hrs.)
Andy Whaloo (3e) (1 AM)
Arbuci (6e) (1 AM)
Aub. Dab (16e) (2 AM)
B*fly (8e) (1 AM)
Bains (3e) (1 AM)
Bar à Huîtres (multi. loc.) (2 AM)
Bar des Théâtres (8e) (1 AM)
Barrio Latino (12e) (2 AM)
Berkeley (8e) (1 AM)
Bistro Melrose (17e) (1 AM)
Boeuf sur le Toit (8e) (1 AM)
Bofinger (4e) (1 AM)
B4 (1er) (1 AM)
Brass. Julien (10e) (1 AM)
Brass. La Lorraine (8e) (12 AM)
Brass. Lipp (6e) (1 AM)
Café de Flore (6e) (1:30 AM)
Café de la Poste (4e) (2 AM)
Café du Passage (11e) (1 AM)
Café Les Deux Magots (6e) (1 AM)
Café Marly (1er) (1 AM)
Café Ruc (1er) (1 AM)
Caviar Kaspia (8e) (1 AM)
Charlot - Roi des Coq. (9e) (1 AM)

Chez André (8e) (1 AM)
Chez Clément (multi. loc.) (1 AM)
Chez Papa (multi. loc.) (1 AM)
Chez Prune (10e) (2 AM)
Chien qui Fume (1er) (1 AM)
China Town Olymp. (13e) (1 AM)
Congrès Maillot (17e) (2 AM)
Costes (1er) (24 hrs.)
Coupe-Chou (5e) (1 AM)
Coupole (14e) (1:30 AM)
Dominique (6e) (1 AM)
Duc de Richelieu (12e) (1 AM)
Ecluse (multi. loc.) (1 AM)
Editeurs (6e) (2 AM)
Etoile (16e) (1 AM)
Flore en l'Ile (4e) (2 AM)
Gamin de Paris (4e) (2 AM)
Gavroche (2e) (2 AM)
Georges (4e) (2 AM)
Grand Café (9e) (24 hrs.)
Grand Colbert (2e) (1 AM)
Grande Armée (16e) (2 AM)
Indiana Café (multi. loc.) (1 AM)
Léon de Bruxelles (multi.) (varies)
Ma Bourgogne (4e) (1 AM)
Maison du Caviar (8e) (1 AM)
Maison Rouge (4e) (2 AM)
Osteria Ascolani (18e) (2 AM)
Pied de Chameau (4e) (1 AM)
Pied de Cochon (1er) (24 hrs.)
Planet Hollywood (8e) (1 AM)
Poule au Pot (1er) (5 AM)
Procope (6e) (1 AM)
Publicis Drugstore (8e) (2 AM)
Rotonde (6e) (1 AM)
Tanjia (8e) (1 AM)
Tav. Maître Kanter (1er) (24 hrs.)
Tav. L'Esprit Blvd. (9e) (1 AM)
Terminus Nord (10e) (1 AM)
Toi (8e) (2 AM)
Vagenende (6e) (1 AM)
Vaudeville (2e) (1 AM)
Verre Bouteille (17e) (4:30 AM)
Viaduc Café (12e) (3 AM)
Vinea Café (12e) (2 AM)
Wepler (18e) (1 AM)

Meet for a Drink
Alcazar (6e)
B*fly (8e)
Bains (3e)

Bar des Théâtres (8e)
Baron Bouge (12e)
Bistrot à Vins Mélac (11e)
Bistrot du Peintre (11e)
Bons Crus (1er)
Bourguignon du Marais (4e)
Café Beaubourg (4e)
Café Burq (18e)
Café Charbon (11e)
Café de Flore (6e)
Café de la Musique (19e)
Café de l'Esplanade (7e)
Café de l'Industrie (11e)
Café Les Deux Magots (6e)
Café Marly (1er)
Café Ruc (1er)
Café Very/Dame Tart. (multi.)
Carr's (1er)
Cloche des Halles (1er)
Closerie des Lilas (6e)
Comptoir Paris-Marrak. (1er)
Coude Fou (4e)
Coupole (14e)
Djoon (13e)
Dôme (14e)
Ecluse (multi. loc.)
Enoteca (4e)
Etoile (16e)
Excuse (4e)
Ferme (1er)
Fish La Boissonnerie (6e)
Fontaines (5e)
Fouquet's (8e)
Fumoir (1er)
Gavroche (2e)
Grande Armée (16e)
Loir dans la Théière (4e)
Ma Bourgogne (4e)
Man Ray (8e)
Maresco (5e)
Murano (3e)
Musichall (8e)
Nemrod (6e)
No Stress Café (9e)
Publicis Drugstore (8e)
River Café (Issy-les-Moul.)
Rubis (1er)
Sauvignon (7e)
Spaghetti Bar/Curieux (4e)
Viaduc Café (12e)
Vinea Café (12e)

Willi's Wine Bar (1er)
Zebra Square (16e)

No Air-Conditioning

A et M Le Bistrot (16e)
Aimant du Sud (13e)
Alivi (4e)
Alsaco (9e)
Amici Miei (3e)
Ami Pierre (11e)
Amognes (11e)
Amuse Bouche (14e)
Anahï (3e)
Anahuacalli (5e)
Angelina (1er)
AOC (5e)
Apollo (14e)
Appennino (13e)
A Priori Thé (2e)
Argenteuil (1er)
Aristide (17e)
Assiette (14e)
Atelier Berger (1er)
Aub. du Champ de Mars (7e)
Aub. Nicolas Flamel (3e)
Authenti© (15e)
Auvergne Gourmande (7e)
Babylone (7e)
Ballon des Ternes (17e)
Bascou (3e)
Biche au Bois (12e)
BIOArt (13e)
Bistro d'Hubert (15e)
Bistrot Baracane (4e)
Bistrot d'à Côté (multi. loc.)
Bistrot d'André (15e)
Bistrot de l'Université (7e)
Bistrot de Marius (8e)
Bistrot de Paris (7e)
Bistrot des Capucins (20e)
Bistrot des Dames (17e)
Bistrot d'Henri (6e)
Bistrot du Dôme (4e)
Bistrot La Catalogne (6e)
Bistrot Vivienne (1er)
Bon Saint Pourçain (6e)
Brass. Balzar (5e)
Brass. de l'Ile St. Louis (4e)
Breakfast in America (5e)
Buisson Ardent (5e)
Ca d'Oro (1er)
Café Beaubourg (4e)

Café Burq (18ᵉ)
Café Charbon (11ᵉ)
Café d'Angel (17ᵉ)
Café de Mars (7ᵉ)
Café des Lettres (7ᵉ)
Café du Commerce (15ᵉ)
Café Max (7ᵉ)
Café Very/Dame Tart. (multi.)
Cagouille (14ᵉ)
Cailloux (13ᵉ)
Caméléon (6ᵉ)
C'Amelot (11ᵉ)
Cap Seguin (Boulogne)
Carr's (1ᵉʳ)
Cartes Postales (1ᵉʳ)
Caveau du Palais (1ᵉʳ)
Caves Pétrissans (17ᵉ)
182 Rive Droite (16ᵉ)
123 (17ᵉ)
Chalet des Iles (16ᵉ)
Chantairelle (5ᵉ)
Chardenoux (11ᵉ)
Charpentiers (6ᵉ)
Chartier (9ᵉ)
Cherche Midi (6ᵉ)
Chez Albert (6ᵉ)
Chez Clément (multi. loc.)
Chez Denise (1ᵉʳ)
Chez Diane (6ᵉ)
Chez Francis (8ᵉ)
Chez Françoise (7ᵉ)
Chez Fred (17ᵉ)
Chez Gérard (Neuilly)
Chez Jean (9ᵉ)
Chez L'Ami Louis (3ᵉ)
Chez la Vieille (1ᵉʳ)
Chez Léon (17ᵉ)
Chez Marcel (6ᵉ)
Chez Marianne (4ᵉ)
Chez Michel (10ᵉ)
Chez Nénesse (3ᵉ)
Chez Omar (3ᵉ)
Chez Paul (11ᵉ)
Chez Paul (13ᵉ)
Chez Pauline (1ᵉʳ)
Chez Prune (10ᵉ)
Chez René (5ᵉ)
Cloche des Halles (1ᵉʳ)
Closerie des Lilas (6ᵉ)
Clown Bar (11ᵉ)
Coco de Mer (5ᵉ)

Coconnas (4ᵉ)
Coin des Gourmets (5ᵉ)
. . . Comme Cochon (12ᵉ)
Comptoir/Saumon (15ᵉ)
Comte de Gascogne (Boulogne)
Contre-Allée (14ᵉ)
Cook Book (7ᵉ)
Cosi (Le) (5ᵉ)
Crus de Bourgogne (2ᵉ)
Dauphin (1ᵉʳ)
Dell Orto (9ᵉ)
Deux Abeilles (7ᵉ)
Devez (8ᵉ)
Dix Vins (15ᵉ)
Djakarta (1ᵉʳ)
Dôme du Marais (4ᵉ)
Duc de Richelieu (12ᵉ)
Durand Dupont (Neuilly)
Ecluse (multi. loc.)
El Palenque (5ᵉ)
Enoteca (4ᵉ)
Entoto (13ᵉ)
Entracte (18ᵉ)
Entredgeu (17ᵉ)
Epi d'Or (1ᵉʳ)
Epi Dupin (6ᵉ)
Famille (18ᵉ)
Fernandises (11ᵉ)
Fins Gourmets (7ᵉ)
Flandrin (16ᵉ)
Flore en l'Ile (4ᵉ)
Florimond (7ᵉ)
Fontaines (5ᵉ)
Foujita (1ᵉʳ)
Fouquet's (8ᵉ)
Gastroquet (15ᵉ)
Gli Angeli (3ᵉ)
Gourmets des Ternes (8ᵉ)
Graindorge (17ᵉ)
Grande Cascade (16ᵉ)
Guinguette/Neuilly (Neuilly)
Il Barone (14ᵉ)
Il Punto (Neuilly)
Jardins de Bagatelle (16ᵉ)
Jumeaux (11ᵉ)
Khun Akorn (11ᵉ)
Louchebem (1ᵉʳ)
Lyonnais (2ᵉ)
Ma Bourgogne (4ᵉ)
Maresco (5ᵉ)
Marius (16ᵉ)

Martel (10ᵉ)
Mascotte (8ᵉ)
Mascotte (18ᵉ)
Maupertu (7ᵉ)
Mauzac (5ᵉ)
Moissonnier (5ᵉ)
Moulin à Vent (5ᵉ)
Muscade (1ᵉʳ)
Natacha (14ᵉ)
No Stress Café (9ᵉ)
Os à Moëlle (15ᵉ)
Ourcine (13ᵉ)
Papinou (Neuilly)
Patrick Goldenberg (17ᵉ)
Pères et Filles (6ᵉ)
Perraudin (5ᵉ)
Petit Bofinger (17ᵉ)
Petite Sirène Copenh. (9ᵉ)
Petit Laurent (7ᵉ)
Petit Lutétia (6ᵉ)
Petit Marché (3ᵉ)
Petit Marguery (13ᵉ)
Petit Niçois (7ᵉ)
Petit Poucet (Levallois)
Petits Marseillais (3ᵉ)
Pharamond (1ᵉʳ)
Pitchi Poï (4ᵉ)
Pomponette (18ᵉ)
Poquelin (1ᵉʳ)
Potager du Roy (Versailles)
Poule au Pot (1ᵉʳ)
Pré Catelan (16ᵉ)
Procope (6ᵉ)
Prosper (8ᵉ)
P'Tit Panisse (11ᵉ)
P'tit Troquet (7ᵉ)
Pure Café (11ᵉ)
Purple (11ᵉ)
R'Aliment (3ᵉ)
Réconfort (3ᵉ)
Relais/l'Entrecôte (8ᵉ)
Relais de Venise (17ᵉ)
Rendez-vous/Camion. (14ᵉ)
Rendez-vous/Chauff. (18ᵉ)
Repaire de Cartouche (11ᵉ)
Rest. du Marché (15ᵉ)
Rest./Palais Royal (1ᵉʳ)
River Café (Issy-les-Moul.)
Robe et le Palais (1ᵉʳ)
Robert et Louise (3ᵉ)
Roi du Pot-au-Feu (9ᵉ)

Romantica (Clichy)
Rouge Tomate (1ᵉʳ)
Rughetta (18ᵉ)
Sale e Pepe (18ᵉ)
Sauvignon (7ᵉ)
Saveurs de Claude (6ᵉ)
Saveurs du Marché (Neuilly)
Scheffer (16ᵉ)
Sept Quinze (15ᵉ)
Si (3ᵉ)
Sinago (9ᵉ)
Soleil (St-Ouen)
Sot l'y Laisse (11ᵉ)
Square Trousseau (12ᵉ)
Table de Lucullus (17ᵉ)
Taka (18ᵉ)
Tastevin (Maisons-Laffitte)
Temps au Temps (11ᵉ)
Temps des Cerises (13ᵉ)
Terrasse Mirabeau (16ᵉ)
Terroir (13ᵉ)
Thanksgiving (4ᵉ)
Timbre (6ᵉ)
Tokyo Eat (16ᵉ)
Tonnelle Saintong. (Neuilly)
Tournesol (16ᵉ)
Train Bleu (12ᵉ)
Triporteur (15ᵉ)
Troquet (15ᵉ)
Truffe Noire (Neuilly)
Tsukizi (6ᵉ)
Vaudeville (2ᵉ)
Viaduc Café (12ᵉ)
Villa Mauresque (8ᵉ)
Vin et Marée (16ᵉ)
Waknine (16ᵉ)
Willi's Wine Bar (1ᵉʳ)
Zéphyr (20ᵉ)
Zygomates (12ᵉ)

Nonsmoking Sections

A et M Le Bistrot (16ᵉ)
Affiche (8ᵉ)
Affriolé (7ᵉ)
Alcazar (6ᵉ)
Al Dar (multi. loc.)
Al Diwan (8ᵉ)
Al Mounia (16ᵉ)
Altitude 95 (7ᵉ)
Ambassadeurs (8ᵉ)
Ambroisie (4ᵉ)
Ampère (17ᵉ)

Amphyclès (17e)
Anacréon (13e)
Annapurna (8e)
AOC (5e)
Appart' (8e)
Appennino (13e)
A Priori Thé (2e)
Arbuci (6e)
Aristide (17e)
Astor (8e)
Astuce (15e)
Atelier Berger (1er)
Atelier Maître Albert (5e)
Atlas (5e)
Aub. Aveyronnaise (12e)
Aub. Dab (16e)
Aub. Etchégorry (13e)
Aub. et Cie (9e)
Aub. Pyrénées Cévennes (11e)
Avenue (8e)
B*fly (8e)
Baan-Boran (1er)
Baie d'Ha Long (16e)
Ballon des Ternes (17e)
Banyan (15e)
Barramundi (9e)
Barrio Latino (12e)
Bar Vendôme (1er)
Basilic (7e)
Bath's (8e)
Bauta (6e)
Beato (7e)
Benkay (15e)
Beudant (17e)
BIOArt (13e)
Bistro 121 (15e)
Bistro de Breteuil (7e)
Bistro du 17ème (17e)
Bistro St. Ferdinand (17e)
Bistrot à Vins Mélac (11e)
Bistrot Baracane (4e)
Bistrot Bigorneau (16e)
Bistrot d'Alex (6e)
Bistrot d'André (15e)
Bistrot de l'Etoile Niel (17e)
Bistrot de l'Université (7e)
Bistrot des Capucins (20e)
Bistrot des Vignes (16e)
Bistrot du Dôme (multi. loc.)
Bistrot du Sommelier (8e)
Bistrot La Catalogne (6e)

Bistrot Papillon (9e)
Blue Elephant (11e)
Bocconi (8e)
Boeuf sur le Toit (8e)
Bon Accueil (7e)
Bon Saint Pourçain (6e)
Bons Crus (1er)
Bouchons/Fr. Clerc (multi. loc.)
Boulangerie (20e)
Bourguignon du Marais (4e)
Braisière (17e)
Brass. Balzar (5e)
Brass. de la Poste (16e)
Brass. de l'Ile St. Louis (4e)
Brass. du Louvre (1er)
Brass. Flo (10e)
Brass. La Lorraine (8e)
Brass. Lutétia (6e)
Brass. Mollard (8e)
Buddha Bar (8e)
Buffalo Grill (multi. loc.)
Buisson Ardent (5e)
Butte Chaillot (16e)
Ca d'Oro (1er)
Café Beaubourg (4e)
Café Burq (18e)
Café Charbon (11e)
Café de Flore (6e)
Café de la Musique (19e)
Café de la Paix (9e)
Café de l'Esplanade (7e)
Café de l'Industrie (11e)
Café du Passage (11e)
Café Etienne Marcel (2e)
Café Faubourg (8e)
Café Flo (9e)
Café Fusion (13e)
Café Guitry (9e)
Café la Jatte (Neuilly)
Café M (8e)
Café Marly (1er)
Café Moderne (2e)
Café Very/Dame Tart. (multi.)
Caffé Toscano (7e)
Cagouille (14e)
Caïus (17e)
Caméléon (6e)
Camélia (Bougival)
Camille (3e)
Cap Seguin (Boulogne)
Cap Vernet (8e)

Carré des Feuillants (1er)
Carr's (1er)
Casa Alcalde (15e)
Casa Hidalgo (11e)
Caveau du Palais (1er)
Cave de l'Os à Moëlle (15e)
Caves Pétrissans (17e)
Caviar Kaspia (8e)
Cazaudehore La For. (St-
    Germain-en-Laye)
Céladon (2e)
Chai 33 (12e)
Chantairelle (5e)
Charlot - Roi des Coq. (9e)
Chartier (9e)
Chen Soleil d'Est (15e)
Cherche Midi (6e)
Chez Albert (6e)
Chez André (8e)
Chez Catherine (8e)
Chez Clément (multi. loc.)
Chez Denise (1er)
Chez Francis (8e)
Chez Françoise (7e)
Chez Fred (17e)
Chez Georges-Maillot (17e)
Chez Gérard (Neuilly)
Chez Gildo (7e)
Chez Janou (3e)
Chez Jean (9e)
Chez Jenny (3e)
Chez L'Ami Louis (3e)
Chez Léon (17e)
Chez Livio (Neuilly)
Chez Marianne (4e)
Chez Michel (10e)
Chez Nénesse (3e)
Chez Omar (3e)
Chez Papa (multi. loc.)
Chez Pauline (1er)
Chez René (5e)
Chez Vong (1er)
Chiberta (8e)
Chicago Pizza (8e)
Chieng Mai (5e)
Chien qui Fume (1er)
China Town Olymp. (13e)
Christine (6e)
Cinq (8e)
Clos Saint-Honoré (1er)
Clovis (8e)

Coin des Gourmets (5e)
Comédiens (9e)
Congrès Maillot (17e)
Contre-Allée (14e)
Cook Book (7e)
Copenhague (8e)
Cordonnerie (1er)
Cosi (6e)
Cosi (Le) (5e)
Costes (1er)
Côté Coulisses (2e)
Coupe Gorge (4e)
Coupole (14e)
Crêperie de Josselin (14e)
Cristal Room (16e)
Dalloyau (multi. loc.)
Da Mimmo (10e)
Dauphin (1er)
Délices de Szechuen (7e)
Dell Orto (9e)
Dessirier (17e)
Deux Abeilles (7e)
Devez (8e)
Diamantaires (9e)
Diep (8e)
1728 (8e)
Djakarta (1er)
Dôme (14e)
Dôme du Marais (4e)
Dominique Bouchet (8e)
Dos de la Baleine (4e)
Drouant (2e)
Duc de Richelieu (12e)
Durand Dupont (Neuilly)
Ebauchoir (12e)
Ecailler du Bistrot (11e)
Ecluse (multi. loc.)
El Mansour (8e)
El Palenque (5e)
Elysées (8e)
Elysées Hong Kong (16e)
Emporio Armani (6e)
Entoto (13e)
Epicure 108 (17e)
Epi Dupin (6e)
Erawan (15e)
Escale du Liban (4e)
Espadon (1er)
Etoile Marocaine (8e)
Excuse (4e)
Fakhr el Dine (16e)

Special Features

Fauchon (8e)
Ferme (1er)
Ferme des Mathurins (8e)
Ferme St-Simon (7e)
Fermette Marbeuf 1900 (8e)
Feuilles/Entrées Libres (Neuilly)
Filo Delle Stagioni (3e)
Findi (8e)
Finzi (8e)
Flora Danica (8e)
Fontaine de Mars (7e)
Fontaine Gaillon (2e)
Fouquet's (8e)
Fous d'en Face (4e)
Fumoir (1er)
Gallopin (2e)
Gare (16e)
Garnier (8e)
Gastroquet (15e)
Georges (4e)
Gitane (15e)
Goumard (1er)
Gourmand (6e)
Graindorge (17e)
Grand Café (9e)
Grand Colbert (2e)
Grande Armée (16e)
Grande Rue (15e)
Grandes Marches (12e)
Grand Véfour (1er)
Grand Venise (15e)
Grill (2e)
Hédiard (8e)
Hélène Darroze (6e)
Hermitage (10e)
Higuma (1er)
Huîtrier (17e)
Il Cortile (1er)
Ile (Issy-les-Moulineaux)
Il Punto (Neuilly)
Jardins de Bagatelle (16e)
Jarrasse (Neuilly)
J'Go (9e)
Joséphine Ch. Dumonet (6e)
Kong (1er)
Lac-Hong (16e)
Ladurée (8e)
Lao Siam (19e)
Lasserre (8e)
Léon de Bruxelles (multi. loc.)
Lescure (1er)
Loir dans la Théière (4e)
Lô Sushi (multi. loc.)
Louchebem (1er)
Macéo (1er)
Magnolias (Perreux-sur-Marne)
Maharajah (5e)
Main d'Or (11e)
Maison Courtine (14e)
Mandalay (Levallois)
Mandarin/Neuilly (Neuilly)
Mansouria (11e)
Market (8e)
Marlotte (6e)
Maupertu (7e)
Mesturet (2e)
Murano (3e)
Murat (16e)
Muses (9e)
Natacha (14e)
Nemrod (6e)
New Nioullaville (11e)
Noces de Jeannette (2e)
Noura (multi. loc.)
Nouveau Village Tao (13e)
O à la Bouche (14e)
Oeillade (7e)
Olivades (7e)
Opportun (14e)
Orenoc (17e)
Orient-Extrême (6e)
Ormes (7e)
Os à Moëlle (15e)
Palanquin (6e)
Pamphlet (3e)
Paolo Petrini (17e)
Paradis Thai (13e)
Parc aux Cerfs (6e)
Paris Seize (16e)
Passy Mandarin (16e)
Paul Chêne (16e)
Paul, Restaurant (1er)
Pavillon Montsouris (14e)
Pearl (13e)
Père Claude (15e)
Perraudin (5e)
Perron (7e)
Petit Bofinger (multi. loc.)
Petit Colombier (17e)
Petit Laurent (7e)
Petit Lutétia (6e)
Petit Marché (3e)

Petit Marguery (13ᵉ)
Petit Niçois (7ᵉ)
Pied de Chameau (4ᵉ)
Pied de Cochon (1ᵉʳ)
Pierre au Palais Royal (1ᵉʳ)
Pinxo (1ᵉʳ)
Pitchi Poï (4ᵉ)
Pizzeria d'Auteuil (16ᵉ)
Point Bar (1ᵉʳ)
Pomponette (18ᵉ)
Port Alma (16ᵉ)
Press Café (2ᵉ)
Procope (6ᵉ)
P'tit Troquet (7ᵉ)
Publicis Drugstore (8ᵉ)
404 (3ᵉ)
Rech (17ᵉ)
Relais/l'Entrecôte (6ᵉ)
Relais de Venise (17ᵉ)
Relais Louis XIII (6ᵉ)
Rest./Palais Royal (1ᵉʳ)
Riad (Neuilly)
Romantica (Clichy)
Rouge Tomate (1ᵉʳ)
Rughetta (18ᵉ)
Saveurs de Claude (6ᵉ)
Saveurs du Marché (Neuilly)
Scoop (1ᵉʳ)
Sébillon (multi. loc.)
16 Haussmann (9ᵉ)
Senso (8ᵉ)
6 New York (16ᵉ)
Sizin (9ᵉ)
Sologne (12ᵉ)
Sormani (17ᵉ)
Soufflé (1ᵉʳ)
Spoon, Food/Wine (8ᵉ)
Stella (16ᵉ)
Stéphane Martin (15ᵉ)
Stresa (8ᵉ)
Sud (17ᵉ)
Table d'Anvers (9ᵉ)
Table du Baltimore (16ᵉ)
Taillevent (8ᵉ)
Tang (16ᵉ)
Tante Louise (8ᵉ)
Tastevin (Maisons-Laffitte)
Taverna de Gli Amici (7ᵉ)
Tav. Maître Kanter (1ᵉʳ)
Tav. L'Esprit Blvd. (9ᵉ)
Temps des Cerises (13ᵉ)

Terrasse (18ᵉ)
Tête Ailleurs (4ᵉ)
Thaï (1ᵉʳ)
Thanksgiving (4ᵉ)
Thoumieux (7ᵉ)
Toque (17ᵉ)
Toupary (1ᵉʳ)
Tourelle (1ᵉʳ)
Train Bleu (12ᵉ)
Tricotin (13ᵉ)
Trois Marches (Versailles)
Troquet (15ᵉ)
Truffière (5ᵉ)
Tsé-Yang (16ᵉ)
Uitr (15ᵉ)
Vagenende (6ᵉ)
Vaudeville (2ᵉ)
Vieille Fontaine Rôtiss.
  (Maisons-Laffitte)
Vieux Chêne (11ᵉ)
Village d'Ung et Li Lam (8ᵉ)
Vinci (16ᵉ)
Vinea Café (12ᵉ)
Vin et Marée (14ᵉ)
20 de Bellechasse (7ᵉ)
Violon d'Ingres (7ᵉ)
Virgin Café (8ᵉ)
Wally Le Saharien (9ᵉ)
Wepler (18ᵉ)
Yvan (8ᵉ)
Zeyer (14ᵉ)
Zo (8ᵉ)
Zygomates (12ᵉ)

Outdoor Dining
(G=garden; P=patio;
S=sidewalk; T=terrace)
Absinthe (1ᵉʳ) (S,T)
Aimant du Sud (13ᵉ) (S,T)
Al Dar (multi. loc.) (S,T)
Alivi (4ᵉ) (T)
Al Mounia (16ᵉ) (S)
Ampère (17ᵉ) (S)
Angl'Opera (2ᵉ) (S,T)
AOC (5ᵉ) (T)
Apollo (14ᵉ) (T)
A Priori Thé (2ᵉ) (P)
Astuce (15ᵉ) (S)
Atlas (5ᵉ) (S)
Aub. Aveyronnaise (12ᵉ) (S,T)
Aub. du Clou (9ᵉ) (S,T)

Authenti© (15ᵉ) (S,T)
Auvergne Gourmande (7ᵉ) (S)
Avenue (8ᵉ) (T)
Baie d'Ha Long (16ᵉ) (T)
Ballon des Ternes (17ᵉ) (S,T)
Bartolo (6ᵉ) (S,T)
Bar Vendôme (1ᵉʳ) (P)
Basilic (7ᵉ) (G,T)
BE Boulangépicier (17ᵉ) (S)
Bel Canto (14ᵉ) (T)
Bélier (6ᵉ) (P)
Berkeley (8ᵉ) (T)
BIOArt (13ᵉ) (T)
Bistro de Breteuil (7ᵉ) (T)
Bistro d'Hubert (15ᵉ) (T)
Bistro du 17ème (17ᵉ) (S)
Bistro St. Ferdinand (17ᵉ) (T)
Bistrot d'à Côté (multi. loc.) (S,T)
Bistrot d'André (15ᵉ) (S,T)
Bistrot de l'Etoile Niel (17ᵉ) (S,T)
Bistrot de Marius (8ᵉ) (S)
Bistrot des Dames (17ᵉ) (G)
Bistrot du Cap (15ᵉ) (T)
Bistrot La Catalogne (6ᵉ) (S)
Bistrot Vivienne (1ᵉʳ) (T)
Bon 2 (2ᵉ) (S,T)
Bon Saint Pourçain (6ᵉ) (S)
Bouchons/Fr. Clerc (multi.) (S)
Bourguignon du Marais (4ᵉ) (T)
Brass. de la Poste (16ᵉ) (S)
Brass. du Louvre (1ᵉʳ) (T)
Bristol (8ᵉ) (G)
Buisson Ardent (5ᵉ) (S)
Butte Chaillot (16ᵉ) (S)
Ca d'Oro (1ᵉʳ) (S)
Café Beaubourg (4ᵉ) (T)
Café de Flore (6ᵉ) (S,T)
Café de la Musique (19ᵉ) (T)
Café de l'Esplanade (7ᵉ) (S)
Café de l'Industrie (11ᵉ) (S)
Café de Mars (7ᵉ) (S)
Café des Lettres (7ᵉ) (P)
Café Guitry (9ᵉ) (T)
Café la Jatte (Neuilly) (G,T)
Café Lenôtre (8ᵉ) (G,P)
Café Les Deux Magots (6ᵉ) (G,T)
Café Marly (1ᵉʳ) (T)
Café Max (7ᵉ) (S,T)
Café Very/Dame Tart. (multi.) (T)
Cagouille (14ᵉ) (T)
Cantinella (14ᵉ) (S,T)

Cap Seguin (Boulogne) (T)
Cap Vernet (8ᵉ) (T)
Caveau du Palais (1ᵉʳ) (S,T)
Cazaudehore La For. (St-
   Germain-en-Laye) (G,T)
182 Rive Droite (16ᵉ) (T)
123 (17ᵉ) (S,T)
Chai 33 (12ᵉ) (T)
Chalet des Iles (16ᵉ) (G,T)
Chantairelle (5ᵉ) (G)
Chateaubriand (11ᵉ) (S)
Cherche Midi (6ᵉ) (S)
Chez Clément (multi. loc.) (S,T)
Chez Francis (8ᵉ) (S)
Chez Françoise (7ᵉ) (T)
Chez Gégène (Joinville) (S,T)
Chez Georges-Maillot (17ᵉ) (S,T)
Chez Janou (3ᵉ) (T)
Chez Livio (Neuilly) (T)
Chez Marcel (6ᵉ) (S)
Chez Omar (3ᵉ) (T)
Chez Paul (13ᵉ) (S)
Chez Prune (10ᵉ) (S)
Chez Ramulaud (11ᵉ) (S)
Chez René (5ᵉ) (S)
Chez Vong (1ᵉʳ) (T)
Chien qui Fume (1ᵉʳ) (S,T)
Ch'Ti Catalan (9ᵉ) (S)
Cinq (8ᵉ) (T)
59 Poincaré (16ᵉ) (P)
Cloche des Halles (1ᵉʳ) (S,T)
Clos des Gourmets (7ᵉ) (T)
Closerie des Lilas (6ᵉ) (T)
Cô Ba Saigon (8ᵉ) (S)
Coconnas (4ᵉ) (T)
Comptoir/Saumon (multi.) (P,S)
Congrès Maillot (17ᵉ) (S,T)
Contre-Allée (14ᵉ) (S)
Cook Book (7ᵉ) (S,T)
Copenhague (8ᵉ) (T)
Cordonnerie (1ᵉʳ) (S)
Costes (1ᵉʳ) (G,P)
Coupe-Chou (5ᵉ) (T)
Dalloyau (multi. loc.) (S,T)
Délices d'Aphrodite (5ᵉ) (S)
Délices de Szechuen (7ᵉ) (S,T)
Dell 'Angelo (7ᵉ) (S)
Dessirier (17ᵉ) (S,T)
Deux Abeilles (7ᵉ) (S)
Devez (8ᵉ) (S)
Diamantaires (9ᵉ) (T)

Djakarta (1er) (S)
Djoon (13e) (S,T)
Dominique (6e) (S)
Drouant (2e) (S)
Duc de Richelieu (12e) (T)
Durand Dupont (Neuilly) (G)
Écaille de la Fontaine (2e) (S)
Ecluse (multi. loc.) (S,T)
Entracte (18e) (T)
Espadon (1er) (G,T)
Feuilles/Entrées (Neuilly) (S)
Flandrin (16e) (S,T)
Flora Danica (8e) (G,T)
Flore en l'Ile (4e) (S,T)
Fontaine de Mars (7e) (S,T)
Fontaine Gaillon (2e) (T)
Fontaines (5e) (S,T)
Fontanarosa (15e) (T)
Fouquet's (8e) (S,T)
Fous d'en Face (4e) (S)
Gallopin (2e) (S)
Gare (16e) (G,T)
Gauloise (15e) (S,T)
Gaya Rive Gauche (7e) (S)
Georges (4e) (T)
Gitane (15e) (S)
Giulio Rebellato (16e) (S)
Gourmets des Ternes (8e) (S)
Grand Café (9e) (S)
Grande Armée (16e) (S)
Grande Cascade (16e) (T)
Grill (2e) (T)
Grille St-Germain (6e) (S)
Guinguette/Neuilly (Neuilly) (T)
Hangar (3e) (S)
Hermitage (10e) (T)
Hippopotamus (multi. loc.) (S,T)
Il Cortile (1er) (P)
Ile (Issy-les-Moulineaux) (G,T)
Il Punto (Neuilly) (S,T)
Jardin (8e) (S,T)
Jardin des Cygnes (8e) (T)
Jardins de Bagatelle (16e) (G,T)
Jarrasse (Neuilly) (S,T)
Je Thé . . . Me (15e) (S,T)
Khun Akorn (11e) (T)
Kim Anh (15e) (T)
Kiosque (16e) (S,T)
Ladurée (multi. loc.) (S,T)
Lao Tseu (7e) (T)
Laurent (8e) (G,T)

Léna et Mimile (5e) (T)
Lescure (1er) (S,T)
Lina's (multi. loc.) (S,T)
Ma Bourgogne (4e) (S,T)
Maison Blanche (8e) (T)
Maison de l'Amér. Lat. (7e) (G)
Mandarin/Neuilly (Neuilly) (T)
Manufacture (Issy-les-Moul.) (T)
Marée de Versailles (Versailles) (T)
Maresco (5e) (S,T)
Marius (16e) (S,T)
Marius et Janette (8e) (S,T)
Market (8e) (S)
Marlotte (6e) (S,T)
Marty (5e) (S,T)
Mascotte (8e) (S,T)
Mascotte (18e) (S,T)
Mathusalem (16e) (S,T)
Maupertu (7e) (S,T)
Mavrommatis (5e) (S,T)
Méditerranée (6e) (S,T)
Montalembert (7e) (S,T)
Mont Liban (17e) (S,T)
Moulin à Vent (5e) (S,T)
Moulin de la Galette (18e) (P)
Murano (3e) (P)
Murat (16e) (S)
Muscade (1er) (G)
Musichall (8e) (S)
Nemrod (6e) (S,T)
New Nioullaville (11e) (S)
No Stress Café (9e) (S,T)
Noura (multi. loc.) (G,T)
Oulette (12e) (S,T)
Papilles (5e) (S,T)
Parc aux Cerfs (6e) (P)
Patrick Goldenberg (17e) (S,T)
Paul, Restaurant (1er) (S,T)
Pavillon Montsouris (14e) (G,T)
Pearl (13e) (S,T)
Pères et Filles (6e) (S,T)
Pershing (8e) (P)
Petite Chaise (7e) (S)
Petite Cour (6e) (T)
Petites Sorcières (14e) (S)
Petit Marguery (13e) (T)
Petit Poucet (Levallois) (G,P,T)
Petit Victor Hugo (16e) (S,T)
Petit Zinc (6e) (P,S,T)
Pied de Chameau (4e) (T)
Pied de Cochon (1er) (S,T)

Pitchi Poï (4e) (T)
Pizzeria d'Auteuil (16e) (S)
Place (8e) (T)
Point Bar (1er) (S,T)
Pomponette (18e) (S,T)
Pomze (8e) (S,T)
Poule au Pot (1er) (T)
Pré Catelan (16e) (G,T)
Publicis Drugstore (8e) (S,T)
Pure Café (11e) (S,T)
Purple (11e) (S,T)
Quai Ouest (St-Cloud) (T)
R. (15e) (T)
Rech (17e) (S,T)
Relais/l'Entrecôte (multi.) (S,T)
Relais de Venise (17e) (S,T)
Réminet (5e) (S)
Rest. Alain Ducasse (8e) (P)
Rest. du Marché (15e) (S,T)
Rest./Palais Royal (1er) (G)
Restaurant GR5 (16e) (T)
River Café (Issy-les-Moul.) (G,T)
Robe et le Palais (1er) (S)
Roi du Pot-au-Feu (9e) (S)
Romantica (Clichy) (P,T)
Rôtiss. de Neuilly (Neuilly) (S,T)
Rotonde (6e) (S,T)
Rouge Tomate (1er) (T)
Rughetta (18e) (T)
Sauvignon (7e) (S)
Saveurs de Claude (6e) (S)
Sawadee (15e) (S,T)
Scoop (1er) (S)
Senso (8e) (S)
7ème Sud (7e) (S)
Sept Quinze (15e) (S,T)
Sologne (12e) (S,T)
Soupière (17e) (S,T)
Square (7e) (S)
Square Trousseau (12e) (S)
Strapontins (10e) (S,T)
Studio (4e) (P)
Sud (17e) (P)
Table d'Anvers (9e) (S,T)
Table du Lancaster (8e) (G,P,T)
Tastevin (Maisons-Laffitte) (G)
Tav. L'Esprit Blvd. (9e) (S,T)
Télégraphe (7e) (T)
Temps au Temps (11e) (S,T)
Terrasse (18e) (T)
Terrasse Mirabeau (16e) (T)

Thiou (7e) (S)
Tonnelle Saintong. (Neuilly) (G)
Toupary (1er) (T)
Trois Marches (Versailles) (G)
Uitr (15e)
Vagenende (6e) (S,T)
Viaduc Café (12e) (S,T)
Vieille Fontaine Rôtiss.
    (Maisons-Laffitte) (G)
Vieux Chêne (11e) (S)
Villa Corse (15e) (S,T)
Vinea Café (12e) (T)
Vin et Marée (multi. loc.) (S)
20 de Bellechasse (7e) (S)
Zebra Square (16e) (S,T)
Zéphyr (20e) (T)

Parking

A et M Le Bistrot (16e)
Ailleurs (8e)
Al Diwan (8e)
Ambassadeurs (8e)
Ambroisie (4e)
Amphyclès (17e)
Apollo (14e)
Arpège (7e)
Aub. Bressane (7e)
B*fly (8e)
Bains (3e)
Bar Vendôme (1er)
Bath's (8e)
Beato (7e)
Beaujolais d'Auteuil (16e)
Bel Canto (14e)
Benkay (15e)
Bistro 121 (15e)
Bistrot Bigorneau (16e)
Bistrot d'à Côté (17e)
Bistrot de l'Etoile Niel (17e)
Bistrot de Marius (8e)
Bistrot de Paris (7e)
Bocconi (8e)
Boeuf Couronné (19e)
Boeuf sur le Toit (8e)
Bon (16e)
Bouquinistes (6e)
Brass. du Louvre (1er)
Brass. Flo (10e)
Brass. Julien (10e)
Brass. La Lorraine (8e)
Bristol (8e)
Café de la Paix (9e)

Café Faubourg (8ᵉ)
Café la Jatte (Neuilly)
Café Lenôtre (8ᵉ)
Café Terminus (8ᵉ)
Cap Seguin (Boulogne)
Carré des Feuillants (1ᵉʳ)
Caviar Kaspia (8ᵉ)
Céladon (2ᵉ)
123 (17ᵉ)
Chalet des Iles (16ᵉ)
Chen Soleil d'Est (15ᵉ)
Chez Françoise (7ᵉ)
Chez Jenny (3ᵉ)
Chez Livio (Neuilly)
Chez Vong (1ᵉʳ)
Chiberta (8ᵉ)
59 Poincaré (16ᵉ)
Closerie des Lilas (6ᵉ)
Clovis (8ᵉ)
Comte de Gascogne (Boulogne)
Congrès Maillot (17ᵉ)
Copenhague (8ᵉ)
Costes (1ᵉʳ)
Coupole (14ᵉ)
Cristal Room (16ᵉ)
Dagorno (19ᵉ)
Da Mimmo (10ᵉ)
Dessirier (17ᵉ)
Diep (8ᵉ)
Divellec (7ᵉ)
1728 (8ᵉ)
Doobie's (8ᵉ)
Drouant (2ᵉ)
Duc (14ᵉ)
El Mansour (8ᵉ)
Elysées (8ᵉ)
Espadon (1ᵉʳ)
Etoile (16ᵉ)
Feuilles/Entrées Libres (Neuilly)
Findi (8ᵉ)
Flandrin (16ᵉ)
Flora Danica (8ᵉ)
Fontaine Gaillon (2ᵉ)
Fouquet's (8ᵉ)
Gare (16ᵉ)
Georges (4ᵉ)
Goumard (1ᵉʳ)
Grand Café (9ᵉ)
Grand Colbert (2ᵉ)
Grande Armée (16ᵉ)
Grande Cascade (16ᵉ)

Grandes Marches (12ᵉ)
Grand Véfour (1ᵉʳ)
Grand Venise (15ᵉ)
Grill (2ᵉ)
Guy Savoy (17ᵉ)
Hédiard (8ᵉ)
Hélène Darroze (6ᵉ)
Huîtrier (17ᵉ)
Il Carpaccio (8ᵉ)
Il Cortile (1ᵉʳ)
Ile (Issy-les-Moulineaux)
Jacques Cagna (6ᵉ)
Jardin (8ᵉ)
Jardin des Cygnes (8ᵉ)
Jarrasse (Neuilly)
Jules Verne (7ᵉ)
Kong (1ᵉʳ)
Lapérouse (6ᵉ)
Lasserre (8ᵉ)
Lucas Carton (8ᵉ)
Maison Blanche (8ᵉ)
Maison du Caviar (8ᵉ)
Man Ray (8ᵉ)
Marée (8ᵉ)
Marius (16ᵉ)
Marius et Janette (8ᵉ)
Market (8ᵉ)
Marty (5ᵉ)
Maxim's (8ᵉ)
Méditerranée (6ᵉ)
Meurice (1ᵉʳ)
Michel Rostang (17ᵉ)
Montalembert (7ᵉ)
Montparnasse 25 (14ᵉ)
Murano (3ᵉ)
Murat (16ᵉ)
Muses (9ᵉ)
Musichall (8ᵉ)
Obélisque (8ᵉ)
Orangerie (4ᵉ)
Orenoc (17ᵉ)
Paris (6ᵉ)
Passiflore (16ᵉ)
Paul Chêne (16ᵉ)
Pavillon Montsouris (14ᵉ)
Pergolèse (16ᵉ)
Pershing (8ᵉ)
Petit Pergolèse (16ᵉ)
Petit Poucet (Levallois)
Petrossian (7ᵉ)
Pierre Gagnaire (8ᵉ)

Pinxo (1er)
Place (8e)
Pré Catelan (16e)
Pressoir (12e)
Quai Ouest (St-Cloud)
R. (15e)
Relais d'Auteuil/Pignol (16e)
Relais Plaza (8e)
Rest. Alain Ducasse (8e)
River Café (Issy-les-Moul.)
Romantica (Clichy)
Rôtiss. de Neuilly (Neuilly)
Rôtiss. d'en Face (6e)
Rue Balzac (8e)
Salon d'Hélène (6e)
Sébillon (Neuilly)
Senso (8e)
6 New York (16e)
Sora Lena (17e)
Spicy (8e)
Spoon, Food/Wine (8e)
Stella (16e)
Sud (17e)
Suite (8e)
Table du Baltimore (16e)
Table du Lancaster (8e)
Taillevent (8e)
Tanjia (8e)
Télégraphe (7e)
Terrasse Mirabeau (16e)
Thiou (7e)
Thoumieux (7e)
Timgad (17e)
Toi (8e)
Tong Yen (8e)
Toupary (1er)
Tour d'Argent (5e)
Trois Marches (Versailles)
Truffe Noire (Neuilly)
Villa Corse (15e)
Village d'Ung et Li Lam (8e)
Vin et Marée (multi. loc.)
W, Restaurant (8e)
Zebra Square (16e)
Zo (8e)

People-Watching

Absinthe (1er)
Anahï (3e)
Angle du Faubourg (8e)
Arpège (7e)
Astor (8e)
Astrance (16e)
Atelier Joël Robuchon (7e)
Avenue (8e)
Bains (3e)
Bélier (6e)
Benoît (4e)
Berkeley (8e)
Brass. Balzar (5e)
Brass. Lipp (6e)
Bristol (8e)
Café de Flore (6e)
Café de l'Esplanade (7e)
Café Etienne Marcel (2e)
Café Guitry (9e)
Café Les Deux Magots (6e)
123 (17e)
Chateaubriand (11e)
Chez L'Ami Louis (3e)
Chez Omar (3e)
Cinq (8e)
Copenhague (8e)
Costes (1er)
Divellec (7e)
Dôme (14e)
Drouant (2e)
Duc (14e)
Elysées (8e)
Epi Dupin (6e)
Espadon (1er)
Famille (18e)
Ferme St-Simon (7e)
Flandrin (16e)
Fouquet's (8e)
Gare (16e)
Gauloise (15e)
Georges (4e)
Grande Armée (16e)
Grand Véfour (1er)
Guy Savoy (17e)
Hélène Darroze (6e)
Il Cortile (1er)
Jarrasse (Neuilly)
Joséphine Ch. Dumonet (6e)
Kong (1er)
Ladurée (multi. loc.)
Lasserre (8e)
Ledoyen (8e)
Lucas Carton (8e)
Maison Blanche (8e)
Maison de l'Amér. Lat. (7e)
Maison Prunier (16e)

Maison Rouge (4ᵉ)
Man Ray (8ᵉ)
Market (8ᵉ)
Méditerranée (6ᵉ)
Mum Sabai (6ᵉ)
Murano (3ᵉ)
Musichall (8ᵉ)
Natacha (14ᵉ)
Orangerie (4ᵉ)
Petrossian (7ᵉ)
Pierre Gagnaire (8ᵉ)
Pré Catelan (16ᵉ)
Publicis Drugstore (8ᵉ)
Relais Plaza (8ᵉ)
Rest. Alain Ducasse (8ᵉ)
Salon d'Hélène (6ᵉ)
Senso (8ᵉ)
6 New York (16ᵉ)
Sormani (17ᵉ)
Spoon, Food/Wine (8ᵉ)
Square Trousseau (12ᵉ)
Stresa (8ᵉ)
Table/Joël Robuchon (16ᵉ)
Table du Lancaster (8ᵉ)
Taillevent (8ᵉ)
Tan Dinh (7ᵉ)
Tanjia (8ᵉ)
Terrasse Mirabeau (16ᵉ)
Thiou (7ᵉ)
Tong Yen (8ᵉ)
Tour d'Argent (5ᵉ)
Voltaire (7ᵉ)
Water Bar Colette (1ᵉʳ)

Power Scenes

Ambassadeurs (8ᵉ)
Apicius (8ᵉ)
Arpège (7ᵉ)
Assiette (14ᵉ)
Astor (8ᵉ)
Atelier Joël Robuchon (7ᵉ)
Benoît (4ᵉ)
Brass. Balzar (5ᵉ)
Brass. Lipp (6ᵉ)
Bristol (8ᵉ)
Café de Flore (6ᵉ)
Café Marly (1ᵉʳ)
Carré des Feuillants (1ᵉʳ)
Caviar Kaspia (8ᵉ)
Cazaudehore La For. (St-
    Germain-en-Laye)
Céladon (2ᵉ)

123 (17ᵉ)
Closerie des Lilas (6ᵉ)
Copenhague (8ᵉ)
Costes (1ᵉʳ)
Cristal Room (16ᵉ)
Cuisine (7ᵉ)
Divellec (7ᵉ)
Dôme (14ᵉ)
Duc (14ᵉ)
Elysées (8ᵉ)
Espadon (1ᵉʳ)
Etoile (16ᵉ)
Ferme St-Simon (7ᵉ)
Fouquet's (8ᵉ)
Gare (16ᵉ)
Georges (4ᵉ)
Grande Armée (16ᵉ)
Grande Cascade (16ᵉ)
Grand Véfour (1ᵉʳ)
Guy Savoy (17ᵉ)
Hiramatsu (16ᵉ)
Jamin (16ᵉ)
Jardin (8ᵉ)
Jarrasse (Neuilly)
Jules Verne (7ᵉ)
Lasserre (8ᵉ)
Laurent (8ᵉ)
Ledoyen (8ᵉ)
Lucas Carton (8ᵉ)
Maison Blanche (8ᵉ)
Marée (8ᵉ)
Marius (16ᵉ)
Marius et Janette (8ᵉ)
Market (8ᵉ)
Meurice (1ᵉʳ)
Michel Rostang (17ᵉ)
Montalembert (7ᵉ)
Montparnasse 25 (14ᵉ)
Natacha (14ᵉ)
Paris (6ᵉ)
Pavillon Montsouris (14ᵉ)
Pichet de Paris (8ᵉ)
Pierre Gagnaire (8ᵉ)
Place (8ᵉ)
Pomze (8ᵉ)
Port Alma (16ᵉ)
Pré Catelan (16ᵉ)
Relais d'Auteuil/Pignol (16ᵉ)
Relais Plaza (8ᵉ)
Rest. Alain Ducasse (8ᵉ)
Stresa (8ᵉ)

Table/Joël Robuchon (16e)
Table du Lancaster (8e)
Taillevent (8e)
Tan Dinh (7e)
Terrasse Mirabeau (16e)
Tong Yen (8e)
Tonnelle Saintong. (Neuilly)
Tour d'Argent (5e)
Violon d'Ingres (7e)
Voltaire (7e)

Quick Bites

Altitude 95 (7e)
Angelina (1er)
A Priori Thé (2e)
Bar des Théâtres (8e)
Baron Bouge (12e)
Barrio Latino (12e)
Bar Rouge (9e)
BE Boulangépicier (17e)
BIOArt (13e)
Bistrot à Vins Mélac (11e)
Bons Crus (1er)
Boulangerie/Odéon (6e)
Breakfast in America (5e)
Buddha Bar (8e)
Buffalo Grill (multi. loc.)
Café Beaubourg (4e)
Café de Flore (6e)
Café des Lettres (7e)
Café du Commerce (15e)
Café Flo (9e)
Café Les Deux Magots (6e)
Café Marly (1er)
Café Very/Dame Tart. (multi.)
Cave de l'Os à Moëlle (15e)
Chez Marianne (4e)
Chez Papa (multi. loc.)
Cloche des Halles (1er)
Clown Bar (11e)
Coffee Parisien (multi. loc.)
Congrès Maillot (17e)
Cosi (6e)
Crêperie de Josselin (14e)
Dalloyau (multi. loc.)
Duc de Richelieu (12e)
Ecluse (multi. loc.)
Emporio Armani (6e)
Escale du Liban (4e)
Ferme (1er)
Fous d'en Face (4e)
Fumoir (1er)

Garnier (8e)
Hédiard (8e)
Indiana Café (multi. loc.)
Je Thé . . . Me (15e)
Joe Allen (1er)
Juvéniles (1er)
Léon de Bruxelles (multi. loc.)
Lina's (multi. loc.)
Loir dans la Théière (4e)
Lô Sushi (multi. loc.)
Ma Bourgogne (4e)
Maison du Caviar (8e)
Mariage Frères (multi. loc.)
Mauzac (5e)
Mesturet (2e)
Mirama (5e)
Murat (16e)
Nemrod (6e)
Noura (multi. loc.)
Papilles (5e)
Petite Sirène Copenh. (9e)
Pinxo (1er)
Press Café (2e)
Publicis Drugstore (8e)
Rest./Musée d'Orsay (7e)
Rubis (1er)
Sauvignon (7e)
Scoop (1er)
Taverne Henri IV (1er)
Tsukizi (6e)
Viaduc Café (12e)
Vinea Café (12e)
Vin sur Vin (7e)
Virgin Café (8e)
Wok Cooking (11e)

Quiet Conversation

Affiche (8e)
Aiguière (11e)
Alivi (4e)
Allard (6e)
Allobroges (20e)
Ambassade d'Auv. (3e)
Ami Marcel (15e)
Ampère (17e)
Amuse Bouche (14e)
Anacréon (13e)
Angelina (1er)
Angl'Opera (2e)
A Priori Thé (2e)
Argenteuil (1er)
Aristide (17e)

Armand, Palais Royal (1er)
Assiette (14e)
Astrance (16e)
Astrée (17e)
Atelier Berger (1er)
Aub. du Clou (9e)
Aub. et Cie (9e)
Aub. Pyrénées Cévennes (11e)
Auvergne Gourmande (7e)
Basilic (7e)
Béatilles (17e)
Bélier (6e)
Bellini (16e)
Beudant (17e)
Bistro de Gala (9e)
Bistrot du Peintre (11e)
Boeuf Couronné (19e)
Boeuf sur le Toit (8e)
Bouillon Racine (6e)
Buisson Ardent (5e)
Butte Chaillot (16e)
Ca d'Oro (1er)
Café de Flore (6e)
Café des Lettres (7e)
Café Faubourg (8e)
Café Lenôtre (8e)
Café Les Deux Magots (6e)
Café M (8e)
Café Marly (1er)
Camélia (Bougival)
Cartes Postales (1er)
Cave Gourmande (19e)
Caviar Kaspia (8e)
123 (17e)
Chardenoux (11e)
Charpentiers (6e)
Chez Georges (2e)
Chez Jean (9e)
Chez Maître Paul (6e)
Chez Pauline (1er)
Chez Ramulaud (11e)
Chez René (5e)
Chiberta (8e)
Copenhague (8e)
Coupe-Chou (5e)
Crus de Bourgogne (2e)
Cuisine (7e)
Daru (8e)
Dauphin (1er)
Dessirier (17e)
Djakarta (1er)

Écaille de la Fontaine (2e)
Ecluse (multi. loc.)
El Mansour (8e)
Entoto (13e)
Entracte (18e)
Epi d'Or (1er)
Erawan (15e)
Escargot Montorgueil (1er)
Estaminet Gaya (1er)
Excuse (4e)
Fins Gourmets (7e)
Fontanarosa (15e)
Gamin de Paris (4e)
Garnier (8e)
Gaya Rive Gauche (7e)
Gérard Besson (1er)
Goumard (1er)
Graindorge (17e)
Hermitage (10e)
Huîtrier (17e)
Il Carpaccio (8e)
Il Cortile (1er)
Joséphine Ch. Dumonet (6e)
Jules Verne (7e)
Jumeaux (11e)
Kiosque (16e)
Ladurée (multi. loc.)
Lapérouse (6e)
Legrand Filles et Fils (2e)
Macéo (1er)
Magnolias (Perreux-sur-Marne)
Maison Blanche (8e)
Marée (8e)
Mariage Frères (multi. loc.)
Marlotte (6e)
Marsangy (11e)
Marty (5e)
Maupertu (7e)
Méditerranée (6e)
Montalembert (7e)
Murano (3e)
No Stress Café (9e)
Obélisque (8e)
Orenoc (17e)
Ormes (7e)
Oulette (12e)
Pamphlet (3e)
Pères et Filles (6e)
Petite Sirène Copenh. (9e)
Petrossian (7e)
Pierre au Palais Royal (1er)

Special Features

Pierre Gagnaire (8ᵉ)
Point Bar (1ᵉʳ)
Potager du Roy (Versailles)
Poulbot Gourmet (18ᵉ)
Rest. du Marché (15ᵉ)
Sarladais (8ᵉ)
Saudade (1ᵉʳ)
16 Haussmann (9ᵉ)
Sologne (12ᵉ)
Sot l'y Laisse (11ᵉ)
Stella Maris (8ᵉ)
Table du Lancaster (8ᵉ)
Taïra (17ᵉ)
Tan Dinh (7ᵉ)
Tanjia (8ᵉ)
Terrasse (18ᵉ)
Tête Ailleurs (4ᵉ)
Toupary (1ᵉʳ)
Trou Gascon (12ᵉ)
Tsé-Yang (16ᵉ)
Vieux Bistro (4ᵉ)
Vin dans les voiles (16ᵉ)
Vin sur Vin (7ᵉ)

Romantic Places

Allard (6ᵉ)
Ambassadeurs (8ᵉ)
Ambroisie (4ᵉ)
Amphyclès (17ᵉ)
Arpège (7ᵉ)
Astor (8ᵉ)
Astrance (16ᵉ)
Bélier (6ᵉ)
Blue Elephant (11ᵉ)
Bouillon Racine (6ᵉ)
Bouquinistes (6ᵉ)
Brass. Flo (10ᵉ)
Brass. Julien (10ᵉ)
Bristol (8ᵉ)
Buisson Ardent (5ᵉ)
Café Les Deux Magots (6ᵉ)
Café Marly (1ᵉʳ)
Casa Olympe (9ᵉ)
Caviar Kaspia (8ᵉ)
Chalet des Iles (16ᵉ)
Chardenoux (11ᵉ)
Chez Diane (6ᵉ)
Chez Pauline (1ᵉʳ)
China Club (12ᵉ)
Closerie des Lilas (6ᵉ)
Coconnas (4ᵉ)
Copenhague (8ᵉ)
Costes (1ᵉʳ)
Coupe-Chou (5ᵉ)
Coupole (14ᵉ)
Cristal Room (16ᵉ)
Délices d'Aphrodite (5ᵉ)
Dôme (14ᵉ)
El Mansour (8ᵉ)
Elysées (8ᵉ)
Epi d'Or (1ᵉʳ)
Espadon (1ᵉʳ)
Flora Danica (8ᵉ)
Fontaine de Mars (7ᵉ)
Gavroche (2ᵉ)
Georges (4ᵉ)
Grande Cascade (16ᵉ)
Grand Véfour (1ᵉʳ)
Guy Savoy (17ᵉ)
Il Cortile (1ᵉʳ)
Jacques Cagna (6ᵉ)
Jardin (8ᵉ)
Jardins de Bagatelle (16ᵉ)
Joséphine Ch. Dumonet (6ᵉ)
Jules Verne (7ᵉ)
Ladurée (multi. loc.)
Lapérouse (6ᵉ)
Lasserre (8ᵉ)
Laurent (8ᵉ)
Ledoyen (8ᵉ)
Macéo (1ᵉʳ)
Maison Blanche (8ᵉ)
Maison de l'Amér. Lat. (7ᵉ)
Man Ray (8ᵉ)
Maxim's (8ᵉ)
Meurice (1ᵉʳ)
Moulin de la Galette (18ᵉ)
Mum Sabai (6ᵉ)
Muscade (1ᵉʳ)
Orangerie (4ᵉ)
Paul, Restaurant (1ᵉʳ)
Pavillon Montsouris (14ᵉ)
Petit Prince de Paris (5ᵉ)
Petrossian (7ᵉ)
Potager du Roy (Versailles)
Poulbot Gourmet (18ᵉ)
Pré Catelan (16ᵉ)
Relais Louis XIII (6ᵉ)
Rest. Alain Ducasse (8ᵉ)
Romantica (Clichy)
Rughetta (18ᵉ)
Sormani (17ᵉ)
Stella Maris (8ᵉ)

Tan Dinh (7ᵉ)
Tanjia (8ᵉ)
Tête Ailleurs (4ᵉ)
Timgad (17ᵉ)
Toupary (1ᵉʳ)
Tour d'Argent (5ᵉ)
Train Bleu (12ᵉ)
Trois Marches (Versailles)
Trou Gascon (12ᵉ)

Singles Scenes

Absinthe (1ᵉʳ)
A et M Le Bistrot (16ᵉ)
Ailleurs (8ᵉ)
Alsace (8ᵉ)
Alsaco (9ᵉ)
Amici Miei (3ᵉ)
Angle du Faubourg (8ᵉ)
Apollo (14ᵉ)
Astor (8ᵉ)
Aub. du Clou (9ᵉ)
B*fly (8ᵉ)
Bains (3ᵉ)
Bar des Théâtres (8ᵉ)
Baron Bouge (12ᵉ)
Barramundi (9ᵉ)
Barrio Latino (12ᵉ)
Bélier (6ᵉ)
Berkeley (8ᵉ)
Bistro des Deux Th. (9ᵉ)
Bistrot à Vins Mélac (11ᵉ)
Bistrot d'à Côté (17ᵉ)
Bistrot d'Alex (6ᵉ)
Bon (16ᵉ)
Brass. Balzar (5ᵉ)
Brass. de la Poste (16ᵉ)
Buddha Bar (8ᵉ)
Café Beaubourg (4ᵉ)
Café Burq (18ᵉ)
Café de Flore (6ᵉ)
Café de la Paix (9ᵉ)
Café de l'Esplanade (7ᵉ)
Café du Passage (11ᵉ)
Café Etienne Marcel (2ᵉ)
Café la Jatte (Neuilly)
Café Lenôtre (8ᵉ)
Café Les Deux Magots (6ᵉ)
Café M (8ᵉ)
Café Marly (1ᵉʳ)
Café Ruc (1ᵉʳ)
Carr's (1ᵉʳ)
Cave de l'Os à Moëlle (15ᵉ)

182 Rive Droite (16ᵉ)
Chateaubriand (11ᵉ)
Cherche Midi (6ᵉ)
Chez Gégène (Joinville)
China Club (12ᵉ)
Closerie des Lilas (6ᵉ)
Clown Bar (11ᵉ)
Comédiens (9ᵉ)
Costes (1ᵉʳ)
Djoon (13ᵉ)
Emporio Armani (6ᵉ)
Enoteca (4ᵉ)
Etoile (16ᵉ)
Fumoir (1ᵉʳ)
Grille St-Germain (6ᵉ)
Joe Allen (1ᵉʳ)
Kiosque (16ᵉ)
Kong (1ᵉʳ)
Loir dans la Théière (4ᵉ)
Lô Sushi (multi. loc.)
Maison Rouge (4ᵉ)
Man Ray (8ᵉ)
Mum Sabai (6ᵉ)
Murano (3ᵉ)
Murat (16ᵉ)
Musichall (8ᵉ)
Natacha (14ᵉ)
Pinxo (1ᵉʳ)
Press Café (2ᵉ)
R'Aliment (3ᵉ)
Rubis (1ᵉʳ)
Sauvignon (7ᵉ)
Spaghetti Bar/Curieux (4ᵉ)
Vinea Café (12ᵉ)
Zo (8ᵉ)

Sleepers

(Good to excellent food, but
little known)
Beurre Noisette (15ᵉ)
Boeuf Couronné (19ᵉ)
Camélia (Bougival)
Cartes Postales (1ᵉʳ)
Caveau du Palais (1ᵉʳ)
Cave Gourmande (19ᵉ)
Chez Jean (9ᵉ)
Chez Vincent (19ᵉ)
Clovis (8ᵉ)
Coin des Gourmets (5ᵉ)
Cottage Marcadet (18ᵉ)
Epi d'Or (1ᵉʳ)

Special Features

Etoile Marocaine (8e)
Fogón Saint Julien (5e)
Fontanarosa (15e)
Giulio Rebellato (16e)
Graindorge (17e)
Grand Venise (15e)
Hangar (3e)
Indra (8e)
Isami (4e)
Jardin (8e)
Je Thé ... Me (15e)
Kambodgia (16e)
Kim Anh (15e)
Lozère (6e)
Luna (8e)
Maison Courtine (14e)
Maison du Jardin (6e)
Manufacture (Issy-les-Moul.)
Marius (16e)
Monsieur Lapin (14e)
Montparnasse 25 (14e)
Paolo Petrini (17e)
Paul Chêne (16e)
Pergolèse (16e)
Perron (7e)
Petit Colombier (17e)
Petite Sirène Copenh. (9e)
Petit Laurent (7e)
Pizzeria d'Auteuil (16e)
Poquelin (1er)
Pouilly Reuilly (Le Pré-St-
   Gervais)
Ravi (7e)
Rech (17e)
Rosimar (16e)
Soleil (St-Ouen)
Stéphane Martin (15e)
Taka (18e)
Vieille Fontaine Rôtiss.
   (Maisons-Laffitte)
Villaret (11e)
Zygomates (12e)

Sunday Dining
(B=brunch; L=lunch;
D=dinner)
Al Caratello (18e) (L,D)
Alcazar (6e) (B,L,D)
Al Dar (multi. loc.) (L,D)
Al Diwan (8e) (L,D)
Alivi (4e) (L,D)

Al Mounia (16e) (L,D)
Alsace (8^e) (L,D)
Altitude 95 (7^e) (L,D)
Ambassade d'Auv. (3^e) (L,D)
Ambassadeurs (8^e) (L,D)
Anahuacalli (5^e) (L,D)
Apollo (14^e) (L,D)
Arbuci (6^e) (L,D)
Ardoise (1er) (L,D)
Asian (8^e) (B,L,D)
Assiette (14^e) (L,D)
Assiette Lyonnaise (8^e) (L,D)
Astrance (16e) (L,D)
Atelier Joël Robuchon (7e) (L,D)
Atlas (5e) (L,D)
Aub. Aveyronnaise (12e) (L)
Aub. Bressane (7e) (L,D)
Aub. Dab (16e) (L,D)
Aub. du Clou (9e) (L,D)
Avenue (8e) (L,D)
Azabu (6e) (D)
B*fly (8e) (B,L,D)
Ballon des Ternes (17e) (L,D)
Ballon et Coquillages (17e) (L,D)
Bar à Huîtres (multi. loc.) (L,D)
Bar des Théâtres (8e) (L,D)
Bar Vendôme (1er) (L,D)
Basilic (7e) (L,D)
B-Café (16e) (L,D)
Beaujolais d'Auteuil (16e) (L,D)
Benkay (15e) (L,D)
Benoît (4e) (L,D)
Berkeley (8e) (B,L,D)
Bistro 121 (15e) (L,D)
Bistro de Breteuil (7e) (L,D)
Bistro de l'Olivier (8e) (L,D)
Bistro des Deux Th. (9e) (L,D)
Bistro d'Hubert (15e) (L,D)
Bistro du 17ème (17e) (L,D)
Bistro St. Ferdinand (17e) (L,D)
Bistrot Bigorneau (16e) (L,D)
Bistrot d'à Côté (17e) (L,D)
Bistrot de l'Etoile Laur. (16e) (D)
Bistrot de Marius (8e) (L,D)
Bistrot de Paris (7e) (L,D)
Bistrot des Dames (17e) (L,D)
Bistrot du Dôme (multi.) (L,D)
Bistrot du Peintre (11e) (L,D)
Blue Elephant (11e) (B,L,D)
Boeuf sur le Toit (8e) (L,D)
Bouillon Racine (6e) (L,D)

Boulangerie (20ᵉ) (L,D)
B4 (1ᵉʳ) (B,L,D)
Brass. Balzar (5ᵉ) (L,D)
Brass. de l'Ile St. Louis (4ᵉ) (L,D)
Brass. du Louvre (1ᵉʳ) (L,D)
Brass. Flo (10ᵉ) (L,D)
Brass. Julien (10ᵉ) (L,D)
Brass. La Lorraine (8ᵉ) (L,D)
Brass. Lipp (6ᵉ) (L,D)
Brass. Lutétia (6ᵉ) (B,L,D)
Brass. Mollard (8ᵉ) (L,D)
Bristol (8ᵉ) (L,D)
Buddha Bar (8ᵉ) (D)
Butte Chaillot (16ᵉ) (L,D)
Café Beaubourg (4ᵉ) (B,L,D)
Café Charbon (11ᵉ) (B,L,D)
Café de Flore (6ᵉ) (B,L,D)
Café de la Musique (19ᵉ) (B,L,D)
Café de l'Esplanade (7ᵉ) (B,L,D)
Café de l'Industrie (11ᵉ) (B,L,D)
Café de Mars (7ᵉ) (B)
Café des Lettres (7ᵉ) (B)
Café du Commerce (15ᵉ) (L,D)
Café du Passage (11ᵉ) (D)
Café Etienne Marcel (2ᵉ) (L,D)
Café Faubourg (8ᵉ) (L,D)
Café la Jatte (Neuilly) (B,L,D)
Café Lenôtre (8ᵉ) (L,D)
Café Les Deux Magots (6ᵉ) (L,D)
Café Marly (1ᵉʳ) (L,D)
Café Ruc (1ᵉʳ) (L,D)
Café Terminus (8ᵉ) (L,D)
Café Very/Dame Tart. (multi.) (L,D)
Caffé Toscano (7ᵉ) (L,D)
Cagouille (14ᵉ) (L,D)
Camille (3ᵉ) (L,D)
Casa Alcalde (15ᵉ) (L,D)
Casa Bini (6ᵉ) (D)
Casa Tina (16ᵉ) (L,D)
Casa Vigata (11ᵉ) (L,D)
Caveau du Palais (1ᵉʳ) (L,D)
Cave de l'Os à Moëlle (15ᵉ) (L)
Cazaudehore La For. (St-Germain-en-Laye) (L,D)
Chai 33 (12ᵉ) (B,D)
Chalet des Iles (16ᵉ) (L,D)
Charlot - Roi des Coq. (9ᵉ) (L,D)
Charpentiers (6ᵉ) (L,D)
Chartier (9ᵉ) (L,D)
Cherche Midi (6ᵉ) (L,D)
Chez André (8ᵉ) (L,D)

Chez Clément (multi. loc.) (L,D)
Chez Francis (8ᵉ) (L,D)
Chez Françoise (7ᵉ) (L,D)
Chez Gégène (Joinville) (L,D)
Chez Georges-Maillot (17ᵉ) (L,D)
Chez Janou (3ᵉ) (L,D)
Chez Jenny (3ᵉ) (L,D)
Chez L'Ami Louis (3ᵉ) (L,D)
Chez Livio (Neuilly) (L,D)
Chez Maître Paul (6ᵉ) (L,D)
Chez Marianne (4ᵉ) (L,D)
Chez Ngo (16ᵉ) (L,D)
Chez Papa (multi. loc.) (L,D)
Chez Paul (11ᵉ) (L,D)
Chez Paul (13ᵉ) (L,D)
Chez Ramulaud (11ᵉ) (L,D)
Chieng Mai (5ᵉ) (L,D)
Chien qui Fume (1ᵉʳ) (L,D)
China Club (12ᵉ) (D)
China Town Olymp. (13ᵉ) (L,D)
Cinq (8ᵉ) (L,D)
Closerie des Lilas (6ᵉ) (L,D)
Coin des Gourmets (5ᵉ) (L,D)
Comptoir Paris-Marrak. (1ᵉʳ) (B,L,D)
Costes (1ᵉʳ) (L,D)
Coude Fou (4ᵉ) (L,D)
Coupe-Chou (5ᵉ) (D)
Coupole (14ᵉ) (L,D)
Dagorno (19ᵉ) (L,D)
Dauphin (1ᵉʳ) (L,D)
Délices de Szechuen (7ᵉ) (L,D)
Dessirier (17ᵉ) (L,D)
Devez (8ᵉ) (L,D)
Diamantaires (9ᵉ) (L,D)
Diep (8ᵉ) (L,D)
Dôme (14ᵉ) (L,D)
Durand Dupont (Neuilly) (B,L,D)
Ecluse (multi. loc.) (L,D)
Editeurs (6ᵉ) (B,L,D)
Elysées Hong Kong (16ᵉ) (L,D)
Enoteca (4ᵉ) (L,D)
Espadon (1ᵉʳ) (L,D)
Etoile Marocaine (8ᵉ) (L,D)
Fakhr el Dine (multi. loc.) (L,D)
Fellini (1ᵉʳ) (L,D)
Fermette Marbeuf 1900 (8ᵉ) (L,D)
Findi (8ᵉ) (B,L)
Fish La Boissonnerie (6ᵉ) (L,D)
Flandrin (16ᵉ) (L,D)
Flora Danica (8ᵉ) (L,D)
Flore en l'Ile (4ᵉ) (B,L,D)

Fogón Saint Julien (5^e) (L,D)
Fontaine de Mars (7e) (L,D)
Fontanarosa (15e) (L,D)
Foujita (1er) (L,D)
Fouquet's (8e) (B,L,D)
Fumoir (1er) (B,L,D)
Gamin de Paris (4e) (L,D)
Gare (16e) (L,D)
Garnier (8e) (L,D)
Gauloise (15e) (L,D)
Georges (4e) (L,D)
Giulio Rebellato (16e) (L,D)
Gli Angeli (3e) (L,D)
Goumard (1er) (L,D)
Grand Café (9e) (L,D)
Grand Colbert (2e) (L,D)
Grande Armée (16e) (L,D)
Grande Cascade (16e) (L,D)
Grand Louvre (1er) (L,D)
Grille St-Germain (6e) (L,D)
Guinguette/Neuilly (Neuilly) (L,D)
Higuma (1er) (L,D)
Huîtrier (17e) (L,D)
Il Carpaccio (8e) (L,D)
Ile (Issy-les-Moulineaux) (L,D)
Isami (4e) (D)
Jardin des Cygnes (8e) (B)
Jardins de Bagatelle (16e) (L,D)
Jarrasse (Neuilly) (L,D)
Joe Allen (1er) (B,L,D)
Jo Goldenberg (4e) (B,L,D)
Jules Verne (7e) (L,D)
Khun Akorn (11e) (L,D)
Kim Anh (15e) (D)
Kiosque (16e) (B,L,D)
Kong (1er) (L,D)
Ladurée (multi. loc.) (B,L,D)
Languedoc (5e) (L,D)
Lao Siam (19e) (L,D)
Lao Tseu (7e) (L,D)
Libre Sens (8e) (B,L,D)
Lô Sushi (multi. loc.) (L,D)
Ma Bourgogne (4e) (L,D)
Maharajah (5e) (L,D)
Maison du Caviar (8e) (L,D)
Maison Rouge (4e) (B,L,D)
Marius et Janette (8e) (L,D)
Market (8e) (B,L,D)
Martel (10e) (D)
Marty (5e) (L,D)
Mascotte (18e) (L,D)

Mavrommatis (5e) (L,D)
Méditerranée (6e) (L,D)
Meurice (1er) (L,D)
Mirama (5e) (L,D)
Monsieur Lapin (14e) (L,D)
Mont Liban (17e) (L,D)
Mon Vieil Ami (4e) (L,D)
Moulin de la Galette (18e) (B,L)
Murano (3e) (B)
Murat (16e) (L,D)
New Jawad (7e) (L,D)
New Nioullaville (11e) (L,D)
Nouveau Village Tao (13e) (L,D)
Obélisque (8e) (L,D)
Orangerie (4e) (D)
Orenoc (17e) (L,D)
Paradis Thai (13e) (L,D)
Parc aux Cerfs (6e) (L,D)
Passy Mandarin (16e) (L,D)
Patrick Goldenberg (17e) (L,D)
Paul, Restaurant (1er) (L,D)
Pavillon Montsouris (14e) (L,D)
Père Claude (15e) (L,D)
Petit Bofinger (multi. loc.) (L,D)
Petite Chaise (7e) (L,D)
Petite Cour (6e) (L,D)
Petite Tour (16e) (L,D)
Petit Lutétia (6e) (L,D)
Petit Marché (3e) (L,D)
Petit Niçois (7e) (L,D)
Petit Poucet (Levallois) (L,D)
Petits Marseillais (3e) (L,D)
Petit St. Benoît (6e) (L,D)
Petit Zinc (6e) (L,D)
Pied de Chameau (4e) (B,D)
Pied de Cochon (1er) (L,D)
Pierre Gagnaire (8e) (D)
Pinxo (1er) (L,D)
Pitchi Poï (4e) (B,L,D)
Pizzeria d'Auteuil (16e) (L,D)
Planet Hollywood (8e) (L,D)
Polidor (6e) (L,D)
Publicis Drugstore (8e) (B)
Quai Ouest (St-Cloud) (B,L,D)
404 (3e) (B,L,D)
Relais/l'Entrecôte (multi.) (L,D)
Relais de Venise (17e) (L,D)
Relais Plaza (8e) (L,D)
Réminet (5e) (L,D)
Rendez-vous/Chauff. (18e) (L,D)
Riad (Neuilly) (L,D)

River Café (Issy-les-Moul.) (L,D)
Rôtiss. du Beaujolais (5ᵉ) (L,D)
Rotonde (6ᵉ) (L,D)
Rouge Tomate (1ᵉʳ) (B)
Rughetta (18ᵉ) (L,D)
Scoop (1ᵉʳ) (B)
Sébillon (multi. loc.) (L,D)
Senso (8ᵉ) (L,D)
7ème Sud (multi. loc.) (B,L,D)
Spaghetti Bar/Curieux (4ᵉ) (B)
Spicy (8ᵉ) (B,L,D)
Stella (16ᵉ) (L,D)
Studio (4ᵉ) (B,D)
Terminus Nord (10ᵉ) (L,D)
Terrasse (18ᵉ) (L,D)
Thoumieux (7ᵉ) (L,D)
Timgad (17ᵉ) (L,D)
Toi (8ᵉ) (L,D)
Tong Yen (8ᵉ) (L,D)
Tonkinoise (13ᵉ) (L,D)
Tour d'Argent (5ᵉ) (L,D)
Tournesol (16ᵉ) (D)
Train Bleu (12ᵉ) (L,D)
Tricotin (13ᵉ) (L,D)
Truffière (5ᵉ) (L,D)
Trumilou (4ᵉ) (L,D)
Tsé-Yang (16ᵉ) (L,D)
Vagenende (6ᵉ) (L,D)
Vaudeville (2ᵉ) (L,D)
Verre Bouteille (17ᵉ) (L,D)
Verre Volé (10ᵉ) (L,D)
Viaduc Café (12ᵉ) (B,L,D)
Vieille Fontaine Rôtiss.
 (Maisons-Laffitte) (L)
Vieux Bistro (4ᵉ) (L,D)
Village d'Ung et Li Lam (8ᵉ) (D)
Vinea Café (12ᵉ) (B,L,D)
Wepler (18ᵉ) (B,L,D)
Zebra Square (16ᵉ) (B,L,D)
Zéphyr (20ᵉ) (L,D)
Zinc-Zinc (Neuilly) (L,D)

Tasting Menus

Allobroges (20ᵉ)
Al Mounia (16ᵉ)
Amphyclès (17ᵉ)
Apicius (8ᵉ)
Arpège (7ᵉ)
Astor (8ᵉ)
Astrance (16ᵉ)
Astrée (17ᵉ)
Atelier Berger (1ᵉʳ)

Aub. et Cie (9ᵉ)
Aub. Nicolas Flamel (3ᵉ)
Avant Goût (13ᵉ)
Baie d'Ha Long (16ᵉ)
Bath's (8ᵉ)
Béatilles (17ᵉ)
Bistro de Gala (9ᵉ)
Bistrot du Sommelier (8ᵉ)
Braisière (17ᵉ)
Bristol (8ᵉ)
Carré des Feuillants (1ᵉʳ)
Cartes Postales (1ᵉʳ)
Casa Tina (16ᵉ)
123 (17ᵉ)
Chamarré (7ᵉ)
Chez Jean (9ᵉ)
Chez Michel (10ᵉ)
Chez Vincent (19ᵉ)
Chiberta (8ᵉ)
Cinq (8ᵉ)
Clos Morillons (15ᵉ)
Clos Saint-Honoré (1ᵉʳ)
Clovis (8ᵉ)
Comte de Gascogne (Boulogne)
Copenhague (8ᵉ)
Cuisine (7ᵉ)
Elysées (8ᵉ)
Epicure 108 (17ᵉ)
Espadon (1ᵉʳ)
Filo Delle Stagioni (3ᵉ)
Flora (8ᵉ)
Florimond (7ᵉ)
Fogón Saint Julien (5ᵉ)
Gérard Besson (1ᵉʳ)
Goumard (1ᵉʳ)
Grande Cascade (16ᵉ)
Grand Véfour (1ᵉʳ)
Guy Savoy (17ᵉ)
Hélène Darroze (6ᵉ)
Jacques Cagna (6ᵉ)
Jamin (16ᵉ)
Jardin (8ᵉ)
Jules Verne (7ᵉ)
Lapérouse (6ᵉ)
Lasserre (8ᵉ)
Laurent (8ᵉ)
Ledoyen (8ᵉ)
Lucas Carton (8ᵉ)
Magnolias (Perreux-sur-Marne)
Mavrommatis (5ᵉ)
Maxim's (8ᵉ)

Meurice (1er)
Michel Rostang (17e)
Montparnasse 25 (14e)
Muses (9e)
O à la Bouche (14e)
Olivades (7e)
Os à Moëlle (15e)
Paolo Petrini (17e)
Paris (6e)
Pergolèse (16e)
Pierre Gagnaire (8e)
Potager du Roy (Versailles)
Pré Catelan (16e)
Pressoir (12e)
Relais d'Auteuil/Pignol (16e)
Relais Louis XIII (6e)
Réminet (5e)
Rest. Alain Ducasse (8e)
Romantica (Clichy)
Sawadee (15e)
Sologne (12e)
Sormani (17e)
Stella Maris (8e)
Table d'Anvers (9e)
Table/Joël Robuchon (16e)
Table du Lancaster (8e)
Taillevent (8e)
Tang (16e)
Terrasse Mirabeau (16e)
Thaï (1er)
Thierry Burlot (15e)
Tire-Bouchon (15^e)
Trois Marches (Versailles)
Troquet (15e)
Violon d'Ingres (7e)
W, Restaurant (8e)

Teen Appeal
Alcazar (6e)
Altitude 95 (7e)
Anahuacalli (5e)
Apollo (14e)
Appart' (8e)
Appennino (13e)
Asian (8e)
Avenue (8e)
B*fly (8e)
Barrio Latino (12e)
Bartolo (6e)
BIOArt (13e)
Blue Elephant (11e)
Bon (16e)

Boulangerie/Odéon (6e)
Breakfast in America (5e)
Buddha Bar (8e)
Café Beaubourg (4e)
Café Burq (18e)
Café Charbon (11e)
Café de la Musique (19e)
Café de la Poste (4e)
Café de l'Esplanade (7e)
Café de l'Industrie (11e)
Café de Mars (7e)
Café du Commerce (15e)
Café la Jatte (Neuilly)
Café Lenôtre (8e)
Café Marly (1er)
Café Max (7e)
Café Ruc (1er)
Café Very/Dame Tart. (multi.)
Cailloux (13e)
C'Amelot (11e)
Carr's (1er)
Cave Gourmande (19e)
Chartier (9e)
Chez Clément (multi. loc.)
Chez Marianne (4e)
Chez Omar (3e)
Chez Papa (multi. loc.)
Chez Prune (10e)
Chez Vong (1er)
Chicago Pizza (8e)
China Club (12e)
Coco de Mer (5e)
Coffee Parisien (multi. loc.)
Coin des Gourmets (5e)
Comptoir Paris-Marrak. (1er)
Cosi (6e)
Coude Fou (4e)
Coupole (14e)
Crêperie de Josselin (14e)
Délices d'Aphrodite (5e)
Djoon (13e)
Enoteca (4e)
Entoto (13e)
Etoile (16e)
Ferme (1er)
Fish La Boissonnerie (6e)
Fogón Saint Julien (5e)
Fous d'en Face (4e)
Fumoir (1er)
Gamin de Paris (4e)
Georges (4e)

Gli Angeli (3e)
Hangar (3e)
Hippopotamus (multi. loc.)
Ile (Issy-les-Moulineaux)
Indiana Café (multi. loc.)
Isami (4e)
Joe Allen (1er)
Kiosque (16e)
Kong (1er)
Lao Siam (19e)
Léon de Bruxelles (multi. loc.)
Lina's (multi. loc.)
Loir dans la Théière (4e)
Lô Sushi (multi. loc.)
Ma Bourgogne (4e)
Man Ray (8e)
Mirama (5e)
No Stress Café (9e)
Ostéria (4e)
Paradis Thai (13e)
Petite Sirène Copenh. (9e)
Petits Marseillais (3e)
Pied de Cochon (1er)
Planet Hollywood (8e)
Polidor (6e)
Press Café (2e)
Quai Ouest (St-Cloud)
404 (3e)
Rendez-vous/Camion. (14e)
Rendez-vous/Chauff. (18e)
River Café (Issy-les-Moul.)
Sept Quinze (15e)
Spaghetti Bar/Curieux (4e)
Spicy (8e)
Spoon, Food/Wine (8e)
Square Trousseau (12e)
Tricotin (13e)
Trumilou (4e)
Vaudeville (2e)
Viaduc Café (12e)
Vinea Café (12e)
Virgin Café (8e)
Wok Cooking (11e)
Yen (6e)
Zebra Square (16e)
Zéphyr (20e)

Theme Restaurants

Aub. Nicolas Flamel (3e)
Bar à Huîtres (multi. loc.)
Barrio Latino (12e)
Bel Canto (multi. loc.)

Bellotta-Bellotta (7e)
Bistrot d'André (15e)
Breakfast in America (5e)
Buddha Bar (8e)
Café de la Musique (19e)
Chez Clément (multi. loc.)
Chicago Pizza (8e)
Coco de Mer (5e)
Léon de Bruxelles (multi. loc.)
Lina's (multi. loc.)
Monsieur Lapin (14e)
Planet Hollywood (8e)
Pomze (8e)
Rouge Tomate (1er)
Virgin Café (8e)
Wok Cooking (11e)

Transporting Experiences

Alsaco (9e)
Anahï (3e)
Annapurna (8e)
Asian (8e)
Atlas (5e)
Baie d'Ha Long (16e)
Benkay (15e)
Blue Elephant (11e)
Buddha Bar (8e)
Café la Jatte (Neuilly)
Chalet des Iles (16e)
Chen Soleil d'Est (15e)
Chez Gégène (Joinville)
Chez Vong (1er)
China Club (12e)
Coco de Mer (5e)
Délices d'Aphrodite (5e)
Djakarta (1er)
Enoteca (4e)
Entoto (13e)
Erawan (15e)
Etoile Marocaine (8e)
Fakhr el Dine (multi. loc.)
Fogón Saint Julien (5e)
Isami (4e)
Jardins de Bagatelle (16e)
Man Ray (8e)
Mansouria (11e)
Mavrommatis (5e)
Monsieur Lapin (14e)
Saudade (1er)
Soufflé (1er)
Stella Maris (8e)
Taïra (17e)

Tan Dinh (7ᵉ)
Tanjia (8ᵉ)
Timgad (17ᵉ)
Tricotin (13ᵉ)
Tsé-Yang (16ᵉ)
Wally Le Saharien (9ᵉ)
Yen (6ᵉ)

Trendy
Affiche (8ᵉ)
Alcazar (6ᵉ)
Anahï (3ᵉ)
Andy Whaloo (3ᵉ)
Angle du Faubourg (8ᵉ)
Angl'Opera (2ᵉ)
Apollo (14ᵉ)
Appart' (8ᵉ)
Arpège (7ᵉ)
Astor (8ᵉ)
Astrance (16ᵉ)
Atelier Joël Robuchon (7ᵉ)
Aub. du Clou (9ᵉ)
Auvergne Gourmande (7ᵉ)
Avant Goût (13ᵉ)
Avenue (8ᵉ)
B*fly (8ᵉ)
Bains (3ᵉ)
Bar des Théâtres (8ᵉ)
Barramundi (9ᵉ)
Barrio Latino (12ᵉ)
Bar Rouge (9ᵉ)
Bélier (6ᵉ)
Benoît (4ᵉ)
Beurre Noisette (15ᵉ)
Bistrot de l'Etoile Laur. (16ᵉ)
Bistrot des Dames (17ᵉ)
Bistrot du Peintre (11ᵉ)
Bon (16ᵉ)
Bouquinistes (6ᵉ)
B4 (1ᵉʳ)
Brass. Balzar (5ᵉ)
Brass. de la Poste (16ᵉ)
Brass. Lipp (6ᵉ)
Buddha Bar (8ᵉ)
Butte Chaillot (16ᵉ)
Café Beaubourg (4ᵉ)
Café Burq (18ᵉ)
Café Charbon (11ᵉ)
Café d'Angel (17ᵉ)
Café de Flore (6ᵉ)
Café de l'Esplanade (7ᵉ)
Café des Délices (6ᵉ)

Café du Passage (11ᵉ)
Café Etienne Marcel (2ᵉ)
Café Guitry (9ᵉ)
Café la Jatte (Neuilly)
Café Lenôtre (8ᵉ)
Café Marly (1ᵉʳ)
Café Ruc (1ᵉʳ)
Caffe del Gattopardo (18ᵉ)
Cailloux (13ᵉ)
Cave Gourmande (19ᵉ)
182 Rive Droite (16ᵉ)
Chateaubriand (11ᵉ)
Cherche Midi (6ᵉ)
Chez L'Ami Louis (3ᵉ)
Chez Michel (10ᵉ)
Chez Omar (3ᵉ)
Chez Paul (11ᵉ)
Chez Prune (10ᵉ)
Chez Ramulaud (11ᵉ)
Chez Vong (1ᵉʳ)
Chieng Mai (5ᵉ)
China Club (12ᵉ)
Cinq (8ᵉ)
Clos des Gourmets (7ᵉ)
Coin des Gourmets (5ᵉ)
. . . Comme Cochon (12ᵉ)
Comptoir Paris-Marrak. (1ᵉʳ)
Contre-Allée (14ᵉ)
Costes (1ᵉʳ)
Cristal Room (16ᵉ)
Deux Abeilles (7ᵉ)
Dix Vins (15ᵉ)
Djoon (13ᵉ)
Durand Dupont (Neuilly)
Editeurs (6ᵉ)
Emporio Armani (6ᵉ)
Entredgeu (17ᵉ)
Espadon (1ᵉʳ)
Etoile (16ᵉ)
Famille (18ᵉ)
Fish La Boissonnerie (6ᵉ)
Flandrin (16ᵉ)
Flora Danica (8ᵉ)
Fontaine de Mars (7ᵉ)
Fouquet's (8ᵉ)
Fumoir (1ᵉʳ)
Gare (16ᵉ)
Garnier (8ᵉ)
Georges (4ᵉ)
Gli Angeli (3ᵉ)
Grande Armée (16ᵉ)

Grandes Marches (12e)
Guy Savoy (17e)
Hangar (3e)
Hélène Darroze (6e)
Hiramatsu (16e)
Il Cortile (1er)
Ile (Issy-les-Moulineaux)
Il Viccolo (6e)
Isami (4e)
Joséphine Ch. Dumonet (6e)
Jumeaux (11e)
Kiosque (16e)
Kong (1er)
Ladurée (multi. loc.)
Legrand Filles et Fils (2e)
Magnolias (Perreux-sur-Marne)
Maison Blanche (8e)
Maison Prunier (16e)
Man Ray (8e)
Manufacture (Issy-les-Moul.)
Maresco (5e)
Mariage Frères (multi. loc.)
Market (8e)
Martel (10e)
Mavrommatis (5e)
Méditerranée (6e)
Montalembert (7e)
Mum Sabai (6e)
Murano (3e)
Musichall (8e)
Natacha (14e)
Orangerie (4e)
Ormes (7e)
Ostéria (4e)
Pamphlet (3e)
Passiflore (16e)
Pearl (13e)
Petite Sirène Copenh. (9e)
Petits Marseillais (3e)
Petrossian (7e)
Pierre au Palais Royal (1er)
Pierre Gagnaire (8e)
Point Bar (1er)
404 (3e)
Régalade (14e)
Relais Plaza (8e)
River Café (Issy-les-Moul.)
Rughetta (18e)
Salon d'Hélène (6e)
Sardegna a Tavola (12e)
Sauvignon (7e)

Sept Quinze (15e)
Soleil (St-Ouen)
Sormani (17e)
Spaghetti Bar/Curieux (4e)
Spoon, Food/Wine (8e)
Square Trousseau (12e)
Stresa (8e)
Table/Joël Robuchon (16e)
Table de Lucullus (17e)
Table du Lancaster (8e)
Taillevent (8e)
Taka (18e)
Tan Dinh (7e)
Tanjia (8e)
Tante Louise (8e)
Tante Marguerite (7e)
Télégraphe (7e)
Thiou (7e)
Tong Yen (8e)
Tour d'Argent (5e)
Vin sur Vin (7e)
Voltaire (7e)
Water Bar Colette (1er)
Zebra Square (16e)
Ze Kitchen Galerie (6e)
Zo (8e)

Views

Alsace (8e)
Altitude 95 (7e)
Avenue (8e)
Bar Vendôme (1er)
Benkay (15e)
BIOArt (13e)
Bistro de Breteuil (7e)
Bistrot du Cap (15e)
Bouquinistes (6e)
Brass. de l'Ile St. Louis (4e)
Café Beaubourg (4e)
Café de Flore (6e)
Café de la Musique (19e)
Café de la Poste (4e)
Café de l'Esplanade (7e)
Café la Jatte (Neuilly)
Café Lenôtre (8e)
Café Marly (1er)
Caffe del Gattopardo (18e)
Cap Seguin (Boulogne)
Cap Vernet (8e)
Caviar Kaspia (8e)
Cazaudehore La For. (St-
   Germain-en-Laye)

Chalet des Iles (16e)
Chantairelle (5e)
Charlot - Roi des Coq. (9e)
Chez Francis (8e)
Chez Gégène (Joinville)
Chez Paul (13e)
Chez Prune (10e)
Clos des Gourmets (7e)
Coconnas (4e)
Copenhague (8e)
Cosi (Le) (5e)
D'Chez Eux (7e)
Délices de Szechuen (7e)
Duc de Richelieu (12e)
Durand Dupont (Neuilly)
Emporio Armani (6e)
Etoile (16e)
Flora Danica (8e)
Flore en l'Ile (4e)
Fontaine de Mars (7e)
Fouquet's (8e)
Fumoir (1er)
Georges (4e)
Grande Armée (16e)
Grande Cascade (16e)
Grandes Marches (12e)
Grand Véfour (1er)
Hédiard (8e)
Il Punto (Neuilly)
Isami (4e)
Jardin des Cygnes (8e)
Jardins de Bagatelle (16e)
Jules Verne (7e)
Kong (1er)
Lapérouse (6e)
Lasserre (8e)
Ledoyen (8e)
Maison Blanche (8e)
Maison de l'Amér. Lat. (7e)
Maresco (5e)
Méditerranée (6e)
Murano (3e)
Papilles (5e)
Paul, Restaurant (1er)
Pères et Filles (6e)
Pershing (8e)
Petit Poucet (Levallois)
Petits Marseillais (3e)
Pitchi Poï (4e)
Point Bar (1er)
Port Alma (16e)

P'Tit Panisse (11e)
Quai Ouest (St-Cloud)
R. (15e)
Relais/l'Entrecôte (6e)
Relais de Venise (17e)
Relais Plaza (8e)
Réminet (5e)
Rest. de la Tour (15e)
Rest./Musée d'Orsay (7e)
Rest./Palais Royal (1er)
River Café (Issy-les-Moul.)
Romantica (Clichy)
Rôtiss. de Neuilly (Neuilly)
Rotonde (6e)
Rouge Tomate (1er)
Square Trousseau (12e)
Table du Lancaster (8e)
Taverne Henri IV (1er)
Terrasse (18e)
Terrasse Mirabeau (16e)
Terres de Truffes (8e)
Tonnelle Saintong. (Neuilly)
Toupary (1er)
Tour d'Argent (5e)
Vaudeville (2e)
Voltaire (7e)

Visitors on Expense Account

Ambroisie (4e)
Amphyclès (17e)
Arpège (7e)
Assiette (14e)
Atelier Joël Robuchon (7e)
Auguste (7e)
Bath's (8e)
Béatilles (17e)
Benoît (4e)
Café Faubourg (8e)
Carré des Feuillants (1er)
Caviar Kaspia (8e)
123 (17e)
Chen Soleil d'Est (15e)
Chez L'Ami Louis (3e)
Chez Pauline (1er)
Chiberta (8e)
Clovis (8e)
Copenhague (8e)
Cuisine (7e)
Dessirier (17e)
Divellec (7e)
Dôme (14e)

Dominique Bouchet (8e)
Drouant (2e)
Duc (14e)
Estaminet Gaya (1er)
Ferme St-Simon (7e)
Flora Danica (8e)
Fouquet's (8e)
Garnier (8e)
Gaya Rive Gauche (7e)
Gérard Besson (1er)
Goumard (1er)
Grand Véfour (1er)
Guy Savoy (17e)
Hélène Darroze (6e)
Il Carpaccio (8e)
Il Cortile (1er)
Jacques Cagna (6e)
Jamin (16e)
Jarrasse (Neuilly)
Joséphine Ch. Dumonet (6e)
Jules Verne (7e)
Lasserre (8e)
Laurent (8e)
Ledoyen (8e)
Lucas Carton (8e)
Maison Blanche (8e)
Mansouria (11e)
Marée (8e)
Marius (16e)
Maxim's (8e)
Michel Rostang (17e)
Muses (9e)
Natacha (14e)
Obélisque (8e)
Orangerie (4e)
Orenoc (17e)
Oulette (12e)
Petit Colombier (17e)
Pierre au Palais Royal (1er)
Pierre Gagnaire (8e)
Pomze (8e)
Pré Catelan (16e)
Pressoir (12e)
Relais Louis XIII (6e)
Relais Plaza (8e)
Stella Maris (8e)
Table d'Anvers (9e)
Table/Joël Robuchon (16e)
Table du Lancaster (8e)
Taillevent (8e)
Taïra (17e)

Tante Jeanne (17e)
Tante Marguerite (7e)
Terrasse Mirabeau (16e)
Tour d'Argent (5e)
Trois Marches (Versailles)
Trou Gascon (12e)
W, Restaurant (8e)

Waterside
BIOArt (13e)
Brass. de l'Ile St. Louis (4e)
Buffalo Grill (13e)
Cap Seguin (Boulogne)
Chalet des Iles (16e)
Chez Gégène (Joinville)
Chez Prune (10e)
Guinguette/Neuilly (Neuilly)
Petit Poucet (Levallois)
Quai Ouest (St-Cloud)
River Café (Issy-les-Moul.)

Winning Wine Lists
Ambassadeurs (8e)
Ambroisie (4e)
Amphyclès (17e)
Atelier Joël Robuchon (7e)
Bar Rouge (9e)
Bistrot du Sommelier (8e)
Bistrot Paul Bert (11e)
Bouchons/Fr. Clerc (multi. loc.)
Bourguignon du Marais (4e)
Bristol (8e)
Café Burq (18e)
Café Lenôtre (8e)
Cagouille (14e)
Carré des Feuillants (1er)
Cave de l'Os à Moëlle (15e)
Caves Miard (6e)
Caves Pétrissans (17e)
123 (17e)
Chai 33 (12e)
Cinq (8e)
Coupe Gorge (4e)
Dessirier (17e)
Divellec (7e)
Drouant (2e)
Ecluse (multi. loc.)
Elysées (8e)
Enoteca (4e)
Excuse (4e)
Ferme St-Simon (7e)
Fish La Boissonnerie (6e)

Special Features

Fogón Saint Julien (5e)
Gérard Besson (1er)
Grande Cascade (16e)
Grand Véfour (1er)
Guy Savoy (17e)
Hélène Darroze (6e)
Il Cortile (1er)
Jacques Cagna (6e)
Jamin (16e)
Jardin (8e)
Joséphine Ch. Dumonet (6e)
Jules Verne (7e)
Lasserre (8e)
Laurent (8e)
Lavinia (8e)
Ledoyen (8e)
Legrand Filles et Fils (2e)
Lucas Carton (8e)
Macéo (1er)
Marée (8e)
Marsangy (11e)
Maxim's (8e)
Meurice (1er)
Michel Rostang (17e)
Montparnasse 25 (14e)

Muses (9e)
Oenothèque (9e)
Oulette (12e)
Paris (6e)
Petit Marguery (13e)
Petrossian (7e)
Pierre au Palais Royal (1er)
Pierre Gagnaire (8e)
Pressoir (12e)
Relais Louis XIII (6e)
Rest. Alain Ducasse (8e)
Saudade (1er)
Spoon, Food/Wine (8e)
Stella Maris (8e)
Table d'Anvers (9e)
Taillevent (8e)
Tante Marguerite (7^e)
Taverne Henri IV (1er)
Tour d'Argent (5^e)
Trois Marches (Versailles)
Trou Gascon (12^e)
Vieux Chêne (11^e)
Vin dans les voiles (16^e)
Vin sur Vin (7^e)

Wine Vintage Chart

This chart is designed to help you select wine to go with your meal. It is based on the same 0 to 30 scale used throughout this *Survey*. The ratings (prepared by our friend **Howard Stravitz,** a law professor at the University of South Carolina) reflect both the quality of the vintage and the wine's readiness for present consumption. Thus, if a wine is not fully mature or is over the hill, its rating has been reduced. We do not include 1987, 1991–1993 vintages because they are not especially recommended for most areas. A dash indicates that a wine is either past its peak or too young to rate.

	'85	'86	'88	'89	'90	'94	'95	'96	'97	'98	'99	'00	'01	'02	'03
WHITES															
French:															
Alsace	24	–	22	28	28	27	26	25	25	26	25	26	27	25	–
Burgundy	26	25	–	24	22	–	28	29	24	23	26	25	23	27	24
Loire Valley	–	–	–	–	24	–	20	23	22	–	24	25	23	27	26
Champagne	28	25	24	26	29	–	26	27	24	24	25	25	26	–	–
Sauternes	21	28	29	25	27	–	21	23	26	24	24	24	28	25	26
Germany	25	–	25	26	27	25	24	27	24	23	25	24	29	27	–
California (Napa, Sonoma, Mendocino):															
Chardonnay	–	–	–	–	–	–	–	24	26	25	25	24	27	29	–
Sauvignon Blanc/Semillon	–	–	–	–	–	–	–	–	25	25	23	27	28	26	
REDS															
French:															
Bordeaux	24	25	24	26	29	22	26	25	23	25	24	28	26	23	24
Burgundy	23	–	21	24	26	–	26	28	25	22	28	22	24	27	–
Rhône	25	19	27	29	29	24	25	23	24	28	27	27	26	–	25
Beaujolais	–	–	–	–	–	–	–	–	–	–	23	24	–	25	28
California (Napa, Sonoma, Mendocino):															
Cab./Merlot	27	26	–	21	28	29	27	25	28	23	26	23	27	25	–
Pinot Noir	–	–	–	–	–	–	–	–	24	24	25	24	26	29	–
Zinfandel	–	–	–	–	–	–	–	–	–	–	–	26	26	–	
Italian:															
Tuscany	–	–	–	–	25	22	25	20	29	24	28	26	25	–	–
Piedmont	–	–	27	28	–	23	27	27	25	25	28	23	–	–	–

Latia